The Politics of Sentencing Reform

The Politics of Sentencing Reform

Edited by

CHRIS CLARKSON

and

ROD MORGAN

CLARENDON PRESS · OXFORD

1995

Oxford University Press, Walton Street, Oxford OX2 6DP
Oxford New York
Athens Auckland Bangkok Bombay
Calcutta Cape Town Dar es Salaam Delhi
Florence Hong Kong Istanbul Karachi
Kuala Lumpur Madras Madrid Melbourne
Mexico City Nairobi Paris Singapore
Taipei Tokyo Toronto
and associated companies in
Berlin Ibadan

Oxford is a trade mark of Oxford University Press

Published in the United States
by Oxford University Press Inc., New York

British Library Cataloguing in Publication Data
Data available

Library of Congress Cataloging in Publication Data
The politics of sentencing reform / edited by Chris Clarkson and Rod
Morgan.
p. cm.
Essays prepared for the Colston International Sentencing Symposium
held Apr. 5–7, 1993 at Bristol University.
1. Sentences (Criminal procedure) 2. Law reform. I. Clarkson,
C. M. V. (Christopher M. V.) II. Morgan, Rodney. III. Colston
International Sentencing Symposium (1993: Bristol University)
K5121.P65 1994 345'.0772—dc20 [342.5772] 94–38332
ISBN 0-19-825872-0

1 3 5 7 9 10 8 6 4 2

Typeset by Best-set Typesetters Ltd., Hong Kong

Printed in Great Britain
on acid-free paper by
Biddles Ltd., Guildford and King's Lynn

Acknowledgements

The first drafts of all but two of the ten essays in this collection were prepared for a conference held on 5–7 April 1993 at Bristol University. The Colston International Sentencing Symposium was sponsored both by the Colston Society, a Bristol foundation devoted to the support of research, and the Home Office. We are grateful to Mr Richard Trevor Johnson and Professor Michael Furmston, respectively President and Chairman of the Colston Research Committee, and to Mr Chris Nuttall, Director of the Home Office Research and Statistics Division, for arranging financial support and giving invaluable advice.

The Colston Symposium was attended by 44 experts, either practitioners, researchers, or academic commentators, from 12 countries. It was by common consent a higly successful event: enormously informative and theoretically stimulating. This outcome was due first and foremost to the principal speakers—Anthony Bottoms, Nils Jareborg, Arie Freiberg, David Thomas, Andrew von Hirsch, Anthony Doob, Andrew Ashworth, and Michael Tonry—who without exception provided papers of a standard which conference organizers yearn for but seldom receive. But thanks are also due to all the participants, several of whom came armed with valuable written papers to support their well-informed oral contributions. Unfortunately, space restraints have prevented us from including these further papers here but they, and the discussion at Bristol, have permeated the present collection in four ways. First, to place the essays in context we have written an introductory chapter, much of which was informed by the rigorous debate at the Symposium. Secondly, chapters by Andrew Ashworth and Michael Tonry constitute the conclusions they have drawn from all that was both read and said at Bristol. Thirdly, the six other original papers have been revised in the light of Bristol and subsequent events. And, finally, we asked one of the participants at Bristol, Richard Frase, to write an additional chapter specially for this text. We did so because it became apparent to us that this collection would lack credibility without a thorough empirical review of sentencing reform developments in the various states in the USA. His chapter builds on much that he reported orally at Bristol and is a splendid complement to the other essays. We thank all our contributors for their considerable effort and patience with our many editorial questions.

An international conference of this nature requires considerable planning and organization, and we are grateful to all who assisted in this task. In particular, our thanks go to Andrew Ashworth and Michael Tonry who provided invaluable advice at the stage when we were drawing up a list of speakers and guests. Further, we must also thank our colleagues in the

Bristol Law Faculty for their assistance with this venture: to Wendy Brett, Rosemarie Trowbridge, and Chris Harries for their practical assistance with the organization of the Colston Symposium, and to Pat Hammond for wrestling for many hours with scripts and disks to get everything into a common shape. Our thanks also go to Sir Henry Brooke, Chairman of the Law Commission, for his stimulating address after the Colston Dinner regarding race and sentencing. Finally, thanks to Richard Hart and John Whelan at Oxford University Press for showing faith in a project about which they could with justification have been sceptical when it was first mooted to them. If this sentence is not deleted we shall assume that they have not lived to regret the invaluable support they gave us.

C.C. and R.M.
Faculty of Law
University of Bristol
January 1994

Contents

List of Contributors

ROD MORGAN is Professor of Criminal Justice and Dean of the Faculty of Law at the University of Bristol.

CHRIS CLARKSON is Reader in Law at the University of Bristol.

ANTHONY BOTTOMS is Wolfson Professor of Criminology and Director of the Institute of Criminology at the University of Cambridge.

ARIE FREIBERG is Professor of Criminology at the University of Melbourne.

NILS JAREBORG is Professor of Criminal Law at Uppsala University, Sweden.

D. A. THOMAS is Reader in Criminal Justice at Cambridge University and a Fellow of Trinity Hall.

ANDREW VON HIRSCH is a Senior Research Fellow at the Institute of Criminology and Fellow of Fitzwilliam College, Cambridge University. He is also Professor at the School of Criminal Justice, Rutgers University, Newark, NJ.

RICHARD S. FRASE is Benjamin N. Berger Professor of Criminal Law at the University of Minnesota.

ANTHONY N. DOOB is Professor of Criminology at the Centre of Criminology, University of Toronto.

ANDREW ASHWORTH is Edmund-Davies Professor of Criminal Law and Criminal Justice, King's College, University of London.

MICHAEL TONRY is Professor of Law at the University of Minnesota.

I

The Politics of Sentencing Reform

ROD MORGAN AND CHRIS CLARKSON

I. INTRODUCTION

This book arises out of a conference held at Bristol University in April 1993. The conference was planned eighteen months previously. Our plans were prompted by the passage in England of the Criminal Justice Act 1991, a statute widely heralded as radical, though not as radical as some commentators wished, and the uncertain impact of which was eagerly awaited. The Act was the product of a long gestation during the course of which alternative legislative models were vigorously debated. It seemed to us that it would be timely to organize a conference bringing together international experts knowledgeable about the process of sentencing reform to see what general lessons might be learnt. Several questions preoccupied us. What range of policy problems typically provide the impetus for major sentencing reform initiatives? Why, in the present climate, has the 'just deserts' approach to sentencing come to be so favoured not just by penal philosophers but by civil servants and politicians? Why are some mechanisms for instituting and interpreting 'just deserts' apparently acceptable in some jurisdictions—sentencing commissions and grids in North America, for example—while they are eschewed elsewhere? What are the typical points of resistance to sentencing reform? And, above all, to what extent do changes in the legislative framework achieve changes in sentencing practice?

Spring 1993 seemed a sensible date for the conference. The Criminal Justice Act 1991 was not to be implemented until October 1992. We judged that by April the following year some preliminary data would be available about how the Act was beginning to work. Eighteen months would also give our overseas guests sufficient time to prepare case-studies on the reforms being pursued in their own jurisdictions, some of which were long-standing and others of which were still being developed. In the event the choice of April 1993 seemed almost prescient. No date could have provided a more dramatic illustration of how high profile a political process sentencing reform often now is.

The Criminal Justice Act 1991 was implemented as planned. But from its first days the Act generated considerable controversy. This was somewhat

surprising given that the legislation had been preceded by government
consultative Green and White Papers[1] and an unprecedentedly thorough
and expensive training programme for all judges and magistrates. Yet
judges and magistrates were in the vanguard of the early criticism that was
heaped on the Act. The Lord Chief Justice led the charge. In a widely
reported speech he said that the Act forced sentencers into an 'ill-fitting
straitjacket' and that 'penologists, criminologists and bureaucrats'—he was
careful not to include politicians—had created through the Act a sentencing
framework 'incomprehensible to right-thinking people generally'.[2] His criticisms were echoed by several of his fellow judges. Moreover, a small
number of magistrates resigned with much show over the Act. And the
press, apparently encouraged by dissidents from within the courts, ran a
series of stories purporting to illustrate the ludicrous decisions which the
Act was forcing sentencers to make.

In early May 1993, Mr Kenneth Clark, the then Home Secretary, announced a U-turn the sharpness of which astonished even those who had
serious reservations about the way the Act appeared to be working. He did
not intend to clarify or 'fine tune' the offending provisions. He intended to
strike them out. The government proposed to repeal two key provisions in
the Act: section 18, which provided for unit fines (scaled so that the number
of units imposed was determined by the seriousness of the offence, and the
monetary value of each unit was determined by the offender's weekly
disposable income); and section 29, which limited the relevance of prior
convictions in deciding the seriousness of the current offence and the sentence appropriate for it. These amendments, and other provisions, were
brought in by the Criminal Justice Act 1993, which received the Royal
Assent in July 1993.

Thus within seven months of its implementation, important provisions in
the Act had been renounced by the responsible Minister, and within nine
months they had been repealed. This precipitate somersault generated as
much, if not more, controversy than the original provisions, not least because it was widely argued that modification, not wholesale abandonment,
was what had been required. Indeed several commentators expressed the
view that the politically generated confusion which now surrounded sentencing—both among sentencers and the public at large—had done as
much to damage the credibility of the criminal-justice system as had the
notorious miscarriages of justice that came to light in the late 1980s and
which led to the appointment of a Royal Commission.[3]

---

[1] Home Office, *Punishment, Custody and the Community* (Cm. 434; London, 1988); *Crime,
Justice and Protecting the Public* (Cm. 965; London, 1990).
[2] See Ch. 5, n. 45.
[3] Runciman Report, *Report of the Royal Commission on Criminal Justice* (Chairman, Lord
Runciman) (Cm. 2263; London, 1993).

This was the immediate political context in which the Bristol conference took place. It lent the papers discussed at the conference an immediacy and importance which we had not envisaged. A topic which in England might reasonably have been expected to be of largely academic and historical importance—most commentators presumed that so major a piece of criminal-justice legislation would be the last political word on the matter for several years—suddenly assumed vital policy relevance. Indeed during the deliberations at Bristol lines of policy argument were explored which later surfaced in the political ferment of 'law and order' rhetoric which continued to be deployed by English Ministers and Opposition spokesmen well into the autumn. It appeared that far from providing oil to calm the waters, the reversed decisions about the Criminal Justice Act 1991 had opened up an even keener argument about the purpose of punishment and the value of particular sanctions, notably imprisonment. The controversy broadened and gathered momentum. In October the new Home Secretary, Michael Howard, announced that he intended to introduce yet more criminal-justice legislation, and in December 1993 a further criminal-justice bill was published: it contains new sentencing provisions which though less fundamental than those incorporated in the Criminal Justice Acts of 1991 and 1993 are no less controversial and revisionary in their implications.[4]

All of this has confirmed our view that the issues discussed in this volume are of considerable relevance to those whose interest goes beyond policy analysis and philosophical debate. There is practical wisdom for those who would influence policy to be gathered here. The process of sentencing reform is not capable of being understood simply in terms of jurisprudential logic any more than the acceptability and use made of penal sanctions can be reduced to questions of utilitarian effectiveness. In the same way that the practices of judicial punishment are statements of collective moral feeling ritually expressed, as well as instruments of political power and technical means to ends,[5] so statements of sentencing policy are at once a combination of rationalized principle and administrative managerialism jostled by party political calculation, some of it very short term. Several of the accounts in this volume illustrate the shifting parameters of this fusion very well. Thus, far from becoming redundant as a result of subsequent conjunctions between the developing discourse of sentencing theory and the practical politics of sentencing practice, there are more long-lasting lessons from

[4] During discussion at the Bristol conference, for example, Mr Chris Nuttall, Director of Research and Statistics in the Home Office, made the observation that the massive rise in the United States prison population during the 1980s had recently been accompanied by a decline in recorded crime, a decline conspicuously against the trend in other advanced industrial societies. In the autumn this connection was advanced by the Home Secretary in support of his contention that 'prison works'.

[5] See D. Garland, *Punishment and Modern Society* (Oxford, 1990) for a review of the sociological literature.

the essays that follow. Before allowing our contributors to speak for themselves, we need first to chart some of influences which have brought us to the present point.

2. BACKGROUND

Until two decades ago sentencers in most countries had a wide discretion to impose whatever sentence they deemed appropriate, subject to the maximum penalty. In the United States, this discretion was virtually uncontrolled with a majority of states having no provision for appeal against sentence. Furthermore, in many states sentences for serious offences comprised indeterminate or partially indeterminate periods of custody the duration of which was determined by parole authorities exercising almost unfettered discretion. In other countries, there were constraints. In England, for example, a 'tariff' was developed by the judiciary which broadly indicated a range of sentences for 'normal cases'; defendants had a right of appeal where an excessive penalty beyond the tariff was imposed. In Australia, it would appear, even the idea of a 'tariff' was objectionable to judges in some states: sentencing was said to involve an 'intuitive synthesis' not susceptible to legislative formulae.[6]

Such broad discretionary powers meant several things in most jurisdictions. Different judges could impose different sentences for different reasons without having to give any explanation in open court. For example, some judges could impose a sentence for deterrent reasons, but other judges in similar cases could sentence offenders in order to rehabilitate them. Even the same judge was not always consistent in sentencing. There was no agreement among judges as to what criteria ought to be taken into account in the sentencing decision and what weight ought to be given to factors such as prior record, age, good family, perceived future dangerousness, whether the accused pleaded guilty, and other such matters. Criticism of this lack of consistency was speedily met with the response that sentences were individualized; they were tailored to meet the needs of the defendant and therefore consistency in punishments for similar crimes was not to be expected. The result was widespread sentencing disparity with similar cases being treated differently and, in England in the lower courts, different benches of magistrates developing different sentencing cultures and standards that seemed not to be justified by any differences in the pattern of offending locally.[7]

---

[6] See Ch. 3, pp. 61–63.

[7] For evidence of sentencing disparity in England, see R. Tarling and M. Weatheritt, *Sentencing Practice in Magistrates Courts* (Home Office Research Study No. 56; London, 1979); C. Corbett, 'Magistrates' Court Clerks' Sentencing Behaviour: An Experimental Study',

Another consequence of judges sentencing for a mixture of reasons, many of them utilitarian, was that excessively long sentences were imposed in some cases. In particular, the rationale of exemplary sentencing resulted in some offenders receiving sentences in excess of those imposed on others committing similar crimes.

There also developed what was said to be a lack of 'truth in sentencing'.[8] Offenders sent to prison were entitled to remission of their sentence (in the United States generally referred to as 'good time' for good behaviour) and to release on parole after a specified period (in England, for example, generally after serving one-third of their sentence). The decision whether to release someone on parole often amounted effectively to a prisoner being sentenced a second time—but this time behind closed doors, without due process. This meant that two offenders who originally received the same sentence for the same crime could be released after very different intervals. It also meant that when parole eligibility thresholds were set at different points for sentences of different lengths (as was the case in many jurisdictions), prisoners originally sent to prison for markedly different periods could end up spending much the same time in custody.[9]

These disparities and inconsistencies would no doubt have struck many observers as unjust and unacceptable whatever the empirical evidence of sentencing efficacy. But in many eyes they became steadily more objectionable as the increasing stock of research evidence failed to demonstrate that individualized utilitarian sentencing worked in terms of subsequent law-abiding behaviour. Faith in the rehabilitative ideal was steadily undermined[10] and increasing knowledge of the extent of crime, and the marginal inroads which policing and criminal-justice interventions make into detecting and punishing those responsible, eventually called into question the

---

in D. Pennington and S. Lloyd-Bostock (eds.), *The Psychology of Sentencing* (Oxford, 1987); NACRO, *The Real Alternative* (London, 1989), 10–17; Liberty, *Unequal before the Law: Sentencing in Magistrates' Courts in England and Wales 1981–1990* (London, 1992). For evidence of sentencing disparity in the United States, see American Friends Service Committee, *Struggle for Justice* (New York, 1971); M. Frankel, *Criminal Sentences: Law Without Order* (New York, 1973); E. Van den Haag, *Punishing Criminals* (New York, 1975); Report of the Twentieth Century Fund Task Force on Criminal Sentencing, *Fair and Certain Punishment* (New York, 1976).

[8] This phrase enjoyed a particular vogue in Australia, especially in New South Wales where 'truth in sentencing' was officially said to be the principal objective of the 1989 Sentencing Act (NSW). See Ch. 3, pp. 54–55. The 1989 Act is colloquially known in New South Wales as 'The Truth in Sentencing Act'.

[9] See Ch. 5, p. 131. For a detailed review of the development of parole policy in England, see Carlisle Report, *The Parole System in England and Wales: Report of the Review Committee* (Cm. 532; London, 1988).

[10] See e.g. D. Lipton, R. Martinson, and J. Wilks, *The Effectiveness of Correctional Treatment* (New York, 1975); S. Brody, *The Effectiveness of Sentencing* (Home Office Research Study No. 35; London, 1976). For the penological implications of this research literature, see e.g. N. Morris, *The Future of Imprisonment* (Chicago, 1974); R. Cross, *Punishment, Prison and the Public* (London, 1976).

doctrine of deterrence, understood in an individual calculative sense.[11] As the consequentialist connection which justified individualized sentencing unravelled, the civil libertarian critique gained in strength. In Sweden the various working parties whose recommendations led to the Sentencing Reform Act 1988 proposed that the special preventive measures which had been introduced in the first half of the century be repealed. In this, they followed the course already charted by Finland, where indeterminate incarceration had effectively been abolished in 1975.[12] In England indeterminate orders accompanied by wide executive discretion had been allowed to develop furthest in relation to those offenders—juveniles and the mentally disordered—whose legal responsibility was most obviously questionable. Thus it was precisely in these areas of the criminal law and social policy that the 'back to justice' movement first mounted its most telling assaults.[13] In the field of juvenile justice, legislation providing for extensive intervention, and loss of rights, on the grounds that criminal behaviour may be symptomatic of welfare need, was not implemented.[14] The tide of opinion had turned.

In many jurisdictions concerns about rising prison populations fed this reformulation of opinion. The use of custody is always an expensive penal option[15] and the expense is called into question if the incapacitative, deterrent, and rehabilitative benefits are doubtful and if control or reduction of public spending has a high priority. In the United States, as Anthony Doob's chapter in this volume makes clear, leading politicians appear to have believed, in spite of the contrary evidence, that imprisonment, extensively used, can serve to control and reduce crime: these politicians actively encouraged the greater use of custody. Furthermore, it appears that in Australia in both New South Wales in 1989, and in Victoria following the fall of the Labour Government in the summer 1992, there came to power administrations which perceived a rise in the prison population to be the inevitable consequence of their adopting tough 'law and order' policies

---

[11] For example, what the British Home Office refers to as the attrition rate (the low likelihood that a crime will be reported, recorded, and cleared up, and that the offender will be convicted and sentenced in a particular way (see Home Office, *Digest 2: Information on the Criminal Justice System in England and Wales* (London, 1993), 29)) has undermined Beccaria's ideal four certainties of offence, detection, conviction, and punishment. See e.g. the statement of official scepticism regarding deterrence in Home Office (1990), above, n. 1, para. 2.8.

[12] See Ch. 4, p. 97.

[13] In relation to juveniles, see e.g. A. Morris and H. Giller, *What Justice for Children?* (London, 1979); L. Taylor, R. Lacey, and D. Bracken, *In Whose Best Interests?* (London, 1980); A. Morris, H. Giller, E. Szwed, and H. Geach, *Justice for Children* (London, 1980). And regarding mentally disordered offenders, see e.g. L. Gostin, *A Human Condition*, i and ii (London, 1975, 1977).

[14] For example, Children and Young Persons Act 1969, ss. 4 and 5(1)–(7): introduced by a Labour Government, not implemented by either the hostile Conservative Government elected in 1970, nor the Labour Government returned to power in 1974.

[15] M. Wasik, *Emmins on Sentencing* (London, 1993), 78.

judged to be electorally popular.[16] The same conclusion might be drawn from the stance of the Conservative Government in England at the time of writing.[17] In most countries it has not been so, most of the time. There has been no shortage of tough 'law and order' political rhetoric,[18] but politicians have generally spoken with forked tongues—making tough noises on the public hustings but encouraging custody-reducing policies *sotto voce* behind the scenes. This has been the dissimulating engine encouraging more and more generous use of executive release, thereby building up the temporal disjunction between custodial sentences passed and custodial sentences served which eventually fuelled the 'truth in sentencing' movement. Though some countries have experienced short-term surges in their prison populations, the proportionate use of custody has generally continued to decline. Controlling sentencers' discretion has become an essential part of the emerging armoury of managerialism in criminal-justice systems.

In England, the Conservative administrations which have continuously enjoyed office since 1979 have made efficiency in public administration a central plank of policy. Wherever possible public services have been returned to the private sector so as to benefit from the allegedly keen winds of competition. The list of services considered suitable for privatization has grown as traditional assumptions have been challenged: the unthinkable has become thinkable and the criminal-justice system has not been im- mune.[19] The corollary of privatization is that the residue of dwindling state services has been subjected to bureaucratically imposed disciplines de- signed to mirror those of the market. The three Es—effectiveness, ef- ficiency, and economy—have been made watchwords and have been used to underpin the demand that all services, including the various agencies that make up the criminal-justice system, state their objectives, devise measur- ing-rods for their achievement and regularly report on progress.[20] Within this climate the idea that sentencing, the visible pinnacle of criminal-justice decision-making, and the progenitor of all penal expenditure, should be

[16] See Ch. 3, pp. 77, 93.

[17] Between spring and December 1993, a rise in the prison population from 42, 000 to 47, 000 was the accompaniment of the reversals to the Criminal Justice Act 1991, the 'get-tough' measures announced by the Home Secretary at the Conservative Party Conference in October 1993, and his suggestion that 'prison works'.

[18] See M. Brake and C. Hale, *Public Order and Private Lives* (London, 1991); D. Downes and R. Morgan, 'The Politics of Law and Order', in M. Maguire, R. Morgan, and R. Reiner (eds.), *The Oxford Handbook of Criminology* (Oxford, 1994).

[19] The management of prisons, for example, has been contracted out to the private commer- cial sector: the same is true in Australia and the USA. See M. Ryan and T. Ward, *Privatization and the Penal System* (Milton Keynes, 1989); and C. Logan, *Private Prisons: Pros and Cons* (New York, 1990).

[20] In England, these managerial initiatives derived from the Government's Financial Management Initiative (see Prime Minister, *Efficiency and Effectiveness in the Civil Service* (London, 1982). For a recent discussion, see C. Jones 'Auditing Criminal Justice', (1993) 33 *Brit. J. Criminol.* 187.

subject to broad relatively uncontrolled discretion was managerially anomalous.

Yet sentencing policy presented the Conservative Government in Britain with a fundamental dilemma. Part of the Conservative Party's traditional hegemony in matters of 'law and order' has rested on its perceived alignment with the bastion institutions of social order, of which the law and the judiciary are central. The idea that the law and the courts represent the politically impartial interests of the body politic are central to Conservative thinking, and this conceptualization has traditionally engendered a high degree of deference to not merely the independence but the autonomy which the judiciary has come jealously to guard as its prerogative. It is apparent from Arie Freiberg's account of sentencing reform in Victoria, Australia, in Chapter 3, that the same phenomenon acts as a powerful brake on politicians there also. The unjustified coalescence of judicial independence, a constitutionally reputable doctrine, and judicial autonomy in the sense of freedom from politically determined legal restraint, a doctrine without constitutional foundation, has as a consequence been a matter of growing concern to Conservative Party tacticians, civil-service policy-makers, and academic critics alike. There is a fundamental distinction between executive intervention in sentencing decisions—generally considered a dangerous intrusion—and the legislative articulation of sentencing policy—arguably a much needed framework.[21] Yet in order to maintain its stance as the traditional party of 'law and order', and not be seen to be tying the hands of the judges—which as the Lord Chief Justice's subsequent reference to being forced into an 'ill-fitting straitjacket' was a danger all too apparent—the government initially moved with extreme caution in deciding how sentencing might be brought within its managerialist fold.

It was a combination of all these factors that provided fertile soil for the growth of the 'justice' or 'just deserts' movement. The agenda was set. Judicial discretion had to be controlled. Sentencing disparity had to be eliminated. This would necessarily involve eliminating disproportionately long sentences. There also needed to be 'truth in sentencing': equal sentences imposed in open court had in practice to mean the same thing for different offenders. The concept of just desert with its liberal emphasis on justice involving like cases being treated alike was the obvious facilitator. However, it was clearly not enough simply to embrace the concept of just desert and reduce the importance of utilitarian considerations. Different judges could have different conceptions of what sentence was deserved in any particular case. What was needed was a mechanism for ensuring that judicial discretion was controlled by forcing judges to sentence in accord-

---

[21] This distinction has powerfully been made by A. Ashworth, *Sentencing and Criminal Justice* (London, 1992), chs. 1 and 2.

ance with agreed and objective standards of desert. The object of this collection of essays is to review the response in several jurisdictions that have taken important steps to meet this challenge. As will be seen, the process of achieving sentencing reform has been largely shaped by a mixture of ideological, practical, and pragmatic considerations arising out of the institutional traditions and political cultures in each jurisdiction.

3. THE CASE-STUDIES

The first and most dramatic reforms were introduced in the United States. California was the first state to amend its sentencing laws in 1976 to declare that the elimination of disparity and the provision of uniformity of sentences was to be the main goal of sentencing.[22] The penalty for most offences was fixed at three levels, and when a defendant was sent to prison, the court was normally to impose the middle term. However, if aggravating or mitigating circumstances were found to exist, the judge could impose the upper or lower term respectively. All sentences of imprisonment were subject to appellate review with the object of eliminating sentencing disparity.[23] Some important discretion does remain, however, in the decision whether to incarcerate or grant probation.

More common in the United States, however, has been the development of numerical sentencing guidelines under which specific sentencing proposals based on offence severity and prior criminal history are developed to structure and control judicial discretion. The Oregon and Minnesota guidelines, discussed by Andrew von Hirsch in Chapter 6, and the US Federal Guidelines, discussed by Anthony Doob in Chapter 8, are classic examples of such guidelines. In these jurisdictions, a sentencing commission was created to establish the sentencing guidelines. Sentencing judges are expected to pass sentences within the specified range, but these are only guidelines and can be departed from. In Minnesota, for example, the guidelines provide a list of non-exclusive mitigating and aggravating factors that may be used as reasons for departure. In Chapter 7, Richard Frase discusses the Minnesota provisions and their consequences in great detail.

The essays by Andrew von Hirsch, Richard Frase, and Anthony Doob lead to a consideration of three important matters. First, one of the principal aims of the guidelines in Minnesota, Oregon, and of the Federal system was that of achieving proportionality which would involve the elimination of disparity. However, the guidelines apply only to fairly serious crime.

---

[22] California Penal Code, s. 1170(a)(1).
[23] Ibid., s. 117(f). See generally, M. Fenili, 'California's Disparate Sentencing Review Process', in M. L. Forst (ed.), *Sentencing Reform: Experiments in Reducing Disparity* (Beverly Hills, Calif., 1982).

With regard to all lesser crime falling below the dispositional line for the use of custody (for example, in Minnesota, crime as serious as residential burglary of an occupied building), judicial discretion remains unfettered. With regard to the more serious crimes, the guidelines appear to have been tolerably successful in reducing disparity, but it is here that a marked difference in the operation of the Minnesota and the Federal approaches can be discerned. In the Federal courts, as Doob's essay demonstrates, the US Sentencing Guidelines have become almost mandatory whereas in Minnesota, there is a departure rate of over 30 per cent.[24] This divergence in approach raises one of the central themes addressed in this volume. Assuming that one is aiming at proportionality, control of judicial discretion, and the elimination of sentencing disparity, how much flexibility is to be permitted to sentencers? Justice demands that like cases be treated alike, but it also requires that different cases be treated differently. It is inevitable that in reducing all serious crimes to a limited number of over-generalized solutions, fine-tuning will have to be achieved on a case-by-case basis, and this will involve departing from the guideline penalty. This of course raises the question as to whether numerical guidelines are any better equipped to achieve the desired objectives than the descriptive guidelines that operate in Sweden, which have to a limited extent been developed in England, and which are now provided for in Victoria, Australia, in the Sentencing Act 1991.

Secondly, most of the guidelines that have been formulated in the United States deal only with the control of discretion at the sentencing stage of the criminal-justice process. The consequence is that much discretion has been shifted to the prosecutor who, being able to determine the charge that is brought, is effectively able to determine the sentence that is imposed. This has opened up the scope for bargaining. When the outcome of bargaining is the laying of a reduced charge in return for a guilty plea, the result is that offenders are not sentenced for the crime they committed, but rather for the crime to which they have pleaded guilty. Such practices, coupled with an apparent tendency on the part of prosecutors to insist that offenders plead guilty to a number of charges so that their offender score is raised,[25] can lead to disparity and injustice being removed to an earlier and less visible stage of the process. An alternative approach, adopted in the Federal jurisdiction, is to sentence offenders according to the 'real' crime they committed rather than the one for which they have admitted guilt.[26]

[24] See Ch. 7, pp. 186–187.
[25] See M. Tonry, 'Sentencing Guidelines and Sentencing Commissions: The Second Generation', in K. Pease and M. Wasik (eds.), *Sentencing Reform* (Manchester, 1987), 39. See also D. Parent, *Structuring Criminal Sentences: The Evolution of Minnesotas Sentencing Guidelines* (Stoneham, Mass., 1988).
[26] See A. Doob, below, Ch. 8.

However, the dangers involved in dispensing with the strict evidentiary rules governing the criminal trial hardly need spelling out.

Finally, a very real danger of implementing any numerical guideline system must be emphasized. In Minnesota and Oregon (albeit not in the Federal jurisdiction), the original guidelines were introduced with the avowed intention of reducing or stabilizing prison populations. Parsimony was as important as proportionality, and in Minnesota the Sentencing Commission developed a computer model of the sentencing process with which to test the prison-population consequences of adopting particular presumptive sentences.[27] Such guidelines are, however, subsequently amenable to hijack by politicians intent on increasing penalties. This has occurred in Minnesota where the presumptive penalties have twice been increased since their inception. In the 1989 round of increases, following several highly publicized homicides and considerable legislative pressure, the Sentencing Commission doubled several guideline penalties: the presumptive penalty for aggravated robbery was increased from 24 to 48 months, for example. The Commission also doubled the number of points accorded to prior convictions, thereby again increasing the potential for, and duration of, imprisonment. The result has been an increase in the incarceration rate.[28] Most of the United States guideline schemes accord what is arguably excessive weight to previous convictions. Though it is possible to reconcile the idea of just deserts with some weight being given to previous convictions,[29] allowing too much weight is likely to thwart the achievement of proportionality and mean that as previous convictions accumulate, the aim of parsimony will be defeated.

In England, similar concerns have been entertained but the response has been more guarded, but nevertheless significant. First, the Attorney-General can now refer an unduly lenient sentence to the Court of Appeal which has the power to increase the sentence.[30] A disparate sentence can be an unduly light one as well as an unduly heavy one and so this right of appeal does go some way towards the elimination of unwarranted disparity. However, since leave to appeal is required this mechanism is used only in extreme cases.[31] Secondly, the Criminal Justice Act 1991 has endorsed the concept of just desert in declaring that the sentences must be proportionate to the seriousness of the offence. Thirdly, the threshold for parole eligibility has been raised so as to produce more 'truth in sentencing':[32] it was the hope of the official Working Party recommending this measure that by giving

[27] See D. Parent, above, n. 25.   [28] See Ch. 7.
[29] See A. von Hirsch, *Past or Future Crimes* (Manchester, 1985), 78–84.
[30] Criminal Justice Act 1988, s. 36.
[31] In 1990, for example, there were only twenty-five applications of which four were withdrawn and one was refused leave ([1992] *Crim. LR* 142).
[32] Criminal Justice Act 1991, s. 33.

sentences greater meaning the courts might be persuaded to lower their tariffs, thereby achieving greater parsimony in the use of custody.[33] Fourthly, the Magistrates' Association has drawn up and issued voluntary guidelines for magistrates' courts in an attempt to establish consistency in sentencing both within and between courts.[34] Guidelines for a variety of offences have been drawn up and some offences have been subdivided. For example, there are separate guidelines for general theft, theft from a shop, theft from a vehicle, and theft in breach of trust. The Magistrates' Association Guidelines are entirely voluntary, though a survey has suggested that 75 per cent of magistrates were using the predecessor of the present guidelines.[35] It must be stressed, however, that the guidelines are sufficiently broad and general that two magistrates using the same guidelines in the same case could come up with very different results. Nevertheless, encouraging uniformity of approach must be an improvement on allowing magistrates complete freedom to sentence purely on the basis of their intuitions. Finally, in an attempt to structure sentencing discretion in the Crown Court, the Court of Appeal has begun handing down guideline judgments. These usually occur when a number of appeals are heard at the same time and the Court of Appeal takes the opportunity to make generalized statements about sentencing for that type of offence. There are guideline judgments now on a wide variety of offences.[36]

There is evidence that some of these Court of Appeal decisions have resulted in sharp increases in sentencing levels. For example, 30 per cent of offenders convicted of rape in 1984 received sentences of at least five years' imprisonment. By 1987, the year following the guideline judgment in *Billam*,[37] the figure had risen to 80 per cent.[38] With the enactment of the Criminal Justice Act 1991, guideline judgments could in the future play an important role by identifying the criteria of seriousness upon which most sentencing decisions have to be based. The main defect of such guideline judgments is that each focuses on only a particular offence without considering the relationship of that offence to other offences in terms of seriousness and without any overall strategy or view of the aims of punish-

---

[33] Carlisle Report, above, n. 9, paras. 239–51. This would be to reverse the process over the previous two decades whereby the courts possibly increased sentences so as to discount earlier release.

[34] Magistrates' Association, *Sentencing Guidelines* (London, 1993).

[35] A. Turner, 'Sentencing in the Magistrates' Court', in C. Munro and M. Wasik (eds.), *Sentencing, Judicial Discretion and Training* (London, 1992), 193. There are similar guidelines for traffic offences: the same survey revealed that 89 per cent of magistrates were using these guidelines.

[36] e.g. *Aramah* (1983) 76 Cr. App. R. 190 (drugs); *Boswell* (1984) 6 Cr. App. R. (S.) 257 (causing death by reckless driving); and *Stewart* (1987) 9 Cr. App. R. (S.) 135 (social-security fraud).

[37] (1986) 82 Cr. App. 347.   [38] Home Office (1990), above, n. 1, para. 2.14.

ment.[39] What is needed is an attempt to structure sentencing discretion within a coherent scheme having a clear overall view of the purposes of punishment. Perhaps the English system is more suited to the setting up of a sentencing commission that would lay down statements of principle along the lines of those employed in Sweden, though David Thomas's account in Chapter 5 is clearly grounded on the view that greater progress towards consistent sentencing practice would have been better achieved in England had the judiciary been left untrammelled by repeated, and inept, political interference in successive Acts of Parliament.

It would appear from Nils Jareborg's account in Chapter 4 of the reform process in Sweden that there is a political culture in Sweden in which practitioners and academic experts are deferred to by politicians to a degree inconceivable in England. He suggests that there was no 'pressure' to reform the Criminal Code in the sense that we have implicitly suggested above. Reform is rather one of continuous review. Official Working Parties monitor the working of legislation and revised codifications are agreed on through a consensual process involving extensive consultation. The corollary is that adjustments are relatively marginal and continuity in practice considerable. There was no great swing towards 'just desert' thinking in the 1988 Criminal Code and though some 'special-preventive' measures were repealed, utilitarian considerations are still given a good deal of scope, particularly in relation to the conditional sentence and probation.[40] It follows that though the 1988 Code has laid down precisely what factors aggravate or mitigate the penal value of a crime, with the consequence that the Supreme Court has issued detailed guidance particularly concerning appropriate sanctions, there has been neither a major shift in the distribution of sanctions employed nor, a most telling point, has the government sponsored any research into the impact on sentencing practice of the new Code. The Code is, as Nils Jareborg explains it, 'both revolutionary and leaves everything as it was'.[41] Moreover, though he suggests that the Code has probably ensured that resort to incarceration has been kept within the relatively parsimonious Scandinavian tradition, it is clear that Sweden is not immune to the tougher 'law and order' political climate which has overtaken all the jurisdictions represented in this volume. In 1993 the Swedish Government has also introduced measures to impose longer custodial sentences for selected offences and make parole less generous.[42]

Arie Freiberg's account in Chapter 3 of the introduction of the Sentencing Act 1991 in Victoria, Australia, provides an example of legislative codification which though prompted, as elsewhere, by doubts about the

[39] See A. Ashworth, 'Three Techniques for Reduced Sentence Disparity', in A. von Hirsch and A. Ashworth, *Principled Sentencing* (Edinburgh, 1992), 284.
[40] See Ch. 4, p. 118.   [41] Ibid., p. 122.   [42] Ibid., pp. 119–120.

rehabilitative ideal, the renaissance in retributive thinking, and the demand for 'truth in sentencing', has resulted in legislating for all the competing principles which already informed sentencing practice, albeit in a largely unstated fashion. Retribution, deterrence, rehabilitation, denunciation, and public protection, either alone or in combination, are all provided for in the Act, despite the fact that the Victorian Sentencing Committee had originally found this *mélange* wanting in coherence.[43] The Victorian case-study illustrates beautifully how resistance to reform is often focused on terminology which is taken to be symbolically threatening. The United States reforming baggage train of numerical guidelines and sentencing grids was regarded as an anathema by the judiciary in Victoria. Even tariffs on the English model and the 'tyranny of statistics' were resisted. Neverthe-less, arguably, more was achieved than in England where the 'just desert' principle was superficially given greater prominence. Statutory maxima were revised on the lines of existing sentencing practice, remission of cus-tody was abolished, mitigating and aggravating factors were listed in the legislation, the means for determining the seriousness of offences were defined (as they were not in England), a hierarchy of sanctions was laid down and provision was made for the issue of guideline judgments on the English model. Moreover, whereas in England the abolition of remission and the raising of the threshold for parole eligibility was accompanied by no more than an act of faith that sentencers would lower tariffs so as to offset what would otherwise be an increase in the prison population (an act of faith which seems so far to have been unwarranted[44]), in Victoria there was a legislative injunction that sentencers should discount their sentences in recognition of less generous executive release provisions. The Sentenc-ing Act has resulted in little change in the size of the Victorian prison population.

Arie Freiberg stresses the long lead time which was provided for in Victoria before the Sentencing Act was implemented. Much effort was invested in training sentencers. As we stressed above, exactly the same was true in England,[45] to little purpose it appears. More important, it would seem, for the successful implementation of any sentencing-reform pro-gramme, whatever criteria for success are specified, is the thoroughness of the consultative process. The key constituencies, political and practitioner, have to buy into the reform programme before it is signed and sealed. It is clear that this was a vital ingredient in the Minnesota and Swedish cases. It was less clearly achieved in England. But the size and intimacy of a jurisdic-tion is almost certainly a factor here. As Arie Freiberg points out, most key sentencers in Victoria, in the lower and higher courts, operate out of ad-jacent buildings in Melbourne, Victoria's major city. Larger and more

---

[43] Ch. 3, p. 62.   [44] See Ch. 5, p. 143.   [45] Above, p 2. See also Ch. 5, p. 143.

fractured jurisdictions are obviously prey to the development of different sentencing cultures.

4. SCENE-SETTING AND DRAWING CONCLUSIONS

We need not delay our readers further by summarizing those developments in penal philosophy which have framed the sentencing-reform programmes described in our case-studies. That task has been eloquently undertaken by Anthony Bottoms in Chapter 2. Nor need we summarize the general lessons that emerge from the case-study material. That invaluable contribution has been made in Chapters 9 and 10 by Andrew Ashworth and Michael Tonry. Each has brought a distinctive perspective to bear. Rather there are two interesting methodological questions that hang over the material in this text.

First, there is the point with which implicitly we started. In spite of our best endeavours, it appears that there is no ideal time on which to embark on an examination of sentencing reform. In England the Criminal Justice Act 1991 was not allowed to settle down so that a dispassionate examination of its impact could be undertaken. The research programme planned by the Home Office Research and Planning Unit had effectively to be abandoned as key provisions in the legislation were first questioned, then repudiated and finally overturned. At the time of writing, further legislation is in the pipeline and there is a ferment of uncertainty, particularly in the Prison Service, as to how things will pan out. In Sweden and Victoria events have been less dramatic. But amendments have recently been made to both the 1988 Criminal Code and the Sentencing Act 1991 respectively which seem certain significantly to affect the size of the prison population. In Minnesota the presumptive sentences originally devised by the Sentencing Commission have twice been increased for populist political reasons in response to notorious crimes. Sentencing policy appears generally to have become a high-profile issue increasingly susceptible to politically partisan pressures. It is doubtful whether there will ever be a time when the scene is sufficiently stable for any comparatively taken snap-shot not to be blurred.

The second methodological question is perhaps more intriguing. When we decided to organize the Colston Symposium in Bristol we decided straightforwardly to focus our case-study attentions on jurisdictions which had recently embarked on *legislative* reform. Our implicit assumption was that a political decision to legislate represents a major commitment to review and to change sentencing practice. However, it may not be so. In Victoria, Australia, and Sweden the new legislation has in large measure codified much existing practice and, not surprisingly, the evidence suggests that practice, at least as far as the distribution of sentences is concerned, has little changed. In Minnesota, the reform was designed to change many aspects of practice but in such a fashion that the size of the prison population should be held constant. This raises an interesting question, therefore. Supposing we had chosen to focus on jurisdictions which had in recent years achieved the greatest changes in sentencing practice—the distribution of sanctions employed, the duration of custodial sentences, the degree of reliance on executive release, the weight given to different aggravating and mitigating factors when assessing the seriousness of crime, and so on—might we have alighted on other countries, jurisdictions that have quietly effected a revolution without resort to legislation?

It is an intriguing question to which we do not know the answer. But we cannot help but observe that in England in the 1980s there was truly a revolution (which may now be being rolled back) in the treatment of juveniles in the criminal-justice system. Prosecution became rare and the use of invasive sanctions, particularly custody, diminished dramatically. It happened quietly, behind the scenes, as a result of practitioners agreeing on a new approach. It happened largely without new legislation.[46] The decision to legislate may or may not represent political commitment to reform: but it also opens up sentencing practice to detailed public scrutiny, which may increase the likelihood that sentencing practice will become vulnerable to political fashion and short-termism.

[46] See L. Gelsthorpe and A. Morris, 'Juvenile Justice', in M. Maguire, R. Morgan, and R. Reiner (eds.), above, n. 18.

2

The Philosophy and Politics of Punishment and Sentencing

ANTHONY BOTTOMS

The preliminary information brochure for the Colston International Sentencing Symposium set out very succinctly some key features of the context in which the Symposium was held:

A number of factors—rising crime rates; prison crowding; fiscal crisis; loss of faith in the treatment paradigm; concern that 'just deserts' be delivered; the need for public protection against 'dangerous' offenders—have in recent years sharpened the debate about sentencing policy.

All of the factors listed in this quotation have been influential, to a greater or lesser extent, in most Western countries at some point during the last three decades. However, as the various national case-studies prepared for the Colston Symposium very well illustrate, the details of the response, in terms of sentencing policy, have been quite varied.

To those who have studied earlier historical developments in criminal policy in different countries, this variation will come as no surprise. For example, in the era of the dominance of the positivist paradigm within criminology, legislation and penal practice were in most countries influenced, to a greater or lesser extent, by this intellectual movement, but the precise nature of the policies adopted differed quite markedly from country to country,[1] and can be shown to have been significantly influenced by the particular cultural and political context of the nation in question. Our best understanding of legislative (and other policy) change leads to the conclusion that much of the detail depends upon particular individuals and

Though the main argument remains the same, this chapter is a considerably expanded and amended version of the paper originally given at the Colston International Symposium. I am most grateful for the comments made by a number of participants at the Colston Symposium, by the Editors, and by Richard Jones, a Ph.D. student at the Institute of Criminology, Cambridge University; these comments have resulted in substantial improvements to the paper. The responsibility for any remaining defects rests, of course, with the author only.

[1] Consider, for example, the substantially greater acceptance of the indeterminate sentence in the USA as compared with England; or the more ready acceptance of positivist-inspired conceptions of 'dangerousness' in Continental European countries than was the case in England.

circumstances in different countries, even where general movements of thought are discernible cross-nationally.[2]

Given the above, the task of presenting an opening paper to the Colston Symposium on 'The Philosophy and Politics of Punishment and Sentencing' posed a number of dilemmas. In some respects, what seemed to be needed was a detailed comparative discussion of the differing political contexts of the different countries represented in the Symposium case-studies—a contribution that would indeed have been most illuminating, but which was beyond my competence. On the other hand, the reference to 'the philosophy of punishment' in the suggested title of the paper could be interpreted as requiring some new contribution to the normative literature in that field of study; yet against this, the tendency of many legislators and administrators to ride roughshod over the nuances of penal theory suggested that such an approach would be altogether too ethereal for the occasion in hand. Accordingly, it eventually seemed to me that the most useful contribution that this introductory paper could make was to operate at a very general level, and with a primarily sociological focus—in short, to attempt *to sketch the main movements of thought that seemed to underpin much of modern sentencing change in different countries, to try to understand why these movements of thought have been occurring, and to reflect upon their implications.*

Within this framework, the central argument of this essay is that modern sentencing change in different countries can be principally understood by reference to three main conceptual developments, which I shall describe as *just deserts/human rights*, *managerialism*, and *'the community'*; and also by reference to a fourth and more obviously political factor which I shall call *'populist punitiveness'*. The first three of these concepts, I shall contend, are ones which historical and sociological analysis would lead one to expect to find, in varying forms, in most Western countries in the late twentieth century. Despite this, they do in fact in certain respects conflict with one another at a conceptual level, a point that I shall try to highlight by concentrating especially on the image of personhood that each concept tends to embody. The fourth factor 'populist punitiveness' is, I shall argue, more unpredictable than the other three factors in the dual sense (1) that it grows less obviously than they do out of long-term social change; and (2) that it is particularly susceptible to appropriation by politicians, sometimes at quite short notice and not infrequently in a somewhat undulating or changeable manner. However, the fact that the first three concepts are in one sense more predictable than the fourth as likely general influences on a given Western criminal-justice system in the late twentieth century emphatically

---

[2] See e.g. D. Garland, *Punishment and Welfare* (Aldershot, 1985); T. S. Dahl, *Child Welfare and Social Defence* (Oslo, 1985).

does not mean that the way in which these concepts will influence a particular criminal-justice system can easily be predicted; moreover, given that (see above) there is in fact some conceptual tension between these three concepts, the variety of ways in which they can be used in actual legislation and penal practice is clearly very large.

Out of abundant caution (as the Romans used to say), I must also make it clear that the four matters highlighted in the preceding paragraph do not, of course, exhaust the range of potential influences upon sentencing change. These matters are nevertheless, in my judgment, of special importance and significance; and certainly they are enough to be going on with in terms of the present analysis. I shall first consider each of the four highlighted factors in its own terms, and then try to develop an overall analysis of their significance.

I. JUST DESERTS/HUMAN RIGHTS

As is well known, the 'just deserts' approach to sentencing gained ground initially in the 1970s and has continued to attract attention among criminologists and among policy-makers ever since.[3] The impetus for the initial growth of the approach seems to have been twofold—first, a pessimism about the previously dominant treatment model in the light of the rather negative results of empirical research; and secondly, a growing interest in making claims about offenders' rights, or the obligation of state authorities to treat them with fairness, in a way that would limit the dominant utilitarianism of the day. On this second point, it is worth noting that one of Norval Morris's first forays into just deserts theory (in his case, interpreted primarily as limiting retributivism) came in an essay explicitly entitled 'Penal Sanctions and Human Rights'.[4] That essay contained, *inter alia*, a cogent argument in favour of the proposition that 'power over a criminal's life should not be taken in excess of that which would be taken were his reform not considered as one of our purposes',[5] and arguments of this sort have, without doubt, since the 1960s had a significant influence in many jurisdictions in, for example, limiting the scale of use of the indeterminate

[3] For a useful summary of the early development of this approach, see A. K. Bottomley, 'The "Justice Model" in America and Britain: Development and Analysis', in A. E. Bottoms and R. H. Preston (eds.), *The Coming Penal Crisis* (Edinburgh, 1980).

[4] N. Morris and C. Howard, *Studies in Criminal Law* (Oxford, 1964), ch. 5.

[5] Ibid. 175. It should be noted that Morris's essay was written just five years after H. L. A. Hart's celebrated lecture entitled 'Prolegomenon to the Principles of Punishment' (originally published 1959, see now H. L. A. Hart, *Punishment and Responsibility* (Oxford, 1968), ch. 1). That paper had similarly suggested rights-based blocks on a predominantly utilitarian punishment system, though Hart focused on the question of distribution (who should be punished?) rather than, as Morris did, on the amount of punishment.

sentence, and/or in reforms of welfare-oriented juvenile-justice systems.[6] In this general movement, a particularly powerful early document was *Struggle for Justice*, a report of the American Friends Service Committee which castigated the treatment model on theoretical/political grounds as 'theoretically faulty, systematically discriminatory in application, and inconsistent with some of our most basic concepts of justice'.[7]

As should be clear from the above, Morris's 'power should not . . .' dictum, and the American Friends' report, were especially concerned to emphasize the injustices of what they saw as the excessive power potentially claimed over offenders' lives by the treatment model. For Morris, therefore, and anticipating the later philosophical argument of Lucas,[8] the concepts of 'justice' and 'desert' as applied to sentencing are essentially asymmetric concepts, in the sense that it is reasonably easy to establish what is unjust or undeserved, but not what, precisely, is just or deserved. As Morris and Tonry have put this point of view recently:

Given the reality that people's views of deserved punishment vary widely, it is unlikely that any comprehensive system of sentencing standards will adopt a rigid scheme of *deserved punishments*. Retributive considerations can, however, give guidance on *undeservedly* lenient or severe punishments (emphasis added).[9]

But to some writers, and notably to Andrew von Hirsch,[10] the kind of approach adopted by Morris remains unsatisfactory. For von Hirsch, a central principle of sentencing is that people who have committed similar offences, with similar criminal records,[11] should receive the same sentences—what he calls the 'parity principle'.[12] On an absolute basis, von Hirsch concedes, with Morris, that we cannot say what, precisely, a given

---

[6] For an example of the kind of thinking to which objection was being taken, see the following 1967 comment from a social-work academic, writing about juvenile justice: '[Critics have argued that we should] *limit* what can be done to offenders in the interests of justice and individual liberty . . . [but] it must be said that the whole purpose of the [proposed welfare-oriented] procedure is to concentrate on treatment needs, and therefore what is done for a child is done in the interests of his welfare' (P. Boss, *Social Policy and the Young Delinquent* (London, 1967), 91, emphasis in original).

[7] American Friends Service Committee, *Struggle for Justice* (New York, 1971), 12; see also A. E. Bottoms, 'An Introduction to "The Coming Crisis" ', in A. E. Bottoms and R. H. Preston (eds.), *The Coming Penal Crisis* (Edinburgh, 1980).

[8] J. R. Lucas, *On Justice* (Oxford, 1980).

[9] N. Morris and M. Tonry, *Between Prison and Probation: Intermediate Punishments in a Rational Sentencing System* (New York, 1990), 89.

[10] A. von Hirsch, *Past or Future Crimes* (Manchester, 1986); and id., *Censure and Sanctions* (Oxford, 1993).

[11] Some desert theorists argue that criminal record should play no role in determining the amount of punishment; but A. von Hirsch, above, n. 10, *Past or Future Crimes*, ch. 7, argues that it may legitimately be taken into account to a small (and strictly limited) extent.

[12] He adds to this the further principles of *rank ordering* (more serious crimes should receive more severe penalties) and *appropriate spacing* (crimes only a little different in seriousness should have not-very-different normal penalties; crimes very different in seriousness should have this difference reflected in the respective penalties awarded).

offender 'deserves' by way of punishment—there is no intuitively consensual yardstick, and no credible external standard that can be applied to yield an absolute amount of commensurably deserved punishment for any specified crime. On the other hand, von Hirsch argues, Morris's 'outer desert limits' approach allows free reign to instrumental considerations within the outer desert limits, and therefore allows far too much scope to courts to impose different penalties—for reasons of deterrence, incapacitation, or whatever—upon offenders who have committed similar crimes, with similar past records.[13] And this, he claims, is unfair—and he could, though he does not, cite evidence from surveys of offenders to show that they would (largely) agree with him.[14]

Though the matter is not usually put in this way, it is for present purposes rather important to emphasize that, despite their differences, both Morris and von Hirsch appear implicitly to accept Lucas's proposition that justice is an asymmetric concept.[15] Morris's acceptance of this proposition is obvious (see above) and requires no elaboration. Andrew von Hirsch's position is more complex, and more positive in its espousal of desert, so his relationship to Lucas's proposition is more difficult to establish. However, the fact that he denies any absolute scale of commensurably deserved punishments seems ultimately crucial. For him, there is no absolute scale; but we can establish outer cardinal limits for punishments for a given offence (as does Morris: and, for von Hirsch as for Morris, it would be unfair to offenders to transgress those limits); we can also establish a principle that those who have committed similar offences with similar records should receive similar punishments (and it would be unfair to treat them otherwise); and, finally, and following on from the last point, we can establish a scale of ordinal proportionality through which those who have committed more serious crimes will receive more serious penalties than those who have committed lesser crimes (and it would be unfair on the latter if it were otherwise).

In the course of the discussions at the Colston Symposium, it was pointed out that, in the real world of policy-making, while the broad concept of 'just deserts' had indeed been very influential in a general sense in many jurisdictions in recent years, what had actually counted as 'just deserts' seemed to vary a good deal from one jurisdiction to another. That is indeed the case, and this variation seems to have three main sources. First, as von Hirsch himself concedes, because there are no positive absolute scales, judgments about the 'seriousness' of given offences may vary culturally from one

[13] For Morris's reply to this criticism, see N. Morris and M. Tonry, above, n. 9, 85 ff.
[14] See e.g. the studies of juveniles by A. M. Morris and H. Giller, 'The Juvenile Court: The Client's Perspective', (1977) *Crim. LR* 198–205; R. Anderson, *Representation in the Juvenile Court* (London, 1978), ch. 5; H. Parker, M. Casburn, and D. Turnbull, *Receiving Juvenile Justice: Adolescents and State Care and Control* (Oxford, 1981), chs. 2 and 5.
[15] In the interests of accuracy, I must however make it clear that neither Morris nor von Hirsch cites Lucas, and there is no evidence that either is aware of his work.

country to another.[16] Secondly, there is a continuing and unresolved debate as to what role previous convictions should play in desert theory;[17] hence, different jurisdictions might well take different stances on this matter. Thirdly, no modern version of desert theory completely excludes instrumental considerations in sentencing,[18] though both Morris and von Hirsch wish to constrain the role of instrumental factors by considerations of fairness (von Hirsch's constraints in this regard being substantially the more stringent); and this 'mixed' character of modern desert theory (linked, I would suggest, to implicitly asymmetric concepts of justice—see above) allows in practice for some variation of interpretation as between jurisdictions.[19]

Despite the remarks in the preceding paragraph, one should not underestimate the recent power of the desert-based critique of previous sentencing practice. In many jurisdictions, ranging from Scandinavia to the United Kingdom to the United States, its influence has been substantial, and that influence is seen especially when one compares present philosophies and practices with those adopted by many countries in the early postwar period, when, for example, in some jurisdictions the 'social defence' school of thought was very influential,[20] and the resulting prevailing instrumentalism led some to complain about an excessive 'lawlessness in sentencing'.[21]

So what lies behind the recent powerful influence of desert theory (notwithstanding that that influence has in most countries been of a rather general kind)? For the answer to this question, one has to return, I believe, all the way back to Norval Morris's 1964 essay[22] where, as previously explained, he explicitly linked desert theory to a theory of human rights. It can reasonably be argued that the underpinning concept lying behind human-rights theory is the concept of fairness,[23] and I have tried to show, throughout this section, how central fairness is to desert theory. That being the case,

[16] A von Hirsch, above, n. 10, *Past or Future Crimes*, 66–7.

[17] See n. 11, above. It is also possible, within a version of desert theory, to take previous convictions into account to a greater extent than von Hirsch does, using the concept of 'progressive loss of mitigation': on this see A. J. Ashworth, *Sentencing and Criminal Justice* (London, 1992), 147–50.

[18] See e.g. A. von Hirsch's position on what he calls 'categorial incapacitation' (above, n. 10, *Past or Future Crimes*, ch. 13), and on adjusting punishment levels in relation to the constraints of available prison space (ibid., ch. 8).

[19] So, for example, even if there were two neighbouring jurisdictions that had fully adopted von Hirsch's approach to sentencing, and even if they had made identical judgments about ordinal ranking and the cardinally appropriate penalty for each kind of offence, they might still have some differences in their penalty-scales because they had differentially taken into account the instrumental factors mentioned in n. 18, above.

[20] See M. Ancel, *Social Defence: A Modern Approach to Criminal Problems* (London, 1965).

[21] M. E. Frankel, *Criminal Sentences: Law Without Order* (New York, 1973).

[22] In N. Morris and C. Howard, above, n. 4.

[23] See e.g. J. Rawls, *A Theory of Justice* (Oxford, 1971).

desert theory can perhaps plausibly be regarded as being simply one of a family of 'human rights' developments which have been of growing practical and political significance in many countries since the 1950s—and leading to, among other things, new laws seeking to restrict or eliminate racial and sexual discrimination.[24] In prisons, too, in many jurisdictions the prisoner is now regarded, to a much greater extent than thirty or forty years ago, as a person with rights, and the courts have tended to abandon (or at least greatly modify) their previous 'hands-off' approach as regards what goes on in penal institutions.[25] This change of perception was explicitly recognized by the highest English court in 1993: in a speech in the House of Lords that was approved by all five adjudicating Law Lords, Lord Mustill expressly disagreed with a 1980 case (*Payne* v. *Lord Harris of Greenwich*[26]) in which the Court of Appeal had held that a life-sentence prisoner had no right to know the reasons why the Parole Board had not recommended his release. *Inter alia*, Lord Mustill commented:

Even in such a short time as 13 years the perception of society's obligation towards persons serving prison sentences has perceptibly changed. . . . [moreover, there is a] continuing momentum in administrative law towards openness of decision-making. Sound as it may well have been at the time, the reasoning of *Payne* v. *Lord Harris of Greenwich* cannot be sustained today.[27]

This increasingly influential conception of prisoners, and of defendants facing sentence, as people with rights, of course incorporates, as a dominant conceptual influence, the liberal individualism of the eighteenth-century Enlightenment. Hence, and despite some important differences, in the sphere of criminal justice there is in a real sense a direct line of influence from Beccaria[28] to Morris and von Hirsch. The puzzling question is why this liberal individualism, which has after all been available as an intellectual resource for a long time, should have become substantially more prominent in the sentencing theory and practice, and the prison law, of the period from the mid-1960s onwards. That is a question to which we must return, after other conceptual developments of the modern era have also been examined.

---

[24] Such laws are also increasingly being specifically strengthened in relation to criminal-justice matters. See e.g. in England s. 95 of the Criminal Justice Act 1991, which, *inter alia*, provides that: 'The Secretary of State shall in each year publish such information as he considers expedient for the purpose of . . . facilitating the performance by [persons engaged in the administration of criminal justice] of their duty to avoid discriminating against any persons on the ground of race or sex or any other improper ground.'

[25] For a graphic portrayal of this movement in the context of one American State, see J. Jacobs, *Stateville: The Penitentiary in Mass Society* (Chicago, 1977).

[26] [1981] 1 WLR 754.

[27] [1993] 3 All ER 92 at 111.

[28] On Beccaria, see e.g. E. Monachesi, 'Cesare Beccaria 1738–1794', in H. Mannheim (ed.), *Pioneers in Criminology* (London, 1960); M. Maestro, *Cesare Beccaria and the Origins of Penal Reform* (Philadelphia, 1973); and H. L. A. Hart, *Essays on Bentham* (Oxford, 1982), ch. 2.

2. MANAGERIALISM

The second main concept to be considered is that of managerialism, a term which is used in this essay in a descriptive and not a pejorative sense. The growing importance of managerialism in criminal justice and penal systems has, perhaps, received less academic attention than it deserves, though in different continents Antonie Peters[29] and Feeley and Simon[30] have independently sought to highlight its significance.[31] In what follows, I shall try to illustrate the developing role of managerialism in modern criminal-justice systems by highlighting three distinct (though closely related) aspects of this general development, namely its *systemic*, its *consumerist*, and its *actuarial* dimensions.

One central feature of a managerialist approach is an emphasis on *the criminal-justice system*, conceived as a system rather than a collection of different parts. In most Western countries, conceptualization of this sort has become a great deal more prominent in the last thirty years in official discourse about criminal policy. To give only one example, in Britain a senior Home Office official, speaking at a conference on the probation service in the late 1980s, prefaced his main remarks with the following important introductory paragraph:

The probation service is a *criminal justice service*. It is one of the five criminal justice services, the others being the police, the courts (perhaps more an institution than a service), the Prison Service and, a newcomer to the scene, the Crown Prosecution Service. All five services are about crime and what to do about it—preventing or reducing it, dealing with its consequences and with those who commit it, and mitigating its effect. The different tasks fall on different services in different ways, and at the operational level they are fairly clearly and rightly distinguished; but *at a more general level the services all share or ought to share a common purpose and common objectives*, even though their character is very different. Each can frustrate any of the others, and action or lack of action by any of them can affect the workload and success of each of the others, *so they must understand one another and they must work together. The point is obvious*, but it does not easily happen (emphasis added).[32]

[29] A. A. G. Peters, 'Main Currents in Criminal Law Theory', in J. van Dijk, C. Haffmans, F. Ruter, J. Schutte (eds.), *Criminal Law in Action* (Arnhem, 1986).

[30] M. M. Feeley and J. Simon, 'The New Penology: Notes on the Emerging Strategy of Corrections and its Implications', (1992) 30 *Criminology* 449–74.

[31] Managerialism in criminal justice has also been considered in some texts primarily aimed at a practitioner audience: see e.g. T. Locke, *New Approaches to Crime in the 1990s: Planning Responses to Crime* (Harlow, 1990); R. Statham and P. Whitehead, *Managing the Probation Service: Issues for the 1990s* (Harlow, 1992).

[32] D. E. R. Faulkner, 'The Future of the Probation Service: A View from Government', in R. Shaw and K. Haines (eds.), *The Criminal Justice System: A Central Role for the Probation Service* (Cambridge, 1989), I. Since this speech was made, enhanced co-operation between the various services mentioned by David Faulkner has been sought by the British Government through the establishment of a national Criminal Justice Consultative Council and a series of

In most jurisdictions, this recent emphasis on the systemic character of the criminal justice tends to embrace some or all of the following features:

1. An emphasis on *inter-agency co-operation* in order to fulfil the overall goals of the system (see quotation above);

2. An emphasis on creating, if possible, *an overall strategic plan* for the whole of criminal policy in the given country (including the criminal-justice system), with each separate criminal-justice agency having its own *mission statement*, integrally related to the goals of the remainder of the system;[33]

3. The creation of *key performance indicators*, related to the overall 'mission statement' of each agency, in order to measure aspects of efficiency and effectiveness (such indicators might include, perhaps, 'clear-up rates' and 'response times' for the police; 'hours of constructive regime activity' and '% of population in overcrowded conditions' in the prison service; 'average length of time spent before trial' and 'average length of court hearing' in the courts, and so on);

4. Active *monitoring* of aggregate information about the system and its functioning, at various key decision points or service-delivery points, using modern information technology, and with special (though not exclusive) attention being given to information concerning the 'key performance indicators'.

This kind of systemic approach is often rather more pervasive in any given criminal-justice system than is apparent to the casual observer. So, for example, in England the Criminal Justice Act 1991, in its original form, has often been referred to as primarily a 'just deserts' statute (and indeed rightly so given some of the language in the White Paper that preceded it[34]), yet close analysis shows that in significant respects the Act also contained, or was backed up by, powerful elements of managerialist thinking. As an example of this, we may note the provisions of the Act relating to the setting up of the new Youth Court, which, *inter alia*, created what is often known as an 'overlapping jurisdiction' for community penalties for 16- and 17-year-olds, a concept which necessarily required an element of inter-agency co-operation or 'partnership'.[35] A government circular to local agencies was

---

24 Area Criminal Justice Liaison Committees working under the umbrella of the national Council. This development follows a specific recommendation made in Lord Justice Woolf's report on prison disturbances in England (*Prison Disturbances April 1990: Report of an Inquiry* (Cm. 1456; London, 1991)).

[33] On 'overall strategic plans', see esp. the Netherlands White Paper of 1985 and subsequent developments: see Netherlands Ministry of Justice, *Society and Crime: A Policy Plan for the Netherlands* (The Hague, 1985); A. K. Bottomley, 'Blue-prints for Criminal Justice: Reflections on a Policy Plan for the Netherlands', (1986) 25 *Howard Journal of Criminal Justice* 199–215.

[34] Home Office, *Crime Justice and Protecting the Public* (Cm. 965; London, 1990).

[35] The concept of the 'overlapping jurisdiction' is that sentences previously available only for juveniles (i.e. persons aged 16 or less) were henceforth to be made available for 17-year-olds, who were to be brought within the ambit of the Youth Court; while conversely, sentences

issued in March 1992, six months before the implementation of the Act, giving, *inter alia*, detailed guidance on the development of services relating to 16- and 17-year-old offenders[36] and emphasizing that in all local areas 'monitoring and evaluation are essential for the assessment of performance and to ensure the efficient and effective delivery of services and programmes'.[37] As an Annexe to the circular, a 'checklist of local action' was provided, in a much more detailed form than would have been contemplated twenty or thirty years beforehand; this checklist emphasized, among other things, the importance of partnership arrangements, target dates, and monitoring (see Figure 2.1).

Given examples such as this, it is not hard to see that, as Feeley and Simon note, one result of what I have called the 'systemic' dimension of managerialism can be that, within criminal-justice systems, 'increasing primacy [is] given to the efficient control of internal system processes'.[38] Concentration on such matters can even, in some cases, result in the displacement of more traditional 'external' objectives such as the reduction of reoffending: hence in some contemporary criminal-justice systems, according to the same authors, 'the sense that any external social referent is intended at all is becoming attenuated'.[39]

I shall return in a moment to the specific role of the courts in all this. As a preliminary to such consideration, however, we may note that the new 'systemic managerialism', at least in its most developed form, has many similarities with what Kamenka and Tay once described as 'bureaucratic-administrative law'.[40] 'Bureaucratic-administrative law', these authors usefully explain, is significantly different from '*Gemeinschaft*-type law' (the typical kind of law in pre-modern societies) and '*Gesellschaft*-type law' (the kind of law emerging especially in the Enlightenment period):

Gemeinschaft-type law takes for its fundamental presupposition and concern the organic community. *Gesellschaft*-type law takes for its fundamental presupposition and concern the atomic individual, theoretically free and self-determined, limited

previously available for 17-year-olds, but not for juveniles, should be made available for 16-year-olds. Courts were then expected to select the most appropriate sentence for each individual 16- or 17-year-old defendant, from across this widened range of disposals. Since the probation service previously had sole responsibility for community penalties for 17-year-olds, and local-authority social-services departments had lead responsibility for some aspects of community penalty provision for 16-year-olds, a degree of inter-agency co-operation was required to make these provisions work effectively.

[36] Home office, Department of Health, and Welsh Office, *Criminal Justice Act 1991: Young People and the Youth Court* (Circular 30/1992; London, 1992), paras. 6–28.

[37] Ibid., para. 27.

[38] M. M. Feeley and J. Simon, above, n. 30, 450.

[39] Ibid.

[40] E. Kamenka and A. E.-S. Tay, 'Beyond Bourgeois Individualism: The Contemporary Crisis in Law and Legal Ideology', in E. Kamenka and R. S. Neale (eds.), *Feudalism, Capitalism and Beyond* (London, 1975).

Getting things going
  1. Has the local CPO/Director of Social Services ensured that there are satisfactory local partnership arrangements?
  2. Are all the local services/organizations represented at a sufficiently senior level?
  3. Have other local services/organizations who may need to be involved/consulted been identified?
  4. Is the local Justices' Clerk aware of the arrangements?

Preparing the ground
  5. Has a statement of aims been drawn up including a commitment to avoid discrimination on grounds of sex or race or other improper grounds?
  6. Is it consistent with other work going on locally with older and younger offenders?
  7. Have present local practices and procedures been reviewed?
  8. Have action plans been drawn up with specific targets and realistic timetables?
  9. Does everybody know what they have to do, and by when?
  10. Have arrangements been made to keep local courts informed?

Making the arrangements
  11. Has a list of local facilities for community sentences setting out the purpose and broad target group been prepared?
  12. Have local arrangements been made for:
    — the management of community sentences;
    — the supervision of offenders released from custody;
    — the preparation of pre-sentence reports;
    — court duty officers;
    — liaison in dealing with individual offenders?
  13. Are these arrangements consistent with other work going on locally with older and younger offenders?
  14. Are the arrangements consistent with national standards/other guidance?
  15. Have local arrangements been made for the joint training of probation/social services/voluntary sector staff?
  16. Has the necessary financial provision been made, and have any grants available been applied for?
  17. Have local arrangements been made for monitoring/evaluating
    — these preparations;
    — the impact locally of the 1991 Act?

Reviewing progress
  18. Have arrangements been made to review and (where necessary) revise the arrangements in the light of evaluation?
  19. Have arrangements been made to keep courts (including the Crown Court) informed of local outcomes?

Source: Home Office *et al.* 1992, Annexe D.

FIG. 2.1. Checklist of local action for dealing with 16–17-year-olds in the community, as prepared by the government in England and Wales in connection with the implementation of the Criminal Justice Act 1991

only by the rights of other individuals. . . . In the bureaucratic-administrative type of regulation, the presupposition and concern is neither an organic human community nor an atomic individual; the presupposition and concern is a non-human abstracted ruling interest, public policy or on-going activity, of which human beings are subordinates, functionaries, or carriers. The *Gesellschaft*-type law concerning railways is oriented towards the rights of people whose interests may be harmed by the operation of railways or people whose activities may harm the rights of the owners or operators of railways seen as individuals exercising individual rights. Bureaucratic-administrative regulations concerning railways take for their object the efficient running of railways or the efficient execution of tasks and attainment of goals and norms which are set by the authorities, or the community, or the bureaucracy as its representative (emphasis in original).[41]

Similarly, in the specific field of criminal policy Antonie Peters draws some analytically helpful schematic contrasts between the new systemic managerialism (what he calls the 'School of Social Control') and the earlier criminological 'schools' of classicism and positivism:

The criminal law is no longer a moral code as it was in liberal market society, nor an instrument of social defence as in the period roughly from 1900 to 1950, but it has become one form, among other forms, of social control. The new approach is characterised by a withdrawal from the idea that the problem of crime can be eliminated, or even can be brought under complete control. Emphasis has shifted from maintenance of the criminal code . . . to more general control of volumes of delinquent activity. Criminal policy is no longer occupied primarily with concrete offenders, nor with problems of doing justice, but with the management of aggregate phenomena of social activity, with criteria for selective law enforcement, with quantitative regulation in the organisational processing of offenders. . . . In the Classical School the main concern was with the definition of right and wrong. Punishment served the purpose of moral clarification. The [Positivist] School was intent on acting upon individual criminals, and punishment was conceived as treatment. In the School of Social Control the concern is with systems of action; punishment has become an instrument of policy . . . I believe that today legal rationality in criminal law has, in an important sense, dissolved in, and been replaced by the rationality of organisation.[42]

As Feeley and Simon emphasize, all this can have very significant consequences for the implicit ways in which individual persons within the criminal-justice system are viewed. The tendency of the systemic approach is to 'target offenders *as an aggregate*' (emphasis added);[43] hence the individual within this kind of approach becomes, at least in some respects (see further below), simply a unit within a framework of policy.[44]

Sometimes in life a specific moment occurs that seems suddenly to illuminate much else. One such moment in my professional life is relevant to the present discussion and seems worth repeating. In the late 1980s, I was a co-opted member of a local Probation Committee,[45] for a county probation service which prided itself on being something of a national leader in the

---

[41] Ibid. 138.
[42] A. A. G. Peters, above, n. 29, 32, 34.
[43] M. M. Feeley and J. Simon, above, n. 30, 450.
[44] W. Mc Williams, 'Probation, Pragmatism and Policy', (1987) 26 *Howard Journal of Criminal Justice* 97–121.
[45] Probation Committees are the employing committees for the various (locally organized) Probation Services in England and Wales.

application of information technology as an aid for senior probation managers. On the occasion in question, the local service had just undergone a periodic inspection by Home Office Inspectors, who were present to discuss their findings with the Committee. The Chief Probation Officer began the meeting by pointing out (with an undoubted element of pride) that this was the first-ever occasion when Home Office Inspectors had begun their inspection of a local probation service by interrogating the service's data base. The discussion then proceeded, using much 'aggregating' data and language, such data being in effect treated as performance indicators—for example, what was the percentage of 'special (intensive) requirements' among all probation orders, to what extent was there correspondence between recommendations in pre-sentence reports and eventual sentencing outcomes, and so on. Suddenly, one magistrate member of the Committee, who had herself been trained in social work in the early post-war period, interrupted the discussion to enquire: 'Mr Chairman, I wonder if I could ask the Chief Probation Officer, through you, whether probation officers in this county still see clients?'(!). Clearly, for this magistrate, the aggregational features of systemic managerialism were incompatible with the very individualized, person-centred approach of her social-work training, and indeed of the probation service in an earlier era. It was, in effect, a clash of philosophies, and of ontologies.

At this point in the argument, I can imagine some readers objecting that all this may be true of the executive agencies related to the criminal-justice system (police, probation service, prison service, etc.), but it is surely not nearly so true of the courts, and hence is not of special relevance in the context of a Symposium focusing especially on sentencing. To develop this objection, it might be further noted that seventeenth- and eighteenth-century liberal constitutional theory made much of the doctrine of 'separation of powers' (between legislature, executive, and judiciary), and, while such a doctrine has admittedly been only partially implemented in many countries, nevertheless it remains the case in most Western jurisdictions that the courts are clearly separate from the executive. Hence, whatever the pressures to adopt 'systemic managerialism' in the executive agencies, the courts, as a separate branch of the state, should and can resist them: as one participant at the Colston Symposium argued in the discussion, 'sentences are a matter that shouldn't be managed'.

Four comments may be made about this important objection. First, the objection is to some extent justified; in most countries, at present, courts (and sentencers) are less affected by managerial considerations than (say) police or prison services, precisely because of the doctrine of separation of powers. Secondly, however, we should be clear that the developing language of systemic managerialism tends to embrace courts within it, and hence it is not so interested in deliberate separations of constitutional function as were the eighteenth-century theorists (the quotation from David Faulkner given earlier in this chapter illustrates precisely this point). Thirdly, it is in any case a mistake to believe that courts, and sentencers, can remain totally immune from the effects of systemic managerialism, even if such managerialism does not directly constrain courts' apparent freedom of decision. Consider, for instance, the impact on the courts of a managerially inspired large increase in the use of cautioning, developed for cost-cutting reasons;[46] or, to take a different and more specific example, there is now research evidence in relation to the 'overlapping jurisdiction' for 16- and 17-year-olds in the 1991 Criminal Justice Act (see above) to the effect that courts' intendedly free choice of the 'best available disposal for the individual case', envisaged by the framers of the Act, is in fact in most local areas notably constrained by the way in which local agencies (acting primarily on managerial principles) have structured their supporting provision.[47] Fourthly, and perhaps most importantly, managerialism may in fact directly impinge on the sentencing decision, especially where, within the rules of a given jurisdiction, the sentencing decision can be closely influenced by the legislature, or a sentencing commission acting in the name of the legislature. Hence, arguably North American-style sentencing guidelines are themselves a kind of managerialism, in part often embracing human-rights (fairness) principles, but in part also offering instrumental possibilities for affecting overall state costs by manipulating (say) the 'in/out line' or the lengths of prison terms for certain offences. Indeed, it was pointed out in the Colston Symposium discussion that one of the prime movers in the early development of Minnesota's sentencing guidelines, Kay Knapp, was herself a graduate in public policy, and saw herself as developing, in the state's sentencing guidelines, a set of managerial techniques which would more rationally allocate individuals to a costly and scarce public resource, namely the state prison system.

I indicated at the outset of this discussion of managerialism that three separate (though related) aspects of it could be distinguished, namely the *systemic*, the *consumerist*, and the *actuarial*. So far, attention has been focused only on the first of these matters; hence, the other two must now be turned to, though fortunately then can be discussed in substantially shorter compass.

What I have called the 'consumerist' dimension of managerialism derives, in a way, from some of managerialism's systemic characteristics. Earlier in this chapter, I mentioned James Jacobs's classic study[48] of long-

[46] This example should not, of course, be taken as implying that cost-cutting is the only possible reason for an increase in cautioning.

[47] Based on as yet unpublished research carried out by Kevin Haines and David O'Mahony at the Institute of Criminology, Cambridge University.

[48] J. Jacobs, above, n. 25.

term changes in one American prison (Stateville): Jacobs fascinatingly portrays how, over a fifty-year period, Stateville was governed in a variety of different ways, including a traditionalist/patriarchal approach and a rehabilitation/reform regime, all of which eventually ran into various kinds of difficulties. The book ends with the extremely 'managerialist' regime of Warden Brierton,[49] a regime which, as Jacobs shrewdly noted, 'might succeed where traditional and reform administrations had failed because it was capable of handling the greatly increased demands for rationality and accountability coming from the courts and the political system'.[50]

In other words, the pressure for the effective delivery of individuals' entitlements (in an era of an increasing willingness to see people, especially disadvantaged people, as possessors of rights: see above), together with an increasing pressure from both legislative and executive branches for efficient service delivery, greater productivity, etc., both often tend to push service deliverers into a managerialist approach because it seems to be the most successful method of meeting these kinds of demands. As a corollary of this, however, managers in managerialist systems also tend to become increasingly interested in the views of those to whom services are delivered, to test whether, in their view, the services are being delivered satisfactorily. This interest in the views of 'consumers' is especially likely to develop in the present era given that: first, specific managerial techniques are normally first developed in the private sector and then applied to the public sector, and secondly, that for reasons too complex to go into here, capitalism in the second half of the twentieth century has become increasingly consumer-oriented.[51]

As with the systemic dimension of managerialism, its 'efficient and effective service delivery' (or 'consumerist') dimension is perhaps less likely to affect courts than other penal services, though an impact on courts certainly cannot be ruled out.[52] A particular reason for discussing this 'consumerist' dimension here, however, is that it does embody a somewhat different concept of personhood than does systemic managerialism. The latter, as we have seen above, tends to see the individual as simply a statistical unit within an aggregated policy system, whereas consumerist managerialism sees the individual as someone well able to judge (like a consumer in the

---

[49] 'The new warden has stressed the need to provide basic services through regularized procedures. . . . [He] has committed himself to justice; each prisoner should receive the treatment and opportunities commensurate with law and to which he is entitled. Each month the warden personally speaks to every inmate in the prison on his "call line", and provides a prompt written reply to every inquiry or grievance. He demands the same formal responsiveness of his staff. Written records have proliferated. Each time an inmate showers, the event is documented. . . . Brierton has thus taken the initiative in attempting to fully bureaucratize the prison' (ibid. 209).

[50] M. M. Feeley and J. Simon, above, n. 30, 454.

[51] S. Lash and J. Urry, *The End of Organised Capitalism* (Cambridge, 1987).

[52] For example, through surveys of jurors, prosecuting and defence lawyers, or victims.

private market) whether or not services are being well delivered.[53] Hence, managerialism as an overall approach (and embodying, as it usually does, both the systemic and the consumerist dimension) normally contains both these images of personhood, but differently deployed on different occasions.

That managerialism has a consumerist dimension incidentally also indicates that it is not merely (as some seem to suppose) a 'top-down' approach; for information about the views of 'consumers', assiduously collected, can and does, in a full-blown managerialist system, affect aspects of the higher organization of the system. On a related point, we should also note that middle and lower-level workers in a system can themselves sometimes adopt managerialist perspectives for their own purposes; and this point is very well illustrated when one looks at the decline in custody rates for juvenile offenders in England and Wales in the 1980s,[54] a decline which was, without any doubt, partly achieved by the application of managerialist techniques 'from below' by juvenile-justice practitioners with an anti-custody agenda, determined to influence court outcomes.[55]

The third and final dimension of managerialism to be considered here is the *actuarial* aspect. This is a dimension valuably highlighted by Feeley and Simon:

> A central feature of the new discourse is the replacement of a moral or clinical description of the individual with an actuarial language of probabilistic calculations and statistical distributions applied to populations. . . . (Hence) the new penology is neither about punishing nor rehabilitating individuals, [rather] it is about identifying and managing unruly groups.[56]

While these comments are in part overstated (obviously neither 'punishing' nor 'rehabilitating' impulses are dead in modern criminal-justice systems), nevertheless they contain an important truth. It is clearly the case that the aggregative tendencies of modern managerialism, discussed earlier when considering its systemic dimension, are particularly likely to lead to an interest in the 'actuarial language of probabilistic calculations'. That being so, we may expect this matter to have important implications for modern sentencing systems—such as, for example, a tendency to be inter-

---

[53] Although the subject of privatization of penal services is outside the scope of this essay, it should be noted that, once one has adopted a version of consumerist managerialism in which 'efficient and effective service delivery' is a key concept, then it seems a morally neutral question to ask whether such service delivery would be more efficiently and effectively achieved by private contractors or by public bodies.

[54] R. Allen, 'Out of Jail: The Reduction in the Use of Penal Custody for Male Juveniles 1981–88', (1991) 30 *Howard Journal of Criminal Justice* 30–52.

[55] See N. Tutt and H. Giller, ' "Manifesto for Management"—The Elimination of Custody', (1987) 151 *Justice of the Peace* 200–2; A. E. Bottoms, P. Brown, B. Mc Williams, W. Mc Williams, M. Nellis, *Intermediate Treatment and Juvenile Justice* (London, 1990).

[56] M. M. Feeley and J. Simon, above, n. 30, 452, 455.

ested in the possibilities of selective incapacitation and 'dangerousness',[57] or, in a different sphere, in complex cost-benefit calculations about the value or otherwise of particular sentencing innovations such as electronic monitoring.

It should also be noted that these kinds of actuarial thought-processes do tend to have important ideological effects, as Jonathan Simon has argued.[58] Considered in the abstract, there is in fact no reason why managerialism should be described, as it was by Peters as having as its 'most striking feature' a 'pervasive instrumentalism'.[59] On the contrary, on paper at least, managerial techniques could as well be applied to deliver effectively a fully deontological or retributive criminal-justice policy as they could to deliver an instrumental one. Yet in fact the actuarial tendency of managerialism does tend to produce a predilection—often an unthinking one—in favour of instrumentalism. This is well illustrated by Simon,[60] in the context of a discussion of a US Supreme Court decision on the use of gender as an actuarial variable in establishing the amount of employee contribution to a retirement benefit plan.[61] The Court declared unequal contributions by gender (based on women's greater life expectancy) to violate the Civil Rights Act; to which the reaction of actuarially-oriented commentators was one of

shock that what appeared in their paradigm as a value-free technical decision (to use gender in setting benefit premiums) had been adjudged as discrimination. . . . The . . . decision [seemed] more than wrongly decided, it [was] an assault on what they [conceived] of as scientifically established reality. From their point of view, a neutral, indeed beneficent, process of social policy [had] been unfairly linked to the brutish process of racism and sexism.[62]

Hence, as Simon points out, the ideological effects of the actuarial dimension of modern managerialism may eventually make it 'more difficult to invoke political and moral responses in ourselves and others'. It is not, he suggests, that we are silenced, but rather that increasingly it may become difficult to counterpoise the traditional language of, for example, 'justice', against the aggregative and instrumental assumptions of an actuarial approach.

I began this section on managerialism by noting that I was using the term descriptively rather than pejoratively, and it should by now be very clear that in fact the various dimensions of managerialism can have both positive

[57] On which, see P. W. Greenwood, *Selective Incapacitation* (Santa Monica, Calif., 1982); R. Tarling, *Analysing Offending: Data, Models and Interpretations* (London, 1993), ch. 9.
[58] J. Simon, 'The Ideological Effects of Actuarial Practices', (1988) 22 *Law and Society Review* 772–800.
[59] A. A. G. Peters, above, n. 29, 33.
[60] J. Simon, above, n. 58.
[61] *Los Angeles Water and Power* v. *Manhart* (1977) 435 US 702.
[62] J. Simon, above, n. 58, 779–80.

and negative features.[63] Hence—and this point can usefully conclude this section of the argument—one important task for policy-makers in any given jurisdiction must be to assess the likely positive or negative results (direct or indirect) arising from the adoption of particular managerialist strategies, and to take these possible results into account in shaping their legislative and policy approaches.

3. COMMUNITY

Like the two previous concepts considered, that of 'community' has several facets of potential relevance to sentencing. Indeed, it is the least unified and probably the most vague of the three main concepts discussed in this essay. Nevertheless, different facets of the 'community' concept have in fact been of considerable importance in sentencing reforms in different jurisdictions, and to omit any consideration of this matter would unhelpfully impoverish the overall analysis being attempted in this essay.

Three main aspects of the 'community' concept can usefully be distinguished. As these are more separate from one another than the dimensions of just deserts/human rights and of managerialism, it is appropriate to deal with them under separate sub-headings. These three main aspects are: community penalties and 'diversion'; justice in and for local communities and groups; and devolving decision-making to the community.

3.1. Community Penalties and 'Diversion'

Without much doubt, the last thirty years have seen increased attention being given to what are now increasingly called 'community penalties' (sometimes 'intermediate penalties'). These are seen as ways of providing a credible sanction for the offender, but operated in the community rather than in prison. Some such penalties (most obviously the probation order) have a longer history, but in the period since 1970 we have seen the invention and very rapid spread of the community-service order,[64] and of the curfew order with electronic tagging,[65] as well as the development of a

[63] In this respect, it has considerable similarities with the concept of 'power': see M. McMahon's critique of the one-sided way in which power has been (negatively) viewed by some criminologists (*The Persistent Prison? Rethinking Decarceration and Penal Reform* (Toronto, 1992)).

[64] See e.g. W. A. Young, *Community Service Orders* (London, 1979); K. Pease, 'Community Service Orders', in M. Tonry and N. Morris (eds.), *Crime and Justice: An Annual Review of Research*, vi (Chicago, 1985); D. C. McDonald, *Punishment Without Walls* (New Brunswick, NJ, 1986); G. McIvor, *Sentenced to Serve* (Aldershot, 1992).

[65] See J. M. Byrne, A. J. Lurigio, and J. Petersilia (eds.), *Smart Sentencing: The Emergence of Intermediate Sanctions* (Newbury Park, Calif., 1992), Part II; G. Mair and C. Nee, *Electronic Monitoring: The Trials and their Results* (Home Office Research Study No. 120; London, 1990).

variety of different versions of intensive probation.[66] As often as not, the motivation in all this has been to avoid increased prison overcrowding, and/ or new prison building, at a time of steadily increasing recorded crime rates; and hence to reduce the overall costs to the state at a time of fiscal crisis.[67] Critics[68] have argued that the new emphasis on 'community corrections' has become a way in which the state is exercising more, and more intrusive, control over the lives of its citizens, but in the wake of recent critique[69] this thesis now seems less attractive than it did.

A further, analogous, movement during the same period has been that of so-called 'diversion to the community', especially diversion from court.[70] This movement often shares some of the same philosophical features as the drive towards 'community penalties',[71] though at a 'shallower' point in the criminal-justice system. However, it is normally additionally associated with a labelling theory rationale, i.e. in the belief that diversion from court will provide a better opportunity than would formal entry into the criminal-justice system to help the offender avoid further criminality, because the stigma of conviction will tend to promote negative self-image and therefore enhanced risk of re-offending.[72]

It has to be said that this first element of the 'community' theme, though undoubtedly prominent in many jurisdictions in recent years, might have, in reality, little to do with real communities. That is most obviously the case when diversion from court simply entails non-prosecution, i.e. no action;[73] but it may also be so as regards some forms of community penalty, e.g. those forms of community-service order where the offenders are engaged, as a group, in a kind of 'public works' programme. In that connection, it is undoubtedly of great interest that McIvor's recent research in Scotland has shown that those forms of community-service order that are more oriented to a genuine 'community' theme tend to have higher compli-

---

[66] See e.g. J. M. Byrne, A. J. Lurigio, and J. Petersilia (eds.), above, n. 65, Part I; N. Morris and M. Tonry, above, n. 9, ch. 7; P. Raynor, *Probation as an Alternative to Custody* (Aldershot, 1988).

[67] Whether costs are actually saved by an increase in community penalties is, however, not a wholly straightforward question: see N. Morris and M. Tonry, above, n. 9, 157–9 for a brief summary of the relevant issues.

[68] e.g. S. Cohen, *Visions of Social Control* (Cambridge, 1985).

[69] M. McMahon, above, n. 63.

[70] See e.g. M. Klein, 'Deinstitutionalization and Diversion of Juvenile Offenders: A Litany of Impediments', in N. Morris and M. Tonry (eds.), *Crime and Justice: An Annual Review of Research*, i (Chicago, 1979).

[71] As it did in the 1980s in English juvenile justice, among a powerful practitioner-led alliance often referred to as developing a 'new orthodoxy': see generally A. E. Bottoms *et al.*, above, n. 55.

[72] The empirical evidence for this view is however less positive than is sometimes supposed: see e.g. D. P. Farrington, 'England and Wales', in M. W. Klein (ed.), *Western Systems of Juvenile Justice* (Beverly Hills, Calif., 1984), 92.

[73] Some diversion schemes however entail an element of more community-oriented action, e.g. reparation or counselling.

ance rates and (though the evidence here is more tentative) lower reconviction rates.[74]

In those instances where 'community penalties' or 'diversion' are only tenuously connected to any genuine sense of community, it is of some interest to ask why the 'community' concept is nevertheless applied to them. The answer to this appears to be that 'community', though an infuriatingly imprecise term, remains highly suggestive to most listeners, and with positive connotations of belonging, support, and identity. As such, it may be used in modern societies from a variety of political perspectives, including the left (in which the reference and appeal may be to the idealized working-class community, trade union, or friendly society, etc.) and the new right.[75] It may also be used, more or less consciously, as an attempt to evoke an image of a bygone and allegedly more tranquil/peaceful society, and in this respect there are some obvious potential linkages between the modern use of 'community' as an idealized concept, and the rise of the 'heritage' theme in modern societies.[76]

3.2. Justice in and for Local Communities and Groups

The second dimension of the 'community' theme derives directly from an intervention made by Michael Tonry at the Colston Symposium (see also Tonry's essay in this volume). Tonry pointed out that in the American context (where numerical sentencing guidelines have now been adopted in many states, and these constrain sentencers to a typically greater extent than the narrative guidance/directions embodied in statutes in, say, England or Scandinavia) it is a not infrequent occurrence to find statewide guidelines being resisted in particular local areas, because they are seen by local judges and others to be insufficiently sensitive to the particular local context. That sense of remoteness to local problems may be particularly marked in communities that are rather distant (physically or structurally) from the main locus of power in the given state—for example, remote rural communities or areas with a special concentration of residents from particu-

---

[74] More specifically, in McIvor's (above, n. 64) research the work placements that were perceived most positively by the offenders were those which maximized the potential contact between the offender and the beneficiaries, those which offenders perceived as being of considerable benefit to the recipients, and those in which the offender him/herself was able to acquire new skills; and where there was positive rating of a placement by offenders, compliance and non-offending tended to be higher.

[75] The new right tends to operate with two rather distinct ideological strands: economic *neo-liberalism*, and social *neo-conservatism*, in which there is an appeal to a number of traditional values, including personal morality, the family, and the value of 'community'. See S. Hall and M. Jacques (eds.), *The Politics of Thatcherism* (London, 1983).

[76] Often interestingly linked to consumer culture: see e.g. N. Thrift, 'Images of Social Change', in C. Hamnett, L. McDowell, and P. Sarre (eds.), *The Changing Social Structure* (London, 1989); S. Lash and J. Urry, *Economics of Signs and Space* (London, 1994).

lar ethnic minorities. Relatively powerless groups of a non-geographical sort might also, and analogously, press their claims for a 'special' justice that has not been understood by the rational-legal state legislature, judiciary, or executive—and such groups might include interest groups such as women victimized by serious violent or sexual crimes, or environmental groups. The general point is that we live in an increasingly pluralist world—or at least, in a world where pre-existing pluralisms have become more overt and widely recognized—and that the demands generated by this pluralism do not always fit well with the rationalizing impulses created both by the 'fairness' critique of the rights approach, and by managerialism.

3.3. Devolving Decision-Making to the Community

One possible response to the kinds of concerns highlighted in the preceding paragraph is to try to 'devolve' decision-making in the adjudication of criminal events into a more informal community-oriented forum, where, for example, the cultural norms of an ethnic minority group may be given greater weight than they can be in the formal context of a Western-style criminal court. Exactly this kind of thinking seems to underlie the interestingly widespread development, in different jurisdictions, of attempts to evolve victim–offender mediation schemes, in which the emphasis switches away from (to put the matter in stark terms to make the point) 'state punishment' and moves instead towards a 'negotiated settlement between parties to a dispute'. This kind of reform is sometimes presented as a necessary part of a broader social policy to recover the lost sense of community in modern life.[77]

Although experiments with mediation schemes have been widespread, it has to be said that reforms of this kind have usually been rather marginal to mainstream criminal-justice developments.[78] Perhaps the most significant exception to this to date has been the New Zealand youth justice reform of 1989, in which so-called 'Family Group Conferences' (FGCs) are held in an attempt to seek a consensual solution to the problems created by the offender's crime: these FGCs are now, in New Zealand, the normal way of dealing with juvenile cases too serious for a mere warning or diversion scheme. FGCs normally comprise a meeting, of a relatively informal kind, between the offender, his/her advocate (if any), his/her family and other invitees, the victim or his/her representative, and the police, with a 'Youth Justice Co-ordinator' as convenor. It is clear that part of the motivation for creating the FGC system was a wish to provide services that were more

[77] N. Christie, 'Conflicts as Property', (1977) 17 *Brit. J. Criminol.* 1–15.

[78] See e.g. T. B. Nergard, 'Solving Conflicts outside the Court System: Experiences with the Conflict Resolution Boards in Norway', (1993) 33 *Brit. J. Criminol.* 81–94; T. F. Marshall and S. Merry, *Crime and Accountability: Victim/Offender Mediation in Practice* (London, 1990).

culturally sensitive, and a legal process that was more culturally appropriate, in the context of a resurgence of Maori culture and values.[79] It is also
clear from an initial extensive evaluation of the scheme that it has a number
of positive features, including the generation of a valued sense of participation by many (including victims and offenders), though in certain
respects the original intentions behind the reforms have not been fully
realized in practice.[80]

Throughout this essay, I have been highlighting the concept of
personhood implied by the various concepts discussed. The second and
third dimensions of the 'community' concept essentially see the person
(offender, victim, or whoever) as, ideally, a member of a group of significant
others, where the informal norms and culture of that group may have a
significant impact on the eventual outcome of the legal process. In this
respect, it should be noted that the community concept is, potentially at
least, significantly different from the just deserts/human rights approach
(which sees people as individual rights-carriers) and managerialism (which
sees them as units within a framework of policy, and as customers to whom
services must be delivered effectively and efficiently).

4. THREE CONCEPTS: TENSION AND COMPROMISE

If I am right in arguing that the three themes of just deserts, managerialism,
and community are of special importance in much recent change in criminal-justice systems, then at a normative level some interesting potential
conflicts are revealed, for these three themes do not necessarily sit comfort-
ably together. For example:

1. Desert theory emphasizes rights, and is therefore deontological in
character, whereas managerialism tends to be (though is not necessarily)
overwhelmingly instrumentalist (see above, in the section on the actuarial
dimension of managerialism).

2. Desert theory potentially conflicts with the 'community' theme, both
in its stronger versions (why should parties in victim–offender mediation
meetings choose desert-appropriate penalties, or even consistent penalties
in similar cases?) and in its weaker version (for example, if the community
penalty is selected primarily on treatment grounds, as probation traditionally was).

3. Managerialism potentially conflicts with the community theme, at
least when the term 'community' is taken seriously. 'Community' is a special characteristic of pre-modern forms of social organization, whereas

[79] G. Maxwell and A. M. Morris, *Families, Victims and Culture: Youth Justice in New Zealand* (Wellington, NZ, 1993), 3.
[80] Ibid., *passim*.

managerialism involves an advanced form of bureaucratic rationality; moreover, 'community' is a holistic concept, and managerialism necessarily involves componentiality and abstraction.[81] It is not difficult to see that these differing characteristics can readily generate different normative approaches.

Tensions between the three concepts can also be seen in the different conceptions of personhood that they each tend to embody, and these have been highlighted in earlier sections. On the other hand, it should not be supposed that one cannot attempt to integrate the three outlined themes. An example of just such an attempt is to be found in the English Criminal Justice Act 1991, in its original form. This statute contained a prominent and well-known desert element, but it was also, as shown in an earlier section of this essay, suffused with managerial concerns. Additionally, it encouraged the greater use of 'community penalties', but at the same time reshaped those penalties more in accord with the logic of desert theory;[82] and it introduced also the new 'community penalty' of the curfew order with electronic tagging,[83] to be administered on behalf of the state by private companies, a development with obvious managerialist overtones. In short, convergences between the three identified themes are possible, despite the very real conceptual tensions that exist between them.

5. POPULIST PUNITIVENESS

As previously indicated, I believe that the analysis of general factors influencing sentencing trends in different countries would not be complete without some consideration of a more overtly political dimension which I have described as 'populist punitiveness'. Generally speaking, this factor is probably of appeal to some politicians for one or more of three main reasons: first, because they believe that resort to increased punitiveness will have an effect in reducing the crime rate through general deterrence and/or incapacitation; secondly, because they believe that it may help to strengthen the moral consensus in society against certain kinds of activity—especially where, as in the field of drugs, there is a degree of moral contestation as regards the activity in question; and thirdly, because they believe that the adoption of a 'populist punitive' stance will satisfy a particular electoral

[81] P. L. Berger, B. Berger, and H. Kellner, *The Homeless Mind* (Harmondsworth, 1974).

[82] Section 6 of the Act; see M. Wasik and A. von Hirsch, 'Non-Custodial Penalties and the Principles of Desert', (1988) *Crim. LR* 555–72; A. E. Bottoms, 'The Concept of Intermediate Sanctions and its Relevance for the Probation Service', in R. Shaw and K. Haines (eds.), *The Criminal Justice System: A Central Role for the Probation Service* (Cambridge, 1989).

[83] Sections 12–13.

constituency.[84] The kinds of offences most likely to be the subject of 'populist punitiveness' stances are violent and sexual offences, on the one hand,
and drugs on the other.

At the Colston Symposium, one or two participants were inclined to
translate 'populist punitiveness' into the more familiar idea of 'public opinion'. This is a conceptual shift that I would resist. The concept of 'public
opinion' as regards criminal policy is a very complex one, with its own
literature;[85] and, *inter alia*, it has been shown that, while considerable popular support can be produced for punitive policies when rather general
and abstract survey questions are asked, that is much less likely to be the
case when questions are asked about specific situations concerning which
survey respondents have detailed knowledge (including crimes of which
they are themselves the victims). In these latter cases, suggested penalties
are likely to be much closer to those actually imposed in the courts. Given
all this, it is clear that we cannot speak in any straightforward fashion about
'public opinion' on crime in a way that automatically equates it with a
heavily punitive approach. On the other hand, it is, I believe, appropriate to
speak of politicians or legislatures adopting 'populist punitive' policies, for
these are political stances, normally adopted in the clear belief that they
will be popular with the public (and usually with an awareness that, in
general and abstract opinion polls, punitive policies are favoured by a
majority of the public: see above). Hence, the term 'populist punitiveness'
is intended to convey the notion of politicians tapping into, and using for
their own purposes, what they believe to be the public's generally punitive
stance.

Some countries and parts of countries seem willing to engage in populist
punitiveness almost regardless of the fiscal cost (in this regard the recent
staggering rise in the jail and prison populations in the various states of the
USA comes especially to mind[86]). However, that is certainly not the case in
all jurisdictions, and so we also find politicians in a number of countries
attracted to the classic modern strategy of bifurcation or 'the twin-track
approach'.[87] When this kind of strategy is adopted in its full form, governments simultaneously increase the penalties for serious offenders (often for
reasons of populist punitiveness) and decrease them for less serious of-

[84] Whether any of these objectives will, in a given case, actually be realized is, of course, a
moot point, as a search of the considerable literature on, for example, general deterrence,
incapacitation, and the so-called 'educative effect' will quickly reveal.

[85] See e.g. N. D. Walker and M. Hough, *Public Attitudes to Sentencing: Surveys from Five
Countries* (Aldershot, 1988).

[86] On this, see A. Blumstein, 'Prison Populations: A System out of Control?', in M. Tonry
and N. Morris (eds.), *Crime and Justice: A Review of Research* (Chicago, 1988). M. M. Feeley
and J. Simon, above, n. 30, attribute this growth to managerialism, but in this respect their
analysis appears to be overly ethnocentric, since similar prison population growth has not
necessarily accompanied the growth of managerialism in other jurisdictions.

[87] See A. E. Bottoms, 'Reflections on the Renaissance of Dangerousness', (1977) 16 *Howard
Journal of Penology and Crime Prevention* 70–96.

fenders (normally to ease the fiscal and administrative problems of, say, a rapidly-escalating total prison population). A celebrated example of bifurcation in this full sense occurred in England in 1983–4, when the then Home Secretary (Mr Leon Brittan) announced at his party's annual conference, and then carried into effect, a radical shift in parole policy.[88] The new policy made parole very restrictive indeed for offenders sentenced to long terms of imprisonment for violent, sexual, or drug offences; but at the same time it widened parole eligibility among short-sentence prisoners, leading to an immediate reduction in the total prison population of some 2,000 prisoners. It is worth noting that, at least in the short term, the Home Secretary gained significant political credit for the first part of this policy, with the second part attracting very little comment.[89]

The subject of bifurcation having been raised, it is worth adding that it is not unknown for such a strategy to appeal also to non-political actors such as judges. A good illustration of this is to be found in some guideline sentencing judgments of the English Court of Appeal in the 1980s: they first encouraged courts to think in terms of shorter terms of imprisonment for those property offenders thought to deserve a custodial sentence,[90] and then a few years later gave guidance that many sentences then being passed for rape offences were too short.[91] This non-political appeal of bifurcation seems to depend upon (1) an attempt to reinforce the moral consensus in society against certain kinds of seriously anti-social activity (i.e. a factor similar to one of those that might appeal to politicians—see the beginning of this section[92]); (2) a wish to be as accommodating as possible to politicians faced with the escalating costs of the prison system; and (3) perhaps a diffused ideological effect whereby the concept of bifurcation, originally adopted in a given country for political reasons, becomes in effect a kind of 'received common sense', and therefore easily capable of being adopted by non-political actors.

6. EXPLANATIONS

Up to this point, this essay has been in effect an essay in descriptive sociology, albeit of a rather complex kind; the aim has been to try to

---

[88] See M. Maguire, 'Parole', in E. Stockdale and S. Casale (eds.), *Criminal Justice under Stress* (London, 1992).

[89] In the longer term, however, the second part of the policy did lead to significant perceived difficulties with the whole parole system, resulting eventually in radical reform in the Criminal Justice Act 1991, Part II. See generally M. Maguire, above, n. 88.

[90] See esp. *R. v. Bibi* [1980] 1 WLR 1193; for a discussion, see C. J. Emmins, *A Practical Approach to Sentencing* (London, 1985), 114–19.

[91] *R. v. Billam* (1986) 8 Cr. App. R. (S.) 48.

[92] And also—as perhaps applied in relation to the increase in sentence lengths for rape—adjusting judgments of seriousness in the light of critiques by particular interest groups, in this case the women's movement.

identify, if possible with some precision, some of the main movements of thought that appear to underpin much of modern sentencing change in different countries. In this final section, the nature of my self-imposed task changes, and it becomes necessary to try to explain why it is that these various movements of thought seem to have been of growing importance in the last few decades. In the nature of the case, it is not possible to provide a full answer to this question within the constraints of this essay, and in any case a full answer would require an element of detailed historical research. Nevertheless, perhaps something worthwhile by way of explanation can be said, even if tentatively and a little speculatively.

A useful starting-point for explanation is to note that many commentators speak of the early twentieth century as a turning-point in modern criminal-justice systems in various countries, since at that time a more individualized, special preventive approach was adopted in many jurisdictions.[93] Perhaps the most extensive scholarly exploration of that early-twentieth-century turning-point in modern penality is that offered by David Garland,[94] using British sources. Garland emphasizes, *inter alia*:

1. That the new kind of individualized penality of the early twentieth century had a normalizing, a corrective, and a segregative sector (in England respectively exemplified especially in the probation order, in the Borstal system, and in preventive detention for habitual offenders, all first legislated for in the decade 1900–1910);

2. That the emergence of this new kind of penality can only be understood against the backdrop of wider social change, in which members of the lower classes were incorporated into the body politic in a new way as citizens, and through 'the establishment of mechanisms of security and integration which could overlay and reorganise the effects of the labour market while maintaining its basic capitalistic terms'.[95] This incorporation, however, was conditional upon members of the lower class upholding certain norms of conduct, and those who deviated from these norms would be subjected to various special preventive normalizing and corrective penal devices (or, if incorrigible, segregated). Yet, as Garland emphasizes,

in *representational terms*, [the new] penality extends and completes the positive character of the state's new [integrative and inclusive] self-image. This new kind of social state is 'bent on generating forces, making them grow, and ordering them' (Foucault 1981, p. 136), and the reformative character of the new penal practices reinforces this crucial image: 'the old idea of penal discipline was to crush and break, the modern idea is to fortify and build up force of character' (Blagg and Wilson 1912, p. 5) (emphasis added).[96]

---

[93] See e.g. A. A. G. Peters, above, n. 29; Jareborg's essay, below, Ch. 4.
[94] D. Garland, above, n. 2.   [95] Ibid. 231.   [96] Ibid. 234.

Yet this kind of normalizing and corrective penology, though indeed not designed to crush and break, was in significant ways deeply hierarchical and class-based. Much of this is captured by Foucault's celebrated *Discipline and Punish*, for 'what one is trying to restore in this technique of correction is . . . the obedient subject, the individual subjected to habits, rules, orders, an authority that is exercised continually around him and upon him, and which he must allow to function automatically in him'.[97]

Hence, for Foucault in this kind of penality 'work on the prisoner's soul must be carried out as often as possible',[98] since the intended corrective effect is 'obtained directly through the mechanics of a training'.[99]

While these quotations well capture the hierarchical nature of that particular kind of penality, they refer only implicitly to its class-based character. That that class-based character was very real is however quickly revealed by any number of texts from the first half of this century. To give a flavour of this, the following paragraph from Roger Hood's history of the English Borstal system may suffice—Hood is describing the situation in the 1930s:

The [Borstal] institutions wanted to turn out a strong dependable type [of trainee], with the public school man's sense of honour and loyalty,[100] and the means to achieve this was by a transference of standards and conduct from the housemasters into the [inmate] group. [As an official report put it]: 'He has to be with his lads early and late, sharing in and guiding all their pursuits, and making himself a leader of thought and action in every direction'. The housemaster was to act as a 'father-substitute' and adviser, but above all he was to stand as an example of upright and good living. As one observer [a lawyer] remarked, the [housemasters] were men from 'the well-to-do class quietly showing that a gentleman can do what is asked of him'.[101]

I have gone to some lengths to spell out the hierarchical and class-based character of the normalizing/corrective penology of the early twentieth century, in order to contrast it with more recent developments. For this kind of *de haut en bas* 'normalizing/corrective' penology now seems very anachronistic; hence it seems that our penal imagery (though perhaps not our penal practice) has become less class-based and hierarchical. There is now more of an image of offenders as those who have broken a social contract, formally equal (and hence with rights), but needing to be dealt with efficiently and (preferably fairly) as a result of their infraction.[102] Even those who we seek to rehabilitate (and we should not now rule out some return to

[97] M. Foucault, *Discipline and Punish: The Birth of the Prison* (London, 1977), 128–9.
[98] Ibid. 125.   [99] Ibid. 180.
[100] For non-British readers, 'public schools' in England are (paradoxically) fee-paying private schools, attended especially by the socially élite.
[101] R. Hood, *Borstal Reassessed* (London, 1965), 109–10.
[102] Cf. A. E. Bottoms, 'Neglected Features of Contemporary Penal Systems', in D. Garland and P. Young (eds.), *The Power to Punish* (London, 1983).

rehabilitative strategies, following recent treatment 'meta-analyses'[103]—
even those whom we seek to rehabilitate are now less seen as potentially
'obedient subjects' or (as in a later and more scientific version of normaliz-
ing/corrective penology) 'the recipients of expert treatment', and are more
likely to be appealed to to co-operate in terms of their own longer-term
interests.[104]

The seeming decline in class-based imagery in our penal representations
is of some importance when set against more general understandings of
social developments in the twentieth century. For during this period there
have been significant long-term structural socio-economic changes, involving among other things the relative decline of manufacturing industry, the
growth of the service sector, the growth of new high-tech industries, and the
birth of 'consumerism'. All this has led to major shifts in the relative
fortunes of certain locations, with some traditional cities going into apparently near-terminal decline, and others (normally initially smaller and less
based on heavy industry) experiencing significant growth. A consequence
of much of this has been a growth in female participation in the labour force
in most countries, thus further complicating traditional patterns of social
stratification. To simplify somewhat, this complex kaleidoscope of factors
has led to an erosion, in most countries, of the importance of social class as
traditionally understood, and its partial replacement with alternative indicators of social differentiation. Some of these indicators are group-based
(tenants' groups, environmental groups, women's groups, etc.), while others are more based on individual lifestyle and can be regarded as (at least to
an extent) personally elective. Lifestyle as a differentiator is increasingly
(and for obvious reasons) promoted by astute sales departments and celebrated by the media.[105]

While all this has been going on, those who have lived through the
twentieth century have also seen radical advances in transport, telecom-
munications, and information technology. These have now made it possible
for people to communicate easily across the globe, yet—sometimes—not
even to know who lives in the house next door. In Anthony Giddens's
terms,[106] we have seen a disembedding of social relations from many of their
traditional milieux such as the extended family, the local community, and
the church; hence, there has been a relative erosion in the significance, for

[103] For a summary, see K. McLaren, *Reducing Reoffending: What Works Now?* (Wellington,
NZ, 1992).
[104] In this respect note also the growth of contracts in the probation/social work and the
prison contexts: see e.g. D. Nelken, 'Discipline and Punish: Some Notes on the Margin', (1989)
28 *Howard Journal of Criminal Justice* 245–54 and the Woolf Report, above, n. 32.
[105] See generally S. Lash and J. Urry, above, n. 76; A. E. Bottoms and P. Wiles, 'Crime and
Insecurity in the City', paper presented at the International Society of Criminology International Course on 'Changes in Society, Crime and Criminal Justice in Europe', Leuven,
Belgium, May 1994.
[106] A. Giddens, *The Consequences of Modernity* (Cambridge, 1990).

PRE-MODERN *General context:* overriding importance of localized trust	MODERN *General context:* trust relations vested in disembedded abstract systems
1. *Kinship relations* as an organizing device for stabilizing social ties across time-space	1. *Personal relationships* of friendship or sexual intimacy as means of stabilizing social ties
2. *The local community* as a *place*, providing a familiar milieu	2. *Abstract systems* as a means of stabilizing relations across indefinite spans of time-space
3. *Religious cosmologies* as modes of belief and ritual practice providing a provi– dential interpretation of human life and of nature	3. *Future-oriented,* counter– factual thought as a mode of connecting past and present
4. *Tradition* as a means of connecting present and future; past-oriented in reversible time	

Source: Giddens (1990): 102.

FIG. 2.2. Giddens's characterization of environments of trust in pre-modern and modern societies

most people's daily lives, of these intermediate level social groups. The individual, accordingly, is now more likely than at the beginning of this century to perceive him/herself as an individual, and is correspondingly less likely to define his/her essential self by reference to (fairly permanent) membership of an intermediate-level group: in other words, we all live increasingly, in Raymond Williams's graphic phrase, in a society based on 'mobile privatization'.[107] A perhaps overschematized but nevertheless very thought-provoking set of contrasts, suggested by Giddens,[108] between so-called 'environments of trust' in pre-modern and modern societies is shown in Figure 2.2; despite its schematic nature, it might be of value in throwing light on the problems in hand.

The growth and rapid spread of technology is a key element in Giddens's analysis, and of course information technology is essential to modern managerialism. That being the case, we may also usefully remind ourselves, in trying to solve this extremely complicated jig-saw puzzle, of the analysis

[107] R. Williams, 'Problems of the 'Coming Period', (1983) 140 *New Left Review* 7–18.
[108] A. Giddens, above, n. 106.

of Berger, Berger, and Kellner twenty years ago,[109] when they suggested that technology and bureaucracy were the 'primary carriers of modernization' in advanced societies. Peter Berger being, as is his wont, especially interested in the subjective or phenomenological dimensions of the subject being studied, the authors went on to analyse what they saw as the 'essential concomitants' of technology and bureaucracy on the 'everyday consciousness of ordinary people'—in other words, what difference it makes to the way we think and behave that we (unlike our great-great grandparents) live in a technological and bureaucratic society. Concentrating for present purposes only on technology, it is worth listing in full Berger, Berger, and Kellner's suggested 'concomitants of technology': they are componentiality; interdependence of components and sequences; separability of means and ends; segregation of work from life; anonymous social relations; self-anonymization and a componential self; and possible alienation.[110]

In the preceding three paragraphs I have, in an extremely short compass, sketched some key features of various sociological theories of modernity, which might be (respectively) summarized as the relative erosion of class and its partial replacement by interest-group and lifestyle differentiators; the decline in intermediate-level social groups and hence a general disembedding of social relations; and the subjective concomitants of living in a technological world. These various aspects of theories of modernity, I would suggest, provide at least the outlines of a framework within which one can analyse the rise, in the criminal-justice system, of desert theory/ human rights, managerialism, and 'community', with occasional doses of populist punitiveness.

The explanation, I would tentatively propose, goes something like this. The increasing social emphasis on the individual, the logical outworking of eighteenth-century Enlightenment thinking, and of contemporary 'disembedding' processes, produces (at least from some) a focus on individual rights which naturally rebels against the older utilitarian theories, especially in their more extreme outcomes; and it produces also a requirement for formal equality of treatment. All this is, however, only possible because of the relative decline of class as a social differentiator; hence when, as early in this century, class position was of overwhelming importance in terms of social identity, the formal Enlightenment concept of rights was of substantially less significance in the penal context. The above also perhaps explains the current strong emphasis on race and gender equality, as against equality in terms of class, since both race and gender, as social constructs, are linked to certain biological characteristics, and hence need constant attention as regards fairness in the context of formal individualistic equality (by contrast, class is more easily disregarded as a non-fundamental

[109] P. L. Berger, B. Berger, and H. Kellner, above, n. 81.   [110] Ibid., ch. 1.

characteristic of individuals, now that we have a less immutable class structure than at the beginning of the century).

Meanwhile, the inclusionary/integrative kind of social strategies adopted at the beginning of the twentieth century, after flourishing especially just after the Second World War, have now declined somewhat in most countries, *inter alia*, because of the fiscal crisis they helped to produce. That fiscal crisis has led to a search for alternatives to imprisonment in the form of the new 'community penalties', the title highlighting a nostalgia for community in a period of increased disembedding of social relations from traditional contexts. That 'disembedding' process has itself probably contributed to the increase in crime, there being much evidence that informal social control can be of considerable importance in keeping crime rates low.[111] In a context where we cannot any longer so readily rely on traditional sources of informal social control, nor (as we now know from empirical research) on the normalizing/corrective efficacy of state social control agents, we may instead try to manage individual offenders and the criminal justice system, using the best available modern management techniques and information technology. The use of technology, however, itself has consequential effects on our consciousness, and as a result we are increasingly likely to think actuarially about criminal-justice issues. Management techniques, too, have their ideological effects, and these tend actually to hasten the decline in reliance on intermediate social organizations for the delivery of social control, since management theory seems most at home in dealing with the macro-level corporate plan (systemic managerialism) or with micro-level service delivery (consumerist managerialism), and seems to have more difficulty in dealing with intermediate levels, or with group affiliations.

Given the above, the tendency of modern politicians occasionally to resort to populist punitiveness is relatively easy to understand. The disembedding processes of modernity, together with the other features outlined, have not only probably increased the crime rate, they have also led to a fairly widespread sense of insecurity, especially among older people, as former social certainties are eroded, and the abstract systems on which people are expected to rely (see Figure 2.2) sometimes seem inadequately reassuring. In such a context, a politician seeking popularity can reasonably easily tap into the electorate's insecurities by promising tough action on 'villains'—even if (see the section on populist punitiveness, above), the public are actually rather less punitive than this when confronted with real situations of criminality. But it is quite hard to know when politicians will choose to adopt this particular kind of stance, and this may depend more on the particular political situation (and indeed on the par-

---

[111] See e.g. R. J. Sampson and J. H. Laub, *Crime in the Making* (Cambridge, Mass., 1993); T. Moriyama, 'Crime, Criminal Justice and Social Control: Why do We Enjoy a Low Crime Rate?,' paper presented to the British Criminology Conference, Cardiff, 1993.

ticular politician) than on any objective analysis of the crime problem in the country in question. It is in this sense that popular punitiveness is, as previously noted, more unpredictable than the other three factors discussed in this essay. Given the preceding analysis of modernity, there are reasonable grounds for believing that most criminal-justice systems will contain some features reflecting the themes of just deserts/human rights, managerialism, and community; but that is not necessarily the case as regards populist punitiveness, that factor being potentially more closely tied to short-term political considerations.

We are left, finally, with the second and third dimensions of the 'community' theme, which are not adequately explained by the analysis above. And here it is necessary to extend the discussion of modernity a little, and speak of the globalization–localization thesis.[112] Everyone knows there are 'globalizing' tendencies in the modern world, as a result of developments in the mass media, the increasingly international nature of capital and business, the creation of supra-state organizations such as the European Community, etc. What is sometimes less well recognized is that specific localities, with their special characteristics, are also now of growing importance to social analysis. This is partly for economic reasons—modern capital is less constrained by such matters as the geographical location of raw materials, and, especially in an era of 'high tech', is more able to choose where to locate: hence the variations already referred to between 'decaying' and 'sunrise' cities. If we add to this the shifting patterns of social differentiation, and the increasing tendency to wish to recognize the human rights of disadvantaged groups such as women and ethnic minorities, then one can more readily understand the issues raised in an earlier section as regards 'justice in and for local communities and groups' and 'devolving decision-making to the community' (for example, as regards the FGCs in New Zealand). These factors, however, probably do not adequately explain the growth of interest in victim–offender mediation in advanced societies with no native indigenous culture (such as that of the Maoris in New Zealand): but in this respect it is illuminating to note the findings of empirical research into English mediation schemes, to the effect that there was often little interest in 'any degree of real input [to the mediation] from local people', while on the other hand the individuals concerned in the mediation were sometimes found to develop 'the feeling of being fellow-citizens, of co-operation, of sharing the same society, of mutual respect and help'.[113] In other words, mediation schemes in advanced societies without a strong indigenous culture seem to be about starting with the individuals concerned

[112] See P. Robert, 'The Norms of the Nation-State: The Crisis in Hegemony', paper presented at the GERN European colloquium on the Crisis in Normative Systems, Paris, 1993; S. Lash and J. Urry, above, n. 76.
[113] T. F. Marshall and S. Merry, above, n. 78, 246–7.

(in which respect cf. Figure 2.2, right-hand column, topmost variable), and, from this dyadic base, trying to engender more of a sense of mutuality and community ties. Thus stated, these developments also seem to be explicable, at least tentatively, within the framework of modernity theory.

7. CONCLUSION

Non-habitués entering courtrooms often comment on their timeless quality, or perhaps on a slight sense of anachronism, of moving back in time a generation or two. From such impressions, one might form the view that very modern phenomena such as managerialism, information technology, and rapidly changing social structures are matters that scarcely belong in an analysis of sentencing. As I hope this essay has demonstrated, nothing could be further from the truth. Sentencers, and those who construct the laws and guidelines which sentencers administer, are, whether they like it or not, inextricably connected with developments in modern societies, and these have an influence, however indirectly, on the structures and the content of sentencing decisions. All this occurs especially, I have argued, through the medium of the four concepts of just deserts/human rights, managerialism, community, and populist punitiveness. Yet these factors make their impact very unevenly in different societies, owing to differing cultural histories and contexts, differing political frameworks, and different political and legal actors in particular jurisdictions. In modern Western jurisdictions, our understanding of 'the philosophy and politics of punishment and sentencing' must necessarily, I believe, embrace both general developments of thought and of social structures, and the specific legal frameworks and politics of particular places.

3

Sentencing Reform in Victoria: A Case-Study

ARIE FREIBERG

I. A DECADE OF CHANGE

When, in the dying hours of the autumn parliamentary session of 1991 the Sentencing Bill finally emerged from a tortuous passage through the legislature to become the Sentencing Act 1991 (Vic), it culminated over a decade of sentencing reform in Victoria. That period had seen three major revisions of sentencing legislation representing Victoria's efforts to grapple with the ubiquitous problems confronting the common law world, identified variously as discretion, disparity, desert, severity, and veracity. These issues dominated the sentencing agenda in Australia during the 1980s, and although many originated in the international social and intellectual currents which profoundly influence Australia, they were nourished by a widespread dissatisfaction with the effectiveness of the sentencing process and exploited by sections of the media for whom the responsibility for the decline of civilization as it knew it could be placed at the door of the criminal-justice system.

The Sentencing Act 1991 (Vic), which came into operation in April 1992, was the product of a reformist state Labour Party which came into office in 1982.[1] Victoria is one of eight states or territories in the Australian Federal system. Under Australian constitutional arrangements, the administration of criminal justice is substantially, but not exclusively, a matter for the states, each of which has developed an individual approach to its indigenous problems of crime and punishment in response to its own particular geopolitical circumstances. The Federal Government has no express Federal power to legislate with respect to criminal law. None the less, the Commonwealth Parliament does possess power to create penal offences in relation to any of the subjects upon which it is authorized by the Constitution to legislate. Offenders convicted of offences against the Commonwealth are subject to a mixture of Commonwealth and state sentencing options.[2]

This project is funded by the Criminology Research Council of Australia. My thanks to Mr Stuart Ross, Dr David Tait, and Professor Richard Fox for comments on an earlier draft of this paper.

[1] Which subsequently lost office in October of that year.
[2] A comprehensive sentencing code is slowly developing at the Commonwealth level, but is not discussed in this essay: see Crimes Act 1914 (Cth).

This essay is an attempt to identify and evaluate the impact of the past decade of change on sentencing law and practice by focusing upon those aspects of sentencing reform in Victoria which possibly distinguish it from other jurisdictions. Section 2, below, examines some of the innovative features of the Sentencing Act 1991 (Vic) and its progenitors, namely (1) the form and structure of the legislation; (2) the governing principles and questions of judicial guidance; (3) the maximum penalty structure; (4) the development of sanction hierarchies; (5) the concepts of guilt, conviction, and sentence; (6) statutory sentencing discounts; (7) the abolition of remission and its impact upon the prison population; (8) the use of intermediate sanctions; and (9) the reform of the law relating to dismissals, discharges, and adjournments. In the third section, the impact of the Act upon prison populations and sentencing patterns is evaluated.

2. SENTENCING REFORM

2.1. Background

When the Australian Law Reform Commission received a reference in August 1978 to review a wide range of issues relating to Federal laws concerning the imposition of punishment for offences, the cause of sentencing reform in Australia received a major impetus. Although there had been at least one comprehensive review of state sentencing laws in South Australia,[3] a number of specific inquiries into prisons, parole, and alternatives to imprisonment,[4] as well as the development of a nascent sentencing literature modelled on David Thomas's work in England,[5] sentencing in Australia had not yet emerged from its role as 'Cinderella's illegitimate baby'.[6] Professor Duncan Chappell's Interim Report for the Commission,

---

[3] Which did not come to legislative fruition for over fifteen years: see South Australia, Criminal Law and Penal Methods Reform Committee (Mitchell Committee), *First Report: Sentencing and Corrections* (Adelaide, 1973) and the Criminal Law (Sentencing) Act 1988 (SA).

[4] *Report of the Royal Commission into New South Wales Prisons* (The Nagle Report) 1978; *Report of the Committee Appointed to Review the Parole of Prisoners Act 1966 (NSW)* (The Muir Report) 1979; *A Report on Parole, Prison Accommodation and Leave from Prison in Western Australia* (The Parker Report) 1979; Sentencing Alternatives Committee of Victoria, *Sentencing Alternatives Involving Community Service* (Law Department, 1979).

[5] M. Daunton-Fear, *Sentencing in Western Australia* (Brisbane, 1977); M. Daunton-Fear, *Sentencing in South Australia* (Sydney, 1980). J. Newton, *Sentencing in Queensland* (Canberra, 1979); I. Potas, *Sentencing Violent Offenders in New South Wales* (Sydney, 1980). This tradition has subsequently continued to cover the rest of Australia, see R. Fox and A. Freiberg, *Sentencing: State and Federal Law in Victoria* (Melbourne, 1985); M. Lillas, *Cases and Materials on Sentencing: Tasmanian Supreme Court* (Tasmania, 1986); K. Warner, *Sentencing in Tasmania* (Sydney, 1991).

[6] N. Walker, *Sentencing in a Rational Society* (London, 1969), 1.

published in 1980,[7] was a comprehensive document which, for the first time, placed the 'renaissance of retribution' controversy then fomented in the United States by von Hirsch,[8] Van den Haag,[9] Wilson,[10] and others[11] on the political agenda in Australia. In particular, it highlighted the issues of discretion, disparity, 'truth in sentencing', and the quantum of punishment. For a number of reasons, the final report of the Australian Law Reform Commission did not emerge for another eight years,[12] following the publication of an extensive series of discussion papers.[13]

Sentencing reform during the 1970s and early 1980s in Victoria had focused primarily upon increasing the range of intermediate sentencing options available to the courts. As well as the traditional powers given to the courts to fine and to release offenders on adjournment, absolute or conditional discharge, dismissal, good behaviour bonds, and the like, the major non-custodial option available to the courts was the power to release offenders on probation. The first community-based programme designed specifically to divert offenders from imprisonment was the attendance-centre order. This order, which required offenders to report for a certain number of hours at regular intervals each week at a nominated centre, was introduced by legislation in 1975 after abortive attempts to introduce periodic detention and weekend imprisonment orders in 1973. In 1981, in the first of the major pieces of reform, the Penalties and Sentences Act 1981 (Vic) consolidated a number of disparate sentencing powers in a single Act and created the community-service order which was based upon the performance of community work as a means of punishment and restitution.[14]

In 1982 a Labour Government was elected to office in Victoria on a wide-ranging platform of reform. At this time debate was turning gradually from a predominant concern with the 'alternatives' to imprisonment debate,

---

[7] Australian Law Reform Commission, *Report No. 15: Sentencing of Federal Offenders* (Canberra, 1980).

[8] A. von Hirsch, *Doing Justice: The Choice of Punishments* (New York, 1976).

[9] E. van den Haag, *Punishing Criminals* (New York, 1975).

[10] J. Wilson, *Thinking about Crime* (New York, 1975).

[11] Twentieth Century Fund Task Force on Criminal Sentencing, *Fair and Certain Punishment* (New York, 1976); N. Morris, *The Future of Imprisonment* (Chicago, 1974).

[12] Australian Law Reform Commission, *Report No. 44: Sentencing* (Canberra, 1988).

[13] Australian Law Reform Commission, *Discussion Paper No. 29: Sentencing: Procedure* (1987); *Discussion Paper No. 30: Sentencing: Penalties* (1987); *Discussion Paper No. 31: Sentencing: Prisons* (1987): see also Australian Law Reform Commission, *Report No. 37: Spent Convictions* (1987); Australian Law Reform Commission and Commonwealth Youth Bureau, *Research Paper No. 11: Sentencing Young Offenders* (1988) by A. Freiberg, R. Fox, and M. Hogan.

[14] It came into operation in September 1982. The idea of community work as a sanction came from the recommendations of the Report of the Victorian Sentencing Alternatives Committee, *Sentencing Alternatives Involving Community Service* (1979). This Committee drew inspiration from the United Kingdom where community-service orders had made their appearance in 1973.

which concentrated on decarceration and the ills of imprisonment, to focus upon the nature of the sentencing system itself and the relationship between the various sentencing authorities. Contemporary concern with executive modifications of sentences, and in particular with the gap between sentences imposed and the periods of time actually spent in prison, had surfaced in Australia the late 1970s.[15] In 1979 the Australian Law Reform Commission recommended the abolition of parole, although only partly for reasons to do with 'truth'.[16] The Commission later resiled from this position, but in its final report[17] it recommended that truth in sentencing be enhanced, not by the abolition of parole, but by the abolition of re-missions.[18] In 1982 the abolition of remissions had been considered and rejected in Victoria by the Nelson Committee[19] on the grounds it would generate resentment and discontent among prisoners and that the danger of adverse public reaction to the apparent public leniency was not sufficient to warrant overturning a system which had functioned reasonably well for many years.

By the mid-1980s, however, a significant swing against remissions was perceived.[20] Increasingly, the debate focused upon the expanding range of executive modifications of sentence, including parole, remissions, pre-release,[21] temporary leave, and the like.[22] The genesis of the Sentencing Act 1991 (Vic) can be traced back to one controversial case decided by a Full Bench of five judges[23] of the Supreme Court of Victoria in 1985

[15] For a more detailed discussion, see A. Freiberg, 'Truth in Sentencing?: The Abolition of Remissions in Victoria', (1992) 16 *Crim. LJ* 165.
[16] Australian Law Reform Commission, Report No. 15 Interim, *Sentencing of Federal Offenders* (Canberra, 1980), 211, citing a minority opinion in the *Report of the Committee Appointed to Review the Parole of Prisoners Act 1966 (NSW)* (1978) (the Muir Report) to the effect that members of the community regarded parole as a 'charade'.
[17] Above, n. 12.
[18] As well as other measures such as changes in sentencing terminology and modifications to pre-release measures: see pp. 38 ff. On the changes made to parole systems in other states, see R. Broadhurst, 'Evaluating Imprisonment and Parole: Survival Rates or Failure Rates?', in S. McKillop (ed.), *Keeping People out of Prison* (Australian Institute of Criminology, Canberra, 1991).
[19] Victoria, Sentencing Alternatives Committee, Second Report, *Parole and Remissions* (1982), 26.
[20] See Victorian Sentencing Committee, *Discussion Paper* (April 1987), 111.
[21] Pre-release was a scheme whereby prisoners serving terms of imprisonment over one year could be released on supervision up to six months prior to the commencement of the non-parole period.
[22] See R. Fox, 'Pre-Release Permits: Executive Modifications of Custodial Sentences', (1984) 58 *Law Institute Journal* 542. The matter of 'truth' in sentencing is, of course, much more complex. A full discussion would also encompass such matters as the relationship between statutory maximum penalties and judicially imposed sentences and concurrent and consecutive sentences.
[23] The appellate court is normally comprised of three judges. A Full Bench of five judges is very rare and can be constituted if the court is contemplating overturning one of its own previous decisions.

which centred upon this emerging political issue of 'truth in sentencing'.[24] The central issue in this case was whether a court should take into account the effect of remissions when imposing sentence.[25] The Full Bench refused to overrule its previous policy that remissions were irrelevant to sentencing.[26] However, in passing judgment, the Court observed acerbically:

An intelligent observer who was told about the sentence passed and the period of incarceration actually served would be likely to conclude either that the Court had no authority because little notice was taken of the sentence passed or that the Court was engaged in an elaborate charade designed to conceal from the public the real punishment being inflicted upon an offender. . . . The authority of the court is eroded whenever the Executive is authorised to interfere with its orders.[27]

This case sparked a fierce debate about the nature of the sentencing process and the relationship of subordinate sentencing authorities such as the Parole Board and the correctional agencies to the courts.

Following the decision in *Yates*, the Victorian Government amended the sentencing legislation to permit a court to take remissions into account in sentencing.[28] In addition, in October 1985, the then Attorney-General, Mr Jim Kennan, appointed a Committee chaired by Sir John Starke QC, a retired Supreme Court judge and erstwhile Chair of the Parole Board, to review current sentencing policy and practice in Victoria.[29] Pending the Committee's report, however, the government hurriedly proceeded to legislate a new Penalties and Sentences Act in 1985. This Act relocated the main sentencing provisions of general application previously scattered in a range of legislation.[30] It introduced suspended sentences into Victoria, permitting courts to suspend a sentence of imprisonment of up to one year, either totally or partially. It also introduced a new measure, the community-based order, which replaced probation, attendance-centre orders, and community-service orders.[31] Finally, the Act required the courts in sentencing

---

[24] *Yates* [1985] VR 41.
[25] Remissions effectively reduced a sentence by about one-third.
[26] See *Douglas* [1959] VR 182; *R. v. Governor of Her Majesty's Gaol at Pentridge; Ex parte Cusmano* [1966] VR 583; *Campbell* [1970] VR 120.
[27] *Yates* [1985] VR 41, 47.
[28] This amendment had no significant impact upon sentencing practices.
[29] The Committee was also required to examine the purposes of sentencing, the impact of custodial and non-custodial sentences, the length of sentences, the impact of remissions, pre-release, parole, temporary leaves and other sentencing shortening practices on such matters as correctional administration, police administration, prisoner morale, staff morale, the community, victims and the offender and his family. Other issues required to be examined were Governor's Pleasure prisoners, youth training centres, the role of the media and the provision of information for the courts.
[30] See Community Welfare Services Act 1970, the Crimes Act 1958 (Vic), the Magistrates (Summary Proceedings) Act 1975, and the Penalties and Sentences Act 1981 (Vic).
[31] See Section 2.9, below.

an offender to have regard to that person's plea of guilty, whether or not it was indicative of remorse.[32]

The Sentencing Committee's Report was tabled in April 1988 and contained a comprehensive set of recommendations together with a draft Penalties and Sentences Bill.[33] The Starke Committee recommended the establishment of a Judicial Studies Board to assist the courts in sentencing and to undertake research on sentencing.[34] It also recommended that further research be carried out in relation to statutory maximum penalties. In April 1989 a Sentencing Task Force under the chairmanship of Mr Frank Costigan QC was established and reported in September 1989.[35] The report recommended a rationalization of statutory maximum penalties under the Crimes Act 1958 (Vic) as well as a number of changes in the form of statutory maxima.[36] In November 1989 a Penalties and Sentences Bill was placed before Parliament which embodied many of the recommendations of the Sentencing Committee and the Sentencing Task Force. Because of the controversial nature of the combined set of recommendations, that bill was in turn subject to a comprehensive review in 1990 which compared each clause with the provisions of the Penalties and Sentences Act 1985 (Vic), the recommendations of the Victorian Sentencing Committee, and the recommendations of the Sentencing Task Force.[37] This review produced the Sentencing Bill 1991.

The Sentencing Act 1991 (Vic), as finally enacted, extensively revised the structure of statutory maximum penalties, abolished remissions, created a new sentencing option—the 'intensive correction order'—revised the provisions relating to community-based orders, suspended sentences, fines and

---

[32] Penalties and Sentences Act 1985 (Vic), s. 4 and see Section 2.7, below.

[33] Between the tabling of the report and subsequent legislation and election was called for late 1988 which returned the incumbent government. On its re-election, the government's first response to the report was the Corrections (Amendment) Bill 1989 which proposed to replace remissions with earned 'merit time'. The bill also provided for the phasing out of the pre-release scheme and a home-detention programme for selected prisoners in the last six months of a sentence. Criticisms of the bill ultimately led to its withdrawal.

[34] These recommendations were accepted and the Board was established by the Judicial Studies Board Act 1990 (Vic). The functions of the Board are: to conduct seminars for judges and magistrates on sentencing matters; to conduct research on sentencing matters; to prepare sentencing guidelines and circulate them among judges and others; to develop and maintain a computerized statistical sentencing data base for use by the courts; to provide sentencing statistics to judges, magistrates, and lawyers; to monitor present trends and initiate further developments in sentencing; to assist the courts to give effect to the principles contained in the Sentencing Act 1991 (Vic); to consult with the public, government departments, and other interested people, bodies, or associations on sentencing matters; and to advise the Attorney-General on sentencing matters. As yet this Board has not come into full operation.

[35] See Sentencing Task Force, *Review of Statutory Maximum Penalties: Report to the Attorney-General* (Melbourne, 1989), written for the Task Force by R. Fox and A. Freiberg.

[36] See further below, Section 2.4.

[37] See A. Freiberg, *Review of the Penalties and Sentences Bill 1989*. This review was circulated to members of the judiciary, the Bar, and the legal profession.

fine default, and significantly rationalized and simplified the provisions relating to dismissals, discharges, and adjournments. It did not represent a revolutionary change in sentencing options, nor did it require fundamental changes in sentencing practices. Its options were familiar to sentencers, who had been intimately involved in the process of reform, and it represented a continuation of policies which had been in place for over a decade.[38] However, there were a number of areas in which significant change had occurred.

2.2. Form and Structure

The Act is structurally significant for a number of reasons. First, it represents the culmination of the decade-long process of consolidating all of the major general sentencing provisions in the one piece of legislation. Section 1(b) states that one of the purposes of the Act is

to have within the one Act all general provisions dealing with the power of the courts to pass sentence.

The Act generally meets this aim. Sentencers at all levels of courts in Victoria[39] now draw their sentencing power from this single piece of legislation which was intended by its framers to be clear, logical, intelligible,[40] and easy to use.[41] It was intended to be understandable to those whose function it was to administer it, and to those who were subject to its

[38] For a review of sentencing reform in Victoria, see P. Sallmann, 'In Search of the Holy Grail of Sentencing: An Overview of Some Recent Trends and Developments', (1991) 1 *Journal of Judicial Administration* 125; R. Douglas, 'Rationalising Sentencing: The Victorian Sentencing Committee's Report', (1988) 12 *Crim LJ* 327; I. Freckleton and A. Thacker, 'The New Sentencing Package: Parts I & II', (1991) 65 *Law Institute Journal* 1032 and 1198.

[39] Offences in Victoria are divided into three categories: indictable offences, indictable offences triable summarily and summary offences. Indictable offences are heard in either the Supreme Court or the County Court, whilst summary offences are heard in the Magistrates' Court. The County Court is the major trial court for indictable offences and can hear all cases except treason, murder, and certain other offences. Currently, the Supreme Court confines itself to trials of murder and certain complex or lengthy cases. In 1991 the higher courts tried 1572 offenders while the Magistrates' Court tried 87, 163 offenders. Juvenile justice is dispensed by a Children's Court under separate legislation: see Children and Young Persons Act 1989 (Vic).

[40] The drafters of the Act had in mind the problems created by the convoluted and difficult drafting style adopted by the Commonwealth in its recent reforms. For the deprecating observations of some judges upon this legislation, see *Paull* (1990) 20 NSWLR 427, 437; 49 A. Crim. R. 142 ('unnecessarily complicated and opaque'); *Muanchukingan* (1990) 52 A. Crim. R. 354, 358 ('convoluted, opaque and unnecessarily time consuming'); *El Karhani* (1990) 21 NSWLR 370, 372.

[41] In particular, the Act consolidated sentencing powers relating to the mentally disordered (see Sentencing Act 1991 (Vic), ss. 90–94 and the Mental Health Act 1986 (Vic)); the intellectually disabled (see Sentencing Act 1991 (Vic), ss. 80–83 and the Intellectually Disabled Persons' Services Act 1986 (Vic)) and the alcoholic and drug-dependent (see Sentencing Act 1991 (Vic), s. 28 and the Alcoholics and Drug-Dependent Persons Act 1968 (Vic)).

provisions. The drafting principles underlying the Act were that provisions of general application, such as sentencing guidance, would precede specific provisions, and that all provisions relating to each sanction should be grouped within the one division. Provisions guiding the use of a specific sanction precede the sanction provisions and administrative and procedural matters. Where provisions relate to any particular sanction, they follow the sanction provisions.

Secondly, the Act lists all of the courts' sentencing powers in one section in the form of a sentencing hierarchy, thus providing courts with a clear description of their powers, and with a logical framework within which to make decisions about which sanction will provide the least restrictive alternative.[42] Finally, the Act states clearly whether a sentencing order is conviction or non-conviction based and provides a basis upon which a court is to exercise its discretion whether or not to convict.[43]

These matters of form and structure create the foundation upon which a coherent sentencing system can be built and, although not spectacular in themselves, have had the effect of sweeping away decades of accumulated anomalies, inconsistencies, and ambiguities. Less successful, however, has been the attempt to limit disparity and discretion.

2.3. Judicial Guidance

The Sentencing Act 1991 (Vic) is intended 'to promote consistency of approach in the sentencing of offenders'.[44] One of the methods by which it is intended that this be done is by providing 'sentencing principles to be applied by courts in sentencing offenders'.[45] These principles are set out in Part 2 of the Act, entitled 'Governing Principles', in particular, in section 5. The Victorian Sentencing Committee was very much concerned with the question of sentencing principles and guidance and nearly three-quarters of the first volume of its report deal with these matters.

Victorian courts have traditionally treated sentencing as an essentially pragmatic exercise. The apotheosis of the Court of Criminal Appeal's approach is found in the leading case of *Williscroft* where Adam and Crockett JJ. stated:

Now, ultimately every sentence imposed represents the sentencing judge's instinctive synthesis of all the various aspects involved in the punitive process. Moreover, in our view, it is profitless . . . to attempt to allot to the various considerations their proper part in the assessment of the particular punishments presently under examination. We are aware that such a conclusion rests upon what is essentially a subjective judgment largely intuitively reached by an appellate judge as to what punishment is appropriate.[46]

---

[42] See further below, Section 2.5.   [43] See further below, Section 2.6.
[44] Sentencing Act 1991 (Vic), s. 1(a).   [45] Ibid.   [46] [1975] VR 292, 300.

This view was recently echoed by the High Court of Australia, when the majority of the court stated:

However, sentencing is not a purely logical exercise, and the troublesome nature of the sentencing discretion arises in large measure from unavoidable difficulty in giving weight to each of the purposes of punishment. The purposes of criminal punishment are various: protection of society, deterrence of the offender and of others who might be tempted to offend, retribution and reform. The purposes overlap and none of them can be considered in isolation from the others when determining what is an appropriate sentence in a particular case. They are guide-posts to the appropriate sentence but sometimes they point in different directions.[47]

The Victorian Sentencing Committee was cognizant of the criticisms which had been directed at the sentencing disparities produced by such a subjective and unstructured approach but was unwilling to contemplate recommending the introduction of sentencing grids, guidelines, tariffs, or fixed penalties which had been tried in other jurisdictions.[48] The Committee's solution was to create a package of measures to guide more closely the exercise of a sentencer's discretion. This package included: (1) clearly defined objectives to be pursued by the sentencing process; (2) clearly set out factors which mitigated or aggravated sentences; (3) the means of determining the seriousness of the offences; (4) the power to hand down guideline sentences; and (5) a clear hierarchy of sanctions.[49]

The Committee's draft bill contained a clause[50] headed 'Sentencing Guidelines' which required a court to impose 'the sentence which it considers to be the most appropriate in the circumstances' having regard to the provisions of the Act, and to have regard to such factors as the gravity of the offence, the offender's culpability, and the presence of aggravating or mitigating factors. It required a court to impose 'the least severe sentence that the court could have imposed to achieve the purpose or purposes for which the sentence is imposed' and specified the purposes of sentencing as the imposition of just punishment, deterrence, rehabilitation, denunciation, the incapacitation of the mentally ill or intellectually disabled, or a combination of these purposes. Finally, it required a court to regard a sentence of confinement as a last resort.

The Committee recognized that the different aims would need to be reconciled and it attempted to resolve the conflict in this manner:

In the Committee's view the just deserts principles ought to set the maximum sentence that can be imposed on an offender in any particular case, however, the

---

[47] *Veen (No. 2)* (1988) 164 CLR 465, 476.
[48] See R. Fox, 'Controlling Sentencers', (1987) 20 *ANZJ Crim* 218; C. Corns, 'Destructuring Sentencing Decision-Making in Victoria', (1990) 23 *ANZJ Crim* 145.
[49] See Victorian Sentencing Committee, above, n. 20, 161, and clauses 5 to 10 in the draft bill attached to the report.
[50] Clause 5.

effects of the just deserts principles should be modified by giving the appropriate weight to the principles of parsimony, relevant aggravating and mitigating factors and the other aims of sentencing—rehabilitation, deterrence and denunciation. In no circumstances should a sentence be increased beyond that which is justified on just deserts principles in order that one or more of the secondary aims are met.[51]

The draft bill provided a scale of penalties[52] and lists of aggravating and mitigating circumstances.[53] It also empowered the Full Court to hand down guideline judgments[54] to be followed by judges and magistrates when sentencing offenders. A guideline judgment would be binding on every judge or magistrate in any subsequent proceeding unless the judge or magistrate was of the opinion that the particular circumstances of the proceedings were so materially different as to require him or her to depart from the guidelines.[55] This clause was excised from the bill in Parliament at the instigation of the Opposition parties on the basis of the Opposition's support for the view of the majority of Supreme Court judges who were of the opinion that such guidelines would unduly restrict the discretion of the courts.

Prior to its introduction into Parliament, the bill based upon the Committee's draft bill was significantly modified, primarily influenced by the work undertaken by the judges of the County Court of Victoria who were developing a 'Sentencing Manual' designed to assist sentencers by providing information about sentencing law, and by developing what they called a sentencing 'methodology'. The methodology involved a 'two-step' or 'two-tier' approach which was purportedly based upon some comments of the High Court of Australia in *Veen (No. 1)*[56] where Jacobs J. had said that the 'sentence should be proportionate to the gravity of the offence' unless the applicant's history warranted some departure from the principle. A court would then determine the appropriate proportionate sentence in reference to all the circumstances of the offence.[57] The revised clause 5 thus required a court first to 'determine what sentence would be proportionate to the offence in the light of the objective circumstances of the offence'[58] and then to 'determine what is the appropriate sentence in all the circumstances of the offence'.[59]

---

[51] Victorian Sentencing Committee, above, n. 20, 122.   [52] Clause 7.
[53] Clauses 8 and 9. These were omitted from the Sentencing Bill.   [54] Clause 6.
[55] Penalties and Sentences Bill 1989, cl. 4(2).   [56] (1979) 143 CLR 458.
[57] This passage was discussed in *Veen (No. 2)* by Mason CJ, Brennan, Dawson, and Toohey JJ. (1988) 164 CLR 465, 472.
[58] Having regard to (*a*) the maximum penalty prescribed for the offence; and (*b*) current sentencing practices; and (*c*) the nature and gravity of the offence; and (*d*) the presence of any other aggravating or mitigating factor in the objective circumstances of the offence.
[59] Having regard to (*a*) the proportionate sentence determined under sub-paragraph (i); and (*b*) the purpose or purposes for which the sentence is imposed; and (*c*) the offender's culpability and degree of complicity in the commission of the offence; and (*d*) whether the offender pleaded guilty to the offence and, if so, the stage in the proceedings at which the offender did

The Penalties and Sentences Bill as introduced into Parliament in November 1989 was subject to the criticism that this attempt to structure judicial discretion was wrong in principle, represented a misreading of the High Court's judgment in the *Veen* cases and was unduly mechanistic. It was also clear that the Victorian Sentencing Committee's attempt to clarify the purposes of punishment had been unsuccessful in that the statements of sentencing principle did little to reconcile the disparate aims of punishment, in particular as any two or more of the purposes could be combined. As had been the case in the past, it was not possible, in the Victorian political or judicial context, to obtain agreement as to whether there should be, and if so what should be, the sole or dominant sentencing purpose. Furthermore, the factors which were said to aggravate or mitigate offences were inconsistent, repetitive, and involved some elements which were already part of the definition of the offence.

In March 1990 the Court of Criminal Appeal of Victoria had before it an appeal from a County Court judge purporting to apply the methodology outlined above, not on any statutory basis but on the ground that this approach merely restated the common law as stated by the High Court in *Veen (No. 2)*. The Court of Criminal Appeal, comprising three judges of the Supreme Court, scathingly rejected the 'methodology'. In the case of *Young*,[60] the Court of Criminal Appeal reaffirmed the 'intuitive synthesis' approach it had articulated in *Williscroft* some fifteen years earlier, noting that 'the task of sentencing cannot be confined, without injustice, within rigid formulae'.[61] In the court's view, the adoption of such a rigid, or formulaic, approach

would be likely to lead either to the imposition of inadequate sentences or injustice. It would certainly lead to an increase in appeals against sentence. What is a sentence proportionate to an offence is a matter of discretion and there must in most cases be a range of sentences open to a sentencing judge which are proportionate to the offence. There cannot be said to be a sentence which is *the* proportionate sentence.[62]

It rejected any notion of a 'tariff' sentence as possibly applied in England,[63] observing that

whatever authority it may have in England, where the problems of sentencing are somewhat different from those in Victoria, we do not think it should . . . be adopted here.

Clause 5 of the Penalties and Sentences Bill 1989 represented a major conflict between the views of the state's two senior courts. In the face of

so or indicated an intention to do so; and (*e*) the offender's previous character; and (*f*) the presence of any other aggravating or mitigating factor concerning the offender or of any other relevant circumstances.

[60] [1990] VR 951.   [61] [1990] VR 951, 955.   [62] [1990] VR 951, 960.
[63] Referring to Thomas's analysis, in *Principles of Sentencing*, 2nd edn. (London, 1979), 35.

such resolute opposition by the Supreme Court to the approach exemplified in clause 5, it was obvious that the bill would not pass in the form presented. A compromise position was struck after the bill was redrafted by a Supreme Court judge at the behest of the Attorney-General. It now appears in section 5 of the Sentencing Act 1991 (Vic).

5. (1) The only purposes for which sentences may be imposed are—
    (a) to punish the offender to an extent and in a manner which is just in all of the circumstances; or
    (b) to deter the offender or other persons from committing offences of the same or a similar character; or
    (c) to establish conditions within which it is considered by the court that the rehabilitation of the offender may be facilitated; or
    (d) to manifest the denunciation by the court of the type of conduct in which the offender engaged; or
    (e) to protect the community from the offender;[64] or
    (f) a combination of two or more of those purposes.

   (2) In sentencing an offender a court must have regard to—
    (a) the maximum penalty prescribed for the offence; and
    (b) current sentencing practices; and
    (c) the nature and gravity of the offence; and
    (d) the offender's culpability and degree of responsibility for the offence; and
    (e) whether the offender pleaded guilty to the offence and, if so, the stage in the proceedings at which the offender did so or indicated an intention to do so; and
    (f) the offender's previous character; and
    (g) the presence of any aggravating or mitigating factor concerning the offender or of any other relevant circumstances.

The current section abandons the concepts of proportionate and appropriate sentences as separate concepts and as part of a 'formulaic' approach to sentencing and, in so doing, ultimately fails to address the problems originally raised by the Victorian Sentencing Committee. By blandly stating all of the purposes of sentencing, it merely restates the common law, which was found so wanting by the Committee.

The significance of the decision in *Young*'s case however, does not lie in a local conflict between two courts, but in the fact that this relatively heated debate goes to the heart of attempts to guide sentencing discretion in common law countries by methods short of those adopted in the United States—methods which have been explicitly rejected in all Australian jurisdictions. *Young*'s case has been reaffirmed in Victoria on a number of occasions and the adoption of such an approach is seen as an error suf-

---

[64] This sub-section was inserted during the bill's passage through Parliament on the motion of the Opposition.

ficiently serious to vitiate the sentencing discretion requiring the appellate court to re-sentence.[65] It has also been adopted by some judges in other states.[66] However, a contrary stream of authority has emerged. As far back as 1987, some judges in the Northern Territory have adopted the idea of looking at the 'objective' and 'subjective' aspects of a sentence,[67] and it appears to be an unobjectionable practice to a number of judges in New South Wales.[68] The High Court, although invited to enter the debate, has so far refused to rule on the 'heretical' methodology.[69]

2.3.1. *Statistical Information*

Sentencing consistency is said to require comprehensive qualitative and quantitative information about the range of sentences imposed in similar cases.[70] The Sentencing Act 1991 (Vic) requires a court, in imposing sentence, to have regard to 'current sentencing practices'[71] which can be taken to mean not only general sentencing principles but also quantitative information about comparable sentences imposed in other cases—the controversial notion of a 'tariff'. The excised clause relating to guideline sentences permitted courts to have regard to statistical research or other similar material submitted to it by the Director of the Judicial Studies Board.

   Australian courts have been fiercely ambivalent about the role of statistical information in guiding judicial discretion. One of the most common grounds of appeal is that a sentence is manifestly excessive. But for a sentence to be classified as excessive, comparison with some norm is required. The Victorian Court of Criminal Appeal, in conformity with its 'intuitive synthesis' approach, generally baulks at references to 'the going rate' or 'the going tariff'[72] for a particular class of offence but recognizes that the determination of what is an appropriate sentence depends upon an awareness of the sentences imposed in the past for the same, or similar

[65] *Atik* 23/8/90 (CCA V); *Bonnano, Dennis and Wilson* 29/3/90 (CCA V); Jarvis and *Jarvis* 15/9/92 (CCA V) (the two-tier approach declared a 'heresy'); *O'Brien* (1991) 55 A. Crim. R. 410; *Nagy* [1992] 1 VR 637; (1991) 57 A. Crim. R. 64.
[66] See e.g. *Gallagher* (1991) 23 NSWLR 220; 53 A. Crim. R. 248 (NSW).
[67] See e.g. *Ireland* (1987) 49 NTR 10, 23 per Nader J. (the objective sentence is the sentence which is appropriate having regard to the circumstances of the crime. It is the appropriate punishment if there were no mitigating factors. The actual sentence will usually be less than the objective sentence, and, sometimes, a mere fraction of it because of the effect of mitigating circumstances); see also *Raggett* (1990) 101 FLR 323, 334 per Kearney J. (the fixing of an 'objective sentence' and then allowing for any proper mitigation—appears to me to be proper, and well-accepted in this jurisdiction); *Jabaltjari* (1989) 64 NTR 1, 20 per Martin J.
[68] See e.g. *Dodd* (1991) 57 A. Crim. R. 349; *El Karhani* (1990) 21 NSWLR 370, 380.
[69] *Bugmy* (1990) 169 CLR 766; 92 ALR 552.
[70] See Australian Law Reform Commission, *Report No. 44: Sentencing* (AGPS, 1988), 147; Sallmann, above, n. 38, at 130.
[71] Sentencing Act 1991 (Vic), s. 5(2)(b).   [72] *Bruce & Watson* 2/6/78; *Zakaria* 18/4/84.

offences.[73] However, this concession is subject to the overriding concern that courts not be exposed to what it calls the 'tyranny of statistics'.[74]

In other jurisdictions, the approach is more flexible. In the Northern Territory, for example, statistical sentencing information appears to be more readily accepted for the purpose of establishing a general level or standard provided that the information is accurate, reliable, and comparable.[75] In recent years a number of judges have expressed the view that the 'need for consistency in the punishment in like cases of like persons overrides the right of the sentencer to impose his idiosyncratic view'.[76] It is probably fair to say that as statistical information becomes more comprehensive and is supplied by state agencies rather than from the researches of the bar,[77] the greater its chance of acceptance by the courts, particularly in view of the High Court's powerful and oft-cited statement in *Lowe* that:

Just as consistency in punishment—a reflection of the notion of equal justice—is a fundamental element in any rational and fair system of criminal justice, so inconsistency in punishment, because it is regarded as a badge of unfairness and unequal treatment under the law, is calculated to lead to an erosion of public confidence in the integrity of the administration of justice. It is for this reason that the avoidance and elimination of unjustifiable discrepancy in sentencing is a matter of abiding importance to the administration of justice and to the community.[78]

However, in Victoria the outlook for the provision of consistent and comprehensive support for the courts by way of an independent Bureau of Crime Statistics appears to be grim. Although legislation for the establishment of an independent bureau was introduced into Parliament in 1989,[79] it was referred to a parliamentary committee for consideration, and although the committee recommended the establishment of an independent statutory body,[80] to date only a rudimentary and under-resourced department of government has been established. Given the fiscal stringency of the current state government, it is unlikely that the hopes for a bureau will be realized.

[73] *Williscroft* [1975] VR 293, 301; *Piercey* [1971] VR 647, 651; *Zouras* 23/7/84. However, even in *Williscroft* the Full Court called for, and was supplied with, statistical data on sentences imposed for the relevant offence; see also *Goulding* (1991) 56 A. Crim. R. 75 (CCA WA) (tariff approach 'undesirable and not within the contemplation of the legislation').

[74] *Bugmy* 21/6/89 (CCA V).

[75] *Breed* v. *Pryce* (1985) 36 NTR 23; *Clair* v. *Brough* (1985) 37 NTR 11; *Allinson* (1987) 49 NTR 38; *Ireland* (1987) 49 NTR 10; *Tarry* v. *Pryce* (1987) 45 NTR 1; *Mason* v. *Pryce* (1988) 53 NTR 1; *Ngulkurr* v. *O'Brien* (1989) 98 FLR 279.

[76] *Tarry* v. *Pryce* (1987) 45 NTR 1, 9; see also *Freeman* v. *Binnekamp* (1987) 44 SASR 114 (CCA SA); *Visconti* [1982] 2 NSWLR 104 (CCA NSW); *Streatfield* (1991) 53 A. Crim. R. 320, 325 (CCA Q); *Boudelah and Charlston* (1991) 53 A. Crim. R. 148; 100 ALR 93 (Federal Court of Australia); *O'Brien* (1987) 6 MVR 75 (CCA T).

[77] See e.g. the work of the Judicial Commission of New South Wales: G. Greenleaf, 'Making the Sentence Fit the Computer—or the Accused?', (1991) 65 *Australian Law Journal* 45.

[78] (1984) 58 ALJR 414, 415 per Mason J.   [79] Criminal Justice (Boards) Bill 1989.

[80] Victoria, Legal and Constitutional Committee, Forty-Sixth Report. Report upon a Bureau of Crime Statistics for Victoria, September 1991.

Overall, it cannot be said that the cause of consistency in sentencing has been much advanced by the Sentencing Act 1991 (Vic) or by any other developments in Australia. Judicial independence and maintenance of a relatively wide discretion are regarded as the hallmarks of a properly functioning criminal-justice system and any extra-curial interventions, as the Victorian experience has shown, will be vigorously resisted.[81]

2.4. Maximum Penalties

The Victorian Sentencing Committee devoted a considerable part of its report to the question of statutory maximum penalties. After reviewing the maximum penalties provided in the Crimes Act 1958 (Vic), the Committee concluded that those engaged in the workings of the criminal-justice system in Victoria were 'acting in a system where many of the maximum penalties set by statute were developed centuries ago, and have no rational basis or relevance to modern views on the seriousness of crimes, the seriousness of penalties and the appropriate policies that ought to guide sentencing'.[82] It was obvious to any student of the criminal-justice system that the penalty structure was inadequate. It was anachronistic,[83] internally inconsistent,[84] divisive,[85] unjust,[86] and unduly complex.[87] One of the Committee's recommendations was that the maxima set by statute be reviewed. Its suggestions were that a seven-part scale be adopted ranging from six months to life. The scale was considerably lower than the existing scale, primarily because of the need to adjust for the progressive abolition of remissions[88] and partly because of its views of current community values.

The Committee's recommendations were not adopted. Rather, a Sentencing Task Force was appointed to undertake a more comprehensive review. There were four main reasons for this:

First, [there was] adverse media and public reaction to the proposed levels of reduction. Secondly, the Starke revision did not refer to the use of non-custodial sanctions, such as fines, which could be used as maxima in their own right or in conjunction with imprisonment. Thirdly, in applying the new maxima to existing

[81] See Victorian Sentencing Committee, Appendix A, Submission of the Majority of the Judges of the Supreme Court.

[82] Victorian Sentencing Committee, above, n. 20, 675.

[83] In that too many of the penalties and many of the offences reflected outdated values and attitudes.

[84] In that there was a lack of congruence between the level of penalty set for similar offences.

[85] In that they create a tension between Parliament and the courts which attempt to create a coherent sentencing practice within an incoherent penalty structure.

[86] In that inconsistent penalties tend to create inconsistent sentences which can lead to a justifiable sense of grievance in offenders whose sentences are unwarrantedly disparate.

[87] In that the range of sanctions, options and combinations had proliferated unnecessarily.

[88] Which was its recommended technique for adjusting for the abolition of remissions.

TABLE 3.1. *Victorian penalty scale Sentencing Act 1991, section 109*

Level	Maximum prison term	Maximum fine penalty units	Community-based order maximum hours of unpaid community work
1	Life	—	—
2	240 months	2,400	500 over 24 months
3	180 months	1,800	500 over 24 months
4	150 months	1,500	500 over 24 months
5	120 months	1,200	500 over 24 months
6	90 months	900	500 over 24 months
7	60 months	600	500 over 24 months
8	36 months	360	
9	24 months	240	375 over 18 months
10	12 months	120	250 over 12 months
11	6 months	60	125 over 6 months
12	—	10	50 over 3 months
13	—	5	—
14	—	1	—

Source: From R. Fox, above, n. 89, at 119. This is not how it appears in the legislation.

Crimes Act offences, the Sentencing Committee obviously modified the seriousness ranking of many of the offences. The report did not indicate how those changes were arrived at. Fourthly, the Committee did not attempt to review other legislation.[89]

The Task Force's methodology is set out in its report and has been published elsewhere.[90] In short, what emerged from Parliament in the Sentencing Act 1991 (Vic), sections 109–110 was a fourteen-level scale ranging from a fine of \$100 to life imprisonment. The scale can be presented as shown in Table 3.1.

There are a number of notable features of the scale. First, the penalty scale is expressed in terms of levels rather than the traditional prescription of a specific maximum penalty for each individual offence. Secondly, the scale is used to distinguish indictable from summary offences. Offences punishable by Levels 1 to 8 inclusive are indictable offences; offences from Levels 5 to 8 inclusive are indictable offences triable summarily, while those at Levels 9 to 14 are summary offences. Thirdly, the sanction unit for imprisonment is expressed in terms of months rather than years. This was intended to smooth out the range of maxima, and it made use of

[89] R. Fox, 'Order out of Chaos: Victoria's New Maximum Penalty Structure', (1991) 17 *Monash University Law Review* 102, 110.

[90] See ibid.; and R. Fox and A. Freiberg, 'Ranking Offence Seriousness in Reviewing Statutory Maximum Penalties', (1990) 23 *ANZJ Crim.* 165.

psychological evidence on the effect of 'least noticeable differences' produced by Fitzmaurice and Pease which suggested that sentencers might be more discriminating in the use of imprisonment when the sanction unit was smaller.[91] It also set up a connection between imprisonment and fine scales. The fine scale in Victoria is expressed in terms of 'penalty units' each of $100. The Sentencing Act 1991 (Vic) equates one month of imprisonment with 10 penalty units ($1,000) and has standardized the fine/imprisonment, imprisonment/fine correlations, which had previously showed no consistency at all. Fourthly, the general level of fines has been increased considerably as the consequence of the policy both to enhance the credibility of the fine as an alternative sanction and to reinforce the policy explicit in the Act that imprisonment is a sanction of last resort. Finally, the application of the scale to the offences in the Crimes Act 1958 (Vic) attempted to rationalize the offence/penalty relationship. Unlike the Victorian Sentencing Committee's massive reductions,[92] the reallocations showed a wide range of changes. Thirty-one offences had their maxima increased, 59 were decreased, and for the majority of offences there was no change at all. Overall, the general level of maxima has been reduced, but this is accounted for by the reduction in the large number of maxima which were never actually used. Many of the changes in fact reflected current judicial sentencing practice and brought the statutory maxima more in line with the prevailing 'tariffs'.[93] In particular, there were major reductions in offences against property and some increases in respect of offences against the person.

The introduction of the penalty scale has not been problem free. The application of the scale to offences outside the Crimes Act 1958 (Vic) remains to be done.[94] Parliament has already broken from the mould in respect of some sexual offences by assigning a maximum penalty of twenty-five years, which is severely out of line with the scale.[95] As yet, no comprehensive set of guidelines have been created by which Parliamentary Counsel can be guided in creating future offences and setting penalty levels and legislation passed subsequent to the Sentencing Act 1991 (Vic) has not adopted the style introduced by section 109. Furthermore, there remains the conceptual problem of penalty equivalence for the courts to solve, for

[91] C. Fitzmaurice and K. Pease, *The Psychology of Judicial Sentencing* (Manchester, 1986), ch. 7.

[92] Which were also intended to compensate for the abolition of remissions.

[93] On the relationship between statutory maxima and judicial sentencing practices, see R. Douglas, 'When Parliament Barks, Do the Magistrates Bite? The Impact of Changes to Statutory Sentence Levels', (1989) 7 *Law in Context* 93.

[94] There are some thousands of statutory offences, but the bulk of cases in fact dealt with by the courts are offences under the Crimes Act 1958 (Vic) and the Road Traffic Act 1986 (Vic).

[95] This penalty level was the result of a 'trade-off' in Parliament in relation to concern expressed by the then Opposition that sentences for sexual offences were too low. The Opposition had proposed that sentences for sexual offences be made cumulative.

although the Task Force clearly did not intend the sanctions to be equivalent all the way up the scale,[96] it does, at the lower levels, starkly raise the question of how penalties are to be combined or substituted.

2.5. Sanction Hierarchies

The issue of how to grade sentencing orders has long been problematic in sentencing theory.[97] The increasing acceptance of more rigorous desert models has necessitated a much closer analysis of the relationship between offence seriousness and penalty across the entire range of offences, summary as well as indictable. Issues of the relative severity of sanctions, of sanction equivalence and sanction additivity have absorbed more appellate time as the range of sentencing options proliferates and as the question of unjustifiable disparity becomes more pressing.

The introduction of the community-based order in Victoria in 1985, which amalgamated a number of discrete orders,[98] rendered the entire middle range of sanctions problematic because of its wide span and ambiguity. The order was criticized on the grounds that without legislative guidance sentencers would be faced by such a conglomeration of sentences that sentencing disparity would be exacerbated.[99] This criticism was soon embraced by the Court of Criminal Appeal of Victoria which observed:

We do wish to draw attention to the consequences of drafting in general terms. No doubt such drafting is often prompted by a desire to simplify legislation. Unfortunately, attempts to do so usually leave a number of questions unanswered. They also very often leave the courts without guidance as to how the question should be answered and when dealing with the legislation the court's only task is to interpret and apply the law laid down by parliament. The courts cannot be legislators.[100]

In response, the Victorian Sentencing Committee recommended that a sentencing hierarchy be adopted in legislative form, a recommendation which ultimately found its way, in a much amended form, in section 7 of the Sentencing Act 1991 (Vic). Section 7 sets out the sentencing orders available to a court.

---

[96] Sentencing Task Force, above, n. 35, 87; R. Fox, above, n. 89, 124.

[97] See generally A. Freiberg and R. Fox, 'Sentencing Structures and Sentencing Hierarchier', (1986) 10 *Crim. LJ* 216; M. Wasik and A. von Hirsch, 'Non-Custodial Penalties and the Principles of Desert', [1988] *Crim. LR* 555; N. Morris and M. Tonry, *Between Prison and Probation: Intermediate Punishments in a Rational Sentencing System* (New York, 1990).

[98] The attendance-centre order, which was an alternative to imprisonment, the community-service order, and probation.

[99] A. Freiberg and R. Fox, 'Sentencing Structures and Sentencing Hierarchies', (1986) 10 *Crim. LJ* 216, 230.

[100] *O'Connor* (1986) 23 A. Crim. R. 50, 54.

7. If a court finds a person guilty of an offence, it may, subject to any specific provision relating to the offence and subject to this Part—
   (a) record a conviction and order that the offender serve a term of imprisonment; or
   (b) record a conviction and order that the offender serve a term of imprisonment by way of intensive correction in the community (an intensive correction order); or
   (c) record a conviction and order that the offender serve a term of imprisonment that is suspended by it wholly or partly; or
   (d) record a conviction and order that the offender be detained in a youth training centre; or
   (e) with or without recording a conviction, make a community-based order in respect of the offender; or
   (f) with or without recording a conviction, order the offender to pay a fine; or
   (g) record a conviction and order the release of the offender on the adjournment of the hearing on conditions; or
   (h) record a conviction and order the discharge of the offender; or
   (i) without recording a conviction, order the release of the offender on the adjournment of the hearing on conditions; or
   (j) without recording a conviction, order the dismissal of the charge for the offence; or
   (k) impose any other sentence or make any order that is authorised by this or any other Act.

Section 7 must be read together with section 5 which provides that:

   (3) A court must not impose a sentence that is more severe than that which is necessary to achieve the purpose or purposes for which the sentence is imposed.
   (4) A court must not impose a sentence that involves the confinement of the offender unless it considers that the purpose or purposes for which the sentence is imposed cannot be achieved by a sentence that does not involve the confinement of the offender.
   (5) A court must not impose an intensive correction order unless it considers that the purpose or purposes for which the sentence is imposed cannot be achieved by a community-based order.
   (6) A court must not impose a community-based order unless it considers that the purpose or purposes for which the sentence is imposed cannot be achieved by imposing a fine.
   (7) A court must not impose a fine unless it considers that the purpose or purposes for which the sentence is imposed cannot be achieved by a dismissal, discharge or adjournment.

The sentencing hierarchy is represented in diagrammatic form in Figure 3.1.

In relation to the problematic community-based order, the Act reinforces the relationship between the hierarchy concept and the principle of proportionality in three ways. First, it provides that a court must not impose

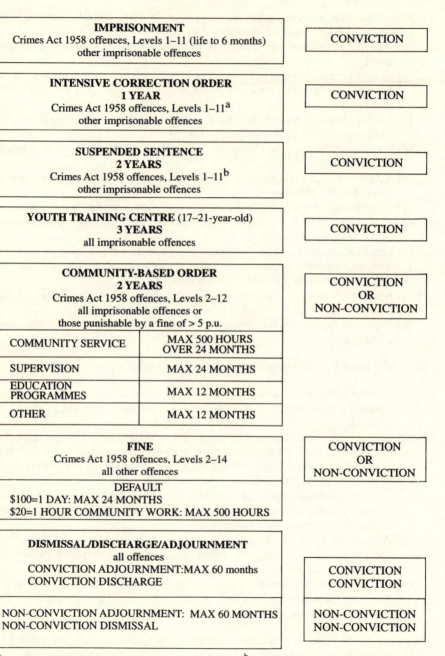

IMPRISONMENT Crimes Act 1958 offences, Levels 1–11 (life to 6 months) other imprisonable offences	CONVICTION
INTENSIVE CORRECTION ORDER 1 YEAR Crimes Act 1958 offences, Levels 1–11[a] other imprisonable offences	CONVICTION
SUSPENDED SENTENCE 2 YEARS Crimes Act 1958 offences, Levels 1–11[b] other imprisonable offences	CONVICTION
YOUTH TRAINING CENTRE (17–21-year-old) 3 YEARS all imprisonable offences	CONVICTION

COMMUNITY-BASED ORDER
2 YEARS
Crimes Act 1958 offences, Levels 2–12
all imprisonable offences or
those punishable by a fine of > 5 p.u.

CONVICTION OR NON-CONVICTION

COMMUNITY SERVICE	MAX 500 HOURS OVER 24 MONTHS
SUPERVISION	MAX 24 MONTHS
EDUCATION PROGRAMMES	MAX 12 MONTHS
OTHER	MAX 12 MONTHS

FINE
Crimes Act 1958 offences, Levels 2–14
all other offences

CONVICTION OR NON-CONVICTION

DEFAULT
$100=1 DAY: MAX 24 MONTHS
$20=1 HOUR COMMUNITY WORK: MAX 500 HOURS

DISMISSAL/DISCHARGE/ADJOURNMENT
all offences
CONVICTION ADJOURNMENT:MAX 60 months
CONVICTION DISCHARGE

CONVICTION
CONVICTION

NON-CONVICTION ADJOURNMENT: MAX 60 MONTHS
NON-CONVICTION DISMISSAL

NON-CONVICTION
NON-CONVICTION

[a] Available at these levels to a maximum of 1 year   [b] Available at these levels to a maximum of 2 years

FIG. 3.1. Victoria: sentence hierarchy

any more programme conditions than are necessary to achieve the purpose or purposes for which the order is made.[101] This is intended to limit the 'smorgasbord' effect and encourage the courts to adopt the most parsimonious approach to non-custodial sentencing. Secondly, it physically separates the programme conditions into separate sections and sets out the purposes of the four major conditions for the guidance of the courts. Finally, through the gradation of the durational limits of the order below Level 9 on the penalty scale, it allows the principle of proportionality to operate in respect of summary offences.

The courts are slowly coming to terms with this relatively new form of guidance. They have held that where an offence is very serious, they do not have openly to consider and reject every sanction from the bottom of the hierarchy to the top, before imposing a sentence of imprisonment, so long as it appears from the judgment that the sentencer has turned his mind to those alternatives.[102] However, they have held that these principles must be applied irrespective of the sentencer's personal opinion as to the relative severity of the sanction.[103] They are also slowly, and hesitatingly, developing a jurisprudence of sentencing combinations, or 'sentencing packages'[104] with a view to ensuring that the totality of penalties imposed are a proper reflection of the totality of offending.[105] Whether these hierarchies have had any impact upon sentencing disparity, however, is open to conjecture and no evidence is available to prove or disprove the structuring effect of sanction hierarchies in the decision-making process.

2.6. Guilt, Conviction, and Sentence

Victorian sentencing law, in common with the law in a number of other jurisdictions, was inconsistent, anomalous, lacking in clarity, productive of disparity, and lacking an overall rationale in relation to whether sentences were conviction or non-conviction based.[106] It had been evident for some

[101] Sentencing Act 1991 (Vic), s. 38(3).
[102] *O'Connor* (1986) 23 A. Crim. R. 50; see also *O'C* (1989) 41 A. Crim. R. 360.
[103] *Hendy* v. *Kraft* (1990) 55 SASR 345. The magistrate in this case had said that in his view the idea that all other sentencing measures should be utilized before imprisonment was totally out of keeping with the expectation of the community. The Supreme Court of South Australia called these comments 'impertinent' and suggested the magistrate study the legislation more closely.
[104] In which, for example, a community-service order may be combined with a fine or suspended sentence of imprisonment.
[105] Most of this jurisprudence has developed in South Australia where appeals from the Magistrates' Court are heard in the Supreme Court and are therefore more likely to be reported. See e.g. *Nieto* v. *Mill* (1991) 54 A. Crim. R. 35; *Lavers* v. *Fauser* (1987) 44 SASR 297; *Holdsworth* v. *Larcombe* (1987) 44 SASR 294 *Siciliano* v. *Tepper* (1985) 19 A. Crim. R. 268; *Elliott* v. *Harris (No. 2)* (1976) 13 SASR 516.
[106] See R. Fox and A. Freiberg, 'Sentences Without Conviction: From Status to Contract in Sentencing', (1989) 13 *Crim. LJ* 297.

time that an increasing number of 'non-conviction' sanctions were being created, primarily motivated by a desire to prevent any permanent stigmatization consequent upon conviction, but at the same time cognizant of the need to preserve the right of the state to impose a range of other sanctions upon an offender found guilty of an offence. Non-conviction sanctions were also seen as a means of preventing irrelevant social and legal discrimination.

In particular Victorian law suffered from the following defects: (*a*) there was inconsistency between sentencing provisions both within and between Acts as to the status of convictions and non-convictions. Some legislation provided that convictions were to be considered convictions unless the court otherwise ordered, whilst others provided that a conviction was not a conviction unless the court otherwise ordered; (*b*) the non-conviction option was being made available higher up the sanction scale, but irrelevant distinctions were being made on the basis of the level in the judicial hierarchy of the court imposing the sanction; (*c*) although courts were given a discretion not to enter a conviction, there was no indication whether ancillary orders could be imposed at the same time; (*d*) there was scant guidance for sentencers as to how the discretion whether not to enter a conviction was to be exercised; (*e*) there was a significant lack of symmetry in the respective positions of the Crown and the accused for the purpose of appealing against 'non-conviction' sentences; and (*f*) the suspect nature of the 'consent' upon which the accused's deprivation of appeal rights was creating severe problems in relation to a range of intrusive 'diversionary' options.

The solution adopted was to premiss the dispositive powers of the courts upon a finding of guilt, and then to state, in legislative form, whether or not the sanction imposed requires the entry of conviction, or whether the court has a discretion.[107] Where a discretion is vested in a court, some guidance is provided by section 8 which sets out some of the factors to which a court must have regard.

These superficially simple changes had a number of consequences which the sentencing reforms attended to and to which future legislators must have regard. These included such matters as whether a non-conviction is to be considered as a prior conviction for the purposes of sentencing; whether an ancillary order[108] can be made in consequence of a non-conviction and whether a right of appeal attaches to the sentencing order. Prior to the amendments made by the Sentencing Act 1991 (Vic), the law in relation to appeals against sentences and orders was piecemeal and unsatisfactory. By standardizing and simplifying the concept of sentencing order and conform-

---

[107] See s. 7.
[108] Such as a compensation order, restitution order, or licence disqualification.

ing appeal rights to sentencing orders, the new legislation has the effect that no differentiation is made between the rights of the Crown and the rights of the defendant, between conviction and non-conviction orders, between non-consensual and 'consensual' sentencing orders, between the sentencing order itself and the conditions attached to the order and between summary and indictable offences.

The Sentencing Act 1991 (Vic) reflects the view that the entry of a conviction on to a person's record is a matter of fundamental importance in the criminal-justice system, signifying a forfeiture of legal rights, a diminution of social status and creating an exposure to a range of potentially detrimental collateral consequences. The revised structure highlights the fact of conviction as part of the sentencing process and clearly identifies and delineates the three fundamental concepts of guilt, conviction, and sentence as basic building-blocks in the structure of sentencing.[109] What is still awaited, however, is complementary legislation providing for the statutory expungement of the consequences of conviction.

2.7. Sentencing Discounts

Delay in bringing cases before the courts is one of the endemic problems of court administration.[110] Australian courts have become sensitive to the need for an efficient use of judicial resources. As Kirby P., in commenting upon one offender's plea of guilty only on the morning of his trial in the face of an overwhelming case against him, observed: 'In the light of the criminal lists awaiting hearing, the public interest demands that greater attention be paid now to the consideration that a plea of guilty saves public time and cost and contributes to reducing delays.'[111] One of the first reports of the recently established Australian Institute of Judicial Administration was the product of an increasing concern over the length and cost of trials. The Institute set up a Shorter Trials Committee whose task was to recommend ways of reducing the time taken by criminal trials and committals and lessening their expense.[112]

Among other mechanisms, the Committee looked at the possibility of reducing the number of trials through the use of a sentencing discount for a guilty plea. Central to the debate was the question whether a plea of guilty, whether or not it was indicative of remorse, repentance, or con-

---

[109] This essay does not canvass the emerging phenomenon of the fixed-penalty system, the latest variation of which in Victoria carries the automatic status of conviction. This latest development was introduced in 1989 as part of a successful campaign against the road toll.

[110] Some of this material is drawn from A. Freiberg, 'Sentencing and Judicial Administration', (1993) 2 *Journal of Judicial Administration* 171.

[111] *Dodge* (1988) 34 A. Crim. R. 325, 331.

[112] Victorian Bar Association and Australian Institute of Judicial Administration, *Report of the Shorter Trials Committee on Criminal Trials* (1985).

trition, was a proper factor to be taken into account when considering the amount of punishment. Whereas it is generally accepted that remorse is considered to be part of the reformative component of a sentence, the question to be considered from the point of view of judicial administration was whether administrative considerations ought to have any role in the sentencing system. The Committee resolved that they should and its recommendations were translated into legislative form in section 4 of the Penalties and Sentences Act 1985 (Vic) which now appears in a slightly modified form as sectoin 5(2)(e) of the Sentencing Act 1991 (Vic). It states:

In sentencing an offender a court must have regard to . . . whether the offender pleaded guilty to the offence and, if so, the stage in the proceedings at which the offender did so or indicated an intention to do so.[113]

The sentencing discount for the guilty plea is controversial[114] requiring a delicate balance between the offender's right to trial on the one hand, and the efficient use of court resources on the other. It is clear from the great number of cases concerning the effect of a guilty plea on sentence[115] that the offering of substantial discounts has affected defendants' decisions whether or not to plead guilty. In a paper prepared by the Chief Judge of the County Court of Victoria and the Registrar of that Court, it was noted that whereas prior to the introduction of section 4 of the Penalties and Sentences Act 1985 (Vic) approximately 11 per cent of accused persons pleaded guilty at committal, currently approximately 21 per cent of accused so pleaded.[116] Another study of guilty pleas at the committal stage has found that after legislative amendments to section 4 of the Penalties and Sentences Act 1985 (Vic) (adding the clause relating to the timeliness of the plea of guilt), the percentage of guilty pleas at committal went from an average of 12 per cent in the six months before to 16.5 per cent in the six months after, rising to 20 per cent in the latter part of that period.[117] According to the Victorian Director of Public Prosecutions, there has been an increase in the percent-

[113] See also Crimes Act 1914 (Cth), s. 16A(2)(g) requiring a court to take into account whether an offender has pleaded guilty.

[114] See J. Willis, 'The Sentencing Discount for Guilty Pleas', (1985) 18 *ANZJ Crim.* 131.

[115] *Morton* [1986] VR 863; *Pickett* [1986] 2 Qd.R. 441; *Ellis* (1986) 6 NSWLR 603; *Stone* [1988] VR 141; *Dodge* (1988) 34 A. Crim. R. 325; *Giakas* (1988) 33 A. Crim. R. 22; *De Zylva* (1988) 33 A. Crim. R. 44; *Jabaltjari* (1989) 64 NTR 1; *Harman* [1989] 1 Qd.R. 414; *Tierney* (1990) 51 A. Crim. R. 446; *Bulger* [1990] 2 Qd.R. 559; *Bond* (1990) 48 A. Crim. R. 1; *Dodd* (1991) 57 A. Crim. R. 349; *Winchester* (1992) 58 A. Crim. R. 345.

[116] His Honour Chief Judge Waldron and J. Denahy, *The County Court of Victoria*, paper presented at the Australia Institute of Judicial Administration, Meeting on Case Management and Delay Reduction in the Higher Courts: Stock-Take and Future Directions, December 1991.

[117] I am indebted to John Willis of Latrobe University for the provision of these unpublished data from the Criminal Delay Reduction Program.

age of guilty pleas as a proportion of total disposals of indictable offences from 51 per cent in 1987 to 62 per cent in 1991.[118]

The controversy over the significance of guilty pleas has become intertwined with that of judicial guidance and the problems raised by *Young*'s case. The problem of how a court is to give effect to the guilty plea in pronouncing sentence has provoked a debate about an acceptable sentencing methodology. If the purpose of such a provision is to encourage pleas of guilty in order to ease the load on the courts, then the nature and extent of the discount should be made manifest so that other accused persons, similarly minded, will be aware of the advantage to them of pleading guilty. However, for a court to state what would have been the sentence in the absence of a guilty plea, and then to state the discount, is a process proscribed in Victoria on the ground that it is another manifestation of the 'two-tier' approach deprecated by the Court of Criminal Appeal in *Young*. Thus, in some cases where a court has either allocated a specific percentage for mitigating factors, or indicated that it has reduced the sentence by a particular amount, the Court of Criminal Appeal has ruled that the sentencing discretion has miscarried.[119]

Similarly in relation to discounts for informers, Victorian courts have set their face against specifically stated discounts. In *Nagy*[120] the majority of the Court of Criminal Appeal held that unless compelled by statute or public policy to do so, a court should avoid the adoption of a process whereby an 'undiscounted' term of imprisonment with regard to which certain mitigating factors are ignored is first of all fixed and announced, on the ground that this involves the 'two-step' process expressly proscribed in *Young*. The majority of the court preferred to take into account all matters of aggravation and mitigation and then to pronounce sentence which the 'intuitive synthesis' produced.[121] However, a strong line of dissent has been articulated by McGarvie J. who argues that discounts can only be effective if made public.[122] Paradoxically, however, by Commonwealth law, a court is required by statute to state the extent of the discount for co-operation,[123] for

---

[118] Director of Public Prosecutions, Victoria, *Annual Report 1991–2*, 76. The percentage decreased slightly in 1992 to 59 per cent.

[119] *Barry* 1/10/92 (CCA V); cf. *Tierney* (1990) 51 A. Crim. R. 446 (CCA V).

[120] [1992] 1 VR 637; (1991) 57 A. Crim. R. 64 (CCA V).

[121] See also *O'Brien* (1991) 57 A. Crim. R. 80.

[122] *Nagy* [1992] 1 VR 637; (1991) 57 A. Crim. R. 64; *Ienco* 29/3/90 (CCA V);

[123] Crimes Act 1914 (Cth), s. 21E(1) states that where a federal sentence or federal non-parole period is reduced by the court imposing the sentence or fixing the non-parole period because the offender has undertaken to co-operate with law enforcement agencies in proceedings, including confiscation proceedings, relating to any offence, the court must (*a*) if sentence is reduced, specify that the sentence is being reduced for that reason and state the sentence that would have been imposed but for that reduction and (*b*) if the non-parole period is reduced, specify that the non-parole period is being reduced for that reason and state the non-parole period that would have been imposed.

TABLE 3.2. *New South Wales and Victoria daily average total prisoners 1981–2 to February 1993*

	New South Wales		Victoria	
	Total prison population	Rate per 100,000 population	Total prison population	Rate per 100,000 population
1981–2	3,357	92.9	1,755	61.4
1982–3	3,511	90.3	1,858	63.9
1983–4	3,511	89.2	1,959	66.3
1984–5	3,492	87.5	1,908	63.6
1985–6	3,851	95.0	1,915	62.8
1986–7	3,969	96.3	1,939	62.5
1987–8	4,122	98.1	2,016	63.8
1988–9	4,369	101.9	2,193	68.1
1989–90	5,006	115.0	2,290	69.8
1990–1	5,712	129.3	2,303	69.1
1991–2	6,102	151.3	2,247	73.6
Feb. 1993	6,004	138.0	2,240	65.7

Source: Data derived from Australian Institute of Criminology, Fact and Figures in Crime and Criminal Justice, Basic Indicators of Imprisonment Trends by Jurisdiction 1981–2 to 1990–1 (August 1992) and subsequent monthly series.

if the co-operation is subsequently refused, the Director of Public Prosecutions may appeal against those reductions. A 'two-tier' approach is thus not only permitted, but is positively required.[124]

This issue of sentencing discounts highlights the sensitive nature of the task of balancing the need for criminal-justice efficiencies, on the one hand, and the protection of basic values such as the presumption of innocence, on the other, and indicates the kinds of difficulties inherent in the giving effect to specific pragmatic imperatives in a loosely structured sentencing system.

2.8. Imprisonment and Remissions

Victoria has long been proud of its record in having the lowest imprisonment rate in Australia,[125] and the financial implications of increasing prison populations is always a factor considered when sentencing reform in mooted. Victoria's imprisonment rate compared with the New South Wales is presented in Table 3.2 and Figure 3.2.

[124] See *Gallagher* (1991) 23 NSWLR 221, 227 (CCA NSW).
[125] Except for the Australian Capital Territory which is not strictly comparable because of its very small population. (Its sentenced prisoners are in fact held in New South Wales gaols.) The daily average rate for Australia between 1980 and 1990 climbed from 67.3 per 100,000

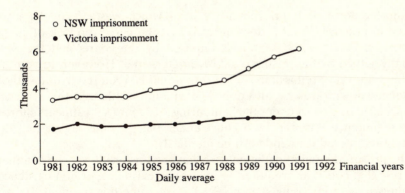

FIG. 3.2. Daily average prisoners: Victoria and New South Wales

As alluded to earlier, one of the most significant factors generating sentencing reform in Australia has been the concern over the executive modification of sentences and the whole constellation of issues encapsulated under the 'truth in sentencing' banner.[126] In obeisance to the perceived public demand for truthful sentences, the Victoria Government decided to abolish remissions.[127]

The government was concerned, however, that the prison population not be increased on account of the abolition of these remissions, as had occurred previously in New South Wales when a similar abolition had taken place.[128] The policy adopted in Victoria was that with the abolition of remissions, adjustments would be made to the length of sentences imposed to take into account their absence. Truth, under the Sentencing Act 1991 (Vic), does not mean that the sentencing patterns prevailing prior to the proclamation of the Act continue so that subsequent to the abolition of remissions prisoners serve the whole of the court's announced, albeit

population in 1980 to 78.0 per 100,000 population in 1990. In comparison, the United States' rate is 426 per 100,000 and the United Kingdom is 97 per 100,000: see D. Chappell, 'Sentencing of Offenders: A Consideration of the Issues of Severity, Consistency and Cost', (1992) 66 *Australian Law Journal* 423.

[126] See generally A. Freiberg, 'Truth in Sentencing?: The Abolition of Remissions in Victoria', (1992) 16 *Crim. LJ* 165: J. Chan, 'The New South Wales Sentencing Act 1989: Where Does Truth Lie?', (1990) 14 *Crim. LJ* 249; D. Brown, 'Battles around Truth: A Commentary on the Sentencing Act 1989', (1992) 3 *Current Issues in Criminal Justice* 329; D. Brown, 'What Truth?', (1989) 14 *Legal Service Bulletin* 161.

[127] See Corrections (Remissions) Act 1991 (Vic). The package of reforms also included the abolition of a pre-release programme which had been introduced in 1983 and which empowered the Parole Board to release a prisoner serving a sentence of three or more who had at least six months, but not more than 12 months, of the prison sentence to serve. This programme had a small, but significant impact upon the prison population.

[128] In New South Wales the prison population had grown from 3,950 in 1988, when a Conservative Government came to power, to 6,109 by September 1992, an increase of about 54 per cent.

unadjusted term of imprisonment, a term which was effectively never served in practice. What it does mean is that the perceived lack of correspondence between the sentences imposed by the courts and the time actually served by the prisoner will be diminished.[129] However, to account for the removal of remissions, sentencers would be required to adjust their sentences downwards by an equivalent amount. Although the sentence pronounced by a court under the Sentencing Act 1991 (Vic) appears shorter than a sentence imposed by a court under the previous legislation, the actual time served is intended to be identical.

The jurisprudential impediment to achieving this result was the common law rule that courts are required to ignore the existence, or non-existence, of remissions in imposing sentence.[130] To overcome this problem the Act clearly states that a court is required to take the abolition of remissions into account and must reduce the sentence to ensure that the offender will not spend more time in custody under the new legislation than he or she would have spent under the previous legislation had he or she been sentenced before the commencement of the Act for a similar offender in similar circumstances.[131] The reduction is mandatory, the amount of reduction is clearly stated as being the period equivalent to full remission entitlements that a prisoner would have received before the abolition of remissions,[132] it applies to both the head sentence and the non-parole period and to suspended as well as executed sentences. The effect of this legislative direction upon Victoria's prison population is discussed in more detail in Section 3, below.

2.9. Intermediate Sanctions

Intermediate sanctions are not a new phenomenon in Victoria. Probation can be traced back to the last century, with the modern system coming into operation in the mid-1950s. Fines and bonds have been extensively used in the lower courts for decades and even back in the early 1980s in Victoria there were nearly twice as many offenders on some form of community order as there were in prison. The sanction options between the fine and the executed sentence of imprisonment have undergone a considerable degree of change over the last two decades. As previously outlined, the major structural change occurred in 1986 when the community-based order was created out of three separate orders, probation, community service, and

[129] It will not be removed completely, because parole will still remain as a form of executive modification of sentence.

[130] See generally *Maguire* (1956) 40 Cr. App. R. 92; *Menz* [1967] SASR 329; *Morgan* (1980) 7 A. Crim. R. 146; *Yates* [1985] VR 41; *Paivinen* (1985) 158 CLR 489; *O'Brien* (1984) 2 NSWLR 449; *Hoare and Easton* (1989) 63 ALJR 505; *Maclay* (1990) 19 NSWLR 112, 126; 46 A. Crim. R. 340, 353–4.

[131] Sentencing Act 1991 (Vic), s. 10(2).   [132] Cf. *El Karhani* (1990) 51 A. Crim. R. 123.

attendance at an attendance centre. These orders could not run for more than two years[133] and required that the offender be convicted of an imprisonable offence. Each order had six 'core conditions' which were similar to those formerly appended to probation orders and permitted a court to attach one or more 'programme conditions'.[134]

The Penalties and Sentences Act 1985 (Vic) also introduced legislation into Victoria allowing for the total or partial suspension of imprisonment for up to one year. The Sentencing Act 1991 (Vic) extended the period of permitted suspension to two years[135] and brought within its confines a previously separate sanction of a suspended sentence of imprisonment for alcoholic and drug-dependent persons which was located in separate legislation.[136]

The Sentencing Act 1991 (Vic) maintained the fundamental structure of the community-based order. Its major reform in this respect was to break the nexus with imprisonment, so that it was no longer a pre-condition for its use that the offence be an imprisonable one. However, considerable concern had been expressed in relation to the place of the community-based order in the sentencing hierarchy—in particular it was felt by a number of criminal-justice practitioners that a 'gap' was emerging between sentences of imprisonment and the community-based order, which was perceived as becoming insufficiently punitive. The suspended sentence was not regarded as a sufficient intermediate option. One suggestion made was to create a conditional suspended sentence, in essence a combination of the suspended sentence and the community-based order. This was opposed on the basis that it would irredeemably confuse the two options and have the likely effect of making the conditional suspended sentence the standard mid-range option, effectively increasing the tariff, as the suspended sentence was still, in theory, a sentence of imprisonment.

A compromise was forged and emerged in the form of the intensive correction order.[137] This order is intended to allow a sentence of imprisonment of up to twelve months to be served in the community through intensive participation in unpaid community work and programmes designed to enhance the offender's personal development.[138] It suspends the

---

[133] Other than in exceptional circumstances.

[134] The programme conditions are (*a*) community work for a maximum of 500 hours over a 24-month period; (*b*) supervision for a period of not more than 24 months; (*c*) attendance for educational or other programmes for not more than 12 months; (*d*) assessment and treatment for alcohol or drug addiction; (*e*) testing for alcohol or drug use; (*f*) participation in special programmes for the intellectually disabled in relevant cases; and (*g*) any other condition considered necessary or desirable: Sentencing Act 1991 (Vic), s. 38.

[135] The impetus for this came from the courts which wanted more scope for its use.

[136] See Alcoholics and Drug-Dependent Persons Act 1968 (Vic), s. 13, now Sentencing Act 1991 (Vic), s. 28.

[137] See D. Richards, 'The Intensive Correction Order', in University of Melbourne and Leo Cussen Institute Seminar, *The Sentencing Act 1991* (Melbourne, 1991).

[138] Sentencing Act 1991, ss. 19–26.

immediate execution of a prison sentence on conditions more onerous than those which attach to a conventional suspended sentence, or to a community-based order. The core conditions provide for closer supervision of the offender than allowed for in the core conditions of a community-based order. Additional special conditions may also be added. It is intended to produce punitive constraints on the offender's liberty while leaving the door open to the possibility of the offender benefiting from special rehabilitative programmes. It is intended to be used ahead of immediate or suspended sentences of imprisonment in the hierarchy of sentences set out in sections 5(2) and 7[139] of the Sentencing Act 1991.

The intensive correction order is designed as a sanction for offenders who are currently being rejected for community-based orders on the basis of their high risk and/or recidivism and who are currently receiving short terms of imprisonment. The target groups for this order are those who were receiving short terms of imprisonment.[140] Research from the Office of Corrections indicated that over 35 per cent of prisoners received for terms of less than 12 months were imprisoned for driving-related offences, predominantly driving whilst disqualified and exceeding .05 per cent blood alcohol level. Most of these offenders have a long history of similar offences, and the courts have tended to impose such sentences because they have run out of other options.[141] Other major offence groups are those convicted of theft, including car theft and burglary. Almost all of the short-term prisoners received in 1990/91 had been imprisoned at least once before and 92 per cent of the target group are men.

2.10. Dismissals, Discharges, and Adjournments

Prior to the Sentencing Act 1991 (Vic), Victorian courts, like courts in other jurisdictions, were faced with a bewildering plethora of non-monetary sentencing options which permitted courts to return offenders to the community without subjecting them to any direct official supervision. These forms of unsupervised release have gone under a confusing variety of names, such as 'adjournment', 'absolute or conditional discharge', 'dismissal', 'deferred sentence', 'conditional release', 'good behaviour bond', 'common law or statutory bond', 'suspended sentence', and others. The terminology varied from jurisdiction to jurisdiction, and the same description often encompasses a number of quite different dispositive orders.[142]

---

[139] Ironically, the form of this sentence harks back to the superseded attendance-centre order which was effectively abandoned in 1985.

[140] That is, under 12 months.

[141] For some offences, a mandatory sentence of imprisonment is required by statute, but as the intensive correction order is regarded as a sentence of imprisonment, it will cover such cases.

[142] Above, n. 7, 451, table 9C.

These orders are not infrequently used, comprising between 6–10 per cent of orders in the higher courts and between 15–20 per cent of all sentencing orders in the Magistrates' Court.

The problems created by this array of orders were many. Some powers were created by statute and some were creatures of the common law. Different courts had access to different powers. It was often not clear whether the release was the product of a conviction or non-conviction order and the terminology did not signify this important distinction. It was not clear at what stage of the proceedings the order was to be made, whether it was a final order or an interim measure as an adjournment of the proceedings. Nor was it clear whether other orders such as restitution or compensation could be made at the same time. Finally there was confusion as to the mechanisms used for enforcing such conditional release. Victorian legislation had hitherto relied on four techniques to punish those who breach conditions attached to an order for release. First, it could be enforced by forfeiting any recognizance or bond which had been formally entered into as a condition of the release. This was basically a financial penalty, a sanction of great antiquity pre-dating the creation of modern police forces and invoking the special procedure for enforcement of debts to the Crown under the Crown Proceeding Act 1958 (Vic). Secondly, it could be enforced by the imposition of a fine for breaching a sentencing order by violating one of its of conditions. Thirdly (particularly if the release was on adjournment), the accused could be subject to recall for sentencing or re-sentencing for the original offence. Fourthly, where the conduct which constituted the breach was itself a criminal offence (which is normally the case), by imposing a further criminal sanction for that offending. This amounted to a form of triple or quadruple jeopardy and seemed an excessively complex and heavy-handed way of responding to breaches of sentencing orders at the lowest level of the sentencing hierarchy. Overall, these provisions represented 'a mismatched collection of poorly drafted sections derived from United Kingdom legislation of the last century' which had been retained for too long without systematic revision.[143]

The solution adopted was to create a simple structure which creates two forms of order: a conditional release and an unconditional release. Each of these must follow a finding of guilt, but may be conviction or non-conviction based. Thus non-conviction orders for release can be either by way of adjournment (in which case they will be subject to conditions, at least one of which is an undertaking to reappear in court when called upon), or final disposition of the case which will be either unconditional or subject to additional orders relating to restitution or compensation. If the require-

[143] R. Fox and A. Freiberg, *Sentencing: State and Federal Law in Victoria* (Melbourne, 1985), 254.

ments of a non-conviction order are adhered to the charges will be recorded as having been dismissed. Similarly, conviction orders for release can be either by way of adjournment (in which case they will be subject to conditions, at least one of which is an undertaking to reappear in court when called upon), or final disposition of the case which will be either unconditional or subject to additional orders relating to restitution or compensation. If the requirements of a non-conviction order are adhered to a conviction will be recorded on the charges, but the defendant will be discharged from any further liability to punishment. After a history of several centuries, recognizances disappear from sentencing law in Victoria so that breaches are now dealt with solely on the basis of the statutory provisions.

3. EVALUATION OF THE SENTENCING ACT

In order to monitor and evaluate the impact of the sentencing legislation a grant was sought and obtained from the Criminology Research Council of Australia for a two-year study of the Act. The major purposes of the study are to identify changes in prison sentence lengths, if any, resulting from the abolition of remissions and to identify changes in prison and community-based corrections sentencing patterns resulting from the introduction of the Sentencing Act 1991 (Vic).

3.1. Effect of Abolition of Remissions

In New South Wales, the Sentencing Act 1989 (NSW) came into operation on 25 September 1989. Under the Act, adult and juvenile offenders sentenced to custodial terms were no longer entitled to remission of their sentences. The Act also introduced a formula whereby for sentences of over six months, a minimum term of custody was to be specified by the courts as well as an 'additional term' during which the offender could be released on parole or remain in custody. The additional period is required to be not more than one-third of the minimum term, unless 'special circumstances' exist which would allow the court to depart from the formula. The stated object of this legislation was

to promote truth in sentencing by requiring convicted offenders to serve in prison (*without any reduction*) the minimum or fixed term of imprisonment set by the court.[144]

In the absence of a binding legislative direction in relation to the account to be taken of the abolition of remissions, the courts have taken the view that

---

[144] Sentencing Act 1989 (NSW), s. 3(a).

no change was required in their sentencing behaviour.[145] The result has been an increase in the New South Wales prison population.[146] To date, three evaluations have been carried out on the impact of the Sentencing Act 1989 (NSW).

In 1990 Gorta and Eyland[147] found that there had been an increase of 19 per cent in the average time to be served by sentenced prisoners, which was equivalent to an overall increase in the prison population of approximately 490 additional sentenced prisoners held on any one day.[148] Although there was an early indication that average minimum and fixed terms handed down by the courts were lower than those set before the Act, this trend did not continue, so that the one result of the changes to sentencing patterns consequent upon the Act has been a massive overcrowding in New South Wales prisons. In 1991 a study by the New South Wales Bureau of Crime Statistics and Research also found that no compensation was being made by sentencers for the abolition of remissions and that there was no significant difference in median lengths of head sentences before and after the intro- duction of the Act.[149] A follow-up report in March 1992 comparing sentenc- ing practices 12 months prior to and 12 months after the Act confirmed that sentencing practices in the higher criminal courts remained unchanged, but that the local courts[150] were setting somewhat shorter sentences than they were before the introduction of the Act.[151]

The Victorian study adopted a similar methodology.[152] If section 10 of the Sentencing Act 1991 (Vic) is working as it should, then the mean time for the aggregate sentence and the minimum after the introduction of the Sentencing Act 1991 (Vic) should be about 67 per cent of that for sentences

[145] *Maclay* (1990) 19 NSWLR 112, 123; 46 A. Crim. R. 340, 351; *Paull* (1990) 49 A. Crim. R. 142, 146.

[146] There are a number of other reasons why the New South Wales imprisonment rate is so much higher. It has been suggested that the primary reason is that New South Wales has a much higher prisoner reception rate due to relatively more people appearing before the courts: see L. Babb, 'Imprisonment Rates in NSW and Victoria: Explaining the Difference', NSW Bureau of Crime Statistics and Research, Contemporary Issues in Crime and Justice, Bulletin No. 14, March 1992.

[147] See A. Gorta and S. Eyland, *Truth in Sentencing: Impact of the Sentencing Act 1989 (Report 1)* (Research and Statistics Division, NSW Department of Corrective Services, June 1990); A. Gorta, 'Impact of the Sentencing Act 1989 on the NSW Prison Population', (1992) 3 *Current Issues in Criminal Justice* 308; A. Gorta, 'Truth in Sentencing', paper presented at the Sixth Annual Conference of the ANZ Society of Criminology, Sydney, 1990.

[148] Ibid.

[149] E. Makta, *NSW Sentencing Act 1989* (Sydney, New South Wales Bureau of Crime Statistics and Research, 1991).

[150] That is, courts of summary jurisdiction.

[151] The median minimum term handed down by Local Courts in the 12 months before the Act was six months, but was 4 months in the 12 months after the Act: information provided by Dr Don Weatherburn, Director of the Bureau of Crime Statistics and Research.

[152] The material which follows is based upon data supplied by Mr Stuart Ross of the Victoria Criminal Justice Statistics Planning Unit and Dr David Tait of the University of Melbourne, who are co-authors of the overall sentencing evaluation study.

TABLE 3.3. *Victoria: daily average number of prisoners January 1992–March 1993*

Jan. 1992	2,222
Feb. 1992	2,196
Mar. 1992	2,183
Apr. 1992	2,222
May 1992	2,250
June 1992	2,247
July 1992	2,258
Aug. 1992	2,234
Sept. 1992	2,251
Oct. 1992	2,253
Nov. 1992	2,248
Dec. 1992	2,249
Jan. 1993	2,243
Feb. 1993	2,236
Mar. 1993	2,232

Source: Data derived from Australian Institute of Criminology, Fact and Figures in Crime and Criminal Justice, Nos. 188–197.

imposed before the Act. The effective time in custody before and after the Act should be identical, that is, the expected value should be 100 per cent.

The data reveal that the average aggregate prison term for all prison receptions dropped from 14.7 months in the 24 months prior to the Act to 10.8 months in the six months after the Act, a drop of 27 per cent. The average non-parole period decreased from 10.4 months to 8.8 months, a reduction of 16 per cent. The average estimated time in custody for all offences remained about the same. Given the difficulty of policing the internal thought processes of the judiciary, and the opportunities for evasion of the legislation by the use of the rules relating to concurrency and cumulation, it would seem that the technique adopted by the Victorian legislature of requiring a mandatory adjustment to sentence lengths has been totally successful in achieving the intended outcome. The results of this study are supported by the aggregate reception data for the period of 12 months before the Act and the 9 months after. These are shown in Table 3.3 which shows the remarkable stability of the Victorian prison population.

3.2. Intermediate Sanctions

The relationship between sentences of imprisonment and other sentences, and that between the various intermediate sanctions, is a complex one. In

TABLE 3.4. *Victoria: higher courts percentage of sentences imposed for principal offence*

	1985	1986	1987	1988	1989	1990	1991
Bond	20.6	19.6	17.5	16.2	17.6	18.0	15.2
Fine	6.6	5.7	4.3	4.6	4.7	3.9	3.3
Suspended	NA	NA	12.0	15.0	15.6	18.4	20.7
CBO	NA	NA	5.2	7.1	4.4	7.2	9.7
Other	0.1	1.7	1.1	0.5	0.4	0.8	0.9
Imprisonment	58.3	50.4	57.6	55.2	54.1	48.5	47.9

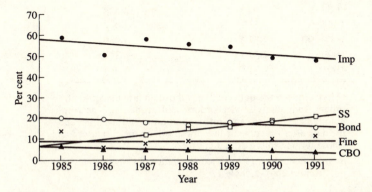

• Imprisonment ○ Bond × Fine □ Suspended sentence ▲ Community-based order

Note: The data in this figure have been smoothed to highlight the trends in dispositional patterns.

FIG. 3.3. Victoria: higher courts dispositions

Table 3.4 and Figure 3.3, the relative changes in the mix of sanctions imposed by the higher courts is presented.

Table 3.4 indicates that even for the higher courts which deal with the most serious cases, less than 50 per cent of offenders are gaoled. The imprisonment rate has decreased from 58.3 per cent of all dispositions in 1985 to 47.9 per cent in 1991, a drop of about 18 per cent. Suspended sentences grew from nil in 1985 to 20 per cent in 1991 while the community-based order grew from 5.2 per cent to 9.7 per cent of orders.

In the Magistrates' Court in 1991,[153] imprisonment orders amounted to 5 per cent of all principal offences disposed of, suspended sentences amounted to 4.71 per cent, community-based orders to 4.29 per cent, fines 43.75 per cent, bonds 20.3 per cent, and sanctions relating to drivers' licences, 20.92 per cent.

---

[153] Reliable figures are not available prior to this date.

TABLE 3.5. *Victoria: trends in prisoner and offender populations 1981–2 to 1991–2*

	Prisoners in custody at end of year	Offenders[a] at end of year
1981–2	1,753	3,267
1982–3	1,996	3,323
1983–4	1,845	3,689
1984–5	1,879	4,348
1985–6	1,955	5,258
1986–7	1,956	5,032
1987–8	2,049	4,423
1988–9	2,256	3,964
1989–90	2,316	3,956
1990–1	2,310	5,368
1991–2	2,277	5,931

[a] Up to 1985–6 the data combines those on attendance-centre orders, community-service orders, and probation. The community-based order came into operation on 1 June 1986 and the data after that date include those still on the earlier orders whose terms expired after June 1986.

Source: Data drawn from Victoria, Office of Corrections, Annual Report 1991–2, table 1.

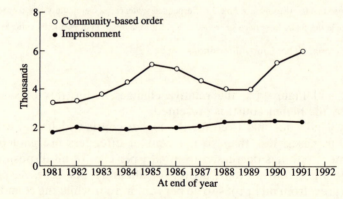
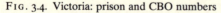

FIG. 3.4. Victoria: prison and CBO numbers

In Table 3.5 and Figure 3.4 the numbers in prison in Victoria over the past decade are contrasted with the numbers on community orders.

Table 3.5 shows a steady increase in the number of offenders on community-based orders. It is of interest to note that over the period 1984–5, a massive increase in resources was devoted to community corrections programmes and became fully available over the whole state in 1985, which would partly explain the peak in the middle part of the decade. The number

TABLE 3.6. *Victoria: community-based corrections offender statistics April 1991–December 1992*

	Community-based order[a]	Intensive correction order
Apr. 1991	4,600	
May 1991	4,847	
June 1991	4,975	
July 1991	5,099	
Aug. 1991	5,198	
Sept. 1991	5,314	
Oct. 1991	5,385	
Nov. 1991	5,447	
Dec. 1991	5,485	
Jan. 1992	5,470	
Feb. 1992	5,467	
Mar. 1992	5,481	
Apr. 1992	5,459	6
May 1992	5,554	58
June 1992	5,601	115
July 1992	5,746	179
Aug. 1992	5,731	211
Sept. 1992	5,754	267
Oct. 1992	5,706	306
Nov. 1992	5,612	310
Dec. 1992	5,530	324

[a] These data record only community-based orders imposed directly by the courts as the sole sanction or where they are combined with imprisonment. They exclude community work as a result of fine default.

Source: Based upon data provided by the Office of Corrections. My thanks to Stuart Ross for compiling the information.

of orders in fact declined over the next three and a half years partly because the new order was shorter than the orders it replaced, such as the probation order[154] and partly because a pre-sentence report was required before making a community-based order. This pre-sentence report gives the community corrections officers some degree of control over the number and type of offenders being admitted to such programmes.[155]

[154] However, it is ironic that the change from probation to the community-based order as the primary intermediate sanction had the effect of increasing the relative severity of the sanction. Community work conditions and supervision make up the majority of conditions of community-based orders.

[155] Sentencing Act 1991 (Vic), s. 96; see D. Richards, 'Maximising Diversion within the Corrections Continuum', in S. McKillop (ed.), *Keeping People out of Prison* (Australian Institute of Criminology: Canberra, 1991); R. Harding, 'Prison Overcrowding: Correctional Policies and Political Constraints', (1987) 20 *ANZJ Crim.* 16.

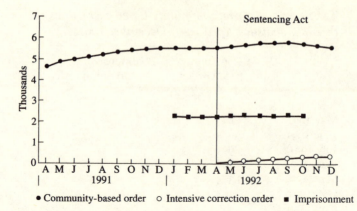

F I G . 3.5. Victoria: prison, CBO, and ICO numbers

Table 3.6 tracks the changes in community-based orders and intensive correction orders in the period immediately before and after the Sentencing Act 1991 (Vic). Figure 3.5 combines the imprisonment data, the community-based order, and the intensive correction order to examine the nature of the changes consequent upon the Act.

It appears that while there have been some fluctuations in numbers, they are within the normal tolerance limits. However, late in 1992 it would seem that the number of community-based orders is decreasing as the number of intensive correction orders increases.

3.3. Intensive Correction Orders

The number of intensive correction orders has grown from six in the first month to 328 in December 1992. In the ten weeks between 22 April and 30 June 1992, courts made 114 intensive correction order sentences and 1,220 community-based order sentences. That is, around 10 per cent of community corrections sentences (excluding fine default sentences) were intensive correction orders. If intensive correction orders are being used by the courts as intended, then one would expect to find them being applied to offenders convicted of more serious offences, with longer or more serious prior criminal histories.

A preliminary analysis of such orders indicates that intensive correction order offences were significantly different from community-based order offences with more being made for break and enter offences, fewer for 'other theft' offences and more for driving offences, the last being a primary target group. The data also seem to indicate that these offenders are not being drawn from the potential community-based order population, but it is

TABLE 3.7. *Victoria: higher courts length of prison sentences imposed 1985–1991, as a percentage of penalty imposed by principal offence*

	1985	1986	1987	1988	1989	1990	1991
<1	10.5	11.2	8.0	9.0	5.5	6.2	6.7
1<2	11.5	7.4	12.8	12.0	11.5	12.3	11.6
2<3	7.9	7.5	10.9	9.3	12.1	9.6	9.0
3<4	9.7	7.6	8.3	6.4	7.6	7.4	9.0
4<5	4.5	4.5	5.9	5.0	4.5	5.2	3.0
5<10	11.7	9.6	10.0	9.5	9.3	6.3	6.8
10+	1.6	2.1	1.3	1.9	3.2	1.5	1.8
Life	1.2	0.5	0.4	0.2	0.4	0.0	0.0

Source: Original table compiled from statistics issued by Attorney-General's Department of Victoria.

as yet unclear as to whether they are having an impact upon the target prison population.

3.4. Some Observations

The level of custodial and non-custodial populations is the result of a very large number of factors, only some of which can be explored in this essay. As noted on a number of occasions, the Sentencing Act 1991 (Vic) built on, and emphasized, a number of trends already evident in Victoria but a number of features need to be highlighted.[156] First, the stability of the prison population has occurred in the face of an increasing crime rate[157] and an increasing number of offences processed by the courts. In the higher courts, from which the prison stock is mainly drawn, the number of offenders sentenced jumped from 1,004 in 1985 to 1,572 in 1991, an increase of nearly 57 per cent. Secondly, it would appear the composition of the prison population is changing, with the courts sentencing fewer people to short terms of imprisonment.[158] This is shown in Table 3.7 and highlighted by the trend data presented in Figure 3.6.

[156] See generally D. Tait, 'Measuring the Impact of Sentencing Changes in Victoria', unpublished paper presented to the Third National Social Research Conference, Hawkesbury, NSW 1992.

[157] Although that rate has, since about 1990, stabilized in Victoria.

[158] On the debate as to whether diverting short-term prisoners to alternative sanctions makes any significant difference to the level of prison populations, see D. Weatherburn, 'Relieving the NSW Prison Population: Sentencing Reform and Early Release', (1987) 11 *Crim. LJ* 119; D. Weatherburn, 'Non-Custodial Sanctions, Prison Costs and Prison Overcrowding', in S. McKillop (ed.), *Keeping People out of Prison* (Australian Institute of Criminology: Canberra, 1991); D. Weatherburn, 'Note: Front-end versus Rear-end Solutions to Prison Overcrowding: A Reply to Professor Harding', (1988) 21 *ANZJ Crim.* 117.

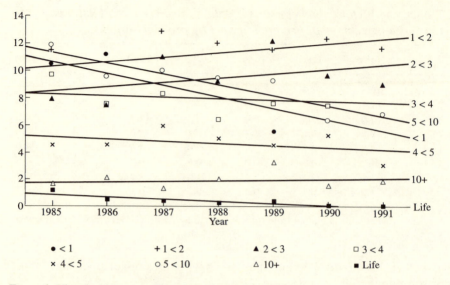

FIG. 3.6. Victoria: higher coupts: sentence lengths

It is apparent that sentences of less than one year have dropped dramatically, from 10.5 per cent of sentences in 1985 to 6.7 per cent in 1991.
Similarly, sentences of between five to ten years have decreased from 11.7
per cent to 6.8 per cent of sentences. Small increases can be noted for the 2–
3 year category and the 1–2 year category. The Sentencing Act 1991 (Vic)
reinforces the move away from short terms of imprisonment by providing
that the lowest maximum statutory sentence of imprisonment should be six
months, thus providing a clear signal that imprisonment should be used only
for the most serious class of offences and only for the more serious examples of imprisonable offences.[159] Thirdly, it would appear that the suspended sentence is having some impact on the lower end of the sentencing
range, but this is focused on what might be called the lesser white-collar
crimes of obtaining property or financial advantage. However, it has also
had an impact on the sentences imposed on persons convicted of assault and
criminal damage. Fourthly, Victoria's prison population may be lower than
other jurisdictions because it has retained a lesser custodial option, the
youth training centre order as an alternative to imprisonment for youths

---

[159] See Sentencing Task Force, above, n. 35, 50–2. The Evaluation study has revealed that in
fact the number of persons received into prison in Victoria has been steadily decreasing, with
an average of 1,619 per six months in the 24 months prior to the Sentencing Act 1991 (Vic), but
with 1,407 prisoners being received in the six months after the Act. This may be due to a
reduced flow of cases through the courts, which is unlikely, or it may be due to the increased
use of non-custodial sanctions.

aged between 17 and 21 years.[160] Finally, it would appear that some real diversion has occurred, with the non-custodial options displacing the custodial option for a range of offenders.

4. PREDICTABLE AND UNPREDICTABLE OUTCOMES

The implementation of the Sentencing Act 1991 (Vic) has taken place generally as predicted. The smooth transition was assisted by the long lead time between the passage of the Act through Parliament and its proclamation. Information about the Act and its implications was widely distributed and in November 1991 a one-day seminar was held at which many of the major innovative features of the Act were explained by those involved in their implementation to an audience of solicitors and barristers, judges, magistrates, and criminal-justice practitioners. The proceedings were immediately available for sale.[161] Comprehensive briefing notes on the Act were prepared, particularly by the Magistracy, and all courts were assisted by the timely publication of the County Court Sentencing Manual which was written in anticipation of the new legislation.

The major unpredictable reform which had the greatest potential for penological and financial disaster was that relating to the abolition of remissions and, as has been indicated, the results of this experiment have exceeded expectations. This outcome occurred in the face of hostility on the part of some judges[162] and the then Opposition which had taken the erroneous view that effective sentence lengths would in fact be decreased by the new legislation. It was also assisted by the preparation of an extensive paper on the legal implications of the abolition of remissions for the sentencing seminar which contained a 'ready reckoner' conversion table from the old to the new sentencing levels. Finally, a change of this magnitude was made possible by the fact that relative to other jurisdictions, Victorian sentencing decision-making is highly centralized. The Supreme Court, the County Court, and the Magistrates' Court are all located within a few city blocks and communication between sentencers at all levels is relatively free.

Unpredictable outcomes have been relatively few. Apparently the Sentencing Act 1991 (Vic) was a factor in Victorian magistrates achieving a pay rise. The Sentencing Act 1991 (Vic) effected some changes in dis-

---

[160] Sentencing Act 1991 (Vic), ss. 32–25; see also V. Duggan, 'Youth Training Centres in Victoria', in S. McKillop (ed.), *Keeping People out of Prison*, n. 158.

[161] See the University of Melbourne and Leo Cussen Institute Seminar, *The Sentencing Act 1991* (Melbourne, 1991).

[162] See 'Outrage on Sentencing Sham', *Herald-Sun*, 6 June 1992; 'Kennan, Judge Clash over Prison Terms', *The Age*, 6 June 1992.

tribution of cases between the higher courts and the Magistrates' Court. The Act amended the Magistrates Court Act 1989 (Vic) so that all offences punishable by imprisonment for ten years or less may be tried summarily. Offences punishable at penalty Level 8 or above (36 months' imprisonment) are presumed to be indictable. Offences between Level 4 and Level 8 are presumed to be indictable offences triable summarily with the consent of the accused and the court.[163] This change meant that a far wider range, and larger number, of serious offences could be heard in the Magistrates' Court, thus creating a greater workload for the magistrates. Because the Magistrates Court Act 1989 (Vic) does not provide any criteria to guide a magistrate in determining which offences should be heard summarily, the Director of Public Prosecutions is preparing draft guidelines to be issued for the guidance of prosecutors to 'enable them to make rational and consistent decisions in determining the attitude of the prosecution to applicants for summary trial made by the defence or offers of summary trial made by the Bench'.[164] According to data produced by the Director of Public Prosecutions, there is some indication that the change in jurisdictional limits may also have led to a decrease in the number of committals for trial in the higher courts.[165]

The nominal and effective reductions in prison-sentence lengths will have a consequential effect upon the parole service. In Victoria, a judge cannot set a non-parole period in relation to sentences of less than 12 months. A non-parole period is optional for sentences of between 12 and 24 months and mandatory for sentences of more than 24 months.[166] With the average term of dropping from 14 months to about 11 months, a large number of offenders who previously would have been eligible for parole now no longer qualify. Although their parole terms may have been short, their exclusion from the parole system altogether may result in a significant decrease in the workload for parole officers.

The only other unpredictable outcome which has come to my notice relates to the fees paid to lawyers. The changes made to maximum sentences has inadvertently changed the fees payable to counsel, as those fees had been set by reference to the maximum penalty applicable to the most serious charge. Because the Act reduced the statutory maxima for a large number of offences to reflect what in reality were the maximum penalties, the Legal Aid Commission of Victoria had to adjust their remuneration scale.

---

[163] See also Magistrates Court Act 1989 (Vic), Schedule 4.

[164] Director of Public Prosecutions, Victoria, *Annual Report 1991/92*, 6–7.

[165] This was based upon only 2 months' evidence to 30 June 1992; see Director of Public Prosecutions, Victoria, *Annual Report 1991/92*, 19.

[166] Sentencing Act 1991 (Vic), s. 11. A court may refuse to fix a non-parole period in the last case if it considers that the nature of the offence or the past history of the offender make the fixing of such a period inappropriate.

5. THE FUTURE

Sentencing structures are built upon unstable foundations. They are the result of, and vulnerable to, shifting social, political, and economic pressures. They will survive as long as they fulfil the needs of the dominant political elements of the society of which they are a product. In October 1992 the Labour Government of Victoria was voted out after ten years in office. The current government campaigned partly on a 'law and order' platform, and it was antagonistic when in Opposition to many of the provisions in the Sentencing Act 1991 (Vic).

In May 1993 it rushed through Parliament an Act which could significantly increase the prison population. Responding to what it perceived to be the community's concern about the inadequacy of custodial sentences imposed upon sexual and violent offenders, the legislation is intended to increase custodial sentences in a number of ways. The first is to create two new classes of offenders: 'serious sexual offenders' and 'serious violent offenders'. Both of these groups are elaborately and widely defined. If these offenders commit certain nominated offences (serious sexual or violent offences), then the court is required to regard the 'protection of the community' as the principal purpose of sentencing and may 'in order to achieve that purpose, impose a sentence longer than that which is proportionate to the gravity of the offence considered in the light of its objective circumstances'. In addition, section 10 of the Sentencing Act 1991 (Vic) will not apply to these offenders, effectively increasing their sentences by one-third. Furthermore, sentences imposed upon serious sexual offenders will be presumptively cumulative. The current legislative presumption is that all sentences are to be served concurrently.

The second method whereby sentence length will be increased is the introduction of indefinite sentences. Adult offenders, who are proved, to a high degree of probability, to be a 'serious danger to the community' and who have been convicted of specified 'serious offences' can, at the discretion of the court, be sentenced to indefinite imprisonment. A court in such cases is required to set a 'nominal sentence', equal to the previous non-parole period, at the expiration of which a judicial review must take place. If the offender is deemed still to be a serious danger to the community, he or she must remain in custody for at least another three years, the minimum period between reviews.

It is difficult, at this early stage, to speculate about the effect of these changes upon prison populations, as much will depend upon the judiciary's attitude to provisions which run so dramatically against the prevailing sentencing culture. In contrast to the intensive consultation which took place prior to the introduction and implementation of the Sentencing Act 1991

(Vic), the 1993 Act was introduced into Parliament and passed within a matter of weeks with no community input at all.

Other than the provision which selectively negates the operation of section 10, the courts retain some discretion in relation to both cumulative sentences and indefinite sentences. However, if implemented wholly as intended, it has been estimated that, on average, sentences imposed on 'serious sexual offenders' will increase by 250 per cent, from 5.4 years to 19 years. Assuming all other variables, such as conviction rates and sentencing practices, remain constant, within ten years or so there may be an additional 400 such offenders in prison.

The Sentencing Act 1991 (Vic) has taken a decade to develop. It is the product of an essentially conservative legal culture and retains, to a large degree, the traditional balance of powers between Parliament, the judiciary, and the executive. It has achieved some advances in the technology of sentencing and has been remarkably successful in accomplishing the transition required by the abolition of remissions. However, the technical successes which it can claim can succumb in a very short time to the endemic public clamour for longer sentences, for the abolition of parole, and for the introduction of a range of newer and more punitive sanctions. The institutional supports needed to maintain the information structure have not been established. The Judicial Studies Board exists in name, but has yet to be given any resources. The proposed Bureau of Crime Research and Statistics exists minutely as the Criminal Justice Statistics Planning Unit within a very large Ministry of Justice. Any on-going monitoring and evaluation of the legislation will need to be undertaken by agencies outside of government.

The direction of sentencing reform in Victoria can best be described as uncertain. Whether the general structure which has evolved over the last decade remains in place with some changes at the periphery or whether the whole system is totally reconstructed remains to be seen. One thing is certain, however, and that is that sentencing change in Victoria will continue unabated.

4

The Swedish Sentencing Reform

NILS JAREBORG

I. THE CRIMINAL CODE OF 1962

A hundred years ago, the general penalties of the Swedish Penal Code (1864) were restricted to capital punishment, fines, and two forms of determinate incarceration, one for longer sentences (penal labour) and one for shorter sentences (imprisonment). The prisons were in principle run according to the Philadelphia system (single-cell prisons). The first decade of the twentieth century witnessed the reluctant and cautious introduction of legal measures based on preventive considerations: compulsory education for criminals aged 15–17 years (1902), the suspended sentence (1906), and parole (1906). Capital punishment was abolished in 1921 (the last execution occurred in 1910[1]). The so-called day-fine system was adopted in 1931. Two forms of indeterminate incarceration for dangerous offenders were introduced in 1927, and another form of indeterminate incarceration for young offenders (youth imprisonment, primarily for offenders aged 18–20 years) in 1935. The English Borstal system served as a model for the latter sanction.

All these changes occurred through legislation outside the Penal Code. Intensive work on a new Penal Code began in the late 1930s, with a view to codifying and modernizing the criminal law. The work of one legislative committee resulted in a Draft Criminal Code, dealing with crimes (1953). The work of another committee resulted in a Draft Protective Code, dealing with sanctions (1956). Some of these committees' proposals had already been enacted as law, but it took until 1962 before an overall codification could be adopted. This Criminal Code, *Brottsbalken*, came into force in 1965.[2]

The Draft Protective Code signifies the peak of 'individual' or 'special-preventive' influence. Even the word 'punishment' was to be abolished.

---

[1] The technical possibility of using capital punishment during war remained until 1973. Sweden has not been at war since 1814.

[2] *Brottsbalken* is abbreviated BrB. BrB 1:1 means The Criminal Code, Chapter 1, section 1. The Code has been translated several times, first in *The Penal Code of Sweden* (translated by Thorsten Sellin, introduction by Ivar Strahl; Ministry of Justice: Stockholm, 1965). The latest translation into English is published by the National Council of Crime Prevention (*The Penal Code*. BRÅ-report 1990:3: Stockholm, 1990). This translation is not always reliable.

This was too much for the politicians and the public to swallow, however, and in the 1965 Code, imprisonment and fines were retained as *punishments*.[3] Other disposals are called other *sanctions for crime*. These included indeterminate incarceration of dangerous recidivists, youth imprisonment, probation, conditional sentence, and commitment to special care. The suspended sentence has disappeared. Confiscation and a number of other sanctions are technically not sanctions for crime, but so-called *special consequences of crime*.

Criminal policy development up to 1962 could, with some over-simplification, be described as a gradual recognition of special-prevention considerations. The first influential force was the so-called 'modern' or 'sociological' school, inspired by the ideas of Franz von Liszt. Later, the so-called 'positive' or 'Italian' school was more influential. After the Second World War, most of the inspiration came from the Social Defence Movement. Although Sweden was a forerunner in criminal policy, the basic ideas were Continental.

Only one section in the Code[4] was designed to guide sentencing:

In the choice of sanctions, the court, bearing in mind what is required to maintain general obedience to the law, shall have regard to the fact that the sanction shall serve to foster the sentenced offender's rehabilitation in society.

Thus the Code appeared to embrace preventive aims, and it seemed that in each individual case the sentencer was expected to amalgamate general-preventive and special-preventive considerations—which, of course, is an impossible task. In reality, things were not that bad. First, it should be emphasized that according to Swedish law, sentencing involves two issues.

1. **Choice of sanction**—selecting the appropriate *type* of sanction.
2. **Measurement of punishment**—meting out a term of imprisonment or a fine in the concrete case (measurement is conceptually excluded if another type of sanction is to be imposed).

The Code's sentencing provision concerned choice of sanction, not measurement of punishment. The struggle between different preventive aims was thus to take place only when considering the appropriate type of sanction. It was openly declared in the preparatory drafts of the Code that when it came to measurement of punishment, the established 'sentencing tradition'—primarily based on judgments relating to the seriousness of the crime—was to be relied upon. In addition, the reference to the need for general prevention was in practice interpreted as a reference to the seriousness or the nature of the crime. Imprisonment was the choice if

---

[3] Penal labour was merged with imprisonment. There were also special forms of punishment of civil servants and military personnel, but these are now abolished.
[4] The now annulled BrB 1:7.

the crime was very serious or belonged to those offences where rehabilitative aims were generally judged to be inappropriate (military offences,
drunken driving, illegal possession of weapons, assault on police officers,
and so on).

It is important to recognize that the influence of special-prevention
considerations in the development of Swedish criminal policy was restricted
to special categories of offenders: young offenders, dangerous offenders,
offenders in need of special care, first-time offenders, and offenders judged
possible to rehabilitate through prescriptions and supervision. The quanti-
tatively most important sanctions—imprisonment and fines—have always
been imposed according to a 'just deserts' model.

By the late 1960s, 'treatment optimism' was beginning to be replaced by
'treatment pessimism'. There had been practically no public debate concerning the penal system adopted under the Code in 1962. From now on,
however, penal matters began to be widely discussed by all sorts of intellec-
tuals, most of them criticizing the so-called treatment ideology on the
grounds that it resulted in more incarceration and stronger repression for
no good reason. The debate took place across the borders of the Nordic
countries. The first country to get an opportunity to legislate was Finland,
where special-preventive considerations had had only a marginal influence.
In 1975, indeterminate incarceration was in practice abolished, and in 1976,
a chapter on sentencing was added to the Finnish Penal Code. (It should be
added that in the end not much happened in Denmark and Norway.)

2. CHAPTER 6 OF THE FINNISH SENTENCING LAW OF 1976: ON THE MEASUREMENT OF SENTENCES

Section 1

In measuring a punishment all the grounds increasing and decreasing the punishment which affect the matter and the uniformness of sentencing practice shall be
taken into consideration. The punishment shall be measured so that it is in just
proportion to the damage and danger caused by the offence and to the guilt of the
offender manifested in the offence.

Section 2

Grounds for increasing punishments are:

1. the degree to which the criminal activity was planned;
2. committing the offence as a member of a group organized for serious offences;
3. committing the offence for remuneration;
4. the previous criminality of the offender, if the previous offence and the new
   offence are similar or if the pattern of offences shows that the offender is apparently heedless of the prohibitions and commands of law.

Section 3

Grounds for decreasing punishments are:

1. significant pressure, threat, or similar influence leading to the perpetration of the offence;
2. strong human sympathy leading to the offence or exceptional and sudden temptation or a similar factor which has been conducive to noticeably lowering the ability of the offender to obey the law; and
3. the voluntary effort of the offender to prevent or remove the effects of the offence or to assist the clearing up of his offence.

Section 4

If the offence has caused, or the resultant punishment has imposed, on the offender another consequence which, together with the punishment given on the basis of the application of the grounds mentioned previously in this chapter, would lead to a result that is unreasonable in comparison with the nature of the offence, such a situation is to be taken into consideration as is reasonable in measuring the punishment.[5]

3. PREPARATIONS FOR A SENTENCING REFORM

Work on reforming the sentencing system in Sweden began in the mid-1970s. In 1977 a Working Group set up by the National Council for Crime Prevention published a discussion report outlining 'a new penal system'.[6] The report contained no draft legislation but played a major role in the ensuing development. It advocated a decreased use of incarceration, a general lowering of the level of repression, abolition of indeterminate incarceration, and increased use of fines and other non-incarcerating sanctions. It emphasized the importance of the penal system being just, consistent, clear, and honest. Also in 1977, a legislative committee proposed that youth imprisonment be abolished. By the end of the decade, the criticism of youth imprisonment and indeterminate incarceration had made these two flagships of the special-prevention era lose their seaworthiness, and they were abolished in 1980 and 1981, respectively. By then, the so-called Imprisonment Committee had begun its work on a more comprehensive sentencing reform, including a revision of the penalty scales for the crimes in the Criminal Code and the most important crimes outside the Code. In 1986 the Committee presented a three-volume study report and a draft bill for

---

[5] The translation is taken, with minor amendment, from *The Penal Code of Finland and the Decree on the Enforcement of the Penal Code* (translated by Matti Joutsen; Research Institute of Legal Policy: Helsinki, 1983). See further e.g. T. Lappi-Seppälä, 'Penal Policy and Sentencing Theory', (1992) 5 *The Canadian Journal of Law and Jurisprudence* 95.

[6] *Nytt straffsystem: Idéer och Förslag.* Brottsförebyggande rådet. Rapport 1977:7. (Stockholm, 1977).

sentencing reform.[7] This proposal was in essence approved by the government and a Sentencing Reform Bill was delivered to Parliament (March 1988).[8] The bill was adopted (June 1988) and the new sentencing law came into force on 1 January 1989.[9]

A non-Swedish reader might find it odd that reform occurred at all. Where did the pressure for reform come from? The correct short answer is: from nowhere. This has to do with the Swedish legislative 'climate'. Most Swedish statutory law is fairly recent, yet statutes are repeatedly reviewed with the aim of finding out whether they are still up to date. Serious political or legal criticism results in a legislative committee being appointed. Nowadays, the members normally have a political background; often they are Members of Parliament. In practice, however, the members have to rely on the advice of the expert advisers. A legislative committee typically works for a number of years; the Imprisonment Committee had sentencing reform on its agenda for six years. All this serves to make the process as rational as possible. The issue is 'cooled down', and political difficulties are normally solved within the committee whose members continuously consult important persons in their respective political parties. In addition, committee reports are sent out to authorities and organizations for comments. The report of the Imprisonment Committee was scrutinized by fifty authorities and organizations, including the Uppsala and Stockholm Faculties of Law. A generally favourable response at this stage is, at least in matters of criminal law, in practice necessary for a decision by the Minister of Justice to prepare a bill for Parliament. The Imprisonment Committee was given a fairly free hand to find the best solution and its report was on the whole well received. The views of the Committee were shared by leading officials in the Ministry of Justice. Having set up the Committee this was all that was needed for reform to happen.

The reform did not include a revision of the penalty scales, and there is no reason to believe that such a revision will occur in the foreseeable future. Nor did it amount to a complete sentencing reform based on just deserts or proportionalist thinking. The law concerning alternatives to imprisonment (conditional sentence[10] and probation) are still guided by special-preventive

---

[7] *Påföljd för Brott.* 1–3. Huvudbetänkande av fängelsestraffkommittén. Statens offentliga utredningar 1986:13–15 (Stockholm, 1986).

[8] *Regeringens proposition 1987/88:120 om ändring i brottsbalken m.m.* (straffmätning och påföljdsval m.m.).

[9] See A. von Hirsch, 'Principles for Choosing Sanctions: Sweden's Proposed Sentencing Statute', (1987) 13 *New England Journal on Criminal and Civil Confinement* 171 (with a translation by von Hirsch and the present author of the central draft legislation); A. von Hirsch, 'Guiding Principles for Sentencing: The Proposed Swedish Law', [1987] *Crim. LR* 746; A. von Hirsch and N. Jareborg, 'Sweden's Sentencing Statute Enacted', [1989] *Crim. LR* 275 (with a translation of the central legislation).

[10] There is no equivalent in common-law countries to the Swedish conditional sentence. It is, paradoxically, a suspended sentence in which nothing is suspended. BrB 27:1 states that: 'A

considerations. Since 1992, however, there has been a new legislative committee, the so-called Penal System Committee, working on the completion of the task—unfortunately in a more repressive criminal policy climate.

4. THE SWEDISH SENTENCING LAW: INTRODUCTION

The 1988 legislation involved major or minor amendments to several existing chapters of the Code, but it mainly comprised two new chapters: Chapter 29 on the measurement of punishment and the remission of sanction; and Chapter 30 on the choice of sanction. The text of these two chapters is set out in full below, in Sections 5 and 9.[11] The provisions concerning particular sanctions are found elsewhere in the Code. Chapter 25 deals with fines, and Chapter 26 with imprisonment. Chapter 27 concerns conditional sentence and Chapter 28 concerns probation. Both these sanctions are sanctions *sui generis*. The suspended sentence does not exist. The provisions on commitment for special care are found in Chapter 31.

So-called 'penalty scales' are attached to the provisions on the specific crimes in the Code or elsewhere, with a particular maximum and a particular minimum sentence. Occasionally the minimum has to be deduced from general rules on minimum sentences. In addition, many types of offences are divided into seriousness levels. For example, the punishment for theft is imprisonment from 14 days to 2 years (BrB 8:1), the punishment for grand theft is imprisonment from 6 months to 6 years (BrB 8:4), and the punishment for petty theft is imprisonment from 14 days to 6 months or a fine (BrB 8:2).[12]

---

conditional sentence may be imposed by a court for an offence for which the penalty of a fine is considered insufficient.' A conditional sentence involves a probationary period of two years.

[11] I have used the translation referred to in n. 9. In choice of words, word order, and style, it differs considerably from the 1990 translation referred to in n. 2. The latter is undoubtedly more elegant, but it suffers from a number of somewhat misleading phrases and a few manifest errors, as when the key term *straffvärde*—'penal value'—is rendered as 'culpability'.

[12] *Section 1*
A person who, with the intent of appropriating it, unlawfully takes what belongs to another shall, if the appropriation involves loss, be sentenced for *theft* to imprisonment for at most two years.

Section 2
If the crime mentioned in section 1 is regarded as petty, considering the value of the stolen goods and other circumstances of the crime, a sentence of a fine or imprisonment for at most six months shall be imposed for *petty theft*.

Section 4
Should the offence envisaged in section 1 be considered serious, the offender shall be convicted of *grand theft* and sentenced to imprisonment for no less than six months and a maximum period of six years.
In assessing the gravity of the offence, special consideration shall be given to whether the unlawful appropriation took place after entry into a dwelling, whether it envisaged the appro-

The scope of the penalty scale is traditionally supposed to reflect the relative seriousness of the specific offence. This is another proportionalist feature of the previous law which facilitated reform: special-prevention considerations were excluded rather than just deserts considerations imported. On the other hand, the legislation is unique in its systematic development of the proportionalist theme.

Another feature of Swedish legal life that should be mentioned is the enormous importance of the *travaux préparatoires* for legal interpretation. Both the Committee report and the bill contain detailed explanations concerning the intentions behind the legislation and how the text should be understood.

I was a member of the Working Group within the Imprisonment Committee that proposed the draft bill on sentencing. It follows that I am, in general, in sympathy with the new law. This does not mean that I approve of every aspect or detail, but it is not the aim of this essay to subject the system or its details to critical analysis. The aim is simply to present the conceptual structures of the new Swedish sentencing law, and to indicate the role of different types of aggravating and mitigating factors within these structures. The bare bones of the system are complicated enough.

5. CHAPTER 29 OF THE SWEDISH CRIMINAL CODE 1988: ON THE MEASUREMENT OF PUNISHMENT AND REMISSION OF SANCTION

Section 1

The punishment shall be imposed within the statutory limits according to the penal value of the crime or crimes, and the interest of uniformity in sentencing shall be taken into consideration.

The penal value is determined with special regard to the harm, offence, or risk which the conduct involved, what the accused realized or should have realized about it, and the intentions and motives of the accused.

Section 2

Apart from circumstances specific to particular types of crime, the following circumstances, especially, shall be deemed to enhance the penal value:

1. whether the accused intended that the criminal conduct should have considerably worse consequences than it in fact had;
2. whether the accused has shown a special degree of indifference to the adverse consequences of the offence;

priation of an object carried on an individual's person, whether the perpetrator was furnished with a weapon, explosive, or similar device, or whether the criminal act was otherwise of an especially dangerous or reckless nature, involved considerable value or entailed severe and substantial loss or damage.

3. whether the accused made use of the victim's vulnerable position, or his other special difficulties in protecting himself;
4. whether the accused grossly abused his rank or position or grossly abused a special trust;
5. whether the accused induced another person to participate in the deed through force, deceit, or abuse of the latter's youthfulness, lack of understanding, or dependent position; or
6. whether the criminal conduct was part of a criminal activity that was especially carefully planned, or that was executed on an especially large scale and in which the accused played an important role.

Section 3

Apart from what is elsewhere specifically prescribed, the following circumstances, especially, shall be deemed to diminish the penal value:

1. whether the crime was provoked by another's grossly offensive behaviour;
2. whether the accused, because of mental abnormality or strong emotional inducement or other cause, had a reduced capacity to control his behaviour;
3. whether the accused's conduct was connected with his manifest lack of development, experience, or capacity for judgment; or
4. whether strong human compassion led to the crime.

The court may sentence below the statutory minimum when the penal value obviously calls for it.

Section 4

Apart from the penal value, the court shall in measuring the punishment, to a reasonable extent take the accused's previous criminality into account, but only if this has not been appropriately done in the choice of sanction or revocation of parole. In such cases, the extent of previous criminality and the time that has passed between the crimes shall be especially considered, as well as whether the previous and the new criminality is similar, or whether the criminality in both cases is especially serious.

Section 5

In determining the punishment, the court shall to a reasonable extent, apart from the penal value, consider:

1. whether the accused as a consequence of the crime has suffered serious bodily harm;
2. whether the accused, according to his ability, has tried to prevent, or repair, or mitigate the harmful consequences of the crime;
3. whether the accused voluntarily gave himself up;
4. whether the accused is, to his detriment, expelled from the country in consequence of the crime;
5. whether the accused as a consequence of the crime has experienced or is likely to experience discharge from employment or other disability or extraordinary difficulty in the performance of his work or trade;

6. whether a punishment imposed according to the crime's penal value would affect the accused unreasonably severely, due to advanced age or bad health;
7. whether, considering the nature of the crime, an unusually long time has elapsed since the commission of the crime; or
8. whether there are other circumstances that call for a lesser punishment than the penal value indicates.

If, in such cases, special reasons so indicate, the punishment may be reduced below the statutory minimum.

Section 6

The sanction is to be remitted entirely when, with regard to circumstances of the kind mentioned in section 5, imposition of a sanction is manifestly unreasonable.

Section 7

If someone has committed a crime before the age of 21, his youth shall be considered separately in the determination of the punishment, and the statutory minimum may be disregarded.

Life imprisonment is never to be imposed in such cases.

6. THE CONCEPT OF PENAL VALUE

It is obvious that penal value has to do with seriousness of crime. But even if there is a close connection between these concepts they are not identical. Seriousness of crime is normally analysed as a function of the criminal conduct's harmfulness and the offender's culpability.[13] This idea is captured in BrB 29:1 para. 2. One should, however, notice that the penal value is determined with special regard to the dimensions of harmfulness and culpability.

The whole of Chapter 29 helps to define the technical term 'penal value'. Factors mentioned in 29:2 and 3 have to do with penal value. Factors mentioned in 29:4, 5, and 7 do not. It follows that not everything that arguably affects the culpability of the offender is a matter of penal value. Some commentators think that a prior criminal record makes an offender more culpable. BrB 29:4 explicitly defines previous criminality as a factor irrelevant for the penal value. Some of the factors mentioned in 29:5 also have a flavour of culpability.

As we have seen, the Swedish sentencing reform was preceded by reform in Finland in 1976 (see Section 2, above). The key sentence of that legislation is found in 6:1 of the Penal Code:

---

[13] See A. von Hirsch, *Past or Future Crimes: Deservedness and Dangerousness in the Sentencing of Criminals* (Manchester, 1986), ch. 6.

The punishment shall be measured so that it is in just proportion to the damage and danger caused by the offence and to the guilt of the offender manifested in the offence.

Similarly, only *culpability manifested in the offence* affects the penal value.

The definition proposed by the Imprisonment Committee was slightly different from the one enacted as law, and very close to the Finnish provision:

The penal value of a crime is determined by its seriousness, with special regard to:
1. the harm or danger which the conduct involved,
2. the guilt of the offender manifested in the crime.

The Committee wanted the terms 'penal value' and 'crime seriousness' to have the same meaning. But as in BrB 29:1, the Committee's formula presupposes that penal value is not exhausted by the criminal conduct's harmfulness and the offender's culpability manifested in the conduct. But what else can there be that influences the penal value?

The Committee based its discussion on a review of arguments used during the last half century in all important cases of determining or amending penalty scales. Ten types of arguments were identified, and their relevance was assessed in the following way.

    1. **Public perceptions or views concerning crime seriousness.** Of basic importance, but in practice normally unsuitable as a ground for penal value deliberations.

    2. **The conduct's social danger, adverse consequences, harmfulness, etc.** Of first-rate importance.

    3. **The need for general prevention.** Irrelevant.

    4. **The need for more powerful measures.** See 2 and 3.

    5. **Comparisons with penalty levels in other countries.** Relevant in cases of international criminality, such as drug offences, hijacking, and terrorism.

    6. **Comparisons with similar crimes.** Relevant.

    7. **Increased frequency or perniciousness of a type of crime.** The frequency argument is irrelevant. The perniciousness argument might be relevant under 2 or 6.

    8. **The criminality is connected with other serious criminality.** Irrelevant, unless it falls under 2.

    9. **A raised maximum will prolong the time for statutory limitation.** Irrelevant.

    10. **A raised maximum will enable the use of coercive measures during the pre-trial investigation.** Irrelevant.

At this stage, the Committee's discussion was primarily concerned with what one might call 'abstract' penal value—the penal value of a type of crime, to be reflected in the penalty scale. But it was also directly relevant for the assessment of the 'concrete' penal value, the penal value of an individual act or omission. In summary, the Committee's opinion seemed to be that the penal value should reflect the reprehensibility of the criminal conduct, which is mainly a function of the conduct's harmfulness and the offender's culpability manifested in the conduct. But the Committee accepted a departure from strict proportionalist thinking: as far as internationally connected criminality is concerned, the penal value to some extent also depends on penalty levels in other countries.

The Committee's report was criticized by some authorities on the basis that the need for general prevention had not been sufficiently considered. The Minister of Justice found the criticism exaggerated, and dissociated herself from, for example, exemplary punishment. However, she saw nothing wrong in considering general-prevention arguments in determining the penalty scales (the abstract penal value): increased frequency or perniciousness were factors of relevance in this context, and she stated that in 'certain cases there may be cause for a change in court practice for such reasons'. We thus have a statement of official policy in the *travaux préparatoires* that sometimes the concrete penal value may be influenced by the need for general prevention. No example was given.[14]

Unfortunately, these two additions to the idea of the penal value being determined by harmfulness and culpability have immense practical importance. Most noteworthy is the fact that the severity of sentences for drug offences is clearly out of proportion to the seriousness of the crime; such a result is clearly attributable to these two factors. However, it must be conceded that this practice was firmly established before the sentencing reform.

An assessment of the penal value of a concrete crime is of importance not only for the measurement of punishment (see Section 8, below) but also for the choice of sanction (see Section 10, below). It is therefore dealt with separately in the next section.

---

[14] The concept of *seriousness of crime* coincides, as already mentioned, approximately with penal value. There is, however, a slight difference when 'crime seriousness' is used technically. As mentioned above (see section 4) many crime types are divided into seriousness levels. There are three levels of assault, two levels of murder, three levels of theft, two levels of robbery, and so on.

What kinds of factors determine the subsumption of a particular offence under a specific level? First, it is clear that only penal-value factors are relevant, and only those penal-value factors that have to do with harmfulness and culpability. Circumstances of the kind referred to in BrB 29:4, 5, and 7 are irrelevant. Secondly, harmfulness factors seem to be more important than culpability factors. The same may be true when we are talking about penal value, but there is a difference in emphasis. Thirdly, some of the factors mentioned in BrB 29:3 are irrelevant. While provocation and human compassion may affect the seriousness level, mental abnormality and immaturity may not.

7. THE ASSESSMENT OF PENAL VALUE

The penal value of a particular crime, as well as the punishment for that crime, is rendered as a certain quantity of imprisonment or money to be paid. Money can be divided into very small units and time can be divided infinitely. In practice, relatively few positions within the penalty scales are used. As far as imprisonment is concerned, the minimum step at the bottom (14 days) is one week, and the minimum step at the top (ten years, or in special circumstances up to eighteen years) is one year. In between we find moves in half months, whole months, two or three months, and six months. In reality, no more than twenty steps are used from 14 days up to ten years. The moves on the scale of day-fines are normally ten or twenty, occasionally five, day-fines. This practice is certainly lacking in sophistication, and it is to be hoped that the sentencing reform will eventually lead to a greater degree of discrimination. Nevertheless, it is quite clear that the number of steps within the scales will remain fairly few. Moral assessment does not lend itself to quantification beyond rough ranking. Differences in quantity (e.g. the value of stolen goods) may reflect differences in quality, but we are really only interested in quality differences when we judge the goodness or badness of conduct, things, events, and so on. Accordingly, the steps within the penalty scales will have to represent quality differences worthy of consideration.

Two things follow from this. First, there is no reason to care about differences between particular offences, aggravating or mitigating circumstances, that are too unimportant to affect the sentence. This 'quantum theory of aggravation and mitigation' is taken for granted by the Swedish law. It is expressed in some of the phrases used in BrB 29:2 and 3: 'considerably worse consequences', 'special degree of indifference', 'grossly abused', 'especially carefully planned', 'especially large scale', 'grossly offensive behaviour', 'manifest lack', and 'strong human compassion'. There are similar qualifications in BrB 29:5. Secondly, since there is no need to consider and weigh every little aggravating or mitigating factor, it is not that difficult to assess the penal value or arrive at a conclusion concerning the appropriate punishment.

The penal value is in principle a function of the harmfulness of the conduct and the culpability manifested in the conduct. The three main types of consideration are: first, the importance of the value or interest harmed or threatened; secondly, the closeness to actual infringement of the value or interest (actual harm, danger of harm, risk-taking, or only protective-rule violation); and thirdly, the kind of general culpability manifested (criminal intent or negligence).[15]

---

[15] See N. Jareborg, *Brotten*, i, 2nd edn. (Stockholm, 1984), 34–45.

In assessing the penal value, the factors mentioned in BrB 29:2 and 3 come in at a late stage. 29:2 uses the expression 'Apart from circumstances specific to particular types of crime'[16] and 29:3 says 'Apart from what is elsewhere specifically prescribed'. To begin with, attention must be drawn to offence-specific aggravating and mitigating factors.

Many offence descriptions contain terms referring to features of harmfulness or culpability. Theft presupposes economic harm (BrB 8:1). Assault in principle presupposes bodily injury, illness, or pain (BrB 3:5). Arson presupposes danger to another's life or health or extensive destruction of another's property (BrB 13:1). Espionage presupposes an intention to aid a foreign power (BrB 19:5). And so on. For most crimes, the penal value is assessed on the basis of parameters provided by the crime definitions and the general culpability requirements.

A second set of offence-specific aggravating and mitigating factors come into play if the type of crime has more than one seriousness level. The example provided above (theft, petty theft, grand theft)[17] should be sufficient to illustrate the point. It is no wonder that the degree of harm is glaringly absent in the enumerations in BrB 29:2 and 3.

Several factors mentioned in BrB 29:2 and 3 are such that they may be used as a ground for placing criminal conduct on a seriousness level with a more severe or more lenient penalty scale than the one attached to the basic crime description. For instance, provocation (BrB 29:3(1)) may prompt the classification of a murder as less serious (manslaughter; BrB 3:2). The question arises whether such a factor may be relevant also for sentencing purposes. As is so often the case, the answer is: it depends. If the factor's relevance is exhausted by the offence classification, then it can no longer be considered. But often something 'remains'. For instance, if a stolen picture is worth 200,000 Swedish crowns, the theft is normally classified as grand theft. But, of course, if the picture is worth millions, that will influence the punishment. Similarly, if a drug offence is classified as aggravated because it was executed on an especially large scale and the accused played an important role therein (cf. BrB 29:2(6)) the circumstances may well be such that a lot 'remains' to be taken into consideration at the sentencing stage.

BrB 29:2 and 3 deal with non-offence-specific aggravating and mitigating factors. However, as far as mitigating non-offence-specific factors are concerned there are other more important provisions. There are cases of self-defence, necessity, official use of violence or force, and acting on superior orders, where the actor is neither fully justified, nor fully excused. There are also cases of complicity that have a reduced penal value (BrB 23:5), i.e. where the offender has been induced to be an accessory to a crime by

---

[16] The translation mentioned in n. 2 misleadingly renders this as 'in addition to the provisions prescribed for each individual type of offence'.

[17] See n. 12.

coercion, deceit, or misuse of his youth, lack of comprehension, or dependent status, or where he has been an accessory only to a small degree (but the case is not of minor importance). The Committee proposed the insertion of a special provision to the effect that a partial justification or a partial excuse should be a mitigating circumstance, but, so far, the legislature has not acted on its advice.

The *travaux préparatoires* emphasize an asymmetry between BrB 29:2 and 29:3. The drafting of 29:2 has been done with such care that there is little room for additions to the list, and the courts have been advised to use restraint in interpreting the provisions. There is considerably greater freedom to add to the list in 29:3. One obvious candidate is excusable mistake of law which does not excuse the actor from criminal responsibility.

The explanatory notes also stress that sentencers may not take objective factors, which are not covered by criminal intent or negligence, into consideration in assessing the penal value. The context seems to indicate that the statement concerns aggravating, but not mitigating, circumstances. As a result of the 'quantum approach', an aggravating factor only covered by negligence can rarely affect the sentence for a crime involving criminal intent.

8. MEASUREMENT OF PUNISHMENT

BrB 29:1 urges the courts to consider the need for uniformity in sentencing. In other words, the courts are advised to accept the general evaluations expressed through legislation, and to adjust to principles developed by case-law.

Step A: Assessment of Penal Value

See Sections 6 and 7, above.

Step B: Recidivism Aggravation

BrB 29:4 regulates the relevance of previous criminality, that is, previous criminality that has resulted in a court sentence, a prosecutor's summary punishment by fine, or a prosecutor's decision to forgo prosecution.

Previous criminality has its major role in the *choice of sanction*. As will be clarified in Section 10, below, previous criminality may affect the choice between imprisonment and conditional sentence/probation (or commitment to care within the social services), between conditional sentence and probation, between probation with a fine and probation without a fine, and between probation with a fine and probation with imprisonment.

Repeated criminality may also result in *revocation of parole*. The parole period is, with few exceptions, one year (BrB 26:10). The most important provision in this connection is BrB 34:4 para. 2:

In judging whether parole should be revoked and in deciding on duration of reconfinement on revocation, consideration shall be given to whether the previous and current offences are similar, whether the offences in both cases are serious, and whether the current offence is more or less serious than the previous offence or offences. In addition, the time that has passed between the crimes shall be considered.

Finally, previous criminality may influence ('to a reasonable extent') the *severity of punishment* if it has not been taken 'appropriately' into account in the choice of sanction or revocation of parole. There may be nothing to revoke (the period of parole is fairly short) and/or the new crime may be so serious that imprisonment is the only option. The guidelines given in BrB 29:4 are similar to those just cited concerning revocation. A main difference is that 29:4 speaks of 'especially' serious criminality, which indicates a penal value of at least one year.

There is much in this that deserves criticism, but this is not within the scope of the present chapter. It is, however, worth mentioning that the Committee proposed a provision making previous criminality irrelevant for the length of a prison sentence.

Step C: Equity Mitigation

The somewhat controversial, and mixed, group of reasons for mitigation set forth in BrB 29:5 are normally referred to as 'equity reasons'. They all supposedly have something to do with fair treatment of the offender. The basis for a more lenient treatment is, however, varying, and slippery: it is not easy to say where pardon begins to be more appropriate than mitigation.

If the penal value has to do with the punishment-worthiness of the offence, we are now considering the punishment-worthiness of the offender. In some cases, the culpability judgment has faded somewhat. In a wider perspective, the offender seems less culpable at the time of passing sentence (see BrB 29:5(2) reparation; and BrB 29:5(7) long time between crime and sentence). In other cases, the offender's vulnerability is decisive: BrB 29:5(1) *poena naturalis*, and BrB 29:5(6) advanced age or bad health. One can, of course, question whether 'feeling sorry'—however well grounded such a reaction may be—should be sufficient basis for mitigation. Two clauses concern cumulation of sanctions: BrB 29:5(4) expulsion, and BrB 29:5(5) discharge from employment, loss of driving licence, prohibition to engage in business, and so on. In addition, the catch-all,

BrB 29:5(8), is meant to cover extraordinary cases where a compensation order, a corporate fine, confiscation, or disciplinary punishment may call for mitigation. As examples of other cases where BrB 29:5(8) may be applicable, the explanatory notes mention crimes committed in connection with a suicide attempt, and that a third party (generally a child) may suffer unreasonably.

Swedish law has been reluctant to reward aid to the operation of the criminal justice system. The mitigation provided by BrB 29:5(3) was a novelty for many courts. It should be noted that mitigation may occur because of a voluntary revelation of the offender's own criminality. The Committee advanced strong reasons against rewarding denunciation of someone else. The bill took the same view, but less categorically: in quite exceptional cases the catch-all clause in BrB 29:5(8) might be applicable.

Equity mitigation is of special importance for the choice between imprisonment and an alternative to imprisonment (BrB 30:4); see Section 10, below. This might be a reason for taking a more lenient view of the imperfections of BrB 29:5.

Step D: Youth Mitigation

A young offender is normally less culpable than an adult one. BrB 29:3(3) provides for mitigation because of reduced culpability (reduced penal value). The mitigation provided for in BrB 29:7 is quite different. It is part of a general policy to try to keep young offenders out of prison, and if they are to be incarcerated, to make it short. The theoretical basis for this is far from clear. As a group, young offenders are probably more vulnerable, and maybe the growing generation deserves more chances and toleration than adults.

In practice, the courts often seem to move directly to BrB 29:7, and let the youth mitigation include mitigation because of reduced individual culpability. The deductions for youth are often drastic: down to one-third of what would otherwise be imposed.

Step E: Special Cases of Mitigation

There are a number of provisions designed to prevent unwarranted cumulation of sanctions:

BrB 2:6. Deduction due to a sanction suffered abroad for the same crime.
BrB 34:3. Deduction due to an unlucky combination of prison sentences.
BrB 28:9, 34:6, and 38:2a. Deduction in connection with revocation of probation.

Step F: Remission of Sanction

1. The general rule on remission of sanction is found in BrB 29:6. Note that remission is only possible due to equity mitigation. Youth mitigation or negligible penal value is not sufficient for going below the smallest fine. If there is no penal value the actor should be acquitted and given no penalty.

2. The deduction envisaged in BrB 2:6 (see under Step E) may lead to a remission of sanction.

3. If a fine is called for, but is not an appropriate sanction as a response to a crime committed under the influence of serious mental abnormality, the offender shall be free from sanction (BrB 30:6).

The burden of proof is on the prosecutor. An aggravating factor must be proved beyond reasonable doubt. It is advisable that an alleged aggravating factor is mentioned in the prosecutor's application for a summons, but it is not required. As far as an alleged mitigating factor is concerned, the prosecutor must be regarded as having proved its non-existence if the offender has done nothing more than put forward a naked assertion or tried to support its existence by means of a story out of touch with reality. If the truth of the offender's statement cannot be excluded, it is up to the prosecutor to disprove it.

9. CHAPTER 30 OF THE CRIMINAL CODE: ON THE CHOICE OF SANCTIONS

Section 1

In choosing sanctions imprisonment is considered more severe than a conditional sentence and probation.

Provisions on the use of commitment to special care are set forth in Chapter 31.

Section 2

Unless otherwise provided, no one is to receive more than one sanction for the same crime.

Section 3

Unless otherwise provided, someone convicted of more than one crime is to be given one sanction.

If there are special reasons, however, the court may combine a fine for some criminal conduct with another sanction for other conduct, or combine imprisonment for some conduct with conditional sentence or probation for other conduct.

Section 4

In choosing the sanction, the court shall especially pay heed to circumstances that suggest a less severe sanction than imprisonment. In so doing, the court shall consider circumstances referred to in Chapter 29, section 5.

As a reason for imprisonment the court may consider, in addition to the penal value and the nature of the criminality, the accused's previous criminality.

Section 5

For a crime committed by someone below the age of 18, imprisonment may be imposed only if there are extraordinary reasons.

For a crime committed by someone between the age of 18 and 21, imprisonment may be imposed only if there are, with respect to the penal value of the crime or other grounds, special reasons.

Section 6

A person who has committed a crime under the influence of serious mental abnormality may not be sentenced to imprisonment. If in such a case the court finds that no other sanction should be imposed, the accused shall be free from sanction. [As amended, to be applied from 1992.]

Section 7

In choosing the sanction, the court shall consider, as a reason for conditional sentence, whether there is no special reason to fear that the accused will relapse into criminal conduct.

Section 8

A conditional sentence shall be combined with day-fines, unless a fine would be unduly harsh, considering the other consequences of the crime, or there are other special reasons that militate against imposition of a fine.

Section 9

In choosing sanction, the court shall consider, as a reason for probation, whether there is reason to suppose that such a sanction can contribute to his not committing crimes in the future.

As special reasons for probation the court may consider:

1. whether a considerable improvement has occurred in the accused's personal or social situation that bears upon his criminality;

2. whether the accused is being treated for abuse or other condition that bears upon his criminality; or

3. whether abuse of addictive substances or other special condition that calls for care or other treatment, to a considerable degree explains the criminal conduct and the accused has declared himself willing to undergo adequate treatment, in accordance with an individual plan, that can be arranged in connection with the execution of the sentence.

Section 10

In judging whether probation should be combined with day-fines, the court shall consider whether this is called for with regard to the penal value or nature of the criminal conduct, or the accused's previous criminality.

Section 11

Probation may be combined with imprisonment[18] only if it is unavoidably called for, with regard to the penal value of the criminal conduct, or the accused's previous criminality.

10. THE STRUCTURE OF THE SENTENCING PROCESS

To get a clear view of the role of aggravating and mitigating circumstances we must use a wider perspective than the one involved in the measurement of punishment. Aggravation and mitigation are sometimes also of importance in choosing a sanction. To clarify these issues, it may be wise to give a picture of the whole sentencing process. The structure developed here is an invisible underlying (logical) structure, quite different from the legislative structure. In practice, of course, no sentencer follows in his or her reasoning the steps in the indicated order, but a 'roving' sentencer is bound to make mistakes unless the restrictions of the structure are respected.

Step 1: The Penalty Scale for each Individual Crime

   1. Each provision defining a crime contains a crime description and a penalty scale. Sometimes the minima may have to be deduced from general rules in BrB Chapter 25 (fines) and Chapter 26 (imprisonment). The penalty scales for attempt, preparation, conspiracy, instigation, and aiding and abetting are found in BrB Chapter 23.
   2. There are, however, a number of ways of breaking through the normal statutory minimum:

BrB 23:5. Complicity; reduced penal value.
BrB 24:5. Excess in cases of self-defence, necessity, official use of violence or force; reduced penal value.
BrB 29:3 para. 2. The penal value obviously calls for it.
BrB 29:5 para. 2. Equity mitigation and special reasons.
BrB 29:7 para. 1. Youth mitigation.
BrB 13:11, 14:11, 15:14. Special cases of equity mitigation: voluntary aversion of danger after the completion of the crime.[19]
BrB 2:3 para. 3. Double criminality considerations when a crime is committed abroad.
BrB 2:6 para. 2. Consideration of sanction abroad for the same crime.

---

[18] BrB 28:3 provides that probation may be combined with imprisonment for a minimum period of fourteen days and a maximum period of three months.
[19] An example would be an offender convicted of sabotage who voluntarily averted the danger or effect before considerable inconvenience or nuisance had arisen. He or she could be sentenced to a milder penalty than that prescribed for the offence.

BrB 34:3. A special case of deduction; see Step E in Section 8, above.
BrB 28:9, 34:6, and 38:2a. Special cases of revocation of probation.
BrB 22:8. War offences: mistake of law; reduced penal value.

   3. There is one way of breaking through the normal statutory maximum.
BrB 26:3 prescribes that if

a person has been sentenced to imprisonment for at least two years and, once the
judgment has acquired legal force, he commits a crime for which the penalty is
imprisonment for more than six years, he may be sentenced for the relapse to
imprisonment for a term which exceeds by four years the maximum punishment.

Since the ordinary general maximum is ten years (BrB 26:1) such recidivism
aggravation may raise the maximum to fourteen years.

   4. There are a number of crimes the maximum sentence for which is ten
years imprisonment or imprisonment for life, e.g. grave arson (BrB 13:2).
Ten years or life is the whole of the penalty 'scale' for murder (BrB 3:1). If
such a crime is committed by someone below the age of 21, life imprisonment may not be imposed (BrB 29:7 para. 2 youth mitigation).

Step 2: The Penalty Scale for Multiple Criminality

The main rule is that someone convicted of more than one crime is to be
given one sanction (BrB 30:3). This means that a new penalty scale must be
constructed for the combination of offences. The minimum for combined
offences is the same as for the most severe minimum of the individual
crimes, and the maximum is raised according to fairly detailed rules (BrB
25:6 and 26:2). A maximum of eight or ten years may be raised by up to
four years in cases of multiple offences, for example. This means that
eighteen years is the maximum determinate term of imprisonment (ten plus
four plus four as recidivism aggravation according to BrB 26:3; see Step
1(3): such enhancement relates to the combined offences, not each individual crime). Although the commission of several offences is very frequent, the rules concerning the construction of a penalty scale for the
combined offences are of practical importance only for drug crimes. Otherwise, the penalty scale for the most serious crime is almost always more than
sufficient.

   BrB Chapter 34 should be mentioned in this connection. It deals, among
other things, with the possibility of letting a sanction imposed for a previous
crime apply for the current criminality as well, and of revoking an earlier
sanction and imposing a different kind of sanction for both the previous and
the current offence. In other words, the court may decide to broaden the
scope of criminality under consideration, and include some offence or
offences on which sentence has already been passed.

Step 3: The Sanction Alternatives

The penalty scales mention only the punishments, i.e. fines and imprisonment. The Code lives by the fiction that imprisonment is a more severe punishment than a fine (BrB 1:5). The fine scale and the imprisonment scale are thus not overlapping.

Conditional sentence and probation may be used instead of imprisonment (BrB 1:4, 27:1, and 28:1). Consequently, conditional sentence and probation are also regarded as more severe sanctions than a fine.

Conditional sentence comprises a warning and a registration. The conditional period is two years. Conditional sentences shall, however, be combined with a fine, unless there are special reasons against imposing a fine (BrB 30:8). Probation involves supervision, the probationary time is three years, and it often includes prescriptions and restrictions. Therefore additional reasons are needed for combining a probation order with a fine (BrB 30:10). Probation, but not conditional sentence, may also be combined with imprisonment up to three months (BrB 28:3, 30:11).

Commitment to special care (BrB Chapter 31) is an alternative to both imprisonment and fines, but it has no practical importance as an alternative to a fine.

A minimum age and a sane mind are no crime prerequisites in Swedish criminal law (a hangover from the 1956 Draft Protective Code). A sanction may not, however, be imposed on someone who has committed a crime before the age of 15 (BrB 1:6).[20]

The rules on limitations on sanction (so-called negative prescription) are found in BrB Chapter 35.

Step 4: Choice of Sanction: Commitment for Special Care

Commitment for special care does not really fit in with the rest of the sanction system. The Committee wanted to designate commitment for special care not as a penal sanction, but as an alternative to a penal sanction. The Committee's reasons for a change were not sufficiently understood by the legislature, and the Code still classifies commitment for special care within the social-welfare or mental-health services as a penal sanction (a sanction for a crime).

Since this form of sanction is a foreign element in the system it is advisable to determine at an early stage whether BrB Chapter 31 can be applied.

---

[20] Someone below 15 must not be prosecuted but is legally 'competent' to commit a crime (in a technical sense). An insane person can be prosecuted, but the penalty options are limited. No one can be acquitted because of insanity, but the offender cannot be sent to prison, and he may well be free from sanction.

The details of this chapter need not concern us, but it might be mentioned that according to BrB 31:1, any offender under the age of 21 may be surrendered for care within the social-welfare services, and if the offender is under 18 there is a strong presumption that such care is the appropriate sanction. This could be seen as part of the youth mitigation. Penal-value considerations may prompt imposition of an additional fine.

Some of the legislation mentioned under Step 7, below, is of importance in determining whether Chapter 31 should be applied, at least as far as young persons and alcohol and drug abusers are concerned.

Step 5: Choice of Sanction: Fines v. Imprisonment

This choice is not regulated by the choice-of-sanction chapter (BrB Chapter 30), but by Chapter 29. Since there is no overlap in severity between fines and imprisonment, there is no difference between measurement of punishment and choice of sanction. If the outcome is that a fine should be imposed, one moves to Step 6. If the outcome is that a fine is not sufficient, one moves to Step 7.

Step 6: Measurement of a Fine

The relevant factors have been dealt with above (Sections 6, 7, and 8). The limits are set out in BrB Chapter 25. This is not the place for a discussion of these.

Step 7: Choice of Sanction: Imprisonment v. an Alternative

The alternatives to imprisonment are conditional sentence and probation. (Commitment for special care of young persons, abusers, and mentally ill persons is treated under Step 4.) BrB 30:1 states that 'in choosing sanctions imprisonment is considered more severe than a conditional sentence and probation'. In relation to fines, however, imprisonment is not considered as more severe than conditional sentence and probation. The rule in BrB 30:1 has the function of laying a basis for a presumption against the use of incarceration.

    1. **BrB 30:6** prohibits the use of imprisonment if the crime was committed under the influence of serious mental abnormality.

    2. **BrB 30:4 para.** 1 urges the court to pay special heed to circumstances that suggest a less severe sanction than imprisonment. In so doing, the court shall consider circumstances referred to in BrB 29:5, i.e. equity mitigation.

    3. **BrB 30:4 para.** 2 indicates where the presumption against imprisonment loses its power:

a reason for imprisonment the court may consider, in addition to the penal value and the nature of the criminality, is the accused's previous criminality.

The explanatory notes state as a guideline that a penal value of one year or more indicates that imprisonment should be used. The relation between this statement and the reference to BrB 29:5 in 30:4 para. 1 remains somewhat obscure, at least in some cases where the penal value is one year or more, but where a measurement of punishment would lead to a considerably less severe punishment, the presumption against imprisonment would seem to be still in force because of BrB 29:5-factors. A better solution would have been to connect the one-year guideline, not with the penal value, but with the result of measuring punishment. At present, there is a risk that BrB 29:5-factors will be disregarded and imprisonment imposed in violation of legislative intent.

The reference to the nature of the crime makes it possible to choose imprisonment instead of conditional sentence/probation for general-preventive reasons. Finally, repetition of criminality of intermediate gravity will eventually lead to imprisonment (recidivism aggravation).

4. For young offenders, the presumption against imprisonment is to a certain extent restored by BrB 30:5.

If the offender at the time of the crime belonged to the age group 18–20, there must be special reasons for imposing imprisonment. The provision mentions the penal value as one important factor, but also the nature of the crime and recidivism aggravation are relevant considerations.

If the offender at the time of the crime belonged to the age group 15–17, the presumption against imprisonment is extremely strong. There must be extraordinary reasons, in practice a very high penal value. Less than fifty persons in this age group are sentenced to imprisonment or imprisonment combined with probation each year, and they get huge deductions due to youth mitigation. The normal disposition is commitment for care within the social-welfare services (BrB 31:1).

5. There are more ways to escape imprisonment. BrB 30:9 para. 2 enumerates special reasons for probation. According to the explanatory notes, the enumeration is not exhaustive, and although not easy to deduce from the text, this paragraph is, within limits, meant to rebut the presumption for imprisonment that BrB 30:4 para. 2 establishes. As far as the penal value is concerned, the practice of the courts suggests that the one-year guideline (mentioned under Step 7 (3) above) is replaced by a two-year guideline.

6. Are there still more possibilities to avoid imprisonment? Since the system plays with presumptions in different directions, there should logically remain a category of cases where BrB 30:4 para. 1 so to speak gets the last word. As indicated above under Step C very strong equity reasons may

rebut all presumptions for imprisonment. Such cases must, however, be infrequent if the alternative is a sentence of imprisonment for more than one year. Otherwise the system of argumentation is undermined.

If the choice results in imprisonment, one moves to Step 8. If the choice results in an alternative, one moves to Step 9 (or Step 4).

Step 8: Measurement of Imprisonment

The relevant factors have been dealt with above (Sections 6, 7, and 8).

Step 9: Choice of Sanction: Conditional Sentence v. Probation

1. In cases covered by BrB 30:9 para. 2—see under Step 7 (5)—only probation is an alternative.[21]

2. At present, the choice between conditional sentence and probation is supposed to be guided by special-prevention considerations (which means that recidivism aggravation may be decisive). The court shall consider, 'as a reason for conditional sentence, whether there is no special reason to fear that the accused will relapse into criminal conduct' (BrB 30:7), and, 'as a reason for probation, whether there is reason to suppose that such a sanction can contribute to his not committing crimes in the future' (BrB 30:9 para. 1). In the bill, the reference to forecasts is played down; it is asserted that in practice the decisive criterion is whether there is any need for support or help.[22] As mentioned above, legislative proposals have been initiated, with a view to making the provisions on conditional sentence and probation harmonize better with a just deserts perspective.

The main rule is that a conditional sentence be combined with a fine (BrB 30:8). Equity mitigation is one reason for avoiding imposing a fine. Another is that the offender has been enjoined to pay compensation.

In judging whether probation should be combined with a fine, the penal value, the nature of the crime, and recidivism aggravation are the relevant considerations (BrB 30:10). A combination of probation with imprisonment is allowed only if it is unavoidably called for, with regard to the penal value or the recidivism aggravation (BrB 30:11)—in other words: when a long

---

[21] In cases of so-called contract care (BrB 30:9 para. 2(3)), the court shall indicate the term of imprisonment to which the offender should have been sentenced had imprisonment been preferred to probation (BrB 28:6a). The same is prescribed for the use of community service as a condition for probation (community service is being used experimentally until the end of 1995).

[22] The Committee's proposal used positive criteria only for probation; the conditional sentence should be employed if imprisonment or probation were not called for. Theoretically, the present law may, in conflict with the spirit of the law, force the sentencer to use imprisonment, because neither the criteria for use of conditional sentence, nor the criteria for use of probation are satisfied.

prison sentence can be avoided only if probation is combined with a short prison sentence.

Step 10: Deduction of Period of Arrest or Detention

Any period of deprivation of liberty shall be deducted from a sentence of imprisonment, and if the sentence involves a fine, the court may direct that the sentence has been executed in full or in part through deprivation of the offender's liberty (BrB Chapter 33).

11. THE SENTENCING PATTERN

The population of Sweden is 8.7 million. The prison system provides places for less than 5,000 persons, including 1,000 places for pre-trial detention. For some years, it has been fully occupied.

The published official statistics reveal practically nothing with regard to the impact of sentencing reform on sentencing practice. The government consciously refrained from financing any follow-up research. My personal guess is that the reform has helped to counter-balance the increased use of incarceration (see below) and that there has been a considerable 'hidden' redistribution of sanctions.

Over one million crimes are reported annually to the police. This figure does not include some minor traffic offences. Two-thirds of reported crimes are not cleared up. The number of convicted persons was 163,000 in 1988, and 167,000 in 1991. These figures include those who received a waiver of prosecution (which presupposes that a crime was committed), namely, 19,300 in 1988, and 17,700 in 1991. On the other hand, these figures do not include summary police fines for traffic and smuggling offences which amounted to 195,000 in 1988, and 218,000 in 1991. If the latter are excluded, the sentences were distributed as shown in Table 4.1.

The average daily prison population is at present approximately 55 per 100,000 population, which is a comparatively low figure. On the other hand, the reception rate is approaching 200 per 100,000 population, which is a remarkably high figure.

The criminal policy of the present government seems to aim at raising the average daily prison population by 20–25 per cent. The methods envisaged are primarily: (1) making the parole rules more restrictive, (2) returning to short imprisonment as the major sanction for aggravated drunken driving, and (3) increasing prison sentences for recidivists and some other types of offenders. To date, one piece of legislation has been adopted and came into force on 1 July 1993. The parole rules have been made more restrictive for

TABLE 4.1. *Sentence distribution in Sweden in 1988 and 1991*

	1988	1991
Prosecutorial fines	76,000	78,000
Court fines	30,000	32,000
Imprisonment	16,500	14,300[a]
Probation with imprisonment	900	600
Probation with contract care	300	300
Probation (other)	5,300	5,900
Conditional sentence	10,300	13,500
Commitment to special care	4,500	5,100
ALL	144,000	150,000

[a] Between 1988 and 1991, the number of imprisonment sentences for aggravated drunken driving decreased by 2,700. See n. 23.

the range of sentences between two months and two years. This will mean an increase in the prison population of 10–12 per cent. In addition, the courts are beginning to increase the use of imprisonment for aggravated drunken driving.[23] And a war on drugs is being pursued.[24]

None of this will change the fact that, by international standards, prison sentences in Sweden are short. Even in 1991, when imprisonment was comparatively rarely used for drunken driving, the median sentence was two months. Sentences up to four months account for 68 per cent, sentences up to six months for 78 per cent, sentences up to one year for 90 per cent, and sentences up to two years for more than 95 per cent, of the number of sentences to imprisonment. Until the recent parole 'reform', all these were released according to the general rule: obligatory parole after serving half

[23] In 1989 the incarceration rate was 72 per cent, accounting for one-third of the number of prison sentences, and one-tenth of the incarceration space. In 1990 the provision on drunken driving was amended (0.2 per mille alcohol in the blood is now the lower limit). A gloss in the bill suggested that ordinary sentencing rules should apply to a greater extent in the future. The courts immediately seized this opportunity. At its lowest (the first three months of 1991), the incarceration rate for aggravated drunken driving (in principle, 1.5 per mille or more) was 33 per cent. In 1991, the incarceration rate was 42 per cent. It is estimated to have been close to 50 per cent in 1992. The politicians and the public think this is too lenient. A legislative committee has recently proposed that the criteria for aggravated drunken driving should be widened and that imprisonment should be the standard sanction. Adoption of this proposal would probably lead to another 10 per cent rise in the prison population.

[24] Sixteen per cent of the prison sentences concern drug offences. But if we look at the severe sentences we get a different picture. More than 1 year, up to 2 years: 15 per cent. More than 2 years, up to 4 years: 38 per cent. More than 4 years: 54 per cent. In 1991 more than 4 years was imposed in 121 cases of drug offences, 47 cases of murder and manslaughter, 6 cases of aggravated assault, 9 cases of rape, and 37 cases of property crimes.

TABLE 4.2. *Sentence distribution in Sweden in 1987 and 1991 on all offences with penal value level up to one year imprisonment*

	Imprisonment (%)	Probation (%)	Conditional sentence (%)
1987	49	18	33
1991	41	18	41

Total numbers: 31,100 in 1987; 32,400 in 1991.

TABLE 4.3. *Sentence distribution in Sweden in 1987 and 1991 on all offences (excluding drunken driving and drug offences) with penal value level up to one year imprisonment*

	Imprisonment (%)	Probation (%)	Conditional sentence (%)
1987	37	19	44
1991	34	18	48

Total numbers: 21,300 in 1987; 22,500 in 1991.

time (but at least two months, and those sentenced to two months or less were, and still are, excluded from parole).

Let us look finally at the distribution between imprisonment, probation, and conditional sentence on offences with a penal-value level of up to one year imprisonment. It is here that we find the supposedly strong presumption against imprisonment (see Section 10, above, Step 7). How strong is it? A rough estimation gives the distributions set out in Table 4.2.

If we disregard drunken driving and drug offences by excluding the legislation outside the Criminal Code, we get the distributions shown in Table 4.3.

If this increased use of conditional sentence is a result of the sentencing reform, it is not without significance (1 per cent = 225 persons). Unfortunately, the figures for 1992 will probably show 36 per cent imprisonment.

The figures for property crimes generally (i.e. including sentences above the one-year penal-value line) are especially interesting (see Table 4.4).

As explained above, on this level the presumption against imprisonment is rebutted by reasons concerning previous criminality or the nature of the crime. The published statistics do not show what lies beneath the figures, but there is probably nothing much wrong with the use of previous

TABLE 4.4. *Sentence distribution in Sweden in 1987 and 1991 for all property offences*

	Imprisonment (%)[a]	Probation (%)	Conditional sentence (%)
1987	34	21	45
1991	33	19	48

Total numbers: 15,100 in 1987; 15,750 in 1991. The number of conditional sentences increased by 850.

[a] The figures for imprisonment include probation combined with imprisonment (434 cases in 1987, 328 in 1991).

Source: The statistical information for Tables 4.2–4.4 is derived from Lars Dolmen (ed.), *Crime Trends in Sweden 1988* (BRÅ-report 1990:4: Stockholm, 1990); *Rättsstatistisk årsbok 1988* (Statistiska centralbyrån: Stockholm, 1988); *Rättsstatistisk årsbok 1992* (Statistiska centralbyrån: Stockholm, 1992); Jan Ahlberg and Lars Dolmén, *Fängelsedomar 1975–1992* (BRÅ-PM 1992: 5: Stockholm, 1992).

criminality as a reason for imprisonment. The weak spot is 'the nature of the crime'. The bill refers to drunken driving, illegal possession of weapons, illegal hunting, illegal stay in the country, assault, violence against officials, and tax fraud. But sexual offences, driving without a permit, and drug offences have higher imprisonment rates than any of these. The substantial numbers come from assault and other violent conduct, drunken driving, and drug offences.

12. CONCLUSION

The new sentencing law is both revolutionary and leaves everything as it was. The proposed law could be accepted by Parliament because (1) it was not designed to bring about any significant change in the distribution of sanctions, and it was described as a codification of current practice; (2) the possibility of using more severe sentences for recidivists was retained; and (3) the possibility of using imprisonment on general-preventive grounds ('the nature of the crime') was retained. There is nevertheless reason to believe that it has marginally helped to keep the level of repression down. Certainly, it is not responsible for increasing repression.

The great advantages of the reform lie elsewhere, however. We now have a number of fairly detailed legal provisions and a legal structure where we earlier had a black box. Legal argumentation regarding matters of sentencing suddenly became acceptable. It is now possible to detect and attack (unwarranted) disparity. Within a few years, the Supreme Court has delivered an impressive number of precedents, primarily concerning choice of sanction (not measurement of punishment).[25] The courts have been forced to be more explicit in their reasoning, and the advocates have new defence weapons. For many individuals, and for the promotion of justice, the sentencing reform is of great value.

There is no reason to believe that the work of the Penal System Committee (see Section 3, above) will lead to any dramatic changes in the present sentencing framework. The main task of the Committee is to propose new alternatives to imprisonment, electronic tagging being one seriously contemplated measure. Somewhat confusingly, the present government is both for less and for more use of imprisonment. As far as the public is concerned, there is some recent research suggesting that apart from cases involving drunken driving there is no significant difference between court practice and the opinions of so-called ordinary people (if they are confronted with all the details of the case).

---

[25] Unfortunately, a couple of these judgments are less loyal to the spirit of the reform than one had reason to expect.

5

Sentencing Reform: England and Wales

D. A. THOMAS

1. THE BACKGROUND: THE CRIMINAL JUSTICE ACT 1948

The development of the modern English sentencing system begins with the Criminal Justice Act 1948.[1] This statute did away with the lingering traces of nineteenth-century sentencing, abolishing penal servitude, imprisonment with hard labour and whipping, and removed remaining restrictions on the power to impose fines in cases of felony. It set out the statutory law of sentencing (except for maximum penalties) in thirty straightforward sections and two short schedules. The Act stated no philosophy; sentencers were left with the choice between the traditional punitive sanctions of imprisonment (which absorbed the former sentence of penal servitude) and fines, on the one hand, and a variety of measures intended to influence or control the offender's future behaviour—probation, detention in a detention centre, attendance at an attendance centre, Borstal training, corrective training, and preventive detention. Of these, detention in a detention centre, attendance at an attendance centre, and corrective training were new; probation, Borstal training, and preventive detention had been available to the courts for forty years. The background to the 1948 Act, which had originally been introduced as a parliamentary bill in 1938, was the relatively long period of stability in the penal system between the wars, when the daily average prison population varied between about 10,000 and about 12,000. Unlike most subsequent Criminal Justice Acts, the 1948 Act was not a crisis measure; it modernized a body of legislation which had been enacted piecemeal over the previous hundred years, and made a few marginal innovations. It survived, without substantial modification, for almost twenty years.

2. THE CRIMINAL JUSTICE ACT 1961

The next significant piece of sentencing legislation was enacted in 1961. The main purpose of the Criminal Justice Act 1961 was to encourage the use of

---

[1] For an account of the earlier development of the structure of the English sentencing system, see D. Thomas, *The Penal Equation* (Cambridge, 1978) and *Constraints of Judgement* (Cambridge, 1979).

Borstal training for offenders under 21 at the expense of imprisonment. The Act raised the minimum age for imprisonment from 15 to 17, extended the power to order the detention of juveniles guilty of serious offences under section 53(2) of the Children and Young Persons Act 1933 to all offences punishable with fourteen years' imprisonment, and restricted the power of a court to impose imprisonment on an offender under the age of 21 by reference to the length of the sentence. The scheme of the Act was that for an offence justifying a sentence of up to six months, the normal custodial sentence on a young offender would be detention in a detention centre, for an offence justifying a sentence of more than six months and less than three years, the sentence would normally be Borstal training, and a sentence of imprisonment would be permissible (with certain exceptions) only if the offence warranted a sentence of three years or more. Although the Act contained provision for the abolition of the power to impose a sentence of imprisonment of up to six months on a young offender, this provision was never implemented as the necessary detention centres were never built.

The effect of the Act was to change the way in which the sentence of Borstal training was viewed by the courts. Previously seen as a therapeutic sentence to be used selectively for those offenders who were considered suitable for the sentence, in the hope that a period of training would lead to 'reformation and the prevention of crime', the sentence was frequently imposed on those convicted of relatively minor offences which would not have been considered sufficiently serious to warrant an equivalent period of imprisonment. Under the Criminal Justice Act 1961, Borstal training became a dual-purpose sentence, used in some cases on the old principle as a therapeutic sentence unrestricted by concepts of proportionality between offence and sentence, and in others as a punitive sentence awarded by reference to the gravity of the offence and without regard to the training needs of the individual offender.[2]

The 1961 Act was never popular with the judiciary; its historical significance in the context of the present discussion is that it was the first serious attempt to control by legislation the exercise of the discretion in sentencing which judges had become accustomed to think of as their own prerogative. It may be that the idea of Borstal training, once seen as the jewel in the crown of the English penal system, had had its day by the 1960s in any event, but the 1961 legislation was an important factor in the decline of its perceived success, although it survived for a further twenty years.

3. THE CRIMINAL JUSTICE ACT 1967

By the early 1960s the optimistic view of the future of the penal system which was reflected in the 1961 legislation began to give way to a realization

---

[2] See D. Thomas, *Principles of Sentencing*, 1st edn. (London, 1970), 236–46.

that serious problems lay ahead.[3] The incidence of reported crime had increased steadily since the end of the Second World War, and the prison population, which had declined sharply in the last two decades of the nineteenth century and remained relatively stable between the wars, had maintained a constant rate of increase since the end of the war. By 1964, it had reached the level from which it had declined in 1880 and was about double the level of 1947. A Royal Commission was appointed to inquire into the penal system; sadly it failed to report and the chance of a clearly articulated penal strategy was lost.[4] Instead, Parliament enacted the Criminal Justice Act 1967, the first of many omnibus Criminal Justice Acts dealing with a variety of subjects. As well as sentencing, the Act dealt with committal proceedings, proof of intent in criminal cases, proof by written statements, alibi defences, majority verdicts, bail, legal aid, and other matters. Its major innovations in relation to sentencing were the introduction of the suspended sentence and discretionary parole. Courts were empowered to suspend any sentence of imprisonment not exceeding two years, and required to suspend any sentence of imprisonment which did not exceed six months unless the case fell within one of a number of exceptions (offenders convicted of offences involving violence, or with a previous custodial sentence, were the most important exceptions). The parole system allowed a prisoner to be released after serving one-third of his sentence or twelve months, whichever was the longer; it effectively applied to those sentenced to more than eighteen months. All prisoners continued to be entitled to the remission of one-third of the sentence pronounced by the court. Other changes made by the Act were the abolition of preventive detention and its resurrection as the extended sentence, the abolition of corrective training, and the enactment of a provision, never to be brought into force, allowing the Home Secretary to require a court to consider a social inquiry report before passing a custodial sentence of a specified kind.

Following the enactment of the Criminal Justice Act 1967, the prison population fell briefly, but soon resumed the steady increase which had been evident for the previous two decades. The intervals between statutes affecting sentencing became shorter. The Criminal Justice Act 1972 introduced community-service orders and deferment of sentence, and empowered courts to make compensation orders. The obligation to suspend sentences of imprisonment of not more than six months was repealed. Most legislation dealing with the sentencing powers of the courts was consolidated in the Powers of Criminal Courts Act 1973; the Criminal Law Act 1977 included a provision (not brought into force until 1982) allowing a court to suspend a sentence of imprisonment in part. Despite these inno-

---

[3] The attitude of the day is well captured in the White Paper, *Penal Practice in a Changing Society* (Cmnd. 645; London, 1959).

[4] The Royal Commission published a number of volumes of evidence, but no report: see *Royal Commission on the Penal System in England and Wales, Written Evidence* (1967).

vations, the prison population continued to increase steadily, and by 1980 prison overcrowding began to be seen as a major national crisis calling for urgent remedial action.

4. JUDICIAL INITIATIVES

Two non-statutory developments of this period should be mentioned. The first was the appointment of Lord Lane to the office of Lord Chief Justice. His immediate predecessor had made no significant contribution to solving the problems which faced the judiciary as a consequence of the growth of the prison population, but Lord Lane, in one of his first judgments as Chief Justice, gave notice that a rethinking of judicial sentencing practice was in contemplation; a few months later, in giving judgment in the case of *Bashir Begum Bibi*[5] and a series of related cases, he indicated that a reduction in the conventional levels of sentencing in certain types of cases should be effected by judges and magistrates. Although there was room for criticism of the details of the guidance given in these cases, the *Bibi* initiative produced a significant reduction in average sentence lengths until it was submerged by further legislative developments.

At about the same time, the Judicial Studies Board was established.[6] Judicial seminars on sentencing had begun to be held in 1970; by the mid-1970s a regular annual seminar for judges of the Crown Court had become an established event. Individual judges and recorders would be expected to attend such a seminar every five years. The original Judicial Studies Board focused exclusively on criminal matters; by 1982 it offered an induction seminar for those about to be approved to sit as assistant recorders, the bottom rung on the ladder leading to a permanent judicial appointment, and a refresher seminar for experienced circuit judges and recorders. The principal concentration of the seminars was sentencing, although the range of topics covered was quickly expanded to include aspects of evidence and procedure, and substantive criminal law. The Board also began in 1983 to publish a Bulletin, distributed to all judges and recorders of the Crown Court, which dealt with legislation and case-law relating to sentencing, and other similar material.[7] The system of judicial studies was extended by the institution of annual day seminars on each circuit, in which sentencing

---

[5] (1980) 2 Cr. App. R. (S.) 177. The other cases, intended to exemplify what was to be the new approach to custodial sentences, are *Murray, Eastlake, Ingham, Jones, Fox, McCann, Brewster, Robinson*, and *Freeman*, all reported at (1980) 2 Cr. App. R. (S.) 181–96.

[6] The impetus for the creation of the Judicial Studies Board came from a Working Party under the Chairmanship of Lord Justice Bridge; see *Judicial Studies and Information, Report of the Working Party* (Home Office and Lord Chancellor's Department: London, 1978).

[7] Bulletin of the Judicial Studies Board; three issues annually, published by the Judicial Studies Board, 14 Little St James St, London.

exercises and discussions of sentencing problems were prominent. By the mid-1980s, a pattern of judicial studies for judges exercising criminal jurisdiction was in effect. The newcomer was required to take part in an induction programme, consisting of the induction seminar, visits to a prison and an institution for young offenders, and some contact with the probation service. This would be followed by what was in effect a probationary period of part-time service as an assistant recorder, sitting for about three working weeks a year; after three years as an assistant recorder, or thereabouts, appointment to a recordership would follow, again involving a commitment to sit for a period of a few weeks a year while continuing for the rest of the year in legal practice. (Those who were not appointed to recorderships after an appropriate interval would cease to sit as assistant recorders and forget ambitions to become judges.) A full-time judicial appointment, either as a circuit judge or a High Court judge of the Queen's Bench Division, would not normally be made unless the candidate had gone through the processes leading to appointment as a recorder; the days when a Chancery silk would find himself suddenly appointed to be a High Court judge and trying serious criminal cases with no previous experience of the criminal law were over. Following appointment as a recorder or full-time circuit judge, the Crown Court sentencer would continue to attend residential seminars every five years and an annual one-day circuit seminar, as well as receive the increasingly elaborate literature prepared by the Board. By 1985, the idea of judicial studies, which had been received with hostility in some judicial quarters,[8] was well established; the membership of the Judicial Studies Board was expanded and its activities extended to civil and family matters, the work of tribunals, and the supervision of the training of lay magistrates. The work of the original Board was carried on by what became the Criminal Committee.[9]

It may be justifiable to devote a sentence or two to another development of this period. Although the Court of Appeal (Criminal Division) and its predecessor, the Court of Criminal Appeal, had exercised jurisdiction to review sentences passed in the higher criminal courts since 1908, there had been no adequate reporting of decisions on sentencing. The major series of law reports ignored the topic; summaries of selected decisions appeared in the *Criminal Law Review*. This meant that there was no effective vehicle for the communication of sentencing policy from the Court of Appeal to the judges of the Crown Court, and no accessible material for critical analysis of the Court of Appeal's decisions. Apart from a textbook[10] based on a study

[8] See P. Devlin, *The Judge* (Oxford,1979), 34–53. (The author had retired from the bench when this book was written.)
[9] The work of the Board is described in detail in its Report for the years 1987–1991; see Judicial Studies Board, *Report for 1987–1991* (HMSO: London.)
[10] D. Thomas, *Principles of Sentencing* (London, 1970 and 1979).

of the unreported decisions of the Court of Appeal, first published in 1970 and in a second edition in 1979, practitioners and sentencers had little to rely on in preparing mitigation or appeals, or in deciding on sentence, other than a general sense of what was conventional. Systematic reporting of selected sentencing decisions began in 1979,[11] supplemented in 1982 by a looseleaf work[12] collecting decisions under various headings and themes. Although the initial reaction of the judiciary to this innovation was hesitant, within a few years it was common to find reported decisions on sentence cited in decisions of the Court of Appeal[13] (usually with a warning that they were not binding precedents) and the looseleaf work had been provided, in a special binder, to all full-time judges of the Crown Court.

The combination of an activist Lord Chief Justice and the development of improved means of communicating matters related to sentencing policy might have led to some amelioration of the basic problem of the growth of the prison population, if some reasonable time had been allowed; the sentencing habits of upwards of 1,000 judges of the Crown Court and 25,000 lay magistrates could not be changed overnight. Any chances that this would be achieved by judicial self-regulation were dashed by a sequence of enactments which constantly changed the statutory framework and rendered the decisions made by sentencers increasingly meaningless.

5. THE CRIMINAL JUSTICE ACT 1982

The first proposal for a drastic statutory solution to the underlying problem was contained in a review of the parole system published in 1981;[14] it was suggested that all offenders sentenced to custody should be released on licence after serving one-third of the sentence imposed by the court. This proposal was abandoned after a combination of judicial and political opposition; in its place the government brought into force in 1982 the partly suspended sentence, which had remained in limbo since it had been created (as a result of back-bench initiative) by the Criminal Law Act 1977 (the back-bencher concerned was by now Minister of State at the Home Office). Although the partly suspended sentence was rarely used in practice,[15] its implementation (and the immediate amendment of the relevant legislation in the Criminal Justice Act 1982) cut across the judicial initiatives taken in 1980. By providing a temptation to the Court of Appeal to uphold a sen-

[11] The Criminal Appeal Reports (Sentencing) (London, 1979–date).
[12] D. Thomas, *Current Sentencing Practice* (London, 1982–date).
[13] For one example among many, see *Green* (1986) 8 Cr. App. R. (S.) 284.
[14] Home Office, *Review of Parole in England and Wales* (1981).
[15] Just over 1,000 defendants sentenced in the Crown Court in 1991 were dealt with by means of a partly suspended sentence, out of a total of 88,000. See *Criminal Statistics* (England and Wales) for 1991, Supplementary Volume 1, Proceedings in the Crown Court.

tence in principle while releasing the offender on the basis of the time served in custody, it effectively brought to an end the hopes for a more ambitious review of judicial sentencing practice which Lord Lane's early decisions had created.

6. PAROLE CHANGES

A further major blow to the prospect of judicial self-regulation was the implementation of section 33 of the Criminal Justice Act 1982, extending the scope of the parole system. The original parole system, introduced by the 1967 Act, applied to a relatively limited number of prisoners. Eligibility for release on licence was not achieved until the prisoner had served one-third of his sentence or twelve months, whichever was the greater; all prisoners were entitled to the remission of the final third of their sentences. The shortest sentence under which a prisoner could qualify for parole under the original scheme was about twenty months; for an offender sentenced to two years' imprisonment, release on licence at the earliest possible moment meant the difference between twelve months and sixteen months in custody. (The difference was less if he had spent time in custody on remand, as that time would count towards the sixteen months but not the twelve.) The 1982 Act contained a provision (section 33) allowing the Home Secretary to reduce the twelve-month minimum period (the 'specified period') which an offender was required to serve before he could be considered for release on licence; this power was exercised by the Eligibility for Release on Licence Order 1983, which reduced the specified period to six months. The result was that a large number of prisoners sentenced to shorter terms of imprisonment became eligible for parole, and a high proportion—approaching 80 per cent—of those who were eligible were released. The new scheme worked in an arbitrary way. Under the revised scheme, a prisoner became eligible for release after serving one-third of the sentence or six months, whichever was the greater; remission of one-third of the sentence remained an entitlement. What this meant in practice (given the high rate of release) was that there was no significant difference between sentences of nine months, twelve months, fifteen months, and eighteen months' imprisonment—all would in most cases result in six months in custody. The effective difference between a sentence of nine months' imprisonment and two years' imprisonment was reduced to two months (nine months meant six months in custody, two years meant eight months in most cases).

The arbitrariness of the new scheme was enhanced by the interaction between the rules governing eligibility for release on licence and the treatment of time spent in custody on remand before sentence. Time spent in custody on remand counted towards the one-third of the sentence that the prisoner was required to serve, but not towards the six months; it also counted towards the two-thirds of the sentence which had to be served before remission of the final third of the sentence could be claimed. The combination of these rules produced a series of anomalies which turned the whole system of custodial sentencing into a lottery. If two co-defendants, guilty of the same crime, were each sentenced to eighteen months' imprisonment, one after spending six months in custody on remand and the other after being on bail, they would each serve a further six months in custody after sentence; one man's sentence would be twice as long as the other's, although the court had adjudged their culpability to be equal. An offender sentenced to fifteen months after spending a little more than three months in custody on remand would find that his time in custody before sentence actually lengthened his time in custody after sentence. He would become eligible for release on licence after serving six months from the date of sentence, but as his time on remand brought his remission date to within thirty days of his eligibility date, he would not be released as his licence would have lasted for less than thirty days, and it was not the policy to release prisoners on a licence of less than thirty days. His more fortunate co-defendant sentenced to the same term after being on bail would not face this obstacle, and would be likely to be released six months after sentence, leaving his accomplice, already in custody for nine months, to serve another month.

There is no purpose in detailing the further complications which arose from the application of these rules to prisoners sentenced to partly suspended sentences, beyond mentioning that it was often the case that a partly suspended sentence was more severe in its potential effect than an ordinary sentence of the same length. Despite an attempt to rationalize the system by extending the remission of sentences of up to twelve months to one-half (and thereby creating further anomalies), the parole system had lost much of its credibility and the Carlisle Committee[16] recommended a substantial reduction in its scope. The extension of the parole system also brought to an end any serious interest on the part of the judiciary in the realignment of general sentencing conventions, once the judiciary generally became aware of the situation. As the length of the sentence passed by the court made little difference to the time served by the offender in the vast majority of cases, there was no point in seeking to accomplish a complex and difficult process which would have been unpopular with the general public, who remained largely unaware of the change in the real meaning of a sentence of a particular length. Ironically, the extension of the parole system brought no relief to the underlying problem; after a brief downturn, the prison population continued to grow at an increased rate.

[16] *The Parole System in England and Wales: Report of the Review Committee* (Chairman: Lord Carlisle of Bucklow QC) (Cm. 532; London, 1988).

7. STATUTORY CRITERIA

A second important development in sentencing legislation made by the Criminal Justice Act 1982 was the introduction of statutory criteria for sentencing, limited to the imposition of custodial sentences on young offenders. The Act rearranged the powers of the courts to pass custodial sentences on offenders under 21; the sentence of Borstal training was replaced by youth custody, and Borstal institutions were renamed accordingly. The new sentence was similar in form to a sentence of imprisonment; those sentenced to youth custody would be eligible for release after serving the same portions of their sentences as an adult sentenced to imprisonment, but with the additional requirement of supervision for a period of time governed by statutory provisions of remarkable complexity. The introduction of the statutory criteria for the imposition of the sentence which eventually became section 1(4) of the 1982 Act was not government policy and they were not included in the original bill; they were enacted as a result of a back-bench initiative. The original criteria were written in very broad language. A court was prohibited from imposing a custodial sentence (youth custody or detention-centre order) on an offender under 21, unless it was of the opinion that no other method of dealing with him was appropriate because it appeared to the court that 'he is unable or unwilling to respond to non-custodial penalties or because a custodial sentence is necessary for the protection of the public or because the offence was so serious that a non-custodial sentence cannot be justified'. The enactment of the criteria made little impact on sentencing practice, and the proportionate use by the courts of custodial sentences for offenders in the relevant age group increased marginally in the years immediately following the implementation of the legislation. The Court of Appeal was rarely invited to consider the meaning of the new provisions in the first two years after they came into effect, and lay magistrates appeared to be unaware of their existence, despite a statutory obligation on magistrates' courts to identify the criterion by which a custodial sentence was justified.[17]

8. THE CRIMINAL JUSTICE ACT 1988

The criteria were revised in the Criminal Justice Act 1988, which amended section 1(4) of the Criminal Justice Act 1982 and inserted a new section 1(4A). To qualify for a custodial sentence on the first ground, the offender was required to have a history of failure to respond to non-custodial measures, in addition to being unwilling or unable to respond to them; the

---

[17] See E. Burney, *Sentencing Young People: What Went Wrong with the Criminal Justice Act 1982* (Aldershot, 1985).

criterion of public protection was made specific to the individual offender and the nature of the harm from which the public required protection was limited to 'serious harm'. The criterion of seriousness was restricted by an amendment whose effect was to require the court to consider one offence only for the purpose of the criterion, even though the offender had committed many others (this interpretation of the earlier version of the criterion had earlier been adopted by the Court of Appeal).[18]

The effect of the enactment of the revised criteria, which came into effect in October 1988, is difficult to assess; they were followed by a noticeable downturn in the proportionate use of custodial sentences for offenders in the relevant age group, but a similar downturn occurred in the proportionate use of custodial sentences for adult offenders, which were not controlled by statutory criteria. There is no doubt that the judiciary were fully aware of the new provisions, as a result of the efforts of the Judicial Studies Board; the legal profession were more ready to use them as the basis of arguments on appeals, and cases on the meaning of the new criteria began to come before the Court of Appeal frequently within a few months.[19]

The apparent success of the statutory criteria in reducing the use of custody for young offenders persuaded various pressure groups that the way to control the growth of the prison population was to extend them to sentences of imprisonment passed on adults.[20] The assumed prerogative of the judiciary to determine sentencing policy without statutory or other forms of intervention had come increasingly under question,[21] and the respect in which the judiciary were held by the public had been damaged by particular decisions in a small number of cases. The case for a sentencing council had been powerfully argued[22] and had gained a wide range of acceptance, but a proposal to create such a body would undoubtedly have met strong opposition from the higher judiciary (as had the earlier relatively harmless proposal to require the Judicial Studies Board to publish guideline decisions of the Court of Appeal, possibly because it was seen as the first step towards turning the Board into a sentencing council). Extending the statutory criteria for the imposition of custodial sentences on young offenders to adults would suffer from one obvious drawback, as a glance at the *Prison Statistics* made clear. The vast majority of adults sentenced to imprisonment would easily satisfy the first criterion for the imposition of a

[18] See *Davison* (1989) 11 Cr. App. R. (S.) 570; *Scott* (1990) 12 Cr. App. R. (S.) 23.
[19] See for instance *Littler and others* (1990) 12 Cr. App. R. (S.) 143; *Marsden* (1990) 12 Cr. App. R. (S.) 274.
[20] See, in particular, publications of the Penal Affairs Consortium, *Criteria for Imprisonment* and *A Joint Manifesto for Penal Reform* (both 1989).
[21] Principally in the writings of A. Ashworth: see, in particular, *Sentencing and Penal Policy* (London, 1983), chs. 2 and 3.
[22] See ibid. 447–51. An amendment to the Criminal Justice Bill which would have created a sentencing council was defeated in the House of Lords in March 1991.

custodial sentence, 'he has a history of failure to respond to non-custodial penalties and is unable or unwilling to respond to them', and applying the criteria to adults would produce no significant change in the use of custody. The only strategy which would be likely to reduce the use of custody for adults was one in which the recidivist who repeatedly committed offences which were not in themselves in the first order of gravity was not imprisoned.

Just as in 1967 the introduction of discretionary parole was made presentable by the then still respectable theory that prisoners improved while undergoing imprisonment, and might reach their peak before serving two-thirds of their sentence, the introduction of the principle that persistent offenders should continue to be subject to community sanctions without the risk of imprisonment if they complied with the requirements of the community sanction, while continuing to offend, required some justification other than expediency. This lay conveniently at hand in the newly fashionable desert theory which had attracted the support of influential academic writers on penology and sentencing.[23] The basic idea of desert theory, that the punishment of an offender should be proportionate to his crime, was hardly a new one; it had formed the basis of articulated judicial sentencing policy, with recognized exceptions, for many years. To lawyers it was recognizable as the basis of the tariff, itself a reasonably complex body of principle based on case-law and convention. The primary objection to the proposal to enact the principle into law was not that it was revolutionary but that it was redundant, and that the manner in which it was carried out would create more problems than it would solve.

9. THE CRIMINAL JUSTICE ACT 1991

The Criminal Justice Bill introduced in 1990 followed closely the proposals set out in the White Paper, *Crime, Justice and Protecting the Public*.[24] A framework of rules for the imposition of custodial sentences was proposed which differentiated between cases in which the offender (necessarily over the age of 21) was convicted of an offence triable only on indictment and had previously served a sentence of imprisonment; those in which the offender was convicted of an offence triable only on indictment and had not previously served a sentence of imprisonment; those in which the offender was over 21 and was convicted of an either way offence; and those in which

[23] See, in particular, A. von Hirsch, *Past or Future Crimes* (Manchester, 1986); for an illustration of the interaction of American and English thinking on sentencing reform, see the various essays in K. Pease and M. Wasik, *Sentencing Reform: Guidance or Guidelines* (Manchester, 1987).

[24] *Crime, Justice and Protecting the Public* (Cm. 965; London, 1990).

the offender was under 21 and was convicted of an either way offence. Previous convictions and previous sentences were to be disregarded in assessing the seriousness of an offence. The length of a custodial sentence was to be commensurate with the seriousness of the offence or offences concerned, with no scope for mitigation on the grounds of personal considerations not directly related to the offence. The question whether a custodial sentence could be justified on the grounds of the seriousness of the offence was to be judged by reference to one offence only, or at most two offences, considered in combination, however many offences had been committed. Similar provisions were made with respect to what were now to be known as community orders—probation orders, community-service orders, and the new combination orders. Any community order was to be justified on the grounds of the seriousness of the offence (evaluated according to the complex rules of the Act, considering only two offences); the offender's needs were a subsidiary consideration. A new system of unit fines was proposed for the magistrates' courts.

The bill did away with most of the innovations of 1967; the extended sentence was abolished, discretionary parole was restricted to a limited class of cases (prisoners sentenced to a custodial sentence of four years or more would be eligible for discretionary release after serving between half and two-thirds of their sentence, otherwise release would be a matter of entitlement after serving half of the sentence, subject to licence in some cases and the possibility of return to custody in the event of a further offence); the suspended sentence was restricted to cases involving 'exceptional circumstances'.

Mercifully, major changes were made (some at a very late stage) as the bill passed through Parliament. In particular, the complex criteria for custodial sentences, which would have been totally unworkable in practice, were simplified, and a revised set of criteria for all custodial sentences was enacted. Specific provision allowing the court to mitigate a sentence on the grounds of factors not directly related to the offence was introduced. The government refused to abandon the rule that the criterion of seriousness for the imposition of a custodial sentence or a community order (as opposed to the determination of the length of a custodial sentence, or the restrictiveness of a community order) must be judged by reference to two offences only, but made some concession to those who pointed out the difficulties that this would cause in the case of multiple offences by enacting section 29(2), allowing the court to take account of 'aggravating factors of an offence . . . disclosed by the circumstances of other offences committed by the offender'.

In the form in which it was enacted, the Criminal Justice Act 1991 set out criteria for the impositon of a custodial sentence, and for determining the length of a custodial sentence. A court was allowed to impose a custodial sentence only if the offence committed by the offender, considered in isolation or combination with one other offence for which he was to be sentenced at the same time, was so serious that only a custodial sentence could be justified for the offence.[25] No definition or explanation of the concept of seriousness was offered, but it was provided that a court in assessing the seriousness of an offence might have regard only to the circumstances of the offence[26] (as opposed to information about the offender) and in particular that previous convictions and the offender's response to previous sentences must be disregarded for this purpose.[27] A court dealing with an offender for an either way offence was required to obtain a pre-sentence report prepared by the probation service before imposing a custodial sentence, whether it considered such a report likely to be helpful or not.[28] In determining the length of a custodial sentence, the court was required to impose a sentence which was commensurate with the seriousness of all the offences for which the offender was being sentenced.[29] Again, previous convictions were to be disregarded in assessing the seriousness of the offences. In relation to the imposition of a custodial sentence, and the determination of the length of a custodial sentence, the court was allowed to take account of 'aggravating factors of an offence . . . disclosed by the circumstances of other offences committed by the offender'.[30] Courts were allowed to mitigate a sentence by reference to any factors which were considered relevant in mitigation.[31] Special provision was made for offenders guilty of violent or sexual offences.[32]

Corresponding rules were enacted to govern the imposition of community orders. A court was required to be satisfied that a community order was justified by the seriousness of the offence, again considered in isolation or combination with one other offence for which he was to be sentenced at the same time, that the proposed order was the most suitable for the offender, and that the restrictions on liberty involved in the order were commensurate with the seriousness of the offences.[33] The restrictions on considering previous convictions and response to previous sentences applied in this context as in the case of custodial sentences.

The unit fine system was enacted so as to apply only to the magistrates' courts.[34] In determining the amount of a fine in all but a few exceptional cases, the court was required to determine the number of units which was commensurate with seriousness of the offence or offences concerned, and then calculate the value of the unit in the case of the defendant.

The restrictions on considering previous convictions applied in this context. The unit was to represent the offender's weekly disposable income; it would be at least £4 in the case of an adult and never more than £100. Rules

[25] Section 1(2)(a).   [26] Section 3(3).   [27] Section 29(1).
[28] Section 3(1).   [29] Section 2(2)(a).   [30] Section 29(2).   [31] Section 28.
[32] Section 1(2)(b) and 2(2)(b).   [33] Section 6.   [34] Section 18.

were made under the authority of the Act which required the court to apply the formula I-E/3.[35] The court was to start with the offender's net weekly income, deduct certain standard allowances for housing costs, dependents, and so forth, and divide the result by three to produce the value of the unit. This was then multiplied by the number of units to produce the amount of the fine.

The three Criminal Justice Acts of 1982, 1988, and 1991 were not the only statutes affecting sentencing enacted during recent years. Legislation dealing with specialized aspects of sentencing includes the Drug Trafficking Offences Act 1986, dealing with the confiscation of the proceeds of drug trafficking, and the Football Spectators Act 1989, designed to protect Europe from the invasion of English football hooligans. While Parliament was busy with the Criminal Justice Act 1991, based on the principle of just deserts and the insignificance of previous offences, it was also enacting the Road Traffic Act 1991, reinforcing the principle that disqualification from driving, a form of punishment in the community, should be awarded on the basis of penalty points accumulated by successive convictions. The result was that a magistrates' court dealing with a traffic offence was required to disregard the offender's previous offences in determining the amount of his fine (or the units on which it was based) and then required to take them into account in determining whether there was an obligation to disqualify him.

10. THE STATUTORY FRAMEWORK

Anyone coming to the study of English sentencing law for the first time would be struck by the quantity and complexity of the legislation involved. The maximum penalties for criminal offences are scattered among a large number of criminal statutes dating back in some cases to 1861; even in 1861 the lack of any logical structure or coherence in their arrangement was obvious,[36] and matters have become worse rather than better. It has been the habit of Parliament to change maximum penalties for individual offences in a piecemeal manner, usually by increasing them in response to a particular clamour, occasionally by reducing them. The Criminal Justice Act 1991 increased the maximum sentences for bomb hoaxing and offences in connection with badgers, and reduced the maximum sentences for theft and burglary of non-residential premises. This was intended in some way to indicate a legislative view that offences against property were now to be treated as relatively less serious and offences of violence more so, but the

---

[35] Magistrates Courts (Unit Fines) Rules 1992 (S.I. 1992 No. 1856).

[36] See C. Greaves, *The Criminal Law Consolidation and Amendment Acts* (London, 1862), preface, p. xlv.

message is easily confused when it is remembered that the maximum sentence for obtaining by deception remains what it was previously (ten years, as opposed to the new maximum of seven years for theft) and the maximum sentence for handling property stolen from a woman (or anyone else) is longer (fourteen years) than the maximum for indecent assault (ten years). The maximum sentence for recklessly damaging a man's spectacles (if they are very expensive) is ten years (criminal damage); for recklessly knocking out his eye (malicious wounding) five years.

Other anomalies abound: a man who fondles the breasts of a 15-year-old girl with her consent commits an indecent assault, punishable with ten years' imprisonment; if he goes further and has sexual intercourse with her with her consent, he is guilty of unlawful sexual intercourse, an offence punishable with a maximum of two years' imprisonment. A 16-year-old offender may be sentenced to up to fourteen years' detention for handling stolen property but not more than twelve months for inflicting grievous bodily harm.

In dealing with maximum penalty legislation, Parliament seems often to be at cross-purposes with itself; concern with the apparent increase of 'joy-riding' by young offenders led in 1992 to the Aggravated Vehicle Taking Act 1992, which creates a new offence consisting, *inter alia*, of causing injury by driving a vehicle which has been taken unlawfully (punishable with two years' imprisonment) and causing death by driving a vehicle which has been taken unlawfully, punishable with five years' imprisonment. This legislation came into force on 1 April 1992 and applies to incidents occurring on or after that date; on 1 October 1992 the Criminal Justice Act 1991 came into effect, reducing the maximum term of custody which could be imposed on an offender under the age of 18 (other than for an offence punishable with fourteen years' imprisonment) to twelve months' detention in a young offender institution, however many offences have been committed. Proposals for a comprehensive review of the law relating to maximum penalties were made by the Advisory Council on the Penal System in 1978[37] and in the Law Commission's Draft Criminal Code in 1989.[38] Both sets of proposals are gathering dust.

Apart from the question of maximum sentences, the piecemeal approach to sentencing law reform which has characterized English sentencing legislation since 1948 has resulted in a maze of statutory provisions spread among a large number of statutes, many of them amended so frequently that they bear little or no relationship to the provision as originally enacted. It is often difficult to be confident of the correct text of a statutory provision

[37] Advisory Council on the Penal System, *Sentences of Imprisonment: A Review of Maximum Penalties* (1978).
[38] The Law Commission, *A Criminal Code for England and Wales* (Law Com. No. 177; 1989).

(let alone its interpretation), and the problem of establishing what law applies in a given case is made more difficult by the fact that statutory provisions are often enacted but not brought into force, or brought into force on different dates, or with modifications. Parliament in 1988 enacted a new statutory code under which victims of violent crime would be given a statutory right to compensation from public funds (as opposed to the *ex gratia* system established in 1964). The relevant provisions have not yet been brought into force. The failure to implement the partly suspended sentence for five years after it was enacted may be explained on the basis that it was not a government initiative; but this cannot be said of the curfew order, enacted in the Criminal Justice Act 1991[39] as a significant element in the government's scheme of community penalties but not brought into force for the time being, and probably abandoned permanently.

The preference for long Criminal Justice Bills dealing with a variety of different topics, which tend to increase in length as they pass through the Parliament and Ministers and others have second or further thoughts, or one Minister is replaced by another, means that the finished legislation is often technically deficient in detail and requires instant amendment or patching up. The unit fine system, introduced by the Criminal Justice Act 1991, was not intended to operate in the Crown Court; unfortunately the designers of the Act did not fully appreciate the existence of a number of situations in which the Crown Court was bound to sentence as if it were a magistrates' court and, in trying to solve this problem by means of a limitation in the relevant Commencement Order,[40] created a further difficulty—did the unit fine system apply on an appeal to the Crown Court from a sentence passed by the magistrates' court?

The process of amending sentencing legislation would be easier to understand if parliamentary draftsmen would set out the amended provision as it is intended to read in a schedule, rather than just scattering amendments to a particular provision in different places in the amending statute, leaving the reader to piece them together for himself; this might also help to avoid mistakes in the drafting of the Act itself.[41]

An illustration of the practical problems which the sentencer faces as a result of this aggregation of legislation may be helpful. I have already referred to the illogicality which confronted lay magistrates daily in applying the Criminal Justice Act 1991 and the Road Traffic Act 1991 to traffic cases; one statute required them to ignore previous convictions for the purpose of one part of the sentence and the other required them to take

[39] By section 12.

[40] Criminal Justice Act 1991 (Commencement No. 3) Order 1992, S.I. 1992 No. 333.

[41] Criminal Justice Act 1991 makes three separate amendments to the Magistrates' Courts Act 1980 section 36, by section 17(2)(a), schedule 8 para. 6(1)(c), and schedule 13.

them into account for the purpose of another, although both parts were punitive in intention.

This is child's play compared to the not uncommon situation of a court—probably a youth court consisting of lay magistrates—dealing with a 16-year-old for a relatively serious offence. Suppose the court has decided that the case falls just short of a custodial sentence and that supervision of the offender under a community order is the best way to deal with him. The first step is to decide between a probation order and a supervision order, both of which are available. The differences between the two types of order are that in the case of a probation order the offender must consent (strictly speaking, express his willingness to comply with) to the whole of the order including any particular requirements, while consent is not necessary in the case of a supervision order except in relation to certain types of requirements; under a probation order supervision must be by a probation officer, while under a supervision order it may be by either a probation officer or a social worker; in the case of a probation order but not a supervision order the court must be of the opinion that supervision is desirable in the interests of securing the rehabilitation of the offender or protecting the public from harm from him, or preventing the commission by him of further offences; in the case of a probation order the court may impose special requirements on those convicted of sexual offences or those dependent on drugs or alcohol; in the case of a probation order, the sanction for failure to comply with the order may include a custodial sentence, while this will be possible in the case of a supervision order only if a statement is made that the supervision order is made as an alternative to a custodial sentence, and the breach relates to certain types of conditions. If a supervision order is made, the court may include a 'night restriction', if the offender consents, for a limited period; under a probation order the court may include an equivalent requirement (under section 3(2) of the Powers of Criminal Courts Act 1973) for an unlimited period, again with the consent of the offender.

Suppose that having mastered this detail, the court has decided to make a supervision order with a requirement that the offender attends at a specified place and takes part in specified activities. The court must now consider whether the statutory requirements for making a community order are satisfied. These are set out in section 6 of the Criminal Justice Act 1991. In its original form, this section provided that the court must be of the opinion that the offence or the combination of the offence and one other offence associated with it was serious enough to warrant a community order (or a supervision order, according to which interpretation of this section is correct). In making this decision, the court was required by the 1991 Act to ignore the offender's previous convictions and response to previous sentences, and any other offences for which the offender was before the court, except to the extent that aggravating factors of the two primary offence were disclosed by the circumstances of other offences committed by the offender. Personal information about the offender's background must be ignored at this stage. The next step is to consider whether the proposed order is 'the most suitable for the offender'. In making this decision, the court is allowed to take account of any information about the offender which is before it, including his previous convictions and response to previous sentences, any other offences for which he is before the court, and any information about his personal background. The third stage is to consider whether 'the restrictions on liberty imposed by the order . . . are commensurate with the seriousness of the offence, or the combination of the offence and other offences associated with it'. In making this decision, the court is permitted to take account of all the offences for which the offender is before the court (not just two of them), but was again required to ignore his previous convictions and his response to previous sentences (except to the extent that aggravating factors of the two primary offence 'are disclosed by the circumstances of other offences committed by the offender') and any personal information about the offender's background.

Having reached this stage, the court must consult the supervisor as to the offender's circumstances and the feasibility of securing compliance with them, obtain and consider a pre-sentence report (which may or may not satisfy this requirement), consider whether the proposed requirements are necessary for securing the good conduct of the offender or preventing the repetition of the same offence or the commission of further offences, and obtain the consent of the offender to the proposed requirement.

As the court has made the supervision order in place of a custodial sentence, it must state in open court that it is making the order instead of a custodial sentence, and that it is satisfied that either the offence, or the combination of the offence and one other associated offence, was so serious that only a supervision order containing this type of requirement or a custodial sentence could be justified for the offence, or if the offence was a violent or sexual offence, that only a supervision order containing this type of requirement or a custodial sentence would be adequate to protect the public from serious harm from him.

The court must now turn to the question of compensation. If the offence has caused loss, damage, or personal injury to any person, the court must state in open court its reasons if it fails to make a compensation order. If it does make a compensation order, it must consider whether to order the parent or guardian of the offender to pay the compensation having first heard anything which the parent or guardian has to say on the subject. Finally, the court should consider whether to exercise the power to bind the parent or guardian over to exercise proper control over him. The combined effect of recent legislation is that Parliament has contrived to impose four-teen distinct statutory requirements on the court making such a routine decision.

As this illustration shows, a large part of the problem of modern English sentencing legislation is Parliament's fondness for stating the obvious and turning it into a statutory requirement. No better illustration of this can be found than the amendment of section 43 of the Powers of Criminal Courts Act 1973 by the Criminal Justice Act 1988. Section 43 of the Powers of the Criminal Courts Act 1973 empowers a court to order an offender to be deprived of property which he has used to commit or facilitate the commission of an offence, or which it is unlawful for him to possess. In its earlier form it did require minor amendment, but the 1988 Act expanded its scope, by making it available in respect of any offence and as the only penalty for the offence in question. Unfortunately, Parliament could not resist the temptation to add a statutory requirement that the court should have regard to the value of the property concerned before making such an order. It might have been thought that anyone considered sufficiently intelligent to be worthy of an appointment to the judicial bench in any capacity would have been capable of working this out for himself, without legislative prompting; inevitably, the High Court reached the conclusion that a court could not have regard to something unless there was evidence before the court relating to the matter in question, and that a court intending (for example) to make an order in respect of a car must have evidence of the value of the car.[42] It is highly unlikely that such evidence will be available when the offender appears for sentence, and if the court wants to make an order under section 43, it must adjourn while it is obtained. Meanwhile the offender is free to dispose of the car and defeat the object of the exercise.

II. IMPLEMENTING THE 1991 ACT

The key sentencing provisions of the Criminal Justice Act 1991 were brought into force on 1 October 1992. For once, a relatively long period was allowed to elapse between the enactment of the legislation and its commencement, and an extensive training programme took place for magistrates and judges. Immediately before the Act came into force, the Lord Chief Justice made a practice statement drawing the attention of judges to the changes in the procedure for the release of offenders sentenced to custodial sentences, which would in many cases mean that a given sentence would involve a longer period in custody than under the earlier system, and encouraged sentencers to take this into account in determining the length of

[42] *R. v. Highbury Corner Stipendiary Magistrate ex parte Di Matteo* (1990) 12 Cr. App. R. (S.) 594.

sentences. As early as was possible after the implementation of the Act, a series of cases were listed in the Court of Appeal to allow the court to determine the meaning of some of the controversial provisions of the Act.[43] Among the points decided by the court were that there was no general definition of what constituted an offence which was 'so serious that only a custodial sentence can be justified' for the purposes of the Act; that the prevalence of an offence was a relevant factor in determining its seriousness; that the fact that an offence satisfied the criterion of seriousness did not mean that the court had to pass a custodial sentence, as it was open to the court to mitigate the sentence by reference to factors relating to the offender; and that the fact that the defendant was on bail when the current offence was committed was an aggravating feature of the current offence.

The provisions restricting the consideration of previous convictions and response to previous sentences were elucidated in detail, and it was held that the Act allowed the sentencing court to take account of deterrence, so long as the sentence was commensurate with the seriousness of the offences concerned. The Act did not permit the addition of an extra element to the sentence to make an example of the offender.

Within a short time of its commencement, the sentencing provisions of the 1991 Act began to attract adverse criticism. Judges of the Crown Court complained of the restrictive effect of the rule which limited the court to considering two offences only when deciding whether the case was sufficiently serious to warrant a custodial sentence; the unit fine system attracted extensive media attention as a result of a series of bizarre cases in which enormous fines were imposed for trivial offences. In some of these cases, the difficulty arose simply because the offender failed to supply information about his means and was accordingly assessed as having a unit value of £100. These fines were adjusted, either on appeal or on a reconsideration by the sentencing court, but in other cases the heavy fines were the result of the proper working of the system. It became clear that the rules governing the calculation of the value of the unit were seriously deficient: they produced a high unit value for persons of moderate means, and failed to distinguish between people of moderate means and the very affluent, who benefited from the limitation of the unit value to £100. The rules made no provision for the many cases where the simple concept of weekly income produced a strange result. No guidance was given on the calculation of the weekly income of a person whose income fluctuated significantly from one week to the next, and the rules said nothing about the position of married persons with no independent income but who enjoyed an affluent lifestyle by reason of the income of their spouse. There were obvious problems in

---

[43] The cases are *Cunningham, Robinson, Okinikan, Oliver and Little, Bexley and others, Baverstock*, and *Cox*, all reported at (1992) 14 Cr. App. R. (S.) 444–85.

dealing with women convicted of soliciting as prostitutes. Although it was made an offence to make a false statement in disclosing income for the purpose of the unit fine system, there was no effective procedure for verifying the information provided by the offender in many cases.

There was frequent criticism of the restrictions imposed on courts in considering previous convictions, some of it based on a misunderstanding of the effect of the new law. The relevant section of the 1991 Act, section 29(1), did not prohibit the court from considering previous convictions at all, merely from taking previous convictions into account when assessing the seriousness of an offence. It did not really go much further than established sentencing principle, which allowed a court to take account of previous convictions for the purpose of determining whether to mitigate the sentence justified by the seriousness of the offence, but not to justify a sentence more severe than the current offence would warrant.[44]

Criticism of the Act came to a peak in an address by the Lord Chief Justice of England, Lord Taylor, to the Law Society of Scotland.[45] Congratulating the Scottish judiciary on the fact that the Act did not apply to Scotland, Lord Taylor CJ said that parts of the Act defied common sense and hoped that it would be reviewed and that sanity would be restored. On 13 May 1993, just over seven months after the Act came into force, Mr Kenneth Clarke, briefly holding the office of Home Secretary between a stint as Secretary of State for Education and becoming Chancellor of the Exchequer a few weeks later, announced that changes would be made to the Criminal Justice Act 1991 with unprecedented speed. A further Criminal Justice Bill dealing, *inter alia*, with aspects of sentencing (primarily the confiscation of the proceeds of drug trafficking and serious crime) was in the last stages of its consideration by Parliament. The opportunity would be taken to add provisions to this bill which would abolish the unit fine system, repeal section 29, and do away with the rules restricting the court to the consideration of a maximum of two offences when deciding whether the threshold of seriousness for a custodial sentence or a community order had been reached. These intentions were carried out in the Criminal Justice Act 1993 which received the Royal Assent in July 1993. The Act amended the 1991 Act so as to allow a court to consider all the offender's current offences when deciding whether the seriousness theshold had been reached; section 29(1) was repealed and replaced by a provision which stated that in considering the seriousness of any offence, the court may take into account any previous convictions of the offender or any failure of his to respond to previous sentences. In place of the unit fine system a new section requires

[44] See D. Thomas, *Principles of Sentencing*, 2nd edn. (London, 1979), 41–4, for a discussion of the treatment of previous convictions before the 1991 Act.
[45] The full text of the address is published in the 38 *Journal of the Law Society of Scotland* 129–31.

the court when imposing a fine to fix as the amount of the fine such amount as, in the opinion of the court, reflects the seriousness of the offence, at the same time taking into account the financial circumstances of the offender, whether this has the effect of increasing or reducing the amount of the fine.

Like all legislation assembled in haste, the amending provisions of the 1993 Act seem destined to cause difficulties. The new provision on fines is internally inconsistent, and the section dealing with previous convictions expresses a principle quite different from the principle applied by the courts before the 1991 Act was passed. During the interval between the coming into force of the 1991 Act and the enactment of the 1993 Act, the Court of Appeal has dealt with a considerable number of cases involving custodial sentences passed under the 1991 Act in its original form, and it is possible to see that the requirement of the 1991 Act that a custoidial sentence be passed only if the offence was so serious that only a custodial sentence could be justified is easily satisfied. Every case of unlawful wounding,[46] almost every case of assault occasioning actual bodily harm,[47] almost every case of burglary,[48] every case of reckless driving considered by the court has been found to satisfy the criterion. In some cases relatively minor offences of dishonesty have been considered to be sufficiently serious for this purpose. One example—admittedly an extreme one—was the case of a man who picked up goods worth £35 in a store, pretended to have bought them on a previous occasion, and was allowed to take goods of equivalent value in exchange for them. This offence of obtaining by deception was held to be so serious that only a custodial sentence could be justified (the sentence was one month's imprisonment, with a suspended sentence for a more serious offence activated concurrently).

At the end of a decade of unprecedented legislative activity in the field of sentencing, there can be no room for satisfaction with the legal framework—a mass of statutory provisions, many amended beyond recognition, others incomplete without reference to modifications contained in a Commencement Order, concealing a wide variety of anomalies and technical

[46] Examples include attacking a man in company with others, causing a laceration to the head with a screwdriver and broken ribs (*Broadhurst*, 8 June 1993); a van driver striking a pedestrian a single blow, causing him to fall to the ground and fracture his wrist (*Jarvis*, 11 May 1993); attacking a man with a truncheon, causing cuts to his head (*Office*, 30 March 1993).

[47] For example, punching a young woman in the face, causing her to fall to the ground, kicking her on the leg while she was on ground, causing a bruised jaw and a painful leg (*Adams*, 18 February 1993); punching and butting an opponent in a soccer match (*Shakeshaft*, 16 March 1993); punching and headbutting a neighbour and another person (*Hill*, 16 March 1993); knocking down a man in a dispute between neighbours, and kicking him about the face and head (*Kearslake*, 29 March 1993).

[48] For example, a single offence of burglary of a house while the owners were away for a weekend (*Kyle*, 25 January 1993); burglary of a bungalow while the owners were on holiday (*Reynolds*, 22 February 1993); burglary of a flat and theft of £264 (*Gadd*, 25 February 1993).

difficulties. Constant change inevitably leads to confusion, particularly as cases remaining in the system after a statutory change have often to be dealt with under the former law. The way in which the unit fine system was introduced meant that for some months after 1 October 1992, magistrates' courts were operating two systems of fining side by side, depending on whether the offences were committed before the first of October. During the coming legal year, the Court of Appeal will have to choose between three sets of rules in determining appeals against sentence. Cases in which sentence was passed before 1 October 1992 will be governed by the pre-1991 Act rules; those where sentence was passed between 1 October 1992 and 15 August 1993 will be governed by the 1991 Act in its original form, and those where sentence was passed on or after 16 August 1993 by the 1991 Act as amended by the 1993 Act. A year after Part 1 of the 1991 Act came into effect, it is difficult to view it as anything other than a complete failure. Ironically, the Act and its amendments have removed the restrictions enacted in 1982 and 1988 on the imposition of custodial sentences on young offenders. These were replaced by the general formulae of the 1991 Act, and the widening of the general criteria, together with the broad interpretation of the seriousness criterion by the Court of Appeal, mean that there are now fewer restrictions on the imposition of custodial sentences on young offenders than at any time since 1982.

The future direction of sentencing reform in England and Wales is uncertain. The last thing that is needed is a continuation of the piecemeal approach of the last ten years, although this seems the course which governments are most likely to take. A moratorium on sentencing legislation for a period of years would be desirable, if the system were not in such a poor state. The prospect of a complete overhaul of the system, either by the Law Commission or a Royal Commission, is remote.

At the Conservative Party Conference in October 1993, the Home Secretary announced a further Criminal Justice Bill; this will be introduced in the near future.

6

Proportionality and Parsimony in American Sentencing Guidelines: The Minnesota and Oregon Standards

ANDREW VON HIRSCH

The US Federal Guidelines will be examined in chapter eight of this volume by Professor Doob. The standards' primary aim, he points out, was to get tough: and tough they certainly are. If the Guidelines produce unfair results, fairness was not one of the drafters' major concerns. By and large, the Federal Guidelines have achieved their purpose: sentences imposed by Federal courts are now substantially more severe than they were before the Guidelines' adoption.[1]

In this essay, I wish to look at a different kind of sentencing guidelines—namely, those designed to achieve certain reformist aims. What is a reformist aim is a matter of perspective, of course, and the authors and supporters of the Federal Guidelines apparently consider it a reform to make punishments ever tougher. But I wish to look at a different conception of reform, involving two ideas—ones that the present volume emphasize. One of these ideas is that of proportionality, of sentences scaled to reflect the seriousness of the criminal conduct. The second is that of parsimony, of limiting the severity of punishment.[2]

Only a minority of US states have adopted numerical sentencing guidelines—that is, a systematic set of sentencing presumptions written by a rule-making agency. The four states that have had such guidelines in operation for some time are Minnesota, Oregon, Washington, and Pennsylvania.[3] Of these four, the last two are of less interest for present purposes.

My principal debt is to Bruce Taylor, my graduate assistant at the Rutgers School of Criminal Justice. Mr Taylor's Master's thesis at the School made me aware of the extent and importance of the differences between the Minnesota and Oregon guidelines. And his painstaking research assistance has been most helpful. I am also grateful to David Factor of the Oregon Criminal Justice Council.

[1] See Ch. 8.

[2] For a discussion of these two ideas, and of the relationship between them, see A. von Hirsch, *Censure and Sanctions* (Oxford, 1993), chs. 2, 5 and epilogue.

[3] Kansas and North Carolina have quite recently adopted sentencing guidelines. In addition, Delaware has adopted voluntary guidelines, addressing non-custodial as well as custodial sentences.

Pennsylvania has very broad guideline ranges, and no enunciated set of aims.[4] Washington's guidelines limit discretion more, but do not give much importance to parsimony: the guidelines were designed to be pretty tough from the outset.[5] This leaves two states which I shall address: Minnesota and Oregon.

I. A STRUCTURAL COMPARISON OF THE MINNESOTA AND OREGON GUIDELINES

Minnesota's guidelines took effect in 1980, Oregon's nearly a decade later, in 1989.[6] The two guideline systems are often thought of as quite similar. They have, after all, a similar format, and both purport to be guided by ideas of proportionality and restraint in the use of imprisonment.[7] However, it is their structural dissimilarities with which my essay largely will deal. My purpose is to point out how much the small print—the details of the guidelines—matter.

The dissimilarities are all the more remarkable, given the fact that the two states seem rather alike in many respects: they are demographically analogous, and have somewhat similar political traditions.

The two states' sentencing grids are set forth in Figures 6.1–6.3 in modified format designed to facilitate comprehension and comparison.[8] The offence score, in each grid, grades the gravity of the current conviction offence—with representative offences noted in the margin. The criminal-history score represents the number and gravity of prior convictions. Across

[4] See A. von Hirsch, K. Knapp, and M. Tonry, *The Sentencing Commission and its Guidelines* (Boston, 1987), 23–4.

[5] For an analysis of Washington's guidelines, see D. Boerner, 'The Role of the Legislature in Guidelines Sentencing in "The Other Washington"', (1993) 28 *Wake Forest Law Review* 381.

[6] For discussion of the aims of these two systems, see A. von Hirsch, K. Knapp, and M. Tonry, above, n. 4, ch. 5 (on Minnesota); and L. Kirkpatrick, 'Mandatory Felony Sentencing Guidelines: The Oregon Model', (1992) 25 *UC Davis Law Review* 695. The text of the two states' guidelines are set forth in Minnesota State Bar Association, Continuing Legal Education, *Minnesota Sentencing Guidelines and Commentary* (St Paul, Minn., 1993); Oregon Administrative Rules, ch. 253.

[7] Neither Minnesota nor Oregon deal systematically with non-custodial sentences, as noted below. However, the success of these two systems in regulating and limiting the use of imprisonment is itself a matter of interest.

[8] The two states actually use different grid formats: Minnesota shows the least serious offences at the top of the grid; Oregon shows the least serious criminal-history scores at the grid's right-hand side, and uses letters rather than numbers to rate those scores. Both states' grids have numbers in the cells for non-prison sentences, but those numbers do not represent presumptive sentence ranges. (In Minnesota, those numbers represent the maximum numbers of months that can be served in cases of departure from the guideline ranges or of revocation of probation; in Oregon, they represent the maximum terms of possible jail sentences or maximum severity of probation sentences.)

Offence score	Criminal-history score						
	0	1	2	3	4	5	6 or more
Intentional unpremeditated murder 10	111–121	133–147	153–171	192–214	231–255	270–298	309–339
Reckless homicide 9	94–100	116–122	124–130	143–155	168–184	195–215	218–242
Assault with a weapon and great bodily harm 8	41–45	50–58	60–70	71–81	89–101	106–120	124–140
Residential burglary with weapon; armed robbery 7	23–25	30–34	38–44	45–53	60–70	75–87	90–104
Residential burglary of an occupied dwelling 6	NP	NP	NP	33–35	42–46	50–58	60–70
Residential burglary of an unoccupied dwelling 5	NP	NP	NP	29–31	36–40	43–49	50–58
Non-residential burglary $5,000–$10,000 4	NP	NP	NP	NP	24–26	30–34	37–45
Theft crimes $150–$2,500 3	NP	NP	NP	NP	21–23	25–29	30–34
Theft-related crimes $150–$2,500 2	NP	NP	NP	NP	NP	NP	25–29
Unauthorized use of motor vehicle 1	NP	NP	NP	NP	NP	NP	NP

Fig. 6.1. Minnesota sentencing guidelines: effective 1 May 1980

each grid is a 'dispositional' (or 'in/out') line, dividing presumptive sentences to state prison from lesser sanctions. The numbers above the dispositional line represent the normally prescribed durations of the prison sentence. (These dispositions, however, may be departed from on account of special aggravating or mitigating circumstances.) Below the dispositional line, the cells are marked 'NP'—indicating a sanction other than state imprisonment.[9] Neither grid prescribes a presumptive range for such sanctions.

[9] These dispositions include confinement in a county jail for a period of less than a year. See discussion of jail terms, below.

Offence score		Criminal-history score						
		0	1	2	3	4	5	6 or more
Intentional unpremeditated murder	10	299–313	319–333	339–353	359–373	379–393	399–413	419–433
Reckless homicide	9	144–156	159–171	174–186	189–201	204–216	219–231	234–246
Assault with a weapon and great bodily harm	8	81–91	93–103	105–115	117–127	129–139	141–151	153–163
Residential burglary with weapon; armed robbery	7	44–52	54–62	64–72	74–82	84–92	94–102	104–112
Residential burglary of an occupied dwelling	6	NP	NP	NP	33–35	42–46	50–58	60–70
Residential burglary of an unoccupied dwelling	5	NP	NP	NP	29–31	36–40	43–49	50–58
Non-residential burglary $5,000–$10,000	4	NP	NP	NP	NP	24–26	30–34	37–45
Theft crimes $150–$2,500	3	NP	NP	NP	NP	18–20	21–23	24–26
Theft-related crimes $150–$2,500	2	NP	NP	NP	NP	NP	NP	20–22
Unauthorized use of motor vehicle	1	NP	NP	NP	NP	NP	NP	18–20

FIG. 6.2. Minnesota sentencing guidelines: effective August 1989–present

1.1. The Dispositional ('In/Out') Standard

One major aim in both states is to shift the use of state imprisonment towards the more serious crimes, such as crimes against the person. To what extent have the two standards implemented such an aim?

1. **Elevation of the Dispositional Line**. In achieving the aim just mentioned, one important matter is the 'elevation' of the dispositional line: viz., how serious must a first offence be before imprisonment is invoked?

Offence score	Criminal-history score								
	1	2	3	4	5	6	7	8	9
Intentional unpremeditated murder **11**	120–121	122–128	129–134	135–148	149–177	149–177	178–194	196–224	225–269
Reckless homicide **10**	58–60	61–65	66–70	71–80	81–90	91–110	111–115	116–120	121–130
Residential burglary with weapon armed robbery **9**	34–36	37–38	39–40	41–45	46–50	51–55	56–60	61–65	66–72
Residential burglary of an occupied dwelling **8**	16–18	19–20	21–22	23–24	25–26	27–28	29–34	35–40	41–45
Residential burglary of an unoccupied dwelling **7**	NP	NP	NP	NP	16–18	19–20	21–24	25–30	31–36
Non-residential burglary $50,000 or more **6**	NP	NP	NP	NP	10–12	13–14	15–18	19–24	25–30
Non-residential burglary $10,000–$49.999 **5**	NP	NP	NP	NP	6–8	9–10	11–12	13–14	15–16
Non-residential burglary $5,000–$9.999 **4**	NP	NP	NP	NP	NP	NP	NP	8–9	10–10
Non-residential burglary $1,000–$4.999 **3**	NP	NP	NP	NP	NP	NP	NP	NP	NP
Non-residential burglary less than $1,000 **2**	NP	NP	NP	NP	NP	NP	NP	NP	NP
Possession of marijuana under 150 grams **1**	NP	NP	NP	NP	NP	NP	NP	NP	NP

FIG. 6.3. Oregon sentencing guidelines grid

The Minnesota guidelines, in their original 1980 form, restricted state imprisonment (save for offenders with longer criminal records, to be discussed below) to crimes with a seriousness-rating of '7' or higher (out of a maximum score of 10). Generally, only crimes of actual or potential violence scored this high. Armed robbery was rated as a '7', but residential burglary received a lower rating. For non-drug street crimes, Minnesota has been able to maintain to this standard, even today. The Commission has accommodated demands for tougher penalties by increasing the durations of punishment for crimes above the in/out line, rather than by moving the line downward or reclassifying the gravity of the offences involved.

For drug crimes, however, the Commission has adopted a drastic change of policy, under pressure from the legislature to raise the penalties for such offences. Street-level sales of crack and (powdered) cocaine have been made presumptively imprisonable, even on the first offence. The Commission has achieved this result by reclassifying the gravity of drug selling. Sales (over a 90-day period) of more than 3 grams of crack or powdered cocaine have been rated as '7' in gravity. This is the quantity that may be handled by many street-corner sellers—by those at the bottom end of the selling chain. Giving routine drug sales this rating makes their prescribed prison sentences formally consistent with the guidelines' scheme, but not so in substance. It is not plausible to assert that such small-level drug sales are comparable in gravity to violent crimes such as armed robbery. Even if the drug trade in aggregate is a serious threat to public health or safety, it is difficult to see how the foreseeable injury done by a single small seller—in 3 grams' worth of sales over 90 days—involves injury or threatened injury of anywhere near the dimensions of a robbery.[10] The new rule really amounts to, not a proportionate sanction, but an attempt at exemplary deterrence: small drug sales are punished substantially above what their seriousness would warrant as a means of discouraging drug use.

The Oregon guidelines draw the dispositional line between seriousness-levels '7' and '8' (out of a maximum rating of 11). Residential burglary of an unoccupied building is classified as a '7' , but of an occupied building as an '8'. Most burglars try to commit their offences when the occupant is absent, so the rule is similar to Minnesota's. The major area of difference, however, is in drug crimes. A sale of 3 grams of crack is rated at seriousness-level '6', which is well below the in/out line. The sale would have to involve a considerably larger amount—10 grams—for the crime to qualify for seriousness-level '8' and thus be presumptively imprisonable at the first offence. Because of this larger required amount—and the absence of Minnesota's rule cumulating sales over a 90-day period—street-level drug sales would not ordinarily receive prison sentences on the first offence.

2. **Effect of the Criminal Record on In/Out Decisions**. This is an area where striking differences exist between Minnesota and Oregon. From the outset, Minnesota's dispositional line moved sharply downward on the right: for offenders with a criminal-history score of '4' or more, all felonies

[10] For fuller analysis of the concept of crime seriousness, see A. von Hirsch and N. Jareborg, 'Gauging Criminal Harm: A Living-Standard Analysis', (1991) 11 *Oxford Journal of Legal Studies* 1, and particularly 32–5.

with a seriousness rating of '3' or higher (which includes non-residential burglaries and the larger thefts) are presumptively prison-bound. For those with highest criminal-history scores, all felonies—even those with the lowest seriousness rating—receive prison sentences. The Minnesota Commission took this tough line with recidivists on the assumption that few offenders would have long records of convictions. However, prosecutors have been 'building up' the records of property offenders by obtaining convictions on multiple counts, so that an increasing number of property offenders were going to prison.[11] In 1989—when the durations of imprisonment were increased—the criminal-history score was changed so as to make this 'building up' somewhat more difficult: low-ranking prior felonies (those with seriousness-ratings of '1' or '2') count one-half point on the criminal-history score each, instead of a full point as before.[12] These generally are property offences. However, even this rule will permit some property offenders with long enough records to be imprisoned. And if any of the prior offences were above seriousness-level '5' (which includes burglary), those priors count one-and-a-half points each or more, meaning a faster build-up of the criminal-history score.

From the point of view of proportionality, the sharp drop-off of the in/out line for those with high criminal-history scores is not defensible. Granted, proportionality would permit a modest adjustment for prior record;[13] and if a 'modified-desert' standard is used, the adjustment could be somewhat larger.[14] But it is hard to see how even a modified-desert model would permit routine imprisonment of those convicted of the least serious felonies, merely because of their criminal records. Thus the treatment of the record in dispositional decisions remains both a practical and a theoretical deficit of Minnesota's system.

Oregon's dispositional line also drops down as one goes across the grid, but not nearly as much as Minnesota's. For the first four cells across the grid, the in/out line is located between seriousness-levels '7' and '8'. It then drops down three cells—and again, down another cell for those with the longest records. This, however, still leaves below the in/out line those currently convicted of crimes of seriousness-level '3' or lower. These include fairly substantial thefts, involving amounts below $5,000. Those convicted of routine thefts cannot ordinarily be sent to state prison, no matter how long their records.

[11] See A. von Hirsch, K. Knapp, and M. Tonry, above, n. 4, 129.
[12] For further discussion of this change, see A. von Hirsch and J. Greene, 'When Should Reformers Support Creation of Sentencing Guidelines?', (1993) 28 *Wake Forest Law Review* 329, esp. 331–5.
[13] For a fuller analysis of the role of the criminal record on a desert model, see A. von Hirsch, *Past or Future Crimes* (Manchester, 1986), ch. 7; A. von Hirsch, 'Criminal Record Rides Again', (1991) 10 *Criminal Justice Ethics* 2, 55–6.
[14] See more fully, A. von Hirsch, above, n. 2, ch. 6.

Moreover, the criminal-history score is calculated differently, so that an accumulation of minor felonies cannot result in a high score. A person does not move into the fifth criminal-history category—where the in/out line begins to drop—until he has committed his fourth property felony. And even then, he cannot accumulate any higher criminal-history score by having committed more property crimes. The worst two criminal-history scores, where the in/out line is at its lowest, apply only to those having previously committed two or more felonies against the person.

From the standpoint of restricting use of imprisonment, the Oregon rule is preferable to Minnesota's: prosecutors cannot so readily imprison those convicted of lesser property felonies merely by building up their records. The slope of the line is also more readily squared with a modified-desert rationale.

1.2. Durations of Imprisonment

The standards regarding duration of imprisonment have become different in the two states.

1. **Initial Durations**. For those with not-so-long criminal records, Minnesota and Oregon once had roughly comparable durations. In Minnesota, durations (those for offenders with low criminal-history scores) were moderate, at least by US standards. A person convicted for a first offence of a crime just above the dispositional line—viz., robbery—would receive 24 months (or actually, a range of 23–25 months). With release at two-thirds of the sentence, which is the rule in Minnesota, this is an actual period of confinement of 18 months—which is not far above the one-year boundary between state imprisonment and jail. For the next seriousness-level up— dealing with grave assaultive offences such as rape—the initial term was somewhat under four years (or about three actually served). It was only homicides that drew very long terms.

After a number of extensively publicized sexual homicides and much legislative pressure in 1988, however, Minnesota's Commission literally doubled initial prison terms. Robberies now get a four-year prison sentence, instead of two years, for the first offence; rapes get a seven-year sentence instead of four. Judged from the point of view of parsimony, this is not an attractive result. It also creates a marked discontinuity in the guidelines: moving from seriousness-level '6' to '7' raises the penalty from a maximum of a year in jail to four years in prison! In a robbery, for example, the presence or absence of a weapon pleaded or proven would make this difference.

Oregon's durations are above Minnesota's former ones, but below that state's current levels. For robbery, for example, the prescribed penalty for a first offence is a three-year sentence—as compared with the old Minnesota level of two and the present level of four years. The penalty for rape is five years—between Minnesota's former four and present seven years. The actual durations need a slight adjustment, however, because Oregon has only a maximum 20 per cent reduction for good behaviour, instead of Minnesota's 33 per cent off.

2. **Increased Durations for Prior Offending**. Here, Minnesota compares unfavourably to Oregon: durations rise much more steeply with the record—and durations for those with the longest records are quite Draconian.

Under the original Minnesota guidelines, durations rose very rapidly with the prior criminal record. For robbery, for example, the prescribed prison term rose from two years for a first offender to three-and-a-half years for someone with two prior felonies; and then to eight years for someone with the highest record score—i.e. an eventual quadrupling of the term. For the more serious assaults or rape, the term runs from four to eleven years, depending on the record. Such a heavy emphasis on the record scarcely squares with proportionality—or even a modified version of desert. And the cumulative nature of the criminal-history score makes it tempting for prosecutors to build up offenders' records through multiple charging, in order to achieve long sentences.

The 1989 amendments which raised the prison terms for first offenders did not make corresponding increases for those with longer records—so that the criminal record no longer has quite the leverage it once had. An armed robber with a criminal-history score of '2' would receive five-and-a-half years, as contrasted with the four-year prison sentence a first offender would receive. However, the criminal-history score has been recalibrated so that prior offences against the person would be given more weight. And the reduced leverage of the criminal-history score has been obtained at the cost of high penalty levels for first offenders.

The criminal-history score has considerably less leverage in the Oregon grid. Consider armed robbery again, where a first offender would receive a three-year sentence. If a recidivist's prior offences were property crimes, he would get at most an additional year—and then only if those convictions were rather numerous. To attain the worst criminal-history score he would have had to have has three prior convictions for offences against the person—and even then, six years (i.e. double the first offender's penalty) is the most he would receive. This result seems preferable. The reduced weight given the record squares better with proportionality principles. And it means that very lengthy terms of confinement are restricted better—to those whose current crime of conviction is very serious.

1.3. Jail and Breach Terms

Neither Minnesota nor Oregon provide presumptive sentence ranges below the 'in/out' line—that is, for cases not involving state imprisonment. Thus, as far as the guidelines are concerned, even the least serious felonies can be visited either by a jail term or a non-custodial sentence.[15] However, the two standards have some significant differences in their ancillary provisions relating to such sentences.

The first of these differences relates to jail terms. The Minnesota guidelines treat any disposition other than incarceration in a state institution for one year or more as an 'out' decision. The effect is to permit judges to impose up to a year in county jail on any convicted felon, even a first offender whose offence has the lowest rating. The Oregon guidelines also provide the jail option for any offence below the line, but impose more significant limits on the duration of such terms. For the cells close to the dispositional line, the maximum jail term is 90 or 60 days, as the case may be; for the lesser felonies at the bottom of the grid, the maximum is 30 days. This reduces the extent to which the guidelines' exclusion of state imprisonment for offences below the line can be circumvented by increased jail terms for such offences.

The Oregon guidelines also prescribe a six-month limitation on imprisonment for breaching the terms of a presumptive probationary sentence. Six months is still a rather harsh penalty for technical breaches, but the provision at least rules out the imposition of lengthy prison terms via probation revocation.[16] Minnesota's guidelines likewise supply maximum terms for breach, but those maxima are higher: for offences close to the line, they are 18 and 30 months, less a one-third 'good-time' allowance.

The Minnesota grid, as it now stands, continues to have the virtue of limiting the invocation of imprisonment in non-drug cases to crimes of actual or threatened violence. Even there, however, the grid gives considerably more weight to the prior record than notions of proportionality could

---

[15] However, the Oregon guidelines set certain (rather broad) maximum limits on the permissible severity of non-custodial penalties. For discussion, see L. Kirkpatrick, above, n. 6, 710–11.

[16] For further discussion of the need for limits on penalties for breach, see A. von Hirsch, above, n. 2, ch. 7. The Oregon legislature has just adopted legislation that permits the Corrections Department to adopt rules prescribing community-based sanctions for probation violations. These sanctions would be imposed by the Department administratively. The aim is to visit violators with significant penalties short of confinement, and thus help induce judges to be more sparing in revoking probation.

warrant, and prison terms (when imposed) are quite lengthy. Moreover, the guidelines impose disproportionate sanctions for drug crimes—accomplished by giving such crimes seriousness-ratings that seem difficult to defend. Judged by the twin aims of proportionality and parsimony, the guidelines have become somewhat disappointing—although Minnesota continues to have low rates of imprisonment compared with most other US states.

Oregon restricts the prison sanction mainly to crimes of actual or potential violence. Durations are more moderate and the criminal-history has less leverage. Moreover, the Commission has maintained some kind of minimally defensible stance on drug crimes: routine street-level drug sales are not considered presumptively imprisonable offences. One thing to bear in mind, however, is that Oregon's guidelines are newer—having only been approved in 1989. It remains to be seen whether the guidelines' better features will survive a decade's operation.

This means that, even in states using a similar guideline format and having similar goals, it is difficult to generalize about the degree to which they implement the aims of reform assumed in this discussion. Minnesota's and Oregon's standards seem significantly different when given close scrutiny.

2. IMPLICATIONS OF THESE STRUCTURAL DIFFERENCES

What lessons are there to be drawn from an examination of these structural differences? A number come to mind, relating to the achievability of aims of proportionality and parsimony, and to the benefits and drawbacks of numerical sentencing guidelines.

2.1. Achievability of Proportionality and Parsimony

1. **The Importance of 'Compared to What?'** In assessing the structure of sentencing guidelines, it is important to bear in mind that proportionality and parsimony are relative terms. The proportionality question is what weight the guidelines give to the degree of gravity of the criminal conduct; the parsimony question is how much the guidelines restrain the use of severe punishments, such as imprisonment. The temptation should be resisted of dealing with these issues in all-or-nothing terms: either the guidelines fully implement a 'pure' desert model (however defined) or else they are not proportionality-based at all; either the guidelines prescribe a dramatic reduction in use of imprisonment or parsimony has not been achieved at all.

In the real world of guideline-writing, the alternatives are never so extreme. The Oregon guidelines do not purport to implement any conceptual model in its supposedly 'pure' form, and yet they are designed to emphasize proportionality—by increasing the emphasis given the gravity of the offence, and reducing that given the prior record. The guidelines do not attempt a dramatic reduction in the use of imprisonment, and no such reduction could have survived Oregon's criminal-justice politics. But the standards are designed to generate a sense of restraint concerning increased use of imprisonment.[17]

Richard Frase has suggested that Minnesota's guidelines are not desert-based at all, but reflect instead a rationale of 'limiting retributivism'. The guidelines, he asserts, now employ the gravity of the offence merely to impose upper limits on the permitted punishment, and effectively permit consideration of other factors (including crime-control) in deciding the penalty below those limits.[18]

In fact, different portions of Minnesota's grid are structured differently. In the leftward portion of the grid above the dispositional line[19] (i.e. for cases with presumptive prison sentences but shorter criminal records), the gravity of the crime counts most. Here, the grid furnishes not merely upper limits, but fairly narrow presumptive ranges. Departures (including downward departures) are authorized only in 'substantial and compelling circumstances'. While (as Frase notes[20]) the courts have recently been permitting departures below the presumptive ranges on grounds of 'amenability' to probation, this does not warrant the conclusion that the guidelines were meant only to supply offence-based upper limits. (Were that the aim, why not have a grid that explicitly furnishes only those limits, and permits courts to go below them whenever they believe that utilitarian concerns warrant? Why put the courts to the trouble of invoking departures below the prescribed ranges?) Indeed, Frase concedes that frequent sentence reductions may not have been the intent of the Commission in writing the guidelines.[21] He points out also that downward departures are occurring

[17] That such a sense of restraint is becoming evident is illustrated by the following. The state currently funds 6,527 beds. Projections indicated that—especially because of probation revocations—an additional 800 beds would have been needed by June 1995. To avoid the expense of building that additional space, the legislature adopted legislation designed to prevent that population increase, while permitting the guidelines to remain unchanged. That legislation included authority for new Corrections Department rules concerning probation violations, described in n. 16. It also included a change in the legal status of a number of theft crimes from felonies to misdemeanours—for those on probation for misdemeanours cannot be sent to state prison upon breach.

[18] Below, Ch. 7. For fuller discussion of 'limiting retributivism', see N. Morris, *Madness and the Criminal Law* (Chicago, 1982), ch. 5.

[19] In speaking of 'above' the line, I am referring to the modified grid formats set out in this essay. The actual Minnesota grid looks different, with the more serious offences below the line.

[20] Below, Ch. 7, 182, 192. See also text accompanying n. 28 below.   [21] Ibid. 192.

most frequently with respect to those presumptive prison terms that were increased so much by the 1989 amendments—suggesting that judges may merely be trying to soften the impact of these changes.[22]

As one moves to the right above the dispositional line, matters change. The grid still prescribes ranges and not just maxima, but the criminal record influences the sentence much more. This means, as I mentioned already, a reduced emphasis on proportionality.

Below the dispositional line, the guidelines prescribe that state imprisonment presumptively may not be invoked. However, the guidelines do not purport systematically to regulate jail or non-custodial dispositions; on the contrary, the Commission explicitly refrained from exercising its legislatively granted option to extend the guidelines to this area.[23] Thus the Commission was no more adopting 'limiting retributivism' here than it was any other rationale.

For presumptive non-prison dispositions, the guidelines also set forth various durations of imprisonment, ranging from 12 to 30 months, that represent the maximum term for cases where judges depart upward from the presumptive 'no-prison' disposition. Frase describes these durations as the 'full just deserts' such offenders could receive.[24] He concludes that (since most felony cases fall under the dispositional line and receive no prison term at all) the majority of offenders in Minnesota are receiving less than their full just deserts. I find this conclusion strange. The maximum terms to which Frase is referring do not represent presumptive dispositions at all; instead, they just represent the most that can be imposed in those aggravated cases in which upward departures are called for. The aggravating factors listed in the guidelines relate chiefly to offence seriousness—that is, to increased harm or culpability. Permitting upward dispositional departures on grounds of 'unamenability' to probation was a surprise addition made by the case-law[25]—and even now such departures occur relatively infrequently.[26] Since the Commission was not purporting to regulate offences below the line in systematic fashion, it is implausible to suppose that those durations represent the Commission's view of how much offences below the line ordinarily deserve. (What the Commission was doing, instead, was setting forth a maximum applicable to the worst cases of such offences; and also making sure that the upward-departure cases did not take up too much prison space.) Frase's view seems predicated on the assumption that a desert rationale is intrinsically a severe one and hence only high penalties could represent offenders' 'full' deserts.

---

[22] Ibid. 195.   [23] Ibid. 180.
[24] See R. Frase, 'The Role of the Legislature, the Sentencing Commission, and Other Officials under the Minnesota Guidelines', (1993) 28 *Wake Forest Law Review* 345, esp. 352–4.
[25] See *State* v. *Park*, 305 NW 2d 775 (Minn. 1981).   [26] See below, Ch. 7, 182.

2. **The Details Count.** The comparison of Minnesota and Oregon should make clear how important the details of the guidelines are. Matters of seeming technical detail can make a large potential difference.

An example of this is the manner of scoring the criminal-history score. Minnesota's score is cumulative: if the defendant accumulates a sufficient number of previous property convictions, he ends in the right-hand part of the grid. Oregon's is not cumulative—or is so to a lesser extent. An accumulation of property crimes, no matter how numerous, cannot take the offender beyond halfway to the grid's right. A record of property offences thus makes the offender less likely to receive a prison sentence, and less exposed to lengthy terms.

Once guidelines are written, they can later be amended in some of their specifics, but cannot easily be restructured. Flaws in the initial guideline structure thus will prove sources of continued trouble. Examples of such flaws, noted already, are the Minnesota Commission's decisions to let the in/out line fall sharply downward on the right, and to have durations of confinement rise sharply with increases in the criminal-history score.

This last point links to another issue, that of regression to pre-existing practice. Guidelines, it is sometimes asserted, might alter sentencing practice in the first few years—but then the old patterns reassert themselves. Minnesota is said to provide the textbook example. In the first years, an increasing proportion of violent offenders, and a decreasing proportion of property offenders, received prison sentences—in accordance with the policy of the guidelines. Over the years, however, this effect has been diminishing.[27]

Minnesota, however, had two specific features which made its guidelines vulnerable in this fashion. One has been discussed at length already: the sharp drop-off of the in/out line towards the right-hand section of the grid. This gave prosecutors the opportunity to 'build up' convicted property offenders' criminal-history scores so that, by the time of their second or third court appearance, they would cross the line and be subject to a prison sentence. The 1989 amendments attempt to impede this effect, by giving each prior property conviction less weight. But the cumulative character of the score still will permit some property offenders to cross into the right-hand portion of the grid. Had Minnesota's guidelines had a flatter in/out line, and a less cumulative criminal-history score—as Oregon does—it would have become harder for property offenders to be imprisoned through manipulation of their criminal histories.

The other vulnerable feature concerns aggravation and mitigation. The guidelines provide a list of aggravating and mitigating circumstances, based primarily on the harm and culpability of the criminal conduct: the list

---

[27] A. von Hirsch, K. Knapp, and M. Tonry, above, n. 4, ch. 8.

features such matters as particular cruelty as aggravating, and provocation as mitigating. However, the list is open-ended: the courts may add other factors. Generally, the Minnesota Supreme Court has insisted that aggravating and mitigating factors should relate to the gravity of the criminal conduct, and thus has ruled out dangerousness as grounds for departure. However, it did decide that 'amenability' (or 'unamenability') to probation was a mitigating (or aggravating) circumstance, although that is surely not desert-based.[28] As a result, significant numbers of defendants convicted of offences against the person received probationary sentences, and some property offenders went to prison even when their criminal records were brief.[29]

This result, however, was far from inevitable. The Commission could originally have specified that departures should relate chiefly to offence-related factors, as one of its consultants (myself) suggested.[30] Or else, it could have responded to the Supreme Court's decision by restricting the extent to which 'amenability' (or 'unamenability') to probation could be grounds for departure. (The Supreme Court was interpreting the guidelines in its decision, and thus the Commission had the power to make such a change.[31]) When a regulatory scheme is created, its drafters can expect that those regulated will take steps to avoid the impact of some of the rules and will sometimes be supported by court interpretations. The regulators can respond by changing the rules in such a way as to close those loopholes. Tax agencies, for example, spend much of their time doing just that. It was because the Commission took no such remedial steps that it has become so much easier over the years for courts to depart from the guideline ranges.[32]

---

[28] See *State* v. *Trog*, 323 NW 2d 28 (Minn. 1982). For why I think this does not square with the rationale of the guidelines, see ibid. 104–5.

[29] Ibid. 102–5.   [30] Ibid. 103–4.

[31] The Minnesota Commission has the legal authority to amend the guidelines, subject only to legislative veto.

[32] Frase indicates that, because he favours a rationale in which desert provides only a maximum, the Minnesota courts are doing the right thing, to the extent they invoke downward departures on grounds of 'amenability' to probation (below, Ch. 7). This conclusion, however, is open to two objections. The first relates to the guideline structure: if it were really desirable to adopt 'limiting retributivism', the proper way to do so would be to restructure the grid so as explicitly to provide only upper sentence limits. It is anomalous to retain a grid that prescribes ranges, only to have judges routinely disregard those ranges' lower limits.

A second objection goes to the merits of Frase's proposed sentencing conception. If crime-gravity were to furnish only the upper limit on the sentence, then the sanction actually imposed will depend (as it did in traditional sentencing schemes) chiefly on crime-prevention factors. As a result, the ranking of penalties may be skewed not only occasionally but routinely. If Offence Type A is more serious than Offence Type B, this would merely require that the maximum for the former offence would be higher. Suppose, however, that Offence B, the lesser offence, occurs more frequently or has higher recidivism rates than the more serious Offence A. Then it would be permissible, on deterrence or incapacitation grounds, for judges regularly to impose a sentence near the applicable maximum for Offence B, but more lenient sentences, well below that offence's maximum, for Offence A. As a result, the lesser crime

Whatever their numerous other defects, the US Federal Guidelines do suggest that sentencing practice can be changed through sentencing standards. As Professor Doob shows in his essay,[33] those standards have brought about the change their drafters desired: tougher sentences. Such a change is easier to bring about because it requires less scrutiny of specific sentencing patterns. It does not matter much that the offence score is sloppily drafted (as Doob points out it is), as long as the net result is that most defendants get more prison than before. The Minnesota Commission faced a more difficult task because, in order to promote proportionality, the pattern of sentence matters. But with some wiser choices in the initial drafting of the standards, or a greater willingness to amend the standards later, the Commission could have succeeded better in its aims.

3. **Proportionality and Parsimony**. There has been some recent debate on whether proportionality and parsimony are conflicting or complementary goals.[34] In the experience of these two jurisdictions, the latter seems to be the case: a greater emphasis on desert helps restrain use of imprisonment. Oregon set its initial durations of confinement, as we saw, at levels that lay somewhere between Minnesota's former prescribed durations and its present ones. However, in dealing with the role of prior criminal record, Oregon more closely abided by desert requirements: the record has much less influence—both over the 'in/out' decision and over durations of confinement—than it does in Minnesota's grid. Limiting the impact of the record in this fashion helps prevent the incarceration of property offenders, who cannot so easily be confined merely by 'building up' their criminal records. It also restrains the use of very long periods of confinement for offenders whose current offences are just above the 'in/out' line.

3. ADVANTAGES/DRAWBACKS OF THE SENTENCING COMMISSION

If one looks at the literature on sentencing commissions—which now runs back two decades to Judge Frankel's 1973 book[35]—a variety of reasons have been cited in favour of commission-generated numerical guidelines.[36] A commission is said to be more competent to draft standards than a legislature facing the press of much other business. The commission's standards—because they actually prescribe the normally applicable penalties

would regularly receive the greater punishment. See also A. von Hirsch, *Past or Future Crimes* (Manchester, 1986), chs. 3 and 4.

[33] See Ch. 8.
[34] For a sketch of this debate, see A. von Hirsch, above, n. 2, epilogue.
[35] See M. Frankel, *Criminal Sentencing: Law Without Order* (New York, 1973), 118–23.
[36] See A. von Hirsch, K. Knapp, and M. Tonry, above, n. 4, ch. 1.

—are claimed to be more readily enforceable than broad, legislatively prescribed principles. And the commission supposedly is better insulated from 'law and order' pressures than members of a legislature facing re-election. To what extent does Minnesota's and Oregon's experience bear out such claims?

1. **Technical Competence.** The details of sentencing guidelines, I have emphasized in this essay, matter a great deal. This calls for competent drafters, having the willingness and skill to write principled guidelines with due attention to the important details.

Competence did characterize the work of Minnesota's and Oregon's Sentencing Commissions. The writing of guidelines in these two states was a sophisticated effort: both Commissions explicitly formulated aims relating to proportionality and restraint of prison populations; both undertook statistical projections to gauge their proposed standards' impact; both devoted considerable time and thought to the guidelines' details. If Oregon's guidelines have fewer structural flaws than Minnesota's, it is in part because Oregon had the benefit of hindsight—of being able to review nearly a decade of experience with the Minnesota standards. The competence point should not be overstated, however. Even a competent commission, such as Minnesota's, made serious mistakes. And competence is by no means assured merely by establishing a commission—as the history of such bodies in some other states,[37] as well as in the Federal system,[38] suggests.

Having a commission issuing numerical guidelines, moreover, is not the only way of achieving a well-crafted set of standards. In the present volume, Nils Jareborg describes the Swedish scheme, which consists of legislatively prescribed sentencing principles.[39] The standards, however, were drafted for legislative consideration by a specially constituted governmental commission aided by a panel of expert advisers. The drafting process, therefore, was in many respects comparable to that undertaken by Minnesota's and Oregon's Commissions.

When legislatively prescribed principles are written without the assistance of such a body, in the routine course of legislative business, the results can be disappointing—as England's Criminal Justice Act of 1991 testifies. The Act was preceded by a quite sophisticated White Paper clearly setting out proportionality and restriction of growth of prison populations as goals.[40] The translation of the White Paper's ideas into legislative language was undertaken with little outside consultation. The guiding standard of

[37] See, e.g. the experience of New York's failed Sentencing Commission, ibid. 21–3.
[38] A. von Hirsch, 'Federal Sentencing Guidelines: Do They Provide Principled Guidance?', (1989) 27 *American Criminal Law Review* 367.
[39] See Ch. 4.
[40] UK Government White Paper, *Crime, Justice and Protecting the Public* (London, 1990).

proportionality thus is ill-defined in the Act, the provision on previous convictions still worse drafted:[41] its confusing language generated the widespread misconception that previous criminality could not be considered at all—a perception that helped lead to that provision's subsequent replacement.[42]

2. **Vulnerability.** A system of statutory principles such as England's or Sweden's is subject to two kinds of vulnerabilities. (1) Because the standards are legislative, they are subject to law-and-order pressures: they can readily be amended to suit the political mood of the moment. An example is the UK Parliament's recent decision to dilute the Criminal Justice Act of 1991 by eliminating unit fines and permitting possibly wider scope for consideration of previous convictions.[43] (2) Because the standards are stated in general terms, they can be nullified by the courts: the courts can simply interpret the standards as having little or no effect. An example is a recent Court of Appeal decision holding that the prevalence of an offence, and the need to deter it, may be considered in determining whether it is serious enough to warrant imprisonment under the provisions of the 1991 Criminal Justice Act.[44]

The question is whether numerical guidelines can do better. Consider the first issue—sensitivity to law-and-order pressures. Supposedly, the sentencing commission is more insulated from political pressures than the legislature. But its insulation is only a relative matter. Political actors appoint the members of the commission, control its budget and powers, and have the authority to disapprove its product. When the Minnesota legislature urged the Commission to raise the prison terms for violent crimes and imprison street drug dealers, as it did in 1989, the Commission had little choice but to accede. The most it could do is make some lower-visibility compensating changes—such as that making it harder for property offenders to accumulate high record scores. The Commission has held the line on not imprisoning convicted burglars, but one would have to be optimistic to assume that this limit will continue to be observed were burglary to become a major political issue. Perhaps, the most that can be said is that a commission constitutes a modest fire-break—that allows the less strong political initiatives to be resisted. If Oregon has maintained the integrity of its standards better so far, it is perhaps because they are newer—and because the standards have had stronger gubernatorial and legislative backing, at least to date.

Numerical guidelines, however, are more resistant to judicial nullification. The chief reason, of course, is that the tariff is set forth in the grid—

---

[41] See A. Ashworth, *Sentencing and Criminal Justice* (London, 1992), chs. 9 and 10.
[42] Criminal Justice Act 1993, s. 66(6).   [43] Ibid., ss. 65 and 66.
[44] *Cunningham* (1993) 96 Cr. App. R. 422.

rather than having actively to be developed by the judiciary interpreting the standards. A court in Minnesota wanting to do what the English Court of Appeal did—considering need-for-deterrence as a reason for invoking imprisonment—would have more difficulty, as need-for-deterrence is simply not part of either the seriousness or the criminal-record score.

The one place for possible nullifying moves is in the rules on aggravation and mitigation. Minnesota has a non-exclusive list of aggravating and mitigating factors—allowing the courts to add further factors. Minnesota's Supreme Court used this power to treat 'amenability' or 'unamenability' to probation as mitigating/aggravating factors—although this seems inconsistent with the philosophy of the guidelines.[45] However, the Commission has (though it has not exercised) the power to override such interpretations through clarifying amendments. Moreover, departures from the guidelines are occurring most frequently where Minnesota's standards themselves are most questionable: in the harsh treatment of drug offences. Had Minnesota not prescribed lengthy terms of confinement for street-level drug sellers, we might not be seeing the nearly 50 per cent downward departure rates now occurring for such cases.[46]

While Oregon's grid is less problematic as we have seen, the guidelines' list of aggravating factors include one potentially troublesome one: 'persistent involvement in similar offences'.[47] This plainly has the potential of being used to incarcerate repetitive property offenders. If this factor is invoked by the courts too frequently for that purpose, the guidelines may need to be amended to eliminate this factor or couch it more narrowly.[48]

I hope the reader has not been wearied by my close scrutiny of the two guideline systems, Minnesota's and Oregon's, but a detailed analysis of this kind is essential. The matters here discussed—the elevation of the 'in/out' line, the emphasis given in the grid to the previous criminal record, the manner in which that record is scored, and the recognized types of aggravating and mitigating circumstances—are of the kind that make much difference. It is they that determine how much imprisonment is employed, and to what degree the system visits proportionate sanctions. Writing satisfactory guidelines takes painstaking work, as well as considerable political courage.

[45] See nn. 25 and 28.

[46] In 1990 the mitigated durational departure rate for drug offenders—that is, the rate at which judges departed from the grid to impose shorter periods of confinement—was 27 per cent. However, in crack cocaine cases, where the rule at the time was particularly tough, that rate was 48 per cent. See Minnesota Sentencing Guidelines Commission, *Report to the Legislature on Controlled Substance Offences* (St Paul, Minn., 1992), 7–8.

[47] Oregon Administrative Rules, s. 253-08-002 (1)(b)(D).

[48] Amendment will not be quite so straightforward procedurally as in Minnesota, because guideline amendments require affirmative legislative approval.

7

Sentencing Guidelines in Minnesota and Other American States: A Progress Report

RICHARD S. FRASE

Presumptive sentencing guidelines developed by an independent sentencing commission have, since the late 1970s, represented the dominant approach to sentencing reform in the United States. Although the Federal Guidelines are the best known (and most criticized) example, such guidelines have also been adopted by many of the American states. This essay describes the wide variety of state sentencing guidelines, examines their common themes, and summarizes the available evidence on the impact and evolution of these systems in practice. Greater attention is given to the Minnesota guidelines, since they have been in effect the longest and have generated the most extensive body of sentencing data, interpretive case-law, post-implementation amendments, and evaluative literature.

The essay concludes that the Minnesota and other state guidelines reforms have generally succeeded in achieving their apparent goals, but that the results have varied as widely as have the states' goals and approaches. State reforms also appear to have generally succeeded in maintaining sufficiently broad support to ensure their long-term survival in those states. Moreover, whatever may be the future of sentencing guidelines in the US Federal courts, it appears likely that more and more states will adopt commission-based presumptive sentencing guidelines: primarily as a means of gaining better predictions of and control over rapidly-escalating prison populations; secondly, to ensure more severe punishment of (and available prison space for) violent offenders; and, thirdly, to achieve increased uniformity of sentences received by offenders with comparable conviction offences and prior records. Commission-based guidelines may also merit serious consideration in non-US jurisdictions with similar reform goals, provided those jurisdictions have recent traditions which suggest receptivity to rational sentencing policy.

I. OVERVIEW OF STATE GUIDELINES REFORMS

1.1. Introduction: The Origins of Sentencing Guidelines

The focus of this essay is on presumptive sentencing guidelines designed and implemented by an independent sentencing commission. Minnesota adopted this approach to sentencing in 1978, and many other states have done likewise since then. These reforms were preceded by a period of widespread dissatisfaction with, and attempts to reform, the traditional system of 'indeterminate' sentencing.[1] Under that system, the dominant purposes of punishment were rehabilitation and incapacitation; to achieve these goals, judges and parole boards were given broad discretion to assess the treatability and dangerousness of each individual offender. Judges could impose any sentence from probation to the maximum prison term authorized by law, and parole boards had broad discretion to decide how much of any imposed prison sentence would actually have to be served. Appellate review of sentencing was rarely available.

In the early 1970s, a broad consensus began to develop that indeterminate sentencing was both ineffective and unjust, and that discretion in sentencing must be substantially reduced.[2] Conservatives objected to what they saw as unduly lenient sentencing; liberals argued that broad judicial and parole discretion produced unjust disparities and racial bias. At the same time, some academics were questioning whether treatment programmes were effective, and whether judges and parole authorities could reliably make individualized assessments of each offender's treatment needs, progress in treatment, and degree of dangerousness.[3] Other academics began arguing for a return to sentencing based on retributive ('just deserts') principles—each offender should be punished in direct proportion to the seriousness of the harm caused by the offence and his or her moral culpability in committing that offence, with little or no consideration given to crime-prevention purposes.[4]

In the mid-1970s, states began to enact 'determinate' sentencing laws, which sharply limited judicial and/or parole board discretion. Some states (e.g. California, Connecticut, Illinois, Indiana, and Maine) adopted legislatively prescribed sentences, specifying a narrow sentencing range for each offence and allowing only minor adjustments for aggravating and mitigating circumstances.[5] Other states retained broad judicial discretion, but adopted guidelines to structure parole release decisions. The sentencing guidelines in Minnesota, Oregon, Washington, and the Federal courts were preceded by several years of experimentation with parole guidelines, and such guide-

[1] A. Blumstein, J. Cohen, S. Martin, and M. Tonry (eds.), *Research on Sentencing: The Search for Reform*, i (Washington, DC, 1983); F. Zimring, 'Making the Punishment Fit the Crime: A Consumer's Guide to Sentencing Reform', (1977) 6 *Hastings Centre Report* 13.

[2] A. Blumstein *et al.*, above, n. 1.

[3] F. Allen, *The Decline of the Rehabilitative Ideal: Penal Policy and Social Purpose* (New Haven, Conn., 1981).

[4] D. Fogel, *We are the Living Proof: The Justice Model of Corrections* (Cincinnati, Ohio, 1975); A. von Hirsch, *Doing Justice: The Choice of Punishments* (New York, 1976).

[5] A. Blumstein *et al.*, above, n. 1; M. Tonry, 'Structuring Sentencing', (1988) 10 *Crime & Justice* 267.

lines are still found in a few states which retain indeterminate sentencing systems.[6]

In 1978 the Minnesota legislature took a different approach. Following a suggestion first made by Judge Marvin Frankel,[7] the legislature created a specialized agency—the Sentencing Guidelines Commission—to develop and implement presumptively-correct rules for prison-commitment and prison-duration decisions. Since 1978 commission-based presumptive guidelines have represented the dominant sentencing reform approach. As shown below, however, the states have adopted a wide variety of reforms of this general type.

1.2. Where, When, and What Kinds of State Guidelines?[8]

By Autumn 1993 commission-based sentencing guidelines were in force, or in the process of development, in at least 15 American states. In addition several states had attempted but failed to establish guidelines systems.[9] In one state (Alaska), the legislature directly imposed presumptive sentences for certain cases, without creating a permanent sentencing commission.[10]

---

[6] M. Tonry, 'Sentencing Commissions and their Guidelines', (1993) 17 *Crime & Justice* 137.

[7] M. Frankel, *Criminal Sentences: Law Without Order* (New York, NY, 1973).

[8] This summary is based on the following principal sources: D. Boerner, 'The Role of the Legislature in Guidelines Sentencing in "The Other Washington" ', (1993) 28 *Wake Forest Law Review* 381; *Federal Sentencing Reporter*, vol. 6, no. 3 (collection of papers describing guidelines reforms in Alaska, Minnesota, North Carolina, Ohio, Pennsylvania, Tennessee, Texas, Washington, and Wisconsin); ibid. vol. 4, no. 1 (papers on Delaware and Oregon); D. Gottlieb, 'A Review and Analysis of the Kansas Sentencing Guidelines', (1991) 39 *Kansas Law Review* 65; J. Junker, 'Guidelines Sentencing: The Washington Experience', (1992) 25 *UC Davis Law Review* 715; L. Kirkpatrick, 'Mandatory Felony Sentencing Guidelines: The Oregon Model', (1992) *UC Davis Law Review* 695; *Overcrowded Times* (papers on guidelines reforms in Delaware (vol. 1, vol. 2 (nos. 2 and 4), and vol. 3), Kansas (vol. 3), North Carolina (vol. 4, nos. 2 and 5), Oregon (vol. 2), Pennsylvania (vol. 3), Texas (vol. 4), and Washington (vols. 2 and 4)); *Pennsylvania Bulletin*, 21 Aug. 1993 (summary of proposed guidelines amendments); M. Tonry, above, n. 6; M. Tonry, 'The Politics and Processes of Sentencing Commissions', (1991) 37 *Crime and Delinquency* 307; M. Tonry, above, n. 5; A. von Hirsch, above, Ch. 6 (Oregon); M. Wesson, 'Sentencing Reform in Colorado: Many Changes, Little Progress', (1993) 4 *Overcrowded Times* (no. 6) 1, 14–17, 20; and numerous unpublished letters, papers, and reports on state systems, on file with the author and his colleague, Michael Tonry.

[9] In Connecticut, Maine, and Texas, sentencing commissions recommended against adoption of presumptive guidelines; in Colorado, New York, South Carolina, and Washington, DC, the commission was unable to persuade the legislature to adopt them (M. Tonry, above, n. 6; M. Wesson, above, n. 8). In addition, guidelines were initially rejected by the legislatures in Pennsylvania and Kansas, but a revised version was later accepted in each state.

[10] These presumptive sentences became effective on 1 January 1980. They apply primarily to repeat offenders, and only set maximum prison terms (parole release discretion was retained). Departures from the presumptive rules are heard by a three-judge court (B. Stern, 'Presumptive Sentencing in Alaska', (1985) 2 *Alaska Law Review* 227). In 1989 the legislature created a temporary Sentencing Commission to evaluate the state's sentencing laws; the Commission recommended no major changes.

TABLE 7.1. *Summary of American sentencing guidelines systems as of 1993*

Jurisdiction	Original effective date	Major limitations or distinctive features
Minnesota	1 May 1980	See Section 2 of this essay
Pennsylvania	22 July 1982 [major revisions in process]	Also covers misdemeanours; broad ranges and departure standards; retains parole board (guidelines determine the *minimum* sentence)
Florida	1 October 1983	Formerly voluntary
Michigan	17 January 1984	Voluntary; retains parole board (guidelines = minimum sentence)
Washington	1 July 1984	Includes upper limits on non-prison and probation-revocation sanctions; some defined exchange rates; also includes vague, voluntary charging standards
Utah	1985	Voluntary
Wisconsin	11 January 1985	Voluntary; retains parole board (guidelines = maximum sentence)
Delaware	10 October 1987	Voluntary; narrative (not grid) standards; also covers non-prison sanctions and misdemeanours
FEDERAL COURTS	1 November 1987	Includes misdemeanours; presumptive terms based on 'relevant conduct' (not limited by elements of conviction offence)
Oregon	1 November 1989	Grid includes upper limits on custodial non-prison sanctions, with defined exchange rates
Tennessee	1 November 1989	Also covers misdemeanours; retains parole board (guidelines = minimum sentence)
Louisiana	1 January 1992	Includes intermediate sanction guidelines and exchange rates
Kansas	1 July 1993	'Bad time' adds to presumptive prison durations shown on grid
North Carolina	1 January 1995	Also covers misdemeanours
Arkansas	(in process)	—
Ohio	(in process)	Preliminary commission report rejects grid form

The 15 states with existing or proposed commission-based guidelines are listed in Table 7.1, in the order in which their guidelines became effective.[11]

---

[11] Guidelines reforms are usually prospective, applying to all crimes committed on or after the effective date. Given the delay in processing arrests, it may be a year or more before the majority of offenders are sentenced under the guidelines. The Federal Sentencing Guidelines,

The Federal Guidelines are also listed, for comparison. It should be noted at the outset that the guidelines systems in several states (Delaware, Michigan, Utah, and Wisconsin) are entirely *voluntary*—trial judges have unlimited discretion to 'depart' from the recommended sentences (but must state 'reasons' on the record).[12]

Several other important variations are shown in the table. First, a few state guidelines include coverage of minor offences (misdemeanours), but most are limited to felonies. With a few exceptions, the latter are serious crimes punishable with at least one year of imprisonment; such lengthy terms are normally served in state-run prisons, but felons may also receive shorter custodial terms to be served in local gaols (jails, in the USA) run by county or city authorities. Common examples of felonies include homicide, rape, robbery, kidnapping, arson, aggravated assault, non-petty thefts or stolen-property possession, burglary, forgery, fraud, and non-petty drug, weapons, gambling, and prostitution offences.

Another major variable evident in the table relates to which sentencing decisions are regulated. All states regulate the imposition and duration of prison terms, but in different ways. In most guidelines systems, parole release discretion has been abolished; defendants serve the entire prison term imposed by the trial court, subject only to reduction (usually up to one-third) for good conduct in prison (including, in many states, co-operation with labour or treatment-programme requirements). But several guidelines states (Michigan, Pennsylvania, Tennessee, and Wisconsin) have retained discretionary parole release. In these states, the guidelines prescribe either the minimum prison term or the maximum term; the parole board then decides how much more, or less, time the offender must serve before release.

As for non-prison terms, each state limits the maximum length of jail terms and probationary supervision, but an increasing number of states (e.g. Delaware, Oregon, and Washington) set upper limits on the severity of all intermediate punishments. These limits are defined in terms of allowable 'sanction units' for each case, with defined 'exchange rates' for converting different sentence types into sanction units (e.g. one day in jail equals *x* hours of community service). However, these exchange rates differ considerably from state to state (e.g. one day in jail equals 8 hours of community service in Washington, but 24 hours in Oregon).

All of the states base their guideline sentences primarily on two factors: prior convictions ('criminal history') and the severity of the most serious

effective in November of 1987, were not applied by some courts until early 1989, when the Supreme Court upheld their constitutionality (A. Doob, below, Ch. 8).

[12] Another group of states experimented with voluntary guidelines and then abandoned them (Maryland, Massachusetts, New Jersey, and Florida prior to its adoption of presumptive guidelines) (M. Tonry, above, n. 6).

current conviction offence. The states thus reject the approach of the Federal Guidelines, which give substantial weight to related but uncharged conduct.[13]

All of the states except Delaware and Ohio use numerical standards contained in one or more two-dimensional grids defined by conviction offence and criminal history (e.g. the Minnesota grid, set out below at p. 179. Most states have a single grid, but some have a separate grid for drug offences. The grids also have widely varying layouts (most serious offences on top, or at the bottom; most serious criminal history at left, or at right). Finally, the numbers in the 'cells' of these grids vary in their absolute magnitude (average severity); rates of increase with increasing offence severity and prior record;[14] and breadth of cell ranges (wide in Pennsylvania; quite narrow in Kansas, Minnesota, and Washington). Some grids have overlapping cell ranges, others do not.

Some of the most critical differences in state guidelines, only hinted at in their grids, relate to criminal-history scoring.[15] Variations relate to offences counted (only felonies, in Tennessee); formulas for weighting prior crimes according to their seriousness; 'patterning' rules giving extra weight to the similarity of prior and current crimes; the presence or absence of 'decay' provisions by which very old convictions count less or not at all; and whether extra weight is given to the status of being on probation or similar conditional release at the time of the current offence.

Washington is thus far the only state which has tried to regulate prosecutorial charging decisions, but the standards are vague and entirely voluntary. Charging decisions directly affect the presumptive sentence, by determining into which grid cell an offender falls. Prosecutors have limited power to increase offence severity under conviction-offence guidelines, given the requirements of proof beyond a reasonable doubt, but prosecutors can and often do reduce charge severity (usually in return for a guilty plea). Prosecutors can also reduce, and in some cases increase, the offender's current and/or future criminal-history score—by varying the number and severity of charges filed and retained to conviction. However, the power of prosecutors to 'dictate' an unduly severe or lenient sentence is limited by the fact that these are only presumptive terms, from which courts may, and often do, depart. Prosecutorial discretion under the Minnesota guidelines is discussed more fully later in this essay.

1.3. Purposes and Priorities of Guidelines Reforms

Some broader, but equally important differences among the guidelines states relate to the aims of these reforms. Although all states were con-

---

[13] A. Doob, below, Ch. 8.   [14] A. von Hirsch, above, Ch. 6.
[15] There are also important differences in definitions of offence severity, and in presumptive prison-commit rules (A. von Hirsch, above, Ch. 6).

cerned to increase uniformity of sentences and reduce unwarranted disparities, the most common driving force behind guidelines implementation in
the 1980s was prison overcrowding (usually accompanied by prisoner law-
suits and court-imposed limits on prison populations). In the absence of
sentencing guidelines, soaring prison populations can only be addressed by
post-commitment ('back door') releasing measures, but at some point this
approach breaks down: actual prison time served becomes so derisory,
compared to the original sentence, that both the public and the offenders
lose respect for the sentencing process. Legislators have become increasingly concerned with 'truth in sentencing'—the law should mean what it
says, and keep its promises.

Guidelines make sentences more predictable, and sentencing commissions (if properly funded and staffed) can acquire the technical expertise
to develop sophisticated computerized sentence-monitoring and simulation
models which predict future prison populations based on presumptive sentences and expected caseloads. These models thus provide early warning of
impending increases in prison populations, and allow states to either ex-
pand prison capacity in time to match population increases, reduce those
increases by lowering prison commitments and/or durations (by modifying
presumptive sentences), or pursue a combination of these approaches.

Legislators in guidelines states were also motivated by a desire to ensure
that violent offenders receive more severe penalties (and that adequate
prison space be available for this). Given tight budgets and already-over-
crowded prisons, the only solution was to reduce prison commitment and
durations for non-violent offenders. But legislators are always reluctant to
reduce criminal penalties, and some former prison-bound offenders need
more punishment, or closer supervision, than is provided by traditional
probation. Thus, state guidelines systems have given increased emphasis to
'intermediate sanctions', including one or more of the following: short
custodial terms in a local jail, half-way house, treatment centre, or day-
reporting centre; electronically monitored home detention; intensive supervision probation; means-based ('day') fines; and community service.
However, for a variety of reasons, both practical and theoretical,[16] state
guidelines have thus far done little more than simply authorize such penalties in lieu of prison, sometimes also setting a presumptive maximum
aggregate severity on intermediate sanctions, but rarely imposing minimum
severity requirements.

Although their aims are similar, guidelines states have differed in the
emphasis they appear to give to each aim. Avoiding prison overcrowding
and overuse ('parsimony')[17] was given very high priority in the Minnesota,
Oregon, and Washington reforms, but was not until recently even recog-

---

[16] R. Frase, 'The Uncertain Future of Sentencing Guidelines', (1993) 12 *Law and Inequality*
1; M. Tonry, above, n. 6.
[17] A. von Hirsch, above, Ch. 6.

nized as a goal in Pennsylvania. Increased severity for certain offenders was not initially a major legislative goal in Minnesota, but seems to have been very important to legislators in Pennsylvania and Washington. A related feature of the latter state's reform is the high degree of control which the legislature retained over the determination of specific guidelines sentences;[18] in Minnesota the legislature waited over ten years before it began to take back some of the policy-making authority it had delegated to the Commission.[19] Finally, the states differ in their philosophies of punishment. Minnesota has managed to balance retributive and utilitarian goals, but other states, especially Washington, appear to have gone further in rejecting rehabilitation and requiring minimum sanction severity.[20]

1.4. Implementation: State Guidelines in Practice

Most state systems are still too new to permit reliable assessments of their impact. Even the older systems are difficult to evaluate and compare, for a variety of reasons:[21] Commission budgetary constraints and the scarcity of external evaluations; missing data on pre-guidelines sentences and on changes in prosecutorial charging practices; the complexity of the reforms themselves; and the difficulty of separating out historical shifts. The available evidence suggests that courts generally do 'conform' to their guidelines, but this has little meaning across jurisdictions, given the widely varying definitions of what constitutes a 'departure'. Pre- versus post-guidelines comparisons of 'compliance rates' are also distorted by the failure to account for shifts in charging patterns (see Section 2, below), and by the tendency to measure 'uniformity' only relative to post-guidelines norms.[22]

As for the increasingly important goal of avoiding or reducing prison overcrowding and overuse, the results are mixed. Delaware experienced prison increases from the start, as did Pennsylvania. Minnesota, Oregon, and Washington appear to have been quite successful in limiting state prison populations and avoiding overcrowding in the early years, but in later years the two older systems (Minnesota and Washington) experienced significant growth in prison populations.

The latter increases resulted in part from certain unpredictable factors: sudden increases in felony caseloads (especially drug offences); changes in prosecutorial charging patterns; and periodic, media-fanned 'crime wave'

[18] D. Boerner, above, n. 8.
[19] R. Frase, 'The Role of the Legislature, the Sentencing Commission, and Other Officials under the Minnesota Sentencing Guidelines', (1993) 28 *Wake Forest Review* 345; see also Section 2 below.
[20] For example, the Washington legislature ruled out compelled treatment not only in prison but also as a condition of probation in most cases; suspended prison terms were also limited. See also A. von Hirsch, above, Ch. 6 (lesser role of criminal history in Oregon).
[21] M. Tonry, above, n. 6.   [22] A. Doob, below, Ch. 8.

hysteria, usually prompted by a few highly publicized violent crimes. It also appears that sentencing guidelines reforms tend initially to experience a statistically artifactual 'grace period' of lowered inmate populations. This occurs because increased sentence durations, and charging changes which increase future criminal-history scores, take effect gradually, whereas presumptive probation terms for non-violent offenders have a large and immediate impact (especially if applied retroactively to some or all previously sentenced inmates). In addition, prosecutors and judges can give immediate effect (through charge reductions and mitigated departures) to any disagreements they have with the increased severity proposed to be given to certain offenders.

Minnesota, Oregon, and Washington continue to have significantly lower per-resident rates of imprisonment, compared with the USA as a whole.[23] Of these states, Minnesota was and still is the most 'parsimonious' in its use of state prison sentences, with a per-resident imprisonment rate less than half that of Oregon and Washington. Only part of this difference is due to lower crime rates and criminal caseload (see Section 2, below). Minnesota does make very frequent use of local jail sentences, but even when jail populations are included, Minnesota's incarceration rate is much lower than rates for the country as a whole, both per resident and when adjusted for differing criminal caseloads.

2. THE ORIGINAL PROTOTYPE: ORIGINS, IMPACT, AND EVOLUTION OF THE MINNESOTA SENTENCING GUIDELINES

2.1. The Guidelines Enabling Statute

In response to the broad sentencing reform movement described previously, in 1978 the Minnesota legislature created the Sentencing Guideline Commission.[24] The Commission is a permanent body composed of judges, prosecution and defence attorneys, law enforcement and correctional officials, and members of the public.

The new guidelines were to govern sentencing in all felony cases (crimes punishable by more than one year of imprisonment). The legislature gave

---

[23] In 1992 these rates (per 100,000 residents) were 84, 173, and 193, respectively; the rate for all US states was 303 (Bureau of Justice Statistics, *Prisoners in 1992* (Washington, DC, 1993).

[24] The legislative history of the Minnesota Guidelines Enabling Act, 1978 Laws, ch. 723, and the Sentencing Commission's implementation of its statutory mandate, are described in D. Parent, *Structuring Criminal Sentences: The Evolution of Minnesota's Sentencing Guidelines* (Stoneham, Mass., 1988). See also R. Frase, 'Sentencing Reform in Minnesota, Ten Years After: Reflections on Dale G. Parent's *Structuring Criminal Sentences: The Evolution of Minnesota's Sentencing Guidelines*', (1991) 75 *Minnesota Law Review* 727; and R. Frase, above, n. 19.

the new Commission only two specific directions: the guidelines were to specify presumptively correct prison-commitment and prison-duration rules for each combination of 'appropriate' offence and offender character-istics, and the Commission was to take previous sentencing practices as well as existing correctional resources into 'substantial consideration'. The enabling statute also abolished parole and provided that the entire prison term imposed must be served in prison, subject only to limited reductions for good behaviour. Moreover, prison treatment programmes were made voluntary and were not to affect the duration of the prison term.

The legislative history of the enabling statute reveals few discussions of sentencing theory as such, but the abolition of parole and of compulsory prison treatment programmes indicates a rejection of the traditional model of in-prison rehabilitation and individualized parole assessments of treat-ment progress and offender dangerousness. Beyond this, the legislature did not adopt 'just deserts' or any other particular theory of punishment; in-stead, it seemed to be saying that sentencing should become more uniform and less discretionary in the pursuit of all of the traditional purposes of punishment.[25]

2.2. Formal Law: The Original Guidelines, Major Case-law and Amendments through 1993

2.2.1. *Summary of Key Guidelines Provisions*

Pursuant to its statutory mandate, the Minnesota Sentencing Guidelines Commission developed, and the legislature accepted, a set of guidelines centred around a sentencing grid.[26] The two major determinants of the presumptive sentence are the severity of the most serious conviction of-fence and the defendant's criminal-history score (which is principally based on prior felony convictions). These two factors place each defendant in one of the cells of the grid. The numbers in the cells represent the duration of the recommended prison sentence in months (see Figure 7.1).

The heavy black line running across the grid is called the 'disposition line': in cells below this line, the guidelines recommend that the prison sentence be immediately executed and the defendant committed to prison. The single number at the top of those cells is the single recommended or best sentence, but a range is also provided within which the sentence could fall without being deemed a 'departure'.

---

[25] R. Frase, above, n. 19.

[26] The initial guidelines were contained in Minnesota Sentencing Guidelines Commission (MSGC), *Report to the Legislature* (St Paul, Minn., 1980). The current guidelines are in Minnesota Sentencing Guidelines and Commentary (St Paul, Minn., 1993).

Criminal history score

Severity levels of conviction offence		0	1	2	3	4	5	6 or more
Sale of a simulated controlled substance	I	12[a]	12[a]	12[a]	13	15	17	19 / 18–20
Theft-related crimes ($2,500 or less) Cheque forgery	II	12[a]	12[a]	13	15	17	19	21 / 20–22
Theft crimes ($2,500 or less)	III	12[a]	13	15	17	19 / 18–20	22 / 21–23	25 / 24–26
Non-residential burglary Theft crimes (over $2,500)	IV	12[a]	15	18	21	25 / 24–26	32 / 30–34	41 / 37–45
Residential burglary simple burglary	V	18	23	27	30 / 29–31	38 / 36–40	46 / 43–49	54 / 50–58
Criminal sexual conduct, 2nd degree (a) and (b)	VI	21	26	30	34 / 33–35	44 / 42–46	54 / 50–58	65 / 60–70
Aggravated robbery	VII	48 / 44–52	58 / 54–62	68 / 64–72	78 / 74–82	88 / 84–92	98 / 94–102	108 / 104–112
Criminal sexual conduct, 1st degree Assault, 1st degree	VIII	86 / 81–91	98 / 93–103	110 / 105–115	122 / 117–127	134 / 129–139	146 / 141–151	158 / 153–163
Murder, 3rd degree Murder, 2nd degree (felony murder)	IX	150 / 144–156	165 / 159–171	180 / 174–186	195 / 189–201	210 / 204–216	225 / 219–231	240 / 234–246
Murder, 2nd degree (with intent)	X	306 / 299–313	326 / 319–333	346 / 339–353	366 / 359–373	386 / 379–393	406 / 399–413	426 / 419–433

Note: Italicized numbers within the grid denote the range within which a Judge may sentence without the sentence being deemed a departure.
Under state statutes, 1st Degree Murder has a mandatory life sentence.

[a] one year and one day

FIG. 7.1. Minnesota sentencing guidelines grid, effective 1 August 1989: Presumptive sentence lengths in months

Above the disposition line, the guidelines generally[27] recommend a stayed (i.e. suspended) prison sentence equal to the number of months shown in each cell. A stayed prison sentence is conditional: it will not be served unless the defendant violates the terms of probation and the stay is revoked. Such stayed prison sentences are normally accompanied by several conditions, such as incarceration in a local jail for up to one year (eight months, with 'good time' credit) and/or required participation in a treatment programme; varying degrees of supervision by a probation officer; community service; victim restitution; or payment of a fine. The enabling statute authorized the Commission to adopt presumptive rules for stay conditions, but the Commission chose not to do so initially, in part because it did not have the time and resources. Since 1980, it has returned to this issue many times, but still has not adopted presumptive stay guidelines (which are strongly opposed by judges, attorneys, and probation officers).[28]

It is important to note that the guidelines recommendations as to execution and duration of prison terms are 'presumptive', not mandatory. The prescribed sentence is presumed to be correct, but the court may depart from this recommendation if it finds that 'substantial and compelling circumstances' call for a different sentence. In that case, the judge must state his or her reasons for departing from the guidelines. As provided in the enabling statute, both the defendant and the prosecution may appeal against the sentence, whether or not it is a departure.

If the defendant does go to prison, either initially or later, following revocation of a stayed sentence, the prison term imposed will be reduced by up to one-third, for good behaviour in prison. Thus, a 36-month guidelines sentence becomes a 24-month sentence if the defendant earns the maximum 'good time' reduction. Any reduction the defendant earns becomes a period of post-prison supervision similar to the traditional parole term. Thus in the example above, the defendant released after 24 months would serve a 12-month supervised released term. The conditions of release might include periodic contacts with a supervising officer, random drug tests, curfews, and so on. A violation of those conditions can result in the return of the defendant to prison to serve out his or her remaining term.

2.2.2. *The Commission's Policy Choices*

The Commission made several very important policy decisions in drafting and implementing its guidelines. First, it adopted an open and highly 'politi-

---

[27] A few cases falling above the disposition line carry a presumptive executed prison term (*Guidelines* § II.E). Most of these involve use or possession of a dangerous weapon, which is subject to mandatory minimum prison terms under a state statute (*Minn. Stat. Ann.* § 609.11, subds. 4 to 9).

[28] R. Frase, above, n. 24; R. Frase, above, n. 16.

cal' process, including public hearings and repeated briefings of and input from key legislators, the media, and the major 'constituencies' of sentencing policy (prosecution, defence, judges, correctional agencies, etc.).[29]

Secondly, the Commission interpreted the legislature's directive to 'substantially' consider correctional resources more strictly than the statute required: almost from the beginning, the Commission decided that the guidelines should produce state prison populations that remained well within (no more than 95 per cent of) prison capacity, and it developed a detailed, computerized prediction model to forecast the expected prison populations that would result from each proposed draft of the guidelines.

Thirdly, the Commission chose to base presumptive sentences almost entirely on prior record and current offence severity (which research showed to be the two most important factors in previous judicial and parole decisions). Offence severity was to be measured almost entirely[30] by the elements of the conviction offence, not the 'real offence' or uncharged misconduct. The latter had been considered in pre-guidelines sentencing and continues to play an important, but highly controversial, role under the Federal Guidelines.[31]

Fourthly, the Commission took the position that its specific guidelines rules should be 'prescriptive', not just descriptive of past judicial and parole decisions (or, the average of such decisions)—that is, they were to be norm-changing, not just norm-reinforcing. In particular, the Commission made its own determinations of offence-severity ranking, criminal-history scoring, the relevance of family and employment status (neither may be considered as grounds for departure), and prison-commitment priority (more violent offenders were to be imprisoned, and fewer property offenders). Overall, the Commission stated that it was adopting a sentencing theory of 'modified Just Deserts'; retributive values are the primary determinant of the presumptive sentence, but criminal history also plays an important role—a role which appears to be based more on crime-control goals (incapacitation, community treatment, special deterrence) than on culpability.[32] Crime-control goals were also given explicit recognition as factors to be considered in setting the conditions of stayed sentences (which presumptively apply to about three-quarters of all defendants).

[29] MSGC, above, n. 26; D. Parent, above, n. 24.

[30] Some real-offence sentencing is permitted, under the Minnesota guidelines. For example, mandatory prison terms applicable if the offence was committed with a weapon cover many crimes which do not include weapon use as an element; some severity rankings and aggravating circumstances are based on facts not included in the conviction offence (R. Frase, 'Implementing Commission-Based Sentencing Guidelines: The Lessons of the First Ten Years in Minnesota', (1993) 2 *Cornell Journal of Law and Public Policy* 279).

[31] A. Doob, below, Ch. 8.

[32] MSGC, *The Impact of the Minnesota Sentencing Guidelines: Three Year Evaluation* (St Paul, Minn., 1984); A. von Hirsch, above, Ch. 6.

2.2.3. *Guidelines Case-law*

Most of the major appellate case-law interpreting the guidelines was decided in the first two years after they became effective. The Minnesota
Supreme Court almost immediately reinforced the principle that guidelines
departures should be based on the conviction offence and should not be
based on the details of offences dismissed or never filed ('real offence'
sentencing). The court also established that departures could not be based
on assessments of the individual defendant's dangerousness, nor on special
needs for deterrence.[33]

In another very significant line of cases, the court held that dispositional
departures (but not durational departures) may be based on individualized
assessments of the offender's 'amenability' to probation or prison.[34] Aggravated departures based on this theory (commitment to prison, in lieu of the
presumptive stayed term) are rare, and are usually based on a finding that
the offender has previously failed on probation. Mitigated amenability
departures (stay of imprisonment, in a presumptive-commit case) are much
more common, accounting for half of all downward dispositional departures; they can be based on a finding either of particular amenability to
treatment in a community programme, or on a finding of the offender's
particular suitability for probationary supervision and unamenability to
imprisonment (e.g. a very vulnerable or impressionable offender).

Another important decision related to dispositional departures was *State
v. Randolph*,[35] which held that courts must grant a defendant's request for
execution of the presumptive stayed prison term when the trial court's
proposed conditions of the stay are so onerous that they are, in effect, more
severe than the prison term would be. The *Randolph* rule thus sets a
ceiling on the aggregate severity of non-prison sentences.[36] Such defendant
requests account for about three-quarters of all aggravated dispositional
departures.[37]

Finally, the court held in *State v. Hernandez*[38] that criminal-history points
may accrue on a single day when defendants are sentenced concurrently for
more than one offence. For example, a defendant with no previous convictions who was sentenced concurrently on four separate burglary counts
would have a criminal history of three (moving him across the disposition

[33] R. Frase, above, n. 30.
[34] These cases are discussed in R. Frase, above, n. 24. See also R. Frase, 'Defendant
Amenability to Treatment or Probation as a Basis for Departure under the Minnesota and
Federal Sentencing Guidelines', (1991) 3 *Federal Sentencing Reporter* 328 (very similar line of
cases under the Federal Guidelines). The different types of departure are further discussed
below at nn. 42 to 45.
[35] 316 NW 2d 508 (Minn. 1982).
[36] There are also statutory limitations on the length of jail terms (one year), length of
probationary supervision (maximum prison term authorized), and maximum fine.
[37] R. Frase, above, n. 30.
[38] 311 NW 2d 478 (Minn. 1981).

line) by the time he was sentenced on the fourth count. Prior to *Hernandez*, prosecutors could serialize prosecutions to achieve the same result, and all additional concurrent counts would increase the defendant's future criminal history if he committed further offences, but *Hernandez* sentencing increases the immediate impact (and plea-bargaining leverage) of multiple counts. The *Hernandez* rule also helps prosecutors target 'high-rate' offenders and emphasizes the crime-control purposes and effects of the guidelines criminal-history score (which, as noted above, already implicitly recognized such purposes).

2.2.4. *Major Guidelines and Statutory Changes since 1980*

The most important changes in the guidelines, since their inception, relate to the presumptive durations of stayed and executed prison terms.[39] In 1983, presumptive durations at Severity Levels I to III, with medium to high criminal history, were lowered by from one to seven months, in order to stay within prison-capacity limits. Also that year, and again in 1987, durations in certain cells at Severity Levels IX and X were increased by from eight to 100 months. In 1989 all presumptive durations at Severity Levels VII through X were increased, in response to major concerns over rising violent crime rates (and two highly publicized rape-murders in city parking ramps). The Commission first voted to increase durations at Levels VII and VIII; not satisfied, the legislature directed the Commission also to increase durations at Levels IX and X, by specified amounts. The cumulative effect of these changes in the presumptive durations for Severity Levels VII through X can be seen by comparing the numbers shown at zero criminal history (48, 86, 150, and 306 months, respectively) with the presumptive durations specified under the original 1980 guidelines (24, 43, 97, and 116 months).

The only other major change in the guidelines themselves was the adoption, in 1989, of a system for weighting prior felony convictions according to their guidelines Severity Level. Felonies included in the criminal-history score had previously counted one point each; they now count from one-half point (Severity Level I or II) up to two points (Severity Level VIII or higher). A major goal of this change was to reduce imprisonment rates for property offenders (who tend to have low-severity prior felonies) and make space in prison for violent offenders subject to the higher durations adopted in 1989.

The years since 1980 have also seen important changes in criminal laws and sentencing statutes (which prevail over any inconsistent guidelines rules). Maximum penalties for violent crimes were raised in 1989, and again in 1992 (in response to yet another round of public hysteria, prompted once

---

[39] R. Frase, above, n. 19.

again by two highly publicized rape-murders). Drug penalties were increased steadily, beginning in 1986. The legislature periodically displayed impatience with presumptive guidelines rules by creating or expanding statutes requiring a mandatory minimum prison term (e.g. for use of a dangerous weapon and for certain recidivists). Some of these statutes are truly 'mandatory'—the court has no power to impose any lesser sentence; others have been interpreted merely to prescribe the minimum prison term if the court chooses prison.[40] Similar impatience was revealed when the legislature, in 1989, amended the guidelines enabling statute to specify that the Commission's 'primary' goal in setting guidelines should be public safety; correctional resources remain a factor, but they are no longer to be taken into 'substantial' consideration.

The latter change demonstrates the legislature's continued acceptance of crime-control sentencing goals. Such goals were also reflected in a variety of laws allowing courts to depart from mandatory or presumptive sentences based on individualized assessments of the defendant's dangerousness and/ or 'amenability' to treatment. Similar discretion was given to correctional authorities by the enactment in 1990 and 1992 of new laws authorizing such officials to select certain prisoners for Intensive Community Supervision or a new 'Boot Camp' prison-diversion programme. The latter programmes were intended to curb the growing prison populations which were resulting from the severity increases previously noted (plus rising felony caseloads, discussed below).

2.3. Implementation: Empirical Data on the Guidelines in Practice

The following is a summary of the available empirical data on how the Minnesota guidelines have affected sentencing practices and inmate populations, from 1981 until 1993.[41] There is probably more empirical data on Minnesota sentencing and corrections, and certainly more published evaluations, than are available for any other American jurisdiction. One of the most important goals of commission-based guidelines is to encourage the collection of empirical data on sentencing, and the application of that data to Sentencing Commission and legislative policy decisions; in this respect, the Minnesota guidelines have been extremely successful.

---

[40] However, the Guidelines Commission treats the latter group of offences as presumptively requiring imprisonment for the specified minimum. Normal departure rules then apply.
[41] This summary is an updated version of the author's evaluation of implementation efforts through 1989 (R. Frase, above, n. 30). The most recent sentencing data is for calendar 1991; jail population data is through 30 June 1993; state-prison population data is through 1 November 1993 (R. Frase, 'Big-City Crime and "Get-Tough" Politics Arrive in Minnesota: Changes in the State's Sentencing Guidelines and Practices Since 1989', paper presented at the 1993 Annual Meeting of the American Society of Criminology).

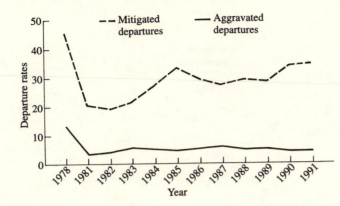

Fig. 7.2. Adjusted dispositional departure rates (% of defendants eligible for each type), 1978 (estimated) and 1981 to 1991

However, despite the huge amount of data, and the large number of internal and external studies of the guidelines, there is much we still do not know about their operation. Evaluation of Minnesota's experience is much easier than for other guidelines states, but it is still subject to most of the problems noted in Section 1, above.

2.3.1. *Effects on Sentencing Uniformity and Neutrality*

Overall Departure rates. Subject to the qualifications noted above, the available data suggests that the Minnesota sentencing guidelines were successful initially, and continue to be successful, in making sentences more uniform for offenders with similar conviction offence and prior record, and have reduced disparities based on race and social class.[42] The Guidelines Commission's principal measures of overall sentencing uniformity have been the rates of departure from presumptive prison-commitment ('disposition') and prison-duration rules. A dispositional departure can be either 'aggravated' or 'mitigated', depending upon whether the presumptive disposition was a stayed or an executed prison sentence. Durational departures can also be either aggravated or mitigated, and are reported separately for (1) all cases, and (2) executed prison terms only. The remainder of this essay reports only the latter rates, since they have much greater practical importance (very few stayed prison terms are ever revoked).

As shown in Figure 7.2, departure rates from guidelines presumptive dispositional rules (prison-commit or stayed sentence) declined sharply in

---

[42] C. Moore and T. Miethe, 'Socio-Economic Disparities under Determinate Sentencing Systems: A Comparison of Pre and Post-Guideline Practices in Minnesota', (1985) 23 *Criminology* 337; T. Miethe and C. Moore, 'Can Sentencing Reform Work? A Four-year Evaluation of Determinate Sentencing in Minnesota', paper presented at the 1987 Annual Meeting of the American Society of Criminology; R. Frase, above n. 30.

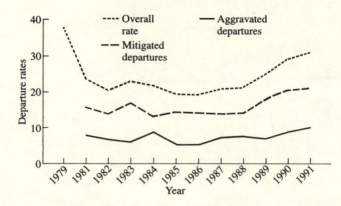

FIG. 7.3. Durational departure rates (executed sentences only), 1979 (estimated) and 1981 to 1991

the first year of the guidelines.[43] Aggravated departures stayed low through 1991, and most involved either defendant requests for prison under the *Randolph* case described above, or cases where the defendant was already in prison (or going there on another charge). Mitigated departures rose sharply in the mid-1980s, remained relatively stable through 1989, and then rose again in 1990 and 1991. The latter increase occurred primarily at Severity Levels VII and VIII, and appears to be a judicial response to the greatly increased presumptive durations adopted in 1989.[44]

It is important to recall that a mitigated dispositional departure means no prison term, but does not necessarily mean the offender avoids incarceration entirely; judges may impose shorter jail terms as a condition of probation in such cases, and they usually do (87 per cent of these departure cases in 1991).

As shown in Figure 7.3, executed-prison durational departure rates fell sharply in the first year of the guidelines, stayed fairly constant through 1989, then rose substantially in 1990 and 1991. Again, the mitigated departure increases occurred primarily at Severity Levels VII and VIII, as judges sought to mitigate the 1989 increases in presumptive durations; nevertheless, average executed durations increased substantially in these cases.[45]

If both dispositional and executed-prison durational departures are included in a single measure, about 16 per cent of all sentences were departures in 1991, three-quarters mitigated, and one-quarter aggravated. About 10 per cent were dispositional departures only; another 5 per cent were

---

[43] For an explanation of why these rates must be computed based on each group of 'eligible' defendants, rather than as a per cent of total cases sentenced that year, see R. Frase, above, n. 30. Until 1993, the Commission used only the latter method in published reports.

[44] R. Frase, above, n. 41.   [45] Ibid.

TABLE 7.2. *Mitigated dispositional departure rates (per cent non-prison sentence), by year and location on the guidelines grid, for defendants with presumptive prison sentences based on conviction offence and on alleged offence (eight-county, in-depth samples)*

	Pre-guidelines 1978	Post-guidelines	
		1981	1984
I. All presumptive-prison cases:			
based on conviction offence	48	20	27
based on alleged offence	53	47	45
II. Cases at Severity Levels VII–X:			
based on conviction offence	39	16	30
based on alleged offence	51	45	50

Source: R. Frase, above, n. 30, at 302.

executed-prison durational departures only; and about 1 per cent of sentences involved both types of departure. Within each of these three groups, mitigated departures greatly outnumbered aggravated departures. The predominance of mitigated departures is evident in all years, both before and after the guidelines (see Figures 7.2 and 7.3), and is one of the indicators of the strong continuing influence of plea bargaining (discussed below).

In fact, mitigated departure rates are even higher than the figures presented above suggest. The figures above measure departures from the presumptive sentence prescribed for the offender's most serious conviction offence and do not take into account additional cases in which leniency was achieved through reduced charges, without any formal departure. If the prosecutor chooses not to file more serious, provable charges, or to dismiss such charges in return for a guilty plea, the result is a *de facto* mitigating departure (dispositional, durational, or both). Moreover, rates of charge reduction are known to have increased in the first year of the guidelines; thus the sudden decline in mitigated dispositional departure rates in 1981 (Figure 7.3) overstates the guidelines' initial success.

In order accurately to assess the extent and degree of change in mitigating departure rates, including both formal and *de facto* mitigations, we need accurate measures of the highest provable offence which could have been filed, in each case. Unfortunately, the Guidelines Commission's 'real offence' data are imprecise,[46] are only available for certain counties (rep-

---

[46] In particular, the Commission's 'alleged offence' variable does not take into account problems of proof which were not evident from the sources used (primarily charging documents and pre-sentence reports).

resenting about 60 per cent of the annual caseload), and since 1984 have only been collected for certain offences.[47] Nevertheless the available data, shown in Table 7.2, suggest that mitigating dispositional departure rates relative to the real offence are much higher than the formal rates alone. Moreover, 'real' departure rates did not fall nearly as much in the first year of the guidelines as did the formal rates, nor did real departures increase as much through 1984.

Race, gender, and socio-economic disparities. Of all the sources and types of disparity, the Minnesota Sentencing Guidelines Commission was particularly concerned that sentencing be neutral with respect to the race, gender, and socio-economic status of offenders. Early evaluations of the guidelines found that they had indeed reduced race and socio-economic disparity; however, females and employed offenders continued to receive less severe sanctions, and minorities as a group received harsher sentences (both because they are less often employed and because they generally have higher criminal histories and are convicted of more serious offences).[48] More recent studies tend to confirm the earlier findings.[49]

Plea bargaining and its attendant disparities. The guidelines state that the exercise of constitutional rights (e.g. trial by jury) is not a legitimate basis for departure. This language may have been successful in preventing aggravated departures in cases of defendants found guilty by trial, but it has done little to prevent the granting of mitigating departures to those who plead guilty. Moreover, the guidelines say nothing about charging concessions related to plea bargaining.

As noted above, charge-bargaining increased under the guidelines. There is also still plenty of room for sentence bargaining, which can take several forms. In return for the defendant's guilty plea or other co-operation, prosecutors can agree to recommend that the court (1) grant a mitigated departure, or (2) overlook factors which would have justified an aggravated departure, or (3) grant lenient conditions of a stayed sentence. Multivariate analysis of guidelines sentencing shows that the defendant's plea, independent of other factors, continues to influence prison and jail sentencing decisions strongly.[50]

Of course, it is impossible to be sure, even with sophisticated multivariate analysis, that plea and trial cases are truly comparable. However, many other factors also point to the continued existence of plea-bargaining leniency and disparity: the similar magnitude of apparent plea-versus-trial disparities, in pre- and post-guidelines periods; the continued high rates of

---

[47] MSGC, above n. 32; R. Frase, above, n. 30.
[48] C. Moore and T. Miethe, above, n. 42.   [49] R. Frase, above, n. 30.
[50] C. Moore and T. Miethe, above, n. 42; R. Frase, above, n. 30.

negotiated guilty pleas; and the consistent tendency to mitigate (or decline to aggravate) presumptive sentences much more often than sentences are aggravated.[51]

Thus, it appears likely that whatever plea–trial disparities there were before the guidelines went into effect continued to exist in the early post-guidelines years, and still exist today. Such disparities are difficult to regulate in an adversary system in which judges are understandably reluctant to second-guess prosecutorial judgments (especially judgments which often reflect evidentiary weakness, trial strategy, and budgetary limitations, as well as considerations of sentencing policy), and in which no one but the prosecutor has standing to appeal cases of undue leniency.

It should not be assumed, however, that Minnesota-style guidelines are useless in the absence of controls over prosecutorial charge and sentence-recommendation concessions, or that conviction-offence guidelines allow prosecutors to 'dictate' the sentencing decision by controlling the severity and number of charges. The guidelines clearly have reduced disparities related to judicial decisions. Moreover, the patterns of charging leniency under the guidelines are quite similar to the patterns of judicial leniency (e.g. in favour of first offenders), which suggests that judges would grant leniency in such cases even if the prosecutor did not.[52] Finally, because the guidelines are not 'mandatory', and are not entirely based on the conviction offence, judges retain substantial power to depart up or down from the presumptive sentence produced by the prosecutor's charging decisions. As noted above, judges have in fact departed quite frequently, especially to mitigate.

However, the continued existence of widespread plea-bargaining concessions, and the high rates of mitigated departure by judges, do have important implications for theories of punishment. These consistent patterns of leniency suggest that lower (i.e. minimum) limits on sanction severity are much less likely to be enforced than upper limits. This finding is consistent with 'limiting' retributive theories which emphasize the importance of setting strict upper limits on sanction severity;[53] it is inconsistent with any more precise, 'defining' retributive model which seeks to ensure that offenders receive no more and no less than they deserve. Widespread mitigation of presumptive penalties is also consistent with the Commission's goal of 'parsimony': offenders should receive the least severe punishment necessary to achieve the purposes of the particular sentence.

2.3.2. *Proportionality (the Commission's Prescriptive Policies)*

The goal of proportionality requires that sanction severity increase in direct proportion to increases in offence severity and criminal history (as defined

---

[51] Ibid.   [52] Ibid. and above, n. 16.
[53] N. Morris, *The Future of Imprisonment* (Chicago, 1974).

by the guidelines). As noted earlier, the Guidelines Commission sought to make a number of prescriptive changes in Minnesota sentencing theory and practice. In particular, the Commission sought to reduce imprisonment rates for property offenders (including most recidivists), increase rates for 'person' (violent) offenders (even those with no prior record), and, in general, increase the importance of retributive, offence-based factors in prison commitment and duration decisions.

Prison rates for person offenders did increase in the early years of the guidelines, but mitigated dispositional departure rates remained very high for those offenders who had usually received probation prior to the guidelines.[54] For example, in cases at Severity Levels VII and VIII, with zero criminal history, prison rates have only been about 50 per cent, since the mid-1980s; in first- and second-degree intra-familial child sex abuse cases (ranked at Severity Levels VII and VIII), prison rates are only 40 per cent; and in above-the-line weapons cases (with presumptive-commit sentences based on a mandatory minimum statute), about 20 per cent of offenders receive prison.

As noted earlier, these conviction-offence-based measures do not include other offenders who avoided prison as a result of charging leniency. When imprisonment rates are examined relative to measures of the 'real offence', prison rates are even lower, and also show much lower rates of change in the first year of the guidelines.[55] For example, prison rates at Severity Level VII, which increased from 60 to 85 per cent based on conviction offence, only increased from 46 to 55 per cent, based on 'real offence' estimates. At Severity Level VIII, conviction offence rates went from 56 to 87 per cent; 'real offence' rates only increased from 45 to 47 per cent.[56]

As for property offenders, the Commission's attempt to reduce prison rates sharply was initially successful but, as shown in Figure 7.4, prison rates were back at their former levels within a few years. The prison-diversion policy was initially successful because prosecutors have limited ability to increase charge severity, and because judges are reluctant to impose aggravating departures (which, unlike mitigating departures, are not plea bargained and are very likely to be appealed). Eventually, however, prosecutors were able to 'run up' average criminal-history scores and push large numbers of property offenders 'across' the disposition line. This was achieved by filing more counts, and/or dismissing fewer in plea bargaining (aided by *State* v. *Hernandez*, above, which allows multiple counts to have

[54] R. Frase, above, n. 30.
[55] See also Table 7.2, above (mitigated dispositional departure rates (per cent not committed) for alleged presumptive-commit cases; prison rate equals 100 minus departure rate).
[56] The seeming disproportion in these prison rates (equal or higher at Level VII than at VIII) is explained by the fact that a large number of the latter are intrafamilial sex abuse cases which judges and prosecutors continue to believe justify probation (to keep the family together and in treatment).

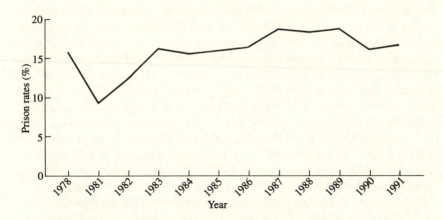

FIG. 7.4. Prison rates for property offenders, 1978 and 1981 to 1991

an immediate impact on criminal history). To counteract these evasions of its policy, the Commission revised its criminal-history scoring system in 1989, to give lesser weight to low-severity property offences. As shown in Figure 7.4, this change did succeed in lowering property offender imprisonment rates in 1990, but the slight rise in 1991 suggests that prosecutors and/ or judges may once again be finding ways to evade the Commission's policy.[57]

The patterns above show that judges and prosecutors continue to give stronger weight to the offender's prior record than the Guidelines Commission intended. Indeed, multivariate analysis of sentencing decisions reveals that criminal history is one of the strongest factors explaining departures from presumptive-prison-commit and presumptive-stay rules (and also explains much of the variation in the use of jail sentences).[58] Advocates of 'just deserts' sentencing have argued that prior record should play only a modest role,[59] but the strong effect of prior record in Minnesota suggests that system actors remain very attached to offender-based sentencing and the pursuit of crime-control sentencing goals. Minnesota has always been a very 'treatment-oriented' state, and there is also strong support among the public, legislators, and system actors, for selective incapacitation of recidivists.

Offender-based, crime-control-oriented sentencing was given explicit judicial approval in the amenable- and unamenable-to-probation departure cases described earlier. As I have argued at greater length elsewhere,[60] such departures are both justifiable and desirable provided they are limited to exceptional cases, and are not granted in a racially discriminatory manner;

---

[57] R. Frase, above, n. 41.   [58] R. Frase, above, n. 30.
[59] A. von Hirsch, above, Ch. 6.   [60] R. Frase, above, n. 24.

thus far, both of the latter conditions seem to have been met.[61] Amenable-to-probation departures avoid unnecessary incarceration (thus serving the Commission's goal of 'parsimony') and conserve scarce prison space for more dangerous offenders. Amenability departures of both types (mitigating and aggravating) also allow the system to deal more honestly with difficult cases, rather than achieving the same results *de facto* by various means, such as charge reduction, multi-count charging, and the granting of probation with the expectation that it will promptly be revoked. Given these substantial, unregulated discretionary powers of prosecutors and judges, formal recognition of amenability departures is not likely significantly to reduce sentencing uniformity and proportionality; instead, it encourages officials to make these decisions more openly, stating reasons.

Amenability departures are clearly consistent with Minnesota statutes (which have always recognized crime-control goals and offender-based sentencing, especially in recent years). They are also consistent with the structure of the guidelines themselves (although perhaps not with the intent of the Commission). Since judges retain broad discretion to set stay conditions and to revoke stays based upon technical violations and other indicia of 'unamenability' to probation, it seems reasonable to conclude that, at least in exceptional (i.e. departure) cases, judges may also consider amenability in deciding whether to grant probation in the first place.

2.3.3. *Prison and Jail Sentencing Rates and Population Changes*

As noted earlier, the Minnesota Commission adopted a goal of never exceeding 95 per cent of prison capacity, developed a sophisticated computerized prison population simulation model, and used the model to assess the prisoner population impact of each major element in the initial guidelines, as well as in all proposed later guidelines amendments and legislative crime bills. The model is necessarily imprecise, but its predictions have been accurate enough to be taken very seriously both by the Commission and by prison administrators and the legislature. Predictions of overcrowding have often required the Commission to modify its rules and have sometimes encouraged the legislature to do likewise. Jail populations were not modelled, in part because there was excess capacity in the early years, but limited jail space in some counties was considered an important reason not to impose presumptive minimum jail terms in stayed-prison cases.

As shown in Figure 7.5, prison-commitment rates have remained remarkably stable (about 20 per cent) in both pre- and post-guidelines years. (The slight dip in 1981 appears to reflect the fact, noted earlier, that the Commission's prescriptive choice to imprison fewer property offenders was initially much more successful than its decision to imprison more person

---

[61] R. Frase, above, n. 30.

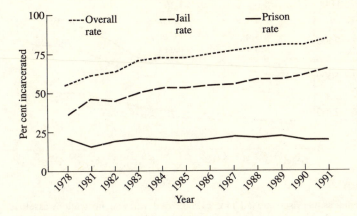

Fɪɢ. 7.5. Prison, jail, and overall custody sentence rates, 1978 and 1981 to 1991

offenders.) However, jail-sentence rates increased steadily under the guidelines, from 35 per cent in 1978 to 66 per cent in 1991; the combined custody rate (prison or jail sentence) rose from 56 per cent to 85 per cent. In comparison with other states, Minnesota uses prison sentences much less often, and jail sentences much more; in 1988, the estimated US felony sentencing rates were: 44 per cent prison; 25 per cent jail; and 69 per cent prison or jail commitment.[62] Since jail terms are much shorter, it appears that Minnesota is 'parsimonious' with respect to length, but not frequency, of custodial terms.

The increase in jail-sentence rates shown in Figure 7.5 partly reflects a trend which began before the guidelines went into effect. As shown in Figure 7.6, jail populations had increased annually for several years before 1981 (the first full year of guidelines sentencing). Moreover, some of the increase in the jail rate during the 1980s may have been due to increases in the average seriousness of felony cases.[63] With limited prison space, and a strong policy of avoiding prison overcrowding, jail sentencing would be expected to increase.

Figure 7.6 also shows that prison populations grew very slowly in the early 1980s, but began to increase more rapidly after 1987, as a result of increases in the felony caseload (number of guidelines cases sentenced). Indeed, throughout the years shown in Figure 7.6, prisoner population increases mirrored caseload increases almost exactly, especially if jail inmates are included in the former measure. For example, in 1982 the average prison-plus-jail inmate population (4,274) equalled 78 per cent of the number of felony cases sentenced in the previous year; in 1992, the average

---

[62] Ibid.   [63] R. Frase, above, n. 16.

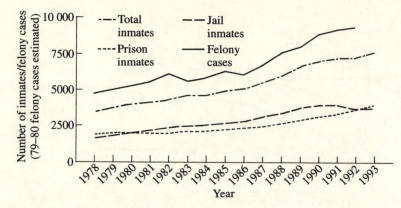

FIG. 7.6. Minnesota prison and jail inmates compared with sentenced felony caseload, 1978 to 1993

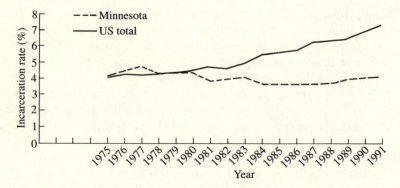

FIG. 7.7. Incarceration rates, US v. Minnesota: Inmates in prisons and jails as a per cent of weighted adult arrests (violent crimes weighted times 10), 1975 to 1991

inmate population (7,182) also equalled 78 per cent of felony cases sentenced in the previous year.

In comparison with other states, Minnesota has much lower per-resident incarceration rates, and its prison and jail populations increased much more slowly during the 1980s. However, Minnesota's low inmate populations are partly due to the state's relatively low crime rates; if incarceration 'rates' are intended as a measure of relative sentencing severity, the rate-base (denominator) needs to reflect criminal caseload levels, not just the number of state residents.

Comparable caseload data is, unfortunately, not available for other states. In the absence of caseload measures, arrest data provide the best

Oxford University Press

Walton Street, Oxford OX2 6DP

Telephone 0865 56767
Telefax 0865 56646
Telex 837330 OXPRES G

A/JAW/rw

13 April 1995

Professor M Tonry
Castine Research Corporation
PO Box 110
Main Street Castine
Maine 04421
USA

Dear Professor Tonry

<u>The Politics of Sentencing Reform</u>

I have pleasure in enclosing an advance copy of the above book. I very much hope you

Yours sincerely

Ros Wallington
Secretary to John Whelan
Commissioning Editor,
Law

Enc

cross-jurisdictional estimate of custody-sentence 'eligibles.' As shown in Figure 7.7,[64] arrest-based incarceration rates increased by 80 per cent for the USA as a whole, between 1975 and 1991, but did not increase at all in Minnesota (4.2 per cent of weighted[65] adult arrests in 1975; 4.1 per cent in 1991, with intermediate years falling in a range of 3.6 to 4.8 per cent). It should also be noted that Minnesota apparently has not always had lower overall incarceration rates than the rest of the country. Minnesota's rate was close to the national average from 1975 until 1981; in that year, Minnesota's incarceration rate began to fall, while national incarceration rates began to increase dramatically. Since Minnesota's sentencing guidelines were just beginning to take effect in 1981, these patterns lend some support to the view that the guidelines were a causal factor in maintaining low incarceration rates.[66]

The sentencing and correctional data in Figures 7.5 to 7.7 do not reflect the full effects of the major increases in statutory and presumptive prison terms, adopted in 1989.[67] Although the prison population impact of these increases has been moderated by increased rates of durational and dispositional departure, prison rates are clearly going to continue to increase; how much they increase, and whether prison construction and expansion can continue to keep pace, remains to be seen. But whatever lies ahead, it is important to appreciate the remarkable success Minnesota had in containing inmate population increases and avoiding overcrowding, for over a decade—a decade which saw not only much greater increases and overcrowding problems elsewhere in the USA, but also startling increases in drug and violent crime in Minnesota.[68] The reasons for Minnesota's continued restraint in custody sentencing are complex, owing in part to luck, progressive political traditions, and legislators with a strong sense of fiscal responsibility. But the guidelines seem to have helped.

[64] The sources for the US data in Figure 7.7 are Bureau of Justice Statistics, *Prisoners in 1992* (Washington, DC, 1993); Bureau of Justice Statistics, *Jail Inmates 1992* (Washington, DC, 1993); and the FBI's annual *Uniform Crime Reports*. Minnesota arrest data was compiled by the State Bureau of Criminal Apprehension; inmate data is from the Department of Corrections. Since increases in arrests do not immediately result in increased inmate populations, a 6-month time lag has been allowed between the former and the latter measures.

[65] Violent arrests need to be weighted more heavily, to reflect their greater expected impact on inmate populations. If no weighting at all is used, Minnesota's incarceration rates are slightly closer to rates for the rest of the country, but the shapes of the Minnesota and US graphs are otherwise very similar to that shown in Figure 7.7.

[66] Despite ever-increasing custody-sentence rates (Figure 7.5), total incarceration rates declined in the mid-1980s (Figure 7.7), and jail populations (numbers) fell in 1992 (Figure 7.6). It appears that increased felony jail sentencing must have been balanced by a decrease in the use of jails for pre-trial detention and/or misdemeanour sentencing (R. Frase, above, n. 16).

[67] R. Frase, 'Prison Population Growing under Minnesota Guidelines', (1993) 4 *Overcrowded Times* 1, 10–12.

[68] R. Frase, above, n. 30.

2.4. Summary

The Minnesota sentencing guidelines have, with varying degrees of success, achieved all of the principal goals of this reform. More violent offenders, and fewer property offenders, were sent to prison (although these shifts were not as dramatic as the Sentencing Commission intended). Sentencing has become more uniform, and racial disparities have been reduced. At the same time, the guidelines still give judges and other officials considerable discretion to tailor sentences to the facts of individual cases, by means of charging discretion as well as formal departure from the presumptive sentence.

The Minnesota guidelines, as implemented by trial judges, attorneys, and the appellate courts, strike an appropriate balance not only between discretion and uniformity, but also between the competing goals of punishment. The duration of presumptive prison terms, departures from those durations, and the maximum severity of probation conditions are limited primarily by the seriousness of the offence and associated offender culpability factors, and secondarily (especially for lower-severity crimes) by the offender's prior record (the 'modified just deserts' theory). However, the vast majority of offenders do not receive their full (modified) desert; presumptive probation terms (without minimum conditions) apply to three-quarters of defendants, and many more cases escape presumptive prison terms by means of charging leniency and mitigated dispositional departures—often based explicitly on offender characteristics unrelated to (modified) desert. Thus, 80 per cent of offenders receive stayed-prison sentences, and the precise conditions and severity of these sentences are determined by all of the traditional purposes of punishment. The guidelines' heavy reliance on such sentences provides a very effective and efficient crime-control device: the power of judges immediately to revoke probation and impose the stayed term gives offenders a strong incentive to co-operate and stay out of trouble.

The guidelines have been particularly successful in promoting the parsimonious use of prison sentences and in preventing prison overcrowding—despite rapidly increasing arrest rates, felony caseloads, and public concern about crime. Increases in sentencing severity for violent and drug offenders were balanced by less severe sentences for property offenders. The key to the Commission's success in controlling the prison population was its inmate population prediction model—an approach to corrections planning which became feasible when sentencing became more uniform. This model allowed the state, for the first time, to link sentencing policy choices with available correctional resources. Advocates of 'get tough' severity increases, both within the Commission and in the political sphere, were forced to confront the full costs of their proposals. This linkage, and the greater degree of fiscal responsibility encouraged by it, is perhaps the most unique and important achievement of the Minnesota guidelines. As discussed above in Section 1, it is also one of the principal reasons why other states are moving to adopt commission-based presumptive guidelines.

3. CONCLUSION

Sentencing guidelines reforms in the American states are very diverse in their goals, details, and impacts, but there seems little doubt that this approach to sentencing is here to stay. More and more states are adopting guidelines, and the American Bar Association has recently amended its recommended 'standards' for criminal justice to adopt all of the essential features of commission-based, presumptive sentencing (without, it must be noted, ever using the term 'guidelines'—such is the negative influence of the Federal version).[69] In particular, the ABA recommends that every state create an 'intermediate' agency (i.e. between the legislature and the courts) to promulgate presumptive sentences, study sentencing practices and effects, predict future correctional populations, and match sentencing policies with correctional resources.

The ABA's approach, like that in Minnesota, reflects a careful balance between the conflicting goals and limitations of punishment. Uniformity and retributive proportionality are given greater emphasis, but sufficient flexibility is retained (especially to mitigate sentences) to accommodate important utilitarian goals, resource limits, and individual offence and offender variations. The ABA, like Minnesota, gives particularly strong emphasis to the matching of sentencing policy to available correctional resources, so as to avoid overcrowding and desperate 'back door' releasing devices which undercut the credibility of legislative and judicial pronouncements. These accomplishments are made possible by the sentencing commission's relative insulation from short-term political pressures, and by its detailed information base, system-wide perspective, and expertise in research, planning, policy formulation, and guidelines implementation. Sentencing commissions can also contribute significantly to the development of more refined sentencing policies, particularly in the emerging areas of non-imprisonment sanctions.[70]

The key features of this model appear suitable for adoption not only in American states without presumptive guidelines, but also in non-US jurisdictions with similar reform objectives. However, the mixed history of

---

[69] American Bar Association, *Criminal Justice Standards for Sentencing Alternatives and Procedures*, 3rd edn. (reprinted in (1993) 52 *Criminal Law Reporter* 2353–70).

[70] N. Morris and M. Tonry, *Between Prison and Probation: Intermediate Punishments in a Rational Sentencing System* (Oxford, 1990).

American guidelines, especially in the Federal system, suggests caution; sentencing guidelines can also be used rapidly to escalate sanction severity, and such guidelines do not guarantee either insulation from short-term politics or parsimonious use of custodial sanctions.[71] The best prospects for achieving the latter benefits would appear to exist in jurisdictions like Minnesota (and perhaps Great Britain) with strong traditions both of centralized research and planning, and of rational (or at least fiscally responsible) sentencing policy.

[71] M. Tonry (1991) above, n. 8; R. Frase, above, n. 24.

8

The United States Sentencing Commission Guidelines: If you don't know where you are going, you might not get there

ANTHONY N. DOOB

I. INTRODUCTION

Sentencing has long been the backwater of the criminal justice system—an ugly little secret veiled from public scrutiny by the myth of rehabilitation and avoided by overworked appellate courts with the same distasteful aversion the Victorians gave to public discussion of sex. A decade of serious criticism has changed much of that.... [T]he remedy of a Sentencing Commission can be more dangerous than the disease it meant to cure.[1]

If one were to characterize the 'problem' that exists in sentencing in common law jurisdictions, one might suggest that there are two problems: (1) What institution is it that should control sentencing policy? (Many jurisdictions—Canada included—have not yet decided who should control sentencing—judges, legislatures, commissions, etc.) (2) How should sentencing be controlled (what goals or purposes, principles, or control mechanisms should be put in place)? Andrew von Hirsch has described how certain states in the USA approached the 'who and how' of sentencing reform.[2] The US Federal jurisdiction is, I think, unique in its approach to these questions. Hence there are different lessons to learn from the US Federal experience than there are from the experiences in sentencing reform in the various states.

The United States Sentencing Commission's efforts have been discussed, analysed, and criticized, more than has the work of any other single criminal-justice institution. Describing the work of the Commission as 'the most controversial and reviled sentencing reform initiative in United States history', Michael Tonry points out, '[T]he Guidelines have no vocal pro-

Preparation of this essay was facilitated by the sustaining contribution to the Centre of Criminology by the Ministry of the Solicitor-General, Canada.

[1] J. Coffee, 'The Repressed Issues of Sentencing: Accountability, Predictability, and Equality in the Era of the Sentencing Commission', (1978) 66 *Georgetown Law Journal* 975 at 977, 980.

[2] See Ch. 6.

ponents except members of the US Sentencing Commission and the US Department of Justice.'[3] Much of the criticism described by Tonry and much of the criticism and commentary which appears in the *Federal Sentencing Reporter*, a publication which quickly became the major source of sentencing decisions under the Guidelines and of discussion of the United States Sentencing Commission and its Guidelines, comes down to the issue of control: who should control sentencing?

In the February/March 1990 issue of the *Federal Sentencing Reporter*, the editors reported their pleasure in welcoming Mr Paul K. Martin, the Director of Communications for the US Sentencing Commission, to the *Federal Sentencing Reporter*'s Advisory Board. Less than two years later, Martin resigned from the Board of the *Federal Sentencing Reporter* suggesting, in effect, that the *Federal Sentencing Reporter* had become an anti-Commission-Guidelines publication. In the exchange between Martin and the editors of the *Federal Sentencing Reporter*, it was noted that the *Federal Sentencing Reporter* had not received 'a single letter from outside the Commission in support of the Guidelines'.

The problem, however, is that in many ways, the Commission might be seen as doing exactly what many people in power seemed to think should be done. If this is the case, it must be difficult and confusing to be a United States Sentencing Commissioner. Nobody seems to think they have done a good job. 'The US Sentencing Commission's Guidelines have failed' is the way in which Michael Tonry[4] begins one assault on them. One commentator noted that the Guidelines that the Commission first promulgated (and subsequently has modified from time to time) 'met with sharp criticism throughout the legal community and [received] virtually no praise'.[5]

One Commissioner who resigned from the Commission because of what he described as a 'lack of commitment by commissioners to base decisions

---

[3] M. Tonry, 'Judges and Sentencing Policy: The American Experience', in M. Wasik and C. Munro (eds.), *Sentencing, Judicial Discretion and Training* (London, 1992), 139; M. Tonry, 'Salvaging the Sentencing Guidelines in Seven Easy Steps', (1992)' 4 *Federal Sentencing Reporter* 355, 359.

[4] M. Tonry, 'The Failure of the U.S. Sentencing Commission's Guidelines', (1993) 39 *Crime and Delinquency* 131.

[5] S. Koh, 'Reestablishing the Federal Judge's Role in Sentencing', (1992) 101 *Yale LJ* 1109. The internal operations of the Commission have also been the subject of conflict and criticism. One of the US Sentencing Commissioners was reported to have described another as a 'maniac'. The recipient of this attack's response, apparently, was to quote the dictionary definition back to her critic, suggesting presumably, that the word didn't describe her (P. Yost, 'Sentencing Panel's Quandary: Whether to Work Part-time', *Washington Post*, 2 Aug. 1989, A17). The Director of 'Administration of Justice Issues' in the United States General Accounting Office described the Commission as suffering from 'significant organizational disarray' (p. 2). For example, he notes that one commissioner admitted that 'she [was] not fully aware whether the [study being carried out by the research staff] will overlap or conflict with the study she is leading' (p. 13). (General Accounting Office, testimony before the Subcommittee on Criminal Justice of the Committee on the Judiciary of the United States House of Representatives, 7 Mar. 1990.)

on research and scientific data when amending sentencing Guidelines'
suggested that 'the festering problem of misconception within the commission as to its proper role has now begun to be manifested in misguided
policy decisions'. More importantly, the ex-Commissioner and his co-author suggested that some amendments to sentencing Guidelines 'increased
punishment levels for no reason other than political expedience'.[6]

One must keep in mind, when understanding what happened with the US
Sentencing Commission, that the setting up of the Commission, and the
nomination of its members, was, of course, a 'political' act. The first director
of the Minnesota Sentencing Guidelines Commission, the first legislatively
created sentencing commission in the United States, suggested that the
'federal [sentencing] commission took an ideological, even political, approach to guideline development that disavowed constructs, suppressed
discussion of purpose, closed decision making to interested and affected
parties, and departed substantially from past sentencing norms'.[7] In one of
the most thoughtful and detailed analyses of the operation of the Commission's Guidelines, Daniel Freed notes that 'when the penalty offends
those charged with the daily administration of the criminal law, tension
arises between the judge's duty to follow the written law, and the judge's
oath to administer justice'.[8] At least one judge, according to Freed, resigned
rather than being forced to impose sentences he saw as unjust.[9] Indeed,
more than 200 federal judges had, within less than two years of the imposition of the Guidelines, 'written or concurred in decisions holding the new
system to be [constitutionally] invalid'.[10]

The Sentencing Commission has not taken criticism lightly. Its 'Communications Director' has said of Michael Tonry, a person whose knowledge of sentencing commissions and their guidelines hardly needs
defending, that 'it is obvious that Mr Tonry has little understanding of the
federal sentencing Guidelines'.[11]

The Commission does not need support from me or anyone else. In the
context of thousands of pages of careful, thoughtful, intelligent analysis
arguing that the Commission has been a failure or a disaster or both,
however, I am going to suggest that in many important ways it has succeeded beyond most of its supporters' wildest dreams. The issue is not
whether the Sentencing Commission succeeded. The issue is whether one
agrees with what they were trying to do. For example, many observers of a

[6] J. Parker and M. Block, 'The Sentencing Commission, P.M. (Post-Mistretta): Sunshine or
Sunset?', (1989) 27 *Am. Crim. L. Rev.* 289, 318.
   [7] D. Parent, 'What Did the United States Sentencing Commission Miss?', (1992) 101 *Yale
LJ* 1773, 1788.
   [8] D. Freed, 'Federal Sentencing in the Wake of Guidelines: Unacceptable Limits on the
Discretion of Sentencers', (1992) 101 *Yale LJ* 1681, 1687.
   [9] Ibid. 1686 n. 14.   [10] Ibid. 1719.
   [11] P. Martin, 'Response to Michael Tonry', (1989) 2 *Federal Sentencing Reporter* 158.

liberal persuasion would not see it as a 'success' that under the Guidelines an already high imprisonment rate went up dramatically. The legislative history of the Commission spans both liberal and conservative Federal administrations and the legislation establishing a 'commission-based' sentencing structure received support from legislators across the political spectrum.

The idea for a sentencing commission is usually traced to Marvin Frankel's 1973 book *Criminal Sentences: Law Without Order*.[12] The goal of the 'guideline' movement that might be seen as having been established by Frankel was to bring sentences under the 'rule of law', to bring a form of accountability to the sentencing process, and to insulate the process from the emotions and short-term interests of politicians. It is important to remember, therefore, that 'structuring' sentencing in the US Federal system did not necessarily have to mean creating longer sentences, or patterns of sentences perceived by many to violate even the roughest concepts of proportionality.

However, one cannot ignore the fact that it was established in the midst of a very conservative 'law and order' era in the United States. The Sentencing Commission, as I will point out, was given a broad mandate to interpret its goals. And, of course, its members were appointed by a conservative administration in an era when most politicians appeared to be concerned about being viewed as 'soft' on crime or criminals. For many—particularly those in a conservative Republican administration—the goal was to have long sentences. Therefore, if imprisoning even more Americans happened to be a goal of the politicians who were responsible for staffing the Commission, one can hardly fault the Commission for accomplishing that goal.

But that is the end of the story; it is important to understand what the United States Sentencing Commission was supposed to do, what it did, and what it accomplished, before we can talk about whether it was a success or failure.

2. PRE-GUIDELINE SENTENCING IN THE US FEDERAL JURISDICTION AND THE SENTENCING REFORM ACT

When one looks at sentencing as it now exists in the US Federal courts and thinks about the way sentences were handed down less than ten years ago, one would be hard pressed to find a sharper contrast. Prior to 1 November 1987, sentencing at the Federal level in the United States was almost completely unstructured. There was no legislative guidance on principles or

---

[12] M. Frankel, *Criminal Sentences: Law Without Order* (New York, 1973).

purposes of sentencing; there were high statutory maxima, and there was very little if any appellate guidance. Although judges would hand down sentences, a prison sentence as expressed in court was, effectively, indeterminate. It was the Parole Board, through a system of guidelines based largely on predictions of recidivism, that in effect determined how much time a person would actually serve in prison. With the decline in belief in rehabilitative possibilities through the sentencing process, and with a Commission that apparently believed that the public was concerned about severity of sentences, it was inevitable that there would be pressure for change.

One implication of the structure that existed in pre-Guidelines days is that there was a very under-developed sentencing[13] and appeal process in place. Clearly, if judicial decisions had very little to do with the length of time that a person was going to serve in prison, then it accomplished very little to appeal a sentence. Appeals courts were not in the business of developing case-law (principles, factors to be considered in applying those principles or in accomplishing the various purposes of sentencing, etc.) on sentencing, particularly as it related to the length of prison terms. When the United States Sentencing Commission's Guidelines came into effect, then, sentencing as we now know it was a new phenomenon for the trial courts and appeal courts. Few judges at either level had the kind of experience with well-developed, though sometimes inconsistent, reported sentencing decisions that judges in Canada or the UK or Australia have. The US Federal system had no person like David Thomas to create order out of chaos in large part because there was no well-developed body of case-law.

One view of the pre-Guidelines sentencing process[14] came from the Chairman of the Sentencing Commission:

[T]he process of punishing persons convicted of federal criminal offences was so manifestly discretionary and so given to unwarranted sentencing disparity that when Congress finally passed legislation in 1984 to change that process, it called the prevailing system 'shameful'. . . . The root of the problem was that sentencing was the one function given to federal judges that was essentially ungoverned by law.[15]

Change was inevitable. In 1984 Congress passed the Sentencing Reform Act (Chapter II of the Comprehensive Crime Control Act). The sentencing

[13] See M. Miller, 'Guidelines are not Enough: The Need for Written Opinions', (1989) 7 *Behavioural Science and the Law 3*.
[14] Many observers of pre-Guidelines sentences believed that parole guidelines had the effect of reducing gross disparities of incarceration times by setting release dates consistent with a fairly coherent 'sentencing' theory. An obvious problem, however, is that the parole board's guidelines had no way of reducing disparity with respect to the decision to incarcerate or not.
[15] Judge William W. Wilkins, Jr., Chairman, United States Sentencing Commission, before the House Subcommittee on Criminal Justice. (Quoted in (1990) 2 *Federal Sentencing Reporter* 214.)

aspects of that Act have been described by the Commission[16] as having a number of quite clear goals:

1. **Creating 'honesty' in sentencing.** The US Sentencing Commission describes this as having been accomplished largely by the legislation abolishing the parole commission, thus making the sentence served more or less equal to the sentence handed down (minus 54 days per year for good behaviour). The Sentencing Commissioners' focus was on imprisonment: after all, imprisonment 'meant something' and under the terms of the Sentencing Reform Act, when someone was sent to prison, that person was to be in prison for almost as long as the judge had indicated.

2. **Creating 'uniformity' in sentencing**, which is interpreted as 'narrowing the wide disparity of sentences imposed by different federal courts for similar criminal conduct by similar offenders'.[17] The use of the term 'uniformity' by the Commission is itself quite interesting, given the legislation establishing the Commission. The actual legislation suggests that

the purposes of the United States Sentencing Commission are to . . . provide certainty and fairness in meeting the purposes of sentencing, avoiding unwarranted sentencing disparities among defendants with similar records who have been found guilty of similar criminal conduct while maintaining sufficient flexibility to permit individualized sentences when warranted by mitigating or aggravating factors not taken into account in the establishment of general sentencing practices.[18]

3. **Creating 'proportionality' in sentencing.** The word 'proportionality', in the context in which the Sentencing Commission often uses it, appears to have a meaning above and beyond the use that von Hirsch and others have given to it. In particular, it seems to be a rather indirect way of saying that offenders are not being punished enough at the sentencing stage of proceedings.

The implication of this construction of the goals of the Act is that these goals were not being met and could not be met within the pre-Guidelines structure. Without going into great detail, it is probably the case that the Commission and Congress were correct in this assessment.

There is little point in reproducing the complete legislation here. However, there are some very important sections that do warrant careful consideration. In particular, section 3553(a) 'Factors to be considered in imposing

---

[16] It is sometimes important to distinguish between what the Sentencing Reform Act says about sentencing and what the United States Sentencing Commission says it says. It is not that the Sentencing Commission has misquoted the Act; however, as Freed (see above, n. 8) and others have pointed out, the interpretation of the Act used by the United States Sentencing Commission is not the same interpretation that many of its critics would have preferred. Freed, as noted later in this essay, makes strong and convincing arguments that the United States Sentencing Commission distorted the purposes of the law.

[17] United States Sentencing Commission, *Federal Sentencing Guidelines Manual* (1987), 1.2.

[18] Section 91(b)(1)(B).

a sentence' demonstrates the way in which the Commission developed an approach that was not inevitable.

Title 18—Crimes and Criminal Procedure, Chapter 227; Subchapter A—General Provisions

Section 3553 Imposition of a Sentence

(a) **Factors to be considered in imposing a sentence.** The court shall impose a sentence sufficient, but not greater than necessary, to comply with the purposes set forth in paragraph (2) of this subsection. The court, in determining the particular sentence to be imposed shall consider—

(1) the nature and circumstances of the offence and the history and characteristics of the defendant;
(2) the need for the sentence imposed—
    (A) to reflect the seriousness of the offence, to promote respect for the law, and to provide just punishment for the offence;
    (B) to afford adequate deterrence to criminal conduct;
    (C) to protect the public from further crimes of the defendant; and
    (D) to provide the defendant with needed educational or vocational training, medical care, or other correctional treatment in the most effective manner;
(3) the kinds of sentence available;
(4) the kinds of sentence and sentencing range established . . . [by the United States Sentencing Commission guideline]
(5) any pertinent policy statement issued by the Sentencing Commission . . .
(6) the need to avoid unwarranted sentence disparity among defendants with similar records who have been found guilty of similar conduct; and
(7) the need to provide restitution to any victim of the offence.

(b) The court shall impose a sentence of the kind, and within the range, referred to in subsection (a)(4) unless the court finds that an aggravating or mitigating circumstance of a kind or to a degree not adequately taken into consideration by the Sentencing Commission in formulating the Guidelines that should result in a sentence different from that described. In determining whether a circumstance was adequately taken into consideration, the court shall consider only the sentencing Guidelines, policy statements, and official commentary of the Sentencing Commission.[19]

. . .

(e) Upon motion of the government, the court shall have the authority to impose a sentence below a level established by the statute as a minimum sentence so as to reflect a defendant's substantial assistance in the investigation or prosecution of another person who has committed an offence. Such a sentence shall be imposed in

---

[19] This second sentence was added in December 1987, and the first sentence was changed at the same time by adding the words 'of a kind or to a degree' to produce the wording reproduced here.

accordance with the Guidelines and policy statement issued by the Sentencing Commission. . . .

. . .

3582(a) The court, in determining whether to impose a term of imprisonment, and, if a term of imprisonment is to be imposed, in determining the length of the term, shall consider the factors set forth in section 3553(a) to the extent that they are applicable, recognizing that imprisonment is not an appropriate means of promoting correction and rehabilitation . . .

Title 28, Chapter 58, Section 991 United States Sentencing Commission; Establishment and Purposes.

(b) The purposes of the United States Sentencing Commission are to—
(1) establish sentencing policies and practices for the Federal criminal justice system that—

(A) assure the meeting of the purposes of sentencing as set forth in section 3553(a)(2) . . .
(B) provide certainty and fairness in meeting the purposes of sentencing, avoiding unwarranted sentencing disparities among defendants with similar records who have been found guilty of similar criminal conduct while maintaining sufficient flexibility to permit individualized sentences when warranted by mitigating or aggravating factors not taken into account in the establishment of general sentencing practices; and

(c) reflect, to the extent practicable, advancement in knowledge of human behaviour as it relates to the criminal justice process . . .

. . .

994(d) The Commission in establishing categories of defendants for use in the Guidelines and policy statements governing the imposition of sentences . . . shall consider whether the following matters, among others, with respect to a defendant, have any relevance to the nature, extent, place of service, or other incidents of an appropriate sentence, and shall take them into account only to the extent that they do have relevance—

(1) age
(2) education
(3) vocational skills
(4) mental and emotional condition to the extent that such condition mitigates the defendant's culpability or to the extent that such condition is otherwise plainly relevant;
(5) physical condition, including drug dependence
(6) previous employment record
(7) family ties and responsibilities
(8) community ties
(9) role in the offence

(10) criminal history; and
(11) degree of dependence on criminal activity for a livelihood.

The Commission shall assure that the Guidelines and policy statements are entirely neutral as to the race, sex, national origin, creed, and socioeconomic status of offenders.

(e) the Commission shall assure that the Guidelines and policy statements, in recommending a term of imprisonment or a length of a term of imprisonment, reflect the general inappropriateness of considering the education, vocational skills, employment record, family ties, and responsibilities, and community ties of the defendant.

. . .

(g) The Commission, in promulgating Guidelines and policy statements . . . shall take into account the nature and capacity of the penal, correctional, and other facilities and services available, and shall make recommendations concerning any change or expansion in the nature or capacity of such facilities and services that might become necessary as a result of the Guidelines. . . . The sentencing Guidelines . . . shall be formulated to minimize the likelihood that the federal prison population will exceed the capacity of the Federal prisons, as determined by the Commission.

(h) The Commission shall assure that the Guidelines specify a sentence to a term of imprisonment at or near the maximum term authorized for categories of defendants in which the defendant is 18 years old or older and
(1) has been convicted of a felony that is

  (A) a crime of violence
  (B) [a drug offence]; and

(2) has previously been convicted of two or more prior felonies each of which is [a violent or drug offence]

(i) The Commission shall assure that the Guidelines specify a sentence to a substantial term of imprisonment for categories of defendants in which the defendant—
(1) has [two or more separate previous felony convictions]
(2) committed the offence as part of a pattern of criminal conduct from which he derived a substantial portion of his income
(3) committed the offence [as part of a racketeering conspiracy]
(4) committed a violent felony [while under some form of criminal-justice control]
(5) committed [a drug offence involving a large quantity of drugs]

(j) The Commission shall insure that the Guidelines reflect the general appropriateness of imposing a sentence other than imprisonment in cases in which the defendant is a first offender who has not been convicted of a crime of violence or an otherwise serious offence and the general appropriateness of imposing a term of imprisonment on a person convicted of a crime of violence that results in serious bodily injury.

. . .

(m) The Commission shall insure that the Guidelines reflect the fact that, in many cases, current sentences do not accurately reflect the seriousness of the offence.

(n) The Commission shall assure that the Guidelines reflect the general appropriateness of imposing a lower sentence than would otherwise be imposed, including a sentence that is lower than that established by statute as a minimum sentence, to take into account a defendant's substantial assistance in the investigation or prosecution of another person who has committed an offence.[20]

. . .

(q) The Commission and the Bureau of Prisons shall submit to Congress an analysis and recommendations concerning maximum utilization of resources to deal effectively with the Federal prison population. Such report shall be based on the consideration of a variety of alternatives including
(1) modernization . . .
(2) [using the lowest level of prison security possible]
(3) use of exiting Federal facilities, such as those currently within military jurisdiction.

. . .

(t) The Commission . . . shall describe what would be considered extraordinary and compelling reasons for sentence reduction, including the criteria to be applied and a list of specific examples. Rehabilitation of the defendant alone shall not be considered an extraordinary and compelling reason.

One must keep in mind, when reading this legislation, that it was passed in the middle of Ronald Reagan's presidency at a time when severity in sentencing was considerably more likely to be politically correct than would be either leniency or rationality in sentencing. The legislation set the stage for what occurred.

A few of the sections could be interpreted as suggesting restraint in the use of penalties. However, one has to use one's imagination, in many cases, to infer that this was the purpose. For example,

- the fact that sentences should be 'sufficient, but not greater' than necessary to comply with the purposes of sentencing.
- the fact that the legislated mandatory minimum penalties could be avoided if there were a motion from the government suggests a latent understanding of one small aspect of the problems such mandatory minima create.

---

[20] This section is particularly interesting because, as noted later in the essay, 'substantial assistance' to the prosecution is one of the few accepted ways of getting an appeal-proof downward departure. An earlier section, 3553(e), allows the court to set a sentence below a *statutory minimum sentence* only on motion of the prosecutor. This section does not require the government motion unless, presumably, the result would be to go below the statutory minimum sentence. However, the United States Sentencing Commission, in its 'substantial assistance' rules for departures, requires a 'motion from the government' for a downward departure for 'substantial assistance' in all cases, thus making downward departures much more difficult for the court to consider.

- the command to the Commission that helping a prosecutor is a reason to lower sentences.
- the statement that prison should not be used for corrective purposes, combined with the fact that rehabilitation could be useful could indicate that a group of people who might otherwise be imprisoned should not be.
- most clearly the statement that the Commission should formulate Guidelines that minimize the likelihood that the Federal prison population will exceed capacity.

Most of the legislation, however, appears to be telling the Commission to be tough, and not to let others undermine their toughness. Examples include the following:

- the provision that decisions concerning prison should generally not take into account 'standard' personal factors.
- the requirement that the Commission make recommendations concerning any change or expansion of facilities as a result of the Guidelines. Indeed, the fact that the Commission is to look into the possibility of using military facilities to imprison civilians suggests that Congress did not have leniency on its mind when passing the legislation.
- the requirements that maximum or near maximum terms of imprisonment be used for large classes of offenders.
- the requirement that the Guidelines specify a 'substantial' prison sentence for large groups of offenders.
- the statement that the Guidelines 'reflect the *fact*' (emphasis added) that in many cases current sentences do not accurately reflect the seriousness of the offence.
- the statement that there should be 'extraordinary and compelling reasons' for sentence reduction, but no parallel statement about sentence enhancement.
- the statement that 'rehabilitation of the defendant alone' shall not be a reason for sentence reduction.

There is some support in the legislation for the view that judges were to retain a fair amount of discretion to hand down sentences appropriate to the case. Freed[21] has focused on section 3553 and has noted that the 'standard' factors that had been used by judges in determining the sentence (e.g. nature and circumstances of the offence and the history and characteristics of the defendant) are listed prior to the guideline and policy statements of the Sentencing Commission. Similarly, as Miller and Freed[22] have noted, section 3553(b), particularly as amended, would seem to invite courts to consider whether the specific aggravating or mitigating circumstance in the

[21] D. Freed, see above, n. 8.
[22] M. Miller and D. Freed, 'Honouring Judicial Discretion under the Sentencing Reform Act', (1991) 3 *Federal Sentencing Reporter* 235, 236.

case at hand was adequately taken into account. In other words, although the Commission might have said that it had taken family obligations into account generally, the particular situation of the case might not have been considered and would, therefore, warrant departure.

Congress never said directly to the Commission that it wanted it to 'set up Guidelines that will have the effect of sending larger numbers of people to prison for longer periods of time than has ever occurred in American history'. However, I do not think it would be stretching things too much to suggest that this was an unspoken part of Congress' political intent.

At least some of the Commissioners appear to have believed, at the time they were doing their work, that the public wanted harsher sentences. In response to some discussion about public attitudes towards sentences at a conference in Canada in 1988, one Commissioner, Ilene Nagel, wrote to the then Canadian Minister of Justice warning him against accepting my argument that the public, when more informed about criminal sentences, did not appear to be quite so far from the judges as simple polling questions would suggest.[23] Perhaps to justify her own Commission's rather harsh Guidelines, Commissioner Nagel pointed out that

in the United States, as in most countries, public opinion surveys consistently show that upwards of three quarters of the public believe that sentences are too lenient and less than proportional to the harm of the offence. The general perception is that the system favours the defendant over the victim. Dr Doob claims that this is not the case in Canada. His reported data are so at odds with all of our experience that I would think it behooves one to examine most critically the data upon which he relies to base this claim.

I, of course, sent Commissioner Nagel a copy of a report based on these data but never heard from her. In any case, I am not sure how productive it would have been to try to choose between her 'experience' and my data. My (then) Minister of Justice, in any case, indicated that he had no real quarrels with my data or my conclusions.

The simple public opinion data that Nagel referred to are important. She is, of course, right about the estimates of public 'approval' of sentences. In the past 20 years or so, about three-quarters of American and Canadian respondents to public-opinion polls indicated that they believe that sentences are too lenient.[24] Roberts looked at a wide range of studies which

---

[23] See e.g. A. Doob and J. Roberts, 'Public Punitiveness and Public Knowledge of the Facts: Some Canadian Surveys', in N. Walker and M. Hough (eds.), *Public Attitudes to Sentencing: Surveys from Five Countries* (Cambridge, 1988); A. Doob and J. Roberts, *An Analysis of the Public's View of Sentencing: A Report to the Department of Justice* (Canada, 1983). Canadian Sentencing Commission, *Sentencing Reform: A Canadian Approach* (Report of the Canadian Sentencing Commission; Canada, 1987).

[24] J. Roberts, 'Public Opinion, Crime, and Criminal Justice', in M. Tonry (ed.), (1992) 16 *Crime and Justice: A Review of Research* 99, 148.

used a variety of methods. He concluded that in four different countries, including the USA, a comparison of public attitudes about punishing offenders with judicial attitudes and practices demonstrates that 'the public are not harsher than the courts, or at least are not consistently harsher as the poll findings would suggest'.[25]

Nevertheless, a public official, or a Commission full of public officials, could easily perceive the public—as well as Congress—as wanting harsher sentences than had been handed down prior to the Sentencing Reform Act. In this context, perceptions seem to have shaped reality. It is worth noting that the Sentencing Reform Act received bipartisan support.[26]

Any legislature that creates a new (and expensive[27]) institution must have lost faith in the ability of existing institutions to deal with the problem. There are indications that Congress had concerns that judges not be given too much freedom of choice in handing down sentences. For example, the legislative language requiring that the Guidelines restrict the use of particular kinds of sentences and the requirement that the range for any guideline involving incarceration be no more than six months or 25 per cent of the lower boundary of the guideline (whichever is greater) are indications of a deep distrust in judicial discretion.[28] Similarly, the use of the words 'extraordinary and compelling' when discussing sentence reductions suggests that the concerned and thoughtful views of judges alone should not guide sentence 'reductions' from guideline ranges.

My point is a simple one. The Sentencing Reform Act must be understood within the political context in which it was written. As Fox has noted:

One point that remains clear is that the Commission emerged from an organizational context which was heavily influenced by both political processes and *a priori* acceptance of the utility of retributive crime control policies . . . [L]iberal and conservative political interests and perspectives have found common ground in the establishment of the Commission. The Commission, in turn, was subject to the ideological influences and imperatives of the incumbent [Reagan] administration, not only in terms of power of appointment, but also in terms of advancing ideology

[25] Ibid. 149.
[26] 'Bipartisan' does not, in the United States, mean 'apolitical'. For example, in an attempt to remove at least party politics from the United States Sentencing Commission's operations, the Sentencing Reform Act requires that in the case of the United States Sentencing Commission, 'Not more than four members of the Commission shall be members of the same political party' (s. 991 (a)).
[27] The Commission spent about $6.5 million in fiscal year 1990 (United States Sentencing Commission, *Annual Report, 1990*).
[28] If the Guidelines had not subsequently been interpreted as being 'mandatory' rather than 'presumptive', this very narrow range might not have been so serious a problem. Nevertheless, 'presumptively' sentences were, in effect, to be 'determined' by the intersection of offence severity and criminal record.

further into the federal criminal justice system. In this context, it is ludicrous to view the Guidelines as being an 'objective' approach intended to resolve widespread dissatisfaction with sentencing.[29]

The United States Congress gave a reasonably clear message to the Commission: get tough on offenders, make sure there is no unwarranted variation in sentencing, and do not let the judges undermine that tough stand by using their discretion. Bring sentencing under control and write tough rigid Guidelines. If the will of Congress was not clear by its words, it certainly was clear by its deeds. Miller and Freed point out that 'Congress has repeatedly overridden the whole idea of structured sentencing discretion. In each election year since 1984 it has enacted new, harsher mandatory sentences, thereby preempting the discretion of both the Commission and the courts.'[30] Congress got what it asked for.

3. FETTERED SENTENCING UNFETTERED BY PRINCIPLES: THE NEW FEDERAL SENTENCING GUIDELINES

In April 1987 the Sentencing Commission released its first set of Guidelines. Two Commissioners—one a voting member (Paul Robinson) and one ex officio (Ronald Gainer)—dissented from the majority of the Commission. Robinson's dissent is part of the public record. Some of the conflicts that occurred in the months leading up to the release of the April 1987 Guidelines have also become part of the public record. Robinson's dissent (1987) is eloquent and detailed and lists as problems with the first set of Guidelines most of the issues that the Commission's critics have discussed since. Re-reading Robinson's dissent almost six years after it was written is a sobering exercise. For example, he suggests that 'the Guidelines are structured in a manner that will not permit the meaningful appellate review necessary for [their] refinement'. Though many of the critics of the Sentencing Commission have not stated their concern in quite that way, the effect has been the same: the appeals courts have not addressed the kinds of concerns that Robinson and most other Commission critics would have wanted them to.

But, in the long run, the dissent is not as important as the Guidelines. What did the Guidelines look like? Remembering that Congress appeared to want severity and inflexibility in sentencing, it is worth noting that the Commission repeated its interpretation of its mandate:

[29] J. Fox, 'Critical Perspectives on Selective Incapacitation and the Prediction of Dangerousness', in D. Champion (ed.), *The US Sentencing Guidelines: Implications for Criminal Justice* (New York, 1989), 148.
[30] M. Miller and D. Freed, 'The Commission under Fire: Constructive Advice or Destructive Attack?', (1990) 2 *Federal Sentencing Reporter* 207.

To understand these Guidelines and the rationale that underlies them, one must begin with the three objectives that Congress, in enacting the new sentencing law, sought to achieve. Its basic objective was to enhance the ability of the criminal justice system to reduce crime through an effective, fair sentencing system.[31]

Given that focus on the Sentencing Reform Act and the Guidelines was on the offence and the offender's record, a focus on crime control through deterrence and incapacitation would appear to signal heavier sentences.

One problem for the Commission, or any group that advocates utilitarian purposes in sentences, is that such purposes shift the focus to the long-term effects of sentences (i.e. actual crime control, if that could conceivably be achieved at the sentencing level). If one were to focus seriously on the utilitarian goals of sentencing (deterrence, incapacitation, rehabilitation) one would have to determine how best to achieve them. Presumably also, one would have to consider the various costs of achieving various goals. For example, one has to ask if long prison sentences really did deter burglars more than intermediate punishments, or whether being convicted is the deterrent and virtually any punishment above and beyond the stigma and costs of going through the criminal process adds nothing. Similarly, one would have to determine, if there was concern about public funds, whether funds expended on incapacitating a burglar would safeguard the community better than some other expenditure of these funds. One can, of course, avoid such a strict 'rational' utilitarian approach to sentencing, but to do so would fly in the face of the basic objective that the Commission had identified as its mandate. Apparently not knowing which way to turn, the Commission avoided the issue completely or, as one commentator delicately described it, the Commission 'did little to create a system of guiding principles'.[32] In the Commission's own words:

A philosophical problem arose when the Commission attempted to reconcile the differing perceptions of criminal punishment. Most observers of the criminal law agree that the ultimate aim of the law itself, and of punishment in particular, is the control of crime. Beyond this point, however, the consensus seems to break down. Some argue that the appropriate punishment should be defined primarily on the basis of the moral principle of 'just deserts'.... Others argue that punishment should be imposed primarily on the basis of practical 'crime control' considerations. Defendants sentenced under this scheme should receive the punishment that most effectively lessens the likelihood of future crime, either by deterring others or incapacitating the defendant.

Adherents of these points of view have urged the Commission to choose between them, to accord one primacy over the other. Such a choice would be profoundly

---

[31] United States Sentencing Commission, *Federal Sentencing Guidelines Manual* (1987), 1.2. Most criminologists would question the ability of any sentencing system to reduce crime. Evidence of the impact of different sentencing patterns (within a plausible range) would appear to favour the view that 'sentencing' and 'crime rates' are more or less independent.

[32] S. Koh, see above, n. 5, 1117.

difficult. The relevant literature is vast, the arguments deep, and each point of view has much to say in its favour. A clear-cut Commission decision in favour of one of these approaches would diminish the chance that the Guidelines would find the widespread acceptance they need for effective implementation. As a practical matter, in most sentencing decisions both philosophies may prove consistent with the same result.

For now, the Commission has sought to solve both the practical and philosophical problems of developing a coherent system by taking an empirical approach that uses data estimating the existing sentencing system as a starting point.[33]

The Commission notes that they did not simply copy previous estimates; they indicate that they departed from them for various reasons.

Various authors[34] have been critical of the Commission's avoidance of this difficult issue. In the end, however, the Commission probably was right: if what it really wanted to do is to put more people in prison for longer periods of time, and if departures from the Guidelines are to be discouraged at almost any cost, then principles and purposes are not worth worrying about.

Lack of principles was a problem that was to haunt the United States Sentencing Commission for years to come. The Commission, under the Sentencing Reform Act, is allowed to amend the Guidelines annually. The number of amendments in each of the years since they were first introduced in 1987 is immense. The problem, however, as one commentator has noted is that 'decisions seem to be made on some amendments without any substantive reasons other than conclusionary statements that certain offence levels "need to be raised"'.[35]

The amendment process appears to be one area where the freedom to act without being fettered by principles becomes quite clear. After pointing out that 'the Commission was designated as an independent agency in the judicial branch to ensure that it would be above the political fray', Weich notes that:

On April 10 and April 13, the Commission received correspondence from Senator Jesse Helms (Republican, North Carolina) and Congressman Thomas Bliley (Republican, Virginia) complaining that the proposed permanent amendments pertaining to cocaine base (crack) and obscenity resulted in insufficiently harsh sentences. *Some Commissioners expressed interest in revising the proposed permanent amendments in response to the Helms/Bliley letters* [emphasis added], but the close proximity of the May 1 deadline for submission of permanent amendments to Congress

[33] United States Sentencing Commission, *Federal Sentencing Guidelines Manual* (1988), 1.3–1.4.
[34] See e.g. A. von Hirsch, 'Federal Sentencing Guidenlines: Do They Provide Principled Guidance?', (1989) 27 *Am. Crim. L. Rev. 367.*
[35] F. Bennett, 'A Direct Participants Perspective on the Guideline Amendment Process', (1990) 3 *Federal Sentencing Reporter* 148, 149.

presented a practical obstacle to that course of action. Instead, the Commission published for public comment four proposed *emergency* [emphasis in the original] amendments that would significantly increase the guideline sentences in crack and obscenity cases.[36]

Professor Michael K. Block, as one of the original Commissioners who had put his name to the report endorsing no particular principles in setting out the initial Guidelines, in the end came to the realization that the lack of principles was a problem. After citing example after example of 'arbitrary change[s] in sentencing policy' he suggested, after resigning from the Commission, in testimony before the House of Representatives Subcommittee on Criminal Justice, that:

The personal preferences of Sentencing Commissioners as to what is 'good' or 'right' or 'just' should not be the basis for the Commission's policy decisions. The basis of those decisions must be information and information in particular on the costs and benefits of various policy options.

In its present form the Commission is at best a waste of the taxpayer's money and more likely . . . a destructive influence.[37]

What concerns me about these unsupported amendments is not only that the substantive changes may not be warranted, but also that the Commission's process for generating guideline amendments is developing in such a way as to hinder rational policy making. . . . The pure increases in offence levels in this amendment were not: (1) required, either explicitly or implicitly, by Congressional action, (2) responsive in any obvious manner to a problem that the Commission or its staff had identified in the operation of the initial guideline, or (3) intended to further the rationalizing of fraud sentencing begun in the initial guideline.[38]

The Commission's persistence in making sentencing law without articulating principles for the original Guidelines (or the changes in them) makes the role of the sentencing judge even more difficult. If judges are to give reasons, there must first be 'a reconsideration of what should count as a reason'.[39]

In any case, as matters stand now, many of the arguments about the Guidelines, amendments to them, principles of departures, etc., can be seen as problems inevitable in a complex system without explicit broadly accepted guiding principles.

[36] R. Weich, 'Emergency Amendments', (1989) 2 *Federal Sentencing Reporter* 71. As far as I can make out, the basis for the 'emergency' was never revealed.

[37] Michael K. Block in testimony before the Subcommittee on criminal justice of the [US] House [of Representatives] Judiciary Committee as reprinted in (1990) 2 *Federal Sentencing Reporter* 221, 222.

[38] M. Block, 'Emerging Problems in the Sentencing Commission's Approach to Guideline Amendments', (1989) 1 *Federal Sentencing Reporter* 451.

[39] A. Ashworth, 'Techniques of Guidance on Sentencing', [1984] *Crim. LR* 519, 528.

4. RELEVANT CONDUCT AND THE UNITED STATES SENTENCING COMMISSION GUIDELINES

On the surface, the Commission Guidelines are deceptively simple. There is a two dimensional grid with 43 rows corresponding to offence levels and six columns (corresponding to six categories of criminal records).[40] All one has to do is to determine the offence level and the record and then read the guideline range off the table.

It is not that simple, however. In grids used in state sentencing guidelines systems (e.g. that of Minnesota), an offence of conviction determines the row and a rather simple calculation of criminal record determines the column. In the United States Sentencing Commission Guidelines, there are serious problems involved in determining the appropriate offence level. The most important problem is the Commission's insistence that the 'relevant conduct' of the offender be used to determine the level of the offence rather than offence of conviction. This has been described by the Chair of the Commission as the 'corner-stone' of the Guidelines.[41]

In order to understand what 'relevant conduct' means, one first has to appreciate the fact that the (offence) rows in the sentencing table do not correspond to criminal offences. They correspond, for the most part, to a kind of 'penal value'. Hence one type of offence—trafficking in drugs, for example—can encompass the whole table, depending on a wide range of factors including the amount and type of drug, the role of the defendant in the deal, and other factors.

'Relevant conduct' sentencing under the Sentencing Commission means, in effect, that a person can be convicted of one count of an indictment and have the 'appropriate' offence level determined by two sets of factors:

1. the judge's assessment of the facts involved directly in the offence of conviction, and

2. a wide range of other related activity that is not covered by that one conviction.

[40] The United States Sentencing Commission was required by the Act that created it to establish 'categories of offences for use in the Guidelines' (s. 994(c) and 'categories of defendants for use in the Guidelines' (s. 994(d)). Hence, it is not surprising that the Commission created, as its basic structure the now familiar 'two-dimensional grid' with various gradations of offences and various levels of criminal record. This structure was, of course, a 'standard' in various state jurisdiction. No other sentencing grid, however, has anything close to the 258 cells contained in the sentencing table. Michael Tonry, referring to the United States Sentencing Commission sentencing table as a 'sentencing machine' ('Salvaging the Sentencing Guidelines in Seven Easy Steps', (1992) 4 *Federal Sentencing Reporter* 355, 358), noted that there are serious problems in both perception and in operation of the high level of specificity of the forty-three offence categories.

[41] W. Wilkins and J. Steer, 'Relevant Conduct: The Cornerstone of the Federal Sentencing Guidelines', (1990) 41 *S. Car. L. Rev.* 495.

If that appears complicated, it is. For example, the United States Sentencing Commission Guidelines Manual specifies that if

a stipulation as a part of a plea of guilty . . . specifically establishes facts that prove a more serious offence or offences than the offence or offences of conviction. . . . the court is to apply the guideline most applicable to the offence or offences established. . . . For example, if the defendant pleads guilty to theft, but admits the elements of robbery as part of the plea agreement, the robbery guideline is to be applied. . . . Similarly, if the defendant pleads guilty to one robbery but admits the elements of two additional robberies as part of a plea agreement, the guideline applicable to three robberies is to be applied.[42]

The rules for calculating the 'relevant conduct' are more complex than this quote would suggest. But it is important to realize that a person can plead guilty to one charge and find, lo and behold, that he is being sentenced for other things. Given that the test of the inclusion of all of these other things is the preponderance of evidence, it can easily be seen that obtaining convictions on all related counts becomes rather unimportant.[43] Being sentenced for behaviour that was not part of the convicted offences may seem strange to those who have not fully resigned themselves to the new world of Federal sentencing. It is, however, true. To quote from the editors of the *Federal Sentencing Reporter*, scholars whose knowledge of the Guidelines is unassailable:

[The relevant conduct rule is highly complex and] requires that despite a plea of guilty to a single crime, or to one count of a multiple-count indictment, a court must enhance the person's sentence by determining some of the 'relevant facts that will make a difference to this sentence' [from Guidelines Manual] even though those 'facts' bear on crimes of which the defendant was not convicted. . . . In the old [pre-Guidelines] system pleas offered some measure of control over information that would reach the court because the litigant could waive the preparation of a presentence report. . . . Such control is less possible where a prosecutor may drop charges at the plea stage and revive them at sentencing. Nor can litigants control pleas where probation officers may generate unexpected information of the kind that was reasonably excluded before. Thus relevant conduct in the guideline system has a powerful capacity to undermine a defendant's reasonable expectations. . . . Defense attorneys . . . have an important role to play in limiting the possibility of

---

[42] United States Sentencing Commission, *Federal Sentencing Guidelines Manual* (1988), 1.16.

[43] Thus, a defendant could plead guilty to one burglary involving very little loss to the victim only to find that a string of unproved burglaries involving large amounts of money determine the sentence. There is, however, still a requirement of at least one conviction before a person can be sentenced, though, if I understand the logic of 'real offence' sentencing correctly, it is not clear why the logic of the United States Sentencing Commission Guidelines would require that one has to be convicted of anything at all. The 'unproved' behaviour that was not part of the offence of conviction could, conceivably, have the impact of moving the guideline sentence from a sentence where probation was available (e.g. a sale of marijuana) to an offence level where a sentence of ten years or more was the 'mandatory' guideline sentence.

illusory bargains. A knowledgeable lawyer, familiar with the Guidelines, ought never plead a client guilty without control over relevant conduct information.[44]

To some extent, the Sentencing Commission relies on a pre-Guidelines case for justification for such a low standard of proof for taking 'relevant conduct' into account. Freed[45] notes that the low standard of proof made sense in the context of a system where rehabilitation was supposed to be the major purpose. It makes less sense when one is being punished and where there is little discretion on the use of such information.

In the context of the Commission Guidelines, however, a low standard of proof has peculiar results. As Freed notes:

Most lawyers as well as ordinary citizens unfamiliar with the [courts] are astonished to learn that a person in this society may be sentenced to prison on the basis of conduct of which a jury has acquitted him, or on the basis of charges that did not result in conviction. . . . [This] allows the prosecutor to increase an offender's sentence more easily by dropping charges than by [proving those charges].[46]

In some US Federal circuits, acquittals do not get an accused person very much. In a 1993 case which the US Second Circuit of Appeals refused to hear, the dissenting judge noted that an accused person

Frais was convicted of two firearms violations and acquitted of a drug conspiracy violation. His applicable guideline range based solely on the convicted conduct would have been 12 to 18 months. His actual guideline range, based in part on the drug conspiracy of which he was acquitted, was 210 to 262 months. This is the same range that would have been applicable had he been convicted of the drug conspiracy. . . . In Frais's case, we permitted acquitted conduct to increase a guideline range by 24 levels. Acquitted conduct was relied on to increase his sentence from 18 months to 20 years. . . . A just system of criminal sentencing cannot fail to distinguish between an allegation of conduct resulting in a conviction and an allegation of conduct resulting in an acquittal.[47]

5. AN EXAMPLE: THE GUIDELINES

Probably the easiest way to understand the mechanical operation of the US Sentencing Commission Guidelines is to take a specific example and work it through. As already pointed out, the Federal Guidelines employ a 258-cell grid. It has 43 different kinds (or levels) of offences and six kinds of offenders (or levels of criminal record). Since 'drugs' are such an important

[44] D. Freed and M. Miller, 'Plea Bargained Sentences, Disparity and Guideline Justice', (1991) 3 *Federal Sentencing Reporter* 175, 177.
[45] D. Freed, see above, n. 8.   [46] Ibid. 1714.
[47] *United States* v. *Nelson Frias*. Dissent from denial of rehearing en banc. (1993) 5 *Federal Sentencing Reporter* 299.

feature of the records of Federal prisoners,[48] I will use the example of a person who has pleaded guilty to the offence of conspiring to traffic in heroin. Let us imagine that our hypothetical offender, Billy, was found to have been in the process of arranging with a friend over the telephone to sell 225 grams of 25 per cent pure heroin to a young woman.

The first thing one learns is that, not surprisingly, the amount of drug makes a difference. Billy's 225 grams of heroin puts him in 'Level 26'. But what about the fact that Billy never actually sold the drug; that he had the misfortune to have been overheard on a wiretapped phone arranging to try to sell it. That makes no difference. Paragraph 2D1.4 ('Attempts and Conspiracies') makes it clear: 'If a defendant is convicted of participating in an incomplete conspiracy or an attempt to commit any offence involving a controlled substance, the offence level shall be the same as if the object of the conspiracy or attempt had been completed.' So far, it is still quite easy. But note that counting conspiracies, attempts, and so on as the same as the completed offence means that this avenue of reducing the seriousness of the charge is made considerably more difficult.

Another aspect of the Guideline system also acts to make things easier. The 'drug quantity table' which lists the amounts of each drug or type of drug for each of sixteen offence categories indicates in a footnote that:

The scale amounts of all controlled substances refer to the total weight of the controlled substance. Consistent with the provisions of the Anti-Drug Abuse Act, if any mixture of a compound contains any detectable amount of a controlled substance, the entire amount of the mixture or compound shall be considered in measuring the quantity.[49] If a mixture of compound contains a detectable amount of

[48] For example, drug offences are described as being the 'primary offence category' for 47% of defendants sentenced for federal offences for the 12 months ending 30 September 1990 (United States Sentencing Commission Annual Report, 1990, p. 43). They account for 53% of all (federal) sentences for prison. (United States Sentencing Commission Annual Report, 1991, cited by S. Schulhofer, 'Excessive Uniformity: How to Fix It', (1992) 5 *Federal Sentencing Reporter* 169.)

[49] A. Alschuler, 'The Failure of Sentencing Guidelines: A Plea for Less Aggregation', (1991) 4 *Federal Sentencing Reporter* 161, notes that the Supreme Court in upholding this aspect of the Guidelines 'noted that the Guidelines sentence for a first offender who sold 100 doses of LSD in sugar cubes would be 188 to 235 months. The dealer's sentence would have dropped by two-thirds had he or she sold the same quantity of LSD in blotter paper. . . . And it would have been [10 to 16 months] if the dealer had sold the LSD in pure form.' Alschuler did not comment on the Supreme Court's view of the effects of ingesting sugar on the health and teeth of America's drug users. He did, however, quote the economic advice given by the Chief Justice of the Supreme Court of the United States of America: 'We note that distributors of LSD make their own choice of carrier, and could act to minimize their potential sentences' (p. 162). Professor Alschuler reports one case where the cocaine a courier was carrying was 'chemically bonded to the suitcase'. The Appeal Court, including one former Sentencing Commissioner, approved of the decision to set the 'base offence level' by weighing the suitcase (conceding, however, that the metal fittings could first be removed). As Professor Alschuler points out, 'These results would have been inconceivable in the old regime of discretionary sentencing. Some judges are odd, but determining how many years to imprison someone by weighing sugar cubes, blotter paper, and suitcases is madness.'

more than one controlled substance, the most serious controlled substance shall determine the categorization of the entire quantity.

This drug table, and accompanying instructions, has a rather surreal quality to it. For example, 'where there are . . . multiple drug types, the quantities are to be added. Tables for making the necessary conversions are provided below.'[50] The actual 'drug equivalency tables' give us, as if it is scientific fact, the following examples of information:

1 gram of Codeine = 0.08 grams of heroin
1 gram of Cocaine = 0.2 grams of heroin
1 gram of Psilocybin = 0.5 grams of heroin or PCP
1 gram of marijuana = 1 mg. of heroin
1 marijuana plant[51] = 0.1 grams of heroin or 100 gm of marijuana
1 gram of Cocaine Base ('Crack') = 100 grams of cocaine/20 grams of heroin.[52]

Poor old Billy was not so smart. He should not have reduced the purity of his drugs before trying to sell them. He should not have tried to sell 225 grams of 25 per cent pure heroin (starting him off as a level 26 offender). He should have tried to find a buyer for the 75 grams of 75 per cent pure heroin he had purchased off the street. Then he would have started at Level 22. Under the Guidelines, 225 grams of any substance that includes *any amount* of heroin is a Level 26 offence. In other words, 220 grams of sugar mixed with 5 grams of heroin is the same as 5 grams of sugar mixed with 220 grams of heroin. For the United States Sentencing Commission, it is the thought that counts.

This is not a trivial difference. Assuming that Billy had no criminal record, it would mean the difference of a sentence of between 41 and 51 months for the Level 22 offence and between 63 and 78 months for the Level 26 offence. But Billy's problems do not stop there.

---

[50] United States Sentencing Commission, *Federal Sentencing Guidelines Manual* (1988), 2.40.

[51] Of any size, apparently.

[52] This particular equivalency is one of the more interesting in the table. Crack is made, I am told, by mixing street cocaine with water and baking soda and then heating the mixture. I understand that the mixture thickens and becomes a 'rock' that 'cracks' when burned. The effect, apparently, is that 100 grams of cocaine makes hundreds of grams of crack. That is, of course, one reason that crack is so cheap to buy: baking soda is cheap. Why then did the United States Sentencing Commission make crack such a high penal-value drug? One obvious reason is that in the USA, crack is seen as the ultimate evil in illicit drugs notwithstanding the fact that recent evidence would suggest that its addictive qualities are not dramatically worse than other drugs. (See e.g. Y. Cheung, P. Erickson, and T. Landau, 'Experience of Crack Use: Findings from a Community-Based Sample in Toronto', (1991) 21 *The Journal of Drug Issues* 121.) Crack also is said to be the drug of choice by the poor and by blacks, whereas cocaine, in its more natural form, has a history of being the drug of choice of the wealthy.

Billy was arranging to sell the drug to a 17-year-old. Paragraph 2D1.3(a)(2)(A) tells us that we should use the offence level corresponding to double the amount of drug involved 'for distributing a controlled substance . . . to an individual under the age of 21'. Billy then is to be considered as bad as someone selling 450 grams of heroin. That puts him in Level 28—where a first-time offender would be sentenced, according to the guideline, between 78 and 97 months.

Fortunately for Billy, he did not actually go out and sell his heroin. If he did, and carried a gun (which he usually did when trafficking in drugs because he was afraid of being mugged on the streets of Washington), he would have had his 'offence level' increased by two levels. This would have taken him to Level 30—97 to 121 months for a first offender.

There are other matters that could make Billy's sentence somewhat harsher. He would go up two more levels if his customer was found to be a pregnant woman (Paragraph 2D1.3.(a)(1)). Similarly, if Billy was distributing or manufacturing his drugs within 1,000 feet of a schoolyard, his offence level would be equivalent to the situation corresponding to double the amount of drugs involved (Paragraph 2D1.3.(a)(2)(B)). And, just to make sure that nobody gets off too lightly, the Commission points out that 'if both subsections . . . apply to a single distribution (e.g., the distribution of 10 grams of a controlled substance to a pregnant woman under 21 years of age), the enhancements are applied cumulatively, i.e., by using four times rather than two times the amount distributed'.[53] However, so as not to look too harsh, one gets only one enhancement for selling the drugs to someone under the age of 21 and selling it within 1,000 feet of a schoolyard.[54]

In Billy's case, there is a problem. The government was not able to determine with absolute certainty whether the woman Billy was arranging to sell to was pregnant. At the sentencing hearing, the judge must decide—using a preponderance of evidence standard—whether Billy's potential customer was under 21 and whether she was more likely pregnant than not. The Guidelines are complete—they contain a metric to imperial measure equivalency table. They give a table of the average weight of standard doses of such drug as LSD. Left out of the latest version of the Guidelines are instructions on determining from a telephone conversation whether an unnamed woman is pregnant.

[53] United States Sentencing Commission, *Federal Sentencing Guidelines Manual* (1988), 2.48.

[54] No explanation is given for this variation in the manner in which 'enhancements' are accumulated. Obviously, one can create *post hoc* reasons. In the absence of stated reasons, or an overall 'theory' of sentencing generally or of drug sentencing in particular, courts undoubtedly have a hard time doing anything but blindly following such directives. If explanations were given, a court could assess whether the particular case fitted the 'theory' behind the rule.

Let us assume, however, that Billy is lucky: either his customer is not pregnant, or else, the preponderance of evidence is that she is not and does not think she is pregnant, or at an absolute minimum, the US attorney knows nothing about her possible pregnancy. And, for the sake of simplicity, let us assume that it was reasonably clear that she was under 21 and that neither she, nor he, nor the planned meeting place was near a school. Let us also assume that Billy has not been charged, as he might have been, with 'using a communication facility in committing a drug offence', a 'base Level 12' offence. Explaining how this additional charge would affect the 'simple' drug conspiracy charge would be too complicated.

We can now move on to the 'adjustments'. Many of these adjustments are irrelevant in Billy's case:

(*a*) Adjustments (up) for victim vulnerability or the victim being a law enforcement or corrections officer or if the victim was physically restrained in the course of the offence.

(*b*) If the offender was a leader of five or more participants, or a manager or supervisor, he would be raised four or three levels, respectively. (Presumably the court will be able to determine, on the preponderance of evidence, whether a person was a 'leader' or a 'manager or supervisor'.)

(*c*) If the defendant's role in the offence was minimal or minor the offence level can be decreased by 4 or 2 points, respectively.

(*d*) If the defendant abused a position of trust, the offence level is increased by two levels.

(*e*) If the defendant impeded, obstructed the administration of justice during the investigation, or attempted to do so, the offence level goes up two levels. (This could be something like destroying or concealing material evidence, according to the official Commission commentary.)

(*f*) If the offender 'clearly demonstrates a recognition and affirmative acceptance of personal responsibility for his criminal conduct' the offence level is reduced two levels.

Generally speaking, with the exception of criminal record, the characteristics of the offender are not relevant in determining the sentence under the Guidelines. The Guidelines Manual contains the following policy statements:

'Age is not ordinarily relevant in determining whether a sentence should be outside the Guidelines. . . . Age *may* [emphasis added] be a reason to go below the Guidelines when the offender is elderly *and* [emphasis in original] infirm and where a form of punishment (e.g. home confinement) might be equally efficient[55] as and less costly than incarceration.' Billy, like most drug dealers, doesn't qualify.

---

[55] I was unable to determine what 'efficient' means.

'Education and vocational skills are not ordinarily relevant in determining whether a sentence should be outside the Guidelines.'

'Mental and emotional conditions are not ordinarily relevant in determining whether a sentence should be outside the Guidelines.'

'Physical condition is not ordinarily relevant in determining whether a sentence should be outside the Guidelines.'

'Employment record is not ordinarily relevant in determining whether a sentence should be outside the Guidelines.'

'Family ties and responsibilities and community ties are not ordinarily relevant in determining whether a sentence should be outside the Guidelines.'

'Race, sex, national origin, creed, religion, and socio-economic status . . . are not relevant in the determination of a sentence.'

A pre-sentence report was done in the case, and it became clear after the probation officer spoke to the police that Billy had experienced the misfortune of having another call wiretapped by the police in which he had attempted to sell drugs. This other case, as it turned out, involved an undercover police officer from another law-enforcement agency as the purchaser. The wiretap evidence had some serious legal deficiencies in it and would probably not be admissible. Even if admissible, the prosecutor thought that it, alone, would not be sufficient to obtain a conviction. In addition, for a variety of reasons it was deemed best not to call the other police officer. Billy's lawyer had told the prosecutor that Billy would not plead guilty to an offence involving this episode.

Billy does not get much of a break, however. The preponderance of evidence suggested that Billy was trying to make another deal, and the amount of this transaction was added to the other one. This particular transaction seemed to involve half an ounce of 'crack'. Half an ounce, according to the Sentencing Commission's 'measurement conversion table',[56] is 14.175 grams. Since one gram of crack is equal to 20 grams of heroin, it is clear that the crack is equivalent (in penal value in the US Federal system, if nothing else) to 283 grams of heroin.

Presumably, had there been adjustments for such matters as Billy's customer being pregnant, this amount would be added after those adjustments had been made. We were, as you will no doubt remember, up to a score of 450 grams of heroin. We now add 283 + 450 to get a penal equivalent of 733 grams which makes Billy a Level 30 offender. The uncharged discussion about the sale of the crack cost Billy somewhere between 24 and 31 extra months in prison.

---

[56] United States Sentencing Commission, *Federal Sentencing Guidelines Manual* (1988), 2.45.

An important power given to the prosecutor (in addition to the enhanced power given to prosecutors to plea bargain) is that 'upon motion of the government stating that the defendant has made a good faith effort to provide substantial assistance in the investigation or prosecution of another person who has committed an offence, the court may depart from the Guidelines'.[57] There are a number of important aspects of this license to depart. The most obvious, of course, is that the departure consideration must be triggered by a 'motion of the government'.[58]

Of equal importance is the fact that one's ability to be considered for a departure in such a situation is limited by one's possession of knowledge that can be of 'substantial assistance' to the prosecutor. Presumably, therefore, if Billy does not really know much about his own source of drugs (he may simply buy them from various people he runs into casually), he can't be of substantial assistance. Alternatively, he cannot be of substantial assistance if the police already know his source (or if his source is, in fact, an undercover drug operation). As various people have pointed out, this provision helps the 'big guys' and gives nothing to the little guys in a crime operation. It also appears to be used to differing extents in different places. Heaney[59] reports rates of downward departures from the Guidelines ranging from 2.3 per cent to 22 per cent in different locations.

Unfortunately, I have thus far only described one of the two dimensions of the one-page grid that determines sentencing in the US Federal criminal jurisdiction. The other dimension is the criminal history. The Commission notes that:

A defendant's record is directly relevant to the [purposes of sentencing]. A defendant with a record of prior criminal behaviour is more culpable than a first offender and thus deserving of greater punishment. General deterrence of criminal conduct dictates that a clear message be sent to society that repeated criminal behaviour will aggravate the need for punishment with each recurrence. To protect the public from further crimes of the particular defendant, the likelihood of recidivism and future behaviour must be considered. Repeated criminal behaviour is an indicator of a limited likelihood of successful rehabilitation.[60]

[57] United States Sentencing Commission, *Federal Sentencing Guidelines Manual* (1988), section 5K1.1.

[58] As noted earlier, the United States Sentencing Commission obviously took this 'formula' from the Sentencing Reform Act provisions that allow sentences below statutory minima for certain offences under similar conditions. Rather than allowing departures any time the judge (alone) thought it appropriate for 'substantial assistance' the Commission decided to restrict it as the Act had restricted departures below statutory minima. This restriction clearly was not mandated by the Sentencing Reform Act, but it does serve the purpose of removing the ability to make judgments away from judges.

[59] G. Heaney, 'Response to William W. Wilkins, Jr., Chairman of the Sentencing Commission', (1992) 4 *Federal Sentencing Reporter* 236.

[60] United States Sentencing Commission, *Guidelines Manual* (1988), ch. 4: 'Criminal History and Criminal Livelihood', 4.1.

Some might not find it all so easy, but clearly the Commission had no trouble justifying heavier sentences for those with criminal records.

I do not want to go into great detail about the calculation of criminal history. Essentially, the previous sentences that the defendant has received determine the outcome. He gets three points for each previous sentence that was over 13 months, two points for each sentence between 2 and 13 months, and one point for any other sentence. And two points are added if the offence for which the sentencing hearing was being held occurred within two years or his being released from prison or if it occurred while on some form of criminal-justice control (probation, parole, etc.).

The highest category of 'criminal history' is for those with 13 or more points. It is a fairly safe criminological bet that the Sentencing Commission's efforts will not reduce re-offending (or at least will not reduce re-conviction). In the near future, with more people being sentenced to prison, people now will be accumulating points at a faster rate than ever before. Hence, the next time they commit a federal crime, they will move even faster than previously to the higher end of the 'criminal-history scale'.

In Billy's case, let us assume that he had twice previously been sentenced to prison for over 13 months and had committed this offence within two years of his most recent release. That would give him eight points and place him in Category IV of the criminal-history dimension. If the criminal-history score does not appear to the judge to reflect adequately how bad the defendant really is (e.g. because he was treated leniently in the past), the judge can depart (upwards, presumably). The Commission does not give any examples under the section 'Adequacy of the Criminal History Category' of people whose criminal-history score exaggerates their past evil deeds.

If Billy were over the age of 18, had twice been previously convicted of felonies involving drugs (or violence), and, as in this instance, was again convicted of a drug (or violence offence), his criminal-history level would be raised and he would be placed, automatically, in the highest criminal-history category.

For purposes of our example, let us give Billy a break and assume that his previous convictions were for property offences.

Billy has now, in effect, been sentenced. The information is all collated by the probation officer and all of the calculations are done by this person as well. The probation officer places all of the information and calculations before the court. The court may have to make some findings (e.g. whether on the preponderance of evidence, Billy's customer is or was pregnant at the time he was talking to her on the telephone). He is a 30-IV offender. Now all that is left for the judge to do is to look it up in the one-page table. Billy's sentence is '135–168' months. The judge can sentence Billy to anything he wants as long as it is between 11.25 years and 14 years. The chances are, according to data from the Commission, Billy will be sentenced at or near the bottom of the range, thus confirming, no doubt, how soft the sentences are that are handed down by US Federal judges.

Billy will not be paroled: there is no parole available now. But if Billy behaves himself, he will be credited with 54 days at the end of each year of his term of imprisonment. Assuming that he was given a sentence of 12 years, and assuming he behaves himself, he will get out in about ten and a half years. The direct costs to the US taxpayer of his incarceration will be close to a quarter of a million dollars. Presumably the Sentencing Commission has determined that this is money well spent.

6. DEPARTURE FROM THE GUIDELINES

Departures from the Guidelines are obviously allowed under certain circumstances; there is, presumably, at least a linguistic difference between 'Guidelines' and mandatory sentences. As noted above, however, the legislation indicated that the reasons to give a reduced sentence had to be 'extraordinary and compelling'.

The Commission's initial statements about departures, however, looked fairly benign. 'Evolutionary' rather than 'revolutionary' was the way they were occasionally described. In its own words:

The new sentencing statute permits a court to depart from a guideline-specified sentence only when it finds 'an aggravating or mitigating circumstance . . . that was not adequately taken into consideration by the Sentencing Commission . . .' 18 U.S.C. §3553(b). Thus, in principle, the Commission, by specifying that it had adequately considered a particular factor, could prevent a court from using it as a grounds for departure. In this initial set of Guidelines, however, the Commission does not so limit the court's departure powers. The Commission intends the sentencing courts to treat each guideline as carving out a 'heartland', a set of typical cases embodying the conduct that each guideline describes. When a court finds an atypical case, one to which a particular guideline linguistically applies but where the conduct significantly differs from the norm, the court may consider whether departure is warranted. . . .

By monitoring when courts depart from the Guidelines and by analyzing their stated reasons for doing so, the Commission, over time, will be able to create more accurate Guidelines that specify precisely where departures should and should not be permitted.[61]

Though such words may have helped encourage judges and others to view the Guidelines as being rather soft on departures, the Commission gave adequate warning of how they saw the Guidelines. In discussing their view

---

[61] United States Sentencing Commission, *Guidelines Manual* (1988), 1.16–1.17.

that certain economic crimes were being dealt with too leniently in pre-Guidelines days, the Commission wrote that:

The Commission's solution to this problem has been to write Guidelines that classify as 'serious' (and therefore subject to *mandatory* [emphasis added] prison sentences) many offences for which probation is now frequently given. At the same time, the Guidelines will permit the sentencing court to impose short prison terms in many such cases. The Commission's view is that the definite prospect of prison, though the term is short, will act as a significant deterrent to many of these crimes, particularly when compared with the status quo where probation, not prison, is the norm.[62]

In other words, the Guideline sentence of a term of imprisonment has now become 'mandatory'.

A central issue, in determining whether a departure can be made, is whether the Commission adequately considered a particular factor before deciding that it should not be given any weight. One set of views on this issue came out as a result of an assessment by a trial court that the Commission had not adequately considered an important characteristic of a convicted drug trafficker. The case, a couple of years after the Guidelines came into place, involved a female addict who was convicted of selling a small amount of cocaine. The sentencing judge remarked that:

For the Guidelines not to make a distinction . . . between the dealer/distributor who preys upon our citizens and the addict who is essentially a medical case and a victim, is to me incomprehensible. . . . [After sentencing Mrs Grant to the bottom of the guideline range—27 months—the judge said] I think that my explication of the matters . . . inadequately considered by the sentencing commission sufficiently explains why I have chosen the bottom of the range.[63]

Judge Broderick's reasons were sent, by the prosecutor, to the Commission for comment. The response is interesting, in view of the early statements that the Commission had no intent to close off departures on the basis of their own assessments that had adequately considered a particular factor.

Section 5H1.4 specifically states that 'drug dependence or alcohol abuse is not a reason for imposing a sentence below the Guidelines.' I certainly respect Judge Broderick's opinion about what should be the appropriate sentence. I disagree with his statement that this is 'a very good example of the inadequate consideration that the Sentencing Commission has given to the role that addiction plays in the commission of crimes.' To the contrary, the Commission spent a great deal of time

[62] Ibid. 1.9. Note that 'mandatory' prison terms are seen as a 'significant deterrent'. 'Certainty' in deterrence theory appears to be equivalent to 'certainty of imprisonment' rather than 'certainty of some punishment'.
[63] Decision of Judge Vincent L. Broderick, Southern District, New York in *US* v. *Andrea Grant* (1989) 2 *Federal Sentencing Reporter* 167.

discussing the issue. Some advocated that it should be a mitigating factor while others advocated that drug abuse was a reliable indicant for propensity to commit crimes and thus should be an aggregating [*sic*] factor. While reasonable people can disagree about the position the Commission took it is not correct to assume that we did not view this issue as important and did not fully consider it.[64]

I am not Judge Broderick, nor, of course, am I even a judge. However, I am not convinced that if I were either I would be very convinced by the Commission's assertion that they had 'spent a great deal of time discussing the issue' and had disagreed about it. This strikes me as being similar to the arguments that some of my students give when they get a bad mark on an exam: 'But I studied a long time for this exam. How can I get a bad mark?' Though one can easily accept the view that the Commission wrestled with the problem, does this automatically mean that their consideration is deemed to be 'adequate'? One point is clear, however: if the Commission asserts that they had adequately considered a point, its own view is that that is enough. They view themselves as having the last word on judging their own work.[65]

Early in the history of the Guidelines, some judges were optimistic about their ability to depart:

Although new federal sentencing Guidelines provide for incarceration for the majority of offences, and departures from the Guidelines must be explained by the judge at the time of sentencing, they do not prevent the courts from acting sensibly. There is no reason why we cannot continue to take advantage of available alternatives to prison by granting permissible downward departures from guideline-mandated prison terms.

[T]he Commission sensibly provided wide discretion to depart from the Guidelines when the particular circumstances of a case so require. Congress recognized in the statute that rehabilitation must be considered by the courts in fashioning individual sentences. The Guidelines are just that: they are not rigid mandates and the judges's discretion remains. . . . The uniqueness of each defendant who comes before us, and the impossibility of mechanically predicting in advance all of the relevant circumstances surrounding every case, have left open myriad permissible grounds for departure. [He then goes on to list 11 factors that he thinks have not been adequately taken into account by the commission, including such things

[64] United States Sentencing Commission Chairman William Wilkins's letter to the US Attorney who prosecuted the case. Reprinted in (1989) 2 *Federal Sentencing Reporter* 169.

[65] In any case, the Sentencing Commission's response to Judge Broderick's criticism should be compared to the first quotation from the Sentencing Commission in this section of my paper: '[I]n principle . . . by specifying that it had adequately considered a particular factor [the Commission] could prevent a court from using it as a grounds for departure. In this initial set of Guidelines, however, the Commission does not so limit the court's departure powers.' The Commission may have changed its view between 'its initial set of Guidelines' and those in place in 1989.

as having young children at home needing supervision, that the defendant's business provides employment for others, 'the good a defendant has done in his lifetime'.][66]

The Guidelines had been in place for less than a year at that point and had not yet been declared constitutional by the US Supreme Court. However, one of the Commissioners, Ilene Nagel, pointed out at the same symposium that Judge Weinstein was, as we used to say when we were children, 'dreaming in Technicolour':

The Guidelines are mandatory rather than voluntary, with the exception of those few instances in which the judge expressly departs; that is, they are binding on the courts. . . . Additionally, there is a statutory provision which permits the judge to depart from the guideline sentence. These departures are triggered by a positive response to a two-tiered test: (1) If there is a factor identified by the judge that was not considered by the Commission, which (2) would justify a sentence *other* than that prescribed by the Guidelines, the judge may depart so long as he justifies and explains the departures with written reasons. Departures may, of course, be appealed by counsel for either side. In general, they are meant to be reserved for the unusual, atypical, extraordinary case.[67]

It is important to note that Commissioner Nagel did not refer to factors that had not been 'adequately' considered by the Commission. In effect, by June of 1988, judges were being told, by the Commission itself, that if a factor had been considered and rejected by the Commission as a ground for departure, then it could not be used as grounds for departure. The 'evolution' of the Guidelines took less than a generation of cases.

Judge Weinstein, who in 1988 had spoken favourably of the Commission's 'sensible provision to depart from the Guidelines', had by 1993 confessed to his mistake. On 12 April 1993 he wrote a memorandum to his fellow judges in the Eastern District of New York saying, in part:

On one day last week I had to sentence a peasant woman from West Africa to 46 months in a drug case. The result for her young children will undoubtedly be, as she suggested, devastating. On the same day, I sentenced a man to 30 years as a second drug offender. . . . These two cases confirm my sense of depression about much of the cruelty I have been party to in connection with the 'war on drugs'. . . . I need a rest from the oppressive sense of futility that these drug cases leave. . . . I have therefore taken my name out of the wheel for drug cases. . . . This resolution leaves me uncomfortable since it shifts the 'dirty work' to other judges. At the moment, however, I simply cannot sentence another impoverished person whose destruction

[66] Eastern District of New York Judge Jack B. Weinstein at a symposium 15 June 1988 reprinted in (1988) 1 *Federal Sentencing Reporter* 96.
[67] United States Sentencing Commissioner Ilene Nagel at a symposium 15 June 1988, reprinted in (1988) 1 *Federal Sentencing Reporter* 102.

has no discernible effect on the drug trade. . . . I am just a tired old judge who has temporarily filled his quota of remorselessness.[68]

Tonry[69] notes the irony of the Commission's position on mandatory Guidelines[70] in that the Commission itself was critical of the US Congress' attraction to mandatory penalties. The Commission suggested that mandatory penalties (or mandatory minimum penalties) have a large number of unfortunate effects on the pre-trial, trial, and sentencing process (e.g. by encouraging plea bargaining to avoid what all parties consider to be inappropriately harsh sentences). Tonry points out that 'these are, of course, precisely the same charges that critics lay against the Commission's Guidelines'.[71] The Guidelines Manual is not the only place the Commission refers to its Guidelines as being 'mandatory'. And clearly the Commission intends its Guidelines to be seen as being mandatory. Here are the words of the Chairman of the Commission and one of its staff:

While the statute begins by listing seven broad factors that courts must 'consider' before imposing sentence, including applicable sentencing Guidelines and policy statements, it immediately follows that listing by directing that courts sentence in accordance with the applicable Guidelines unless the court identifies one or more aggravating or mitigating factors 'not taken into consideration by the Sentencing Commission in formulating the Guidelines that should result in a sentence different from that described.' In other words, under the [Sentencing Reform Act] scheme, the Guidelines are *mandatory*, except in cases that are significantly atypical. This feature has important implications for the ability of the Guidelines significantly to reduce the influence of invidious sentencing factors [emphasis in the original].[72]

The appeal courts have responded to the issue of departures by supporting the Commission's views. One early example of judicial caution in challenging the Commission or its interpretation of the Sentencing Reform Act comes from an appeal of a sentence of 16 months on a charge of conspiracy to create and to supply false immigration documents. The relevant guideline was determined to be imprisonment for 10 to 16 months. The defence wanted a downward departure on the grounds that the defendant was 65 years old, had heart problems, hypertension, diabetes, and alcohol dependence. The prosecutor did not object to suspension of the sentence. The trial court refused, noting that 'the reason we have this Reform Act is that

---

[68] J. Weinstein, 'Memorandum', reprinted in full in (1993) 5 *Federal Sentencing Reporter* 298.

[69] M. Tonry, 'Judges and Sentencing Policy: The American Experience', in C. Munro and M. Wasik (eds.), *Sentencing, Judicial Discretion and Training* (London, 1992), 137, 150.

[70] An oxymoron everywhere except, apparently, in the Commission's offices.

[71] See above, n. 69.

[72] W. Wilkins, Jr., P. Newton (Staff Director, United States Sentencing Commission), and J. Steer (General Counsel, United States Sentencing Commission), 'The Sentencing Reform Act of 1984: A Bold Approach to the Unwarranted Sentencing Disparity Problem', (1991) 2 *Criminal Law Forum* 355, 368–9.

Congress was tired of judges departing from [its] prescribed sentence'. On appeal, the door that had been shut by the trial court was locked up tight by the appeal court: 'We conclude that the district court's discretionary refusal to depart downward from the sentencing Guidelines is not subject to review on appeal. Accordingly, we dismiss this appeal.'[73]

The non-reviewability of a failure to depart means, in effect, that even if there are arguments that the 'wrong' sentence was given, the appeals courts will not consider the appeal.[74]

Similar examples are easy to find. Because the Guidelines do not allow personal characteristics to be taken into account, it is inevitable that appeal courts, who do not have to face the defendant, will be less likely than trial courts to be tolerant of special problems. Schwarzer cites one appeal court decision reversing a downward departure of a female defendant, 'who on entering prison would have to leave her three small children with her ill mother a thousand miles away'. The court's view of this was simple: the case presented nothing unusual because 'imposition of prison sentences normally disrupts family relationships'.[75] In another, the court reversed a downward departure for a pregnant defendant on the ground that 'since time immemorial the sins of parents have been visited on children and to allow such a departure would set a dangerous precedent since it should send an obvious message to all female defendants that pregnancy is a way out'.[76]

Professor Daniel Freed is particularly brutal in his condemnation of the Court of Appeal's role in accepting the Commission's view of the Guidelines. In his carefully argued and well-documented view he concludes that 'the courts have misread the *Guidelines Manual* and [have] not read the Sentencing Reform Act'.[77] He demonstrates that the appeals courts have not assessed whether the Guidelines conform to the Sentencing Reform Act, nor have they ever, it seems, tested the assertion by the Sentencing Commission that they have 'adequately considered' the various factors that they declare to be outside of the role of the sentencing judge to consider. As he points out, the Commission seems to take the view, and the appeals courts appear to accept the view, that simply asserting that they have given adequate consideration to a factor means that they have.

The guideline ranges are narrow, departures are difficult, and the appeal courts have generally accepted the views of the Sentencing Commission. It is not surprising, therefore, that judges 'feel that federal law obligates them to hand down sentences that they strongly believe are inappropriate'.[78]

[73] *US* v. *Lucio Morales* (1990) 2 *Federal Sentencing Reporter* 291.
[74] S. Koh (see above, n. 5) points out that one can then get disparity created by the variation in the willingness of trial judges to take a chance and depart from the Guidelines.
[75] W. Schwarzer, 'Judicial Discretion in Sentencing', (1991) 3 *Federal Sentencing Reporter* 339.
[76] Ibid. 340.   [77] D. Freed, see above, n. 8, 1732.
[78] M. Miller and D. Freed, see above, n. 22, 235.

Miller and Freed point out that section 3553(a) ('Factors to be considered in imposing a sentence') lists the Guidelines as item number four after such traditional factors as '(1) the nature and circumstances of the offence and the history and characteristics of the defendant; (2) the need for the sentence imposed to [achieve the traditional purposes of sentencing]; (3) the kinds of sentences available'. They suggest that the legislative history suggests that these three traditional considerations should come first—i.e. before the Guidelines. The question, then, is why judges surrendered so quickly to the rigid rules stated or implied by the Commission?

The judges' passivity in accepting the Sentencing Commission's rigid view of their own Guidelines is, as Miller and Freed[79] point out, particularly peculiar given that Congress in 1987 amended the section dealing with departures in such a way as to make it seemingly easier to show that a departure from the Guidelines was justified. The original legislation indicated that a sentence within the guideline range was to be imposed 'unless the court finds that an aggravating circumstance exists that was not adequately taken into account by the Sentencing Commission'. In 1987 this section was modified such that the words 'of a kind or to a degree' were inserted after the word 'circumstance'.

Part of the answer lies, I think, in the peculiar history of sentencing in the US Federal system. Unlike the situation in Canada or the UK, sentence appeals are really a new phenomenon. Prior to the implementation of the Commission Guidelines, there were no sentence appeals of the kind that are common in England and in Canada. For incarcerated prisoners, it was the Parole Board that, in effect, did the sentencing. The appeals courts, like the trial courts, were new at the sentencing business. And the Sentencing Commission were the experts. The results seem to have been that the appeals courts were as timid in dealing with the Commission Guidelines as the trial judges were angry. Their timidity led, it would seem, in most circuits, to a case by case surrender to the views of the United States Sentencing Commission. The appeals courts, as one trial judge who was also the Chairman of the Committee on Law and Probation Administration of the Judicial Conference of the United States told the Commission in an open hearing, 'in the area of departures . . . believe that the Guidelines are written in stone and that an act of departure is something which has to be curbed'.[80]

The perception of how the appeals courts would respond to departures was only part of the problem. One former Assistant US Attorney noted:

[79] M. Miller and D. Freed, see above, 235–8.
[80] 'Excerpt from the Testimony of Judge Broderick' [at a public hearing on proposed amendments to the Sentencing Guidelines], reprinted in (1991) 3 *Federal Sentencing Reporter* 289, 290.

Our constitutional anxiety about lost responsibility [for sentencing policy] should be redoubled by the Sentencing Commission's warning that it intends to actively police interpretation of the Guidelines by federal judges. One Commissioner warned last year that should mitigating reductions of guideline sentences run much higher than 15% of cases, the Commission might well amend the Guidelines to forbid 'departures' altogether. This is a heavy club when the Guidelines fail to give weight to so many of the factors that enter into just sentencing, including the deleterious effect that jail may have on some first offenders in minor crimes. The Commission seems to lack confidence in the process of appellate review to guard the integrity of departures.[81]

The concern by practitioners about the closing off of what flexibility still exists in the Guidelines was made quite clear in a letter from one Federal defender to one of the Sentencing Commissioners:

I don't perceive an atmosphere existing where input from people like myself would have much impact on Sentencing Commission policies. Indeed, it seems more likely to me that anything I tell you would only be used to close the 'loopholes' that give the practice under the Sentencing Guidelines the little flexibility that remains . . . I must candidly tell you that I would be unwilling to reveal any 'tricks of the trade' that I have learned . . . because to do so might compromise the cases of the people I currently represent.[82]

7. WHAT IS DISPARITY, WAS IT REDUCED, AND IF IT WAS REDUCED, WAS THAT A GOOD THING?

The problem in evaluating whether unwarranted disparity has been 'reduced' as a result of the Sentencing Guidelines is that we have *in theory and in practice* no appropriate way of assessing levels of disparity before or after the implementation of the Guidelines. Before the implementation of the Guidelines, the model or theory of sentencing held by the sentencing judge presumably varied from judge to judge and from offender to offender. Simulation exercises have, of course, shown variation in sentences given in identical (hypothetical) cases. With the US Sentencing Commission Guidelines, if one ignores the difficulty in determining what the proper guideline would be, one can assess what proportion of sentences are within the guideline range. This is essentially what the Commission did in its December 1991 report on the Guidelines. In that report they compared the proportion of post-Guidelines sentences that were within the appropriate

---

[81] R. Wedgewood, (1989) 1 *Federal Sentencing Reporter* 359.
[82] Letter from M. Katz (Federal defender, Colorado) to United States Sentencing Commissioner Ilene H. Nagel dated 21 February 1990, reprinted in (1990) 2 *Federal Sentencing Reporter* 229, 230.

guideline with the proportion of pre-Guidelines sentences that were within the guideline range. Not surprisingly, 'disparity' (but perhaps, depending on one's point of view, not unwarranted disparity) decreased. The General Accounting Office's August 1992 report is somewhat less glowing than is the Commission on this issue. They found that the amount of sentencing disparity had been reduced, though they suggested that some unwarranted disparity still existed.

There are, however, two serious problems with the Commission's (and the General Accounting Office's) approach. The first is that the test of disparity is inappropriate. The Commission is, in effect, going one step further than comparing apples to oranges. When looking at post-Guidelines sentences, it is comparing real sentences to their notion of 'ideal' sentences (complete compliance with the Guidelines). But pre-Guidelines sentences were handed down on a different model. It is not surprising that pre-Guidelines sentences show more 'disparity' when compared to a standard that did not exist when they were being handed down. Prior to the promulgation of the Guidelines, nobody in the world would ever have used a standard such as the Commission Guidelines as a 'standard of excellence' against which sentences should be evaluated. It is, in effect, asking whether an apple tastes as much like an orange as an orange does.

For example, if pre-Guidelines sentences were reliably being handed down on the basis of a 'perfect' estimate of rehabilitative potential (i.e. the most rehabilitative sentence available was invariably assigned to an offender—a rather far-fetched notion but useful for this example), such sentences would, if assessed in line with that model, show no unwarranted disparity. They would, however, be likely to be uncorrelated with the 'appropriate' US Commission Guideline sentence. The General Accounting Office, for example, noted that the data it had on pre-Guidelines sentences 'focused on personal information, such as socio-economic status and family and community ties, that was supposed to be irrelevant under the Guidelines in all or most cases'. These data were relevant to sentencing prior to 1987 and irrelevant after. Similarly, it seems unlikely that, prior to 1987, files would contain much information on 'relevant conduct'.

Thus one would hardly need to do research to find the answer to the question that the General Accounting Office set itself: 'to determine . . . whether or not the guideline reduced the variation in sentences . . . by groups of offenders who committed similar crimes and who had similar criminal histories'.[83] If the judges were following the Guidelines at all it would be almost inevitable that their post-Guidelines sentences would con-

---

[83] United States General Accounting Office, *Sentencing Guidelines: Central Questions Remain Unanswered* (Report to Congressional Committees, 1992), 9.

form to the Guidelines more than the pre-Guidelines sentences conformed to the yet-to-be-written Guidelines.

The second point that should be made is that the more simple, the more mechanistic, and the less human the judgment involved in the guideline sentencing process, the less potential there would be for 'unwarranted disparity' if one uses 'variation from the guideline' as one's only measure of unwarranted disparity. A system based on the principle that the only thing that mattered was the offence of conviction and which had a single legislated fixed sentence (*n* months for *x* offence) would have no 'unwarranted disparity' if it could be implemented without circumvention. And such a system of measuring disparity that ignored all variation in sentencing created at the charge and plea stages of the proceeding would be able to show that it had 'solved' the disparity problem. I doubt that many people would see this as much of an accomplishment.[84]

The point that I am making is that compliance with the Guidelines is one thing, but in the absence of an agreed upon 'theory' of sentencing, compliance with the Guidelines is not everything.

The Commission's own data show some variation across the country in some of the important indicators. It is, however, a little difficult to know what this variation means without more complete knowledge of the nature of the cases. The rate of downward departures from the guideline range for 'substantial assistance' to the prosecutor (which have to be initiated by the prosecutor) varies from a low in one circuit of 2.4 per cent of cases to a high of 13.9 per cent of cases. These could, of course, reflect differences in the mix of (Federal) cases in the different circuits.

A careful examination of the evidence that the Commission puts forward in its 1991 'self-evaluation' has not convinced most observers that, even using its own definitions, there is convincing evidence of a substantial reduction in disparity, except in that any system that moves towards a 'mandatory' sentence must show some reduction in variation of sentences. As Tonry points out, it would be astonishing if there were not a reduction in variation in sentencing measured in terms of rate of compliance with the applicable Guidelines as 'objectively measured'—the measure the Commission would want us to accept.[85]

The Commission looked carefully at only a small number of offences (bank robbery, embezzlement, and two drug offences). Interestingly enough, a careful look at the statistics presented by the Commission

[84] The United States Sentencing Commission's obsession with excessive, but narrowly defined, disparity (i.e. documentable sentencing outside of the apparently 'appropriate' Guideline range) should be contrasted with the opposing concern expressed by many that, in fact, there are too many cases of different defendants convicted of different types of behaviour being treated with 'excessive uniformity' (see S. Schulhofer, above, n. 48).

[85] M. Tonry, 'GAO Report Confirms Failure of US Guidelines', (1992) 5 *Federal Sentencing Reporter* 147.

suggests that the impact has, remarkably, not been very dramatic. Weisburd[86] notes that for the majority of the analyses that the Commission did (on a very limited number of offences) there were no statistically significant reductions in 'sentencing disparity' as measured by the Commission. Rhodes[87] points out that by including two drug offences in the group of four offences analysed, the Commission took advantage of the fact that Congress had, in its wisdom, virtually ensured that a certain amount of apparent disparity would be removed by creating mandatory minimum sentences.

The Commission argues in its 1991 'self-evaluation' report that factors which were not supposed to affect sentences—race, for example—have been effectively eliminated as sentencing factors as a result of the implementation of the Guidelines. The General Accounting Office, however, was not so convinced. Part of the difference seems to be the metric used to measure sentences. The Commission measure was whether or not the sentence was within the guideline range. The General Accounting Office looked at the actual sentence (i.e. including what small range there was within each guideline). Neither, of course, was able to look at factors such as prosecutorial discretion that could, of course, have a discriminatory impact. If prosecutors were sometimes 'fact bargaining' (i.e. agreeing to suppress possible 'relevant conduct' in exchange for a guilty plea), disparity created by differential access to bargains obviously would not enter into 'disparity' calculations.

More disturbing are some of the results related to race. The General Accounting Office found that 'for heroin distribution both whites and Hispanics were more likely than blacks to have counts reduced or dismissed; there were no significant differences for embezzlement', and furthermore that 'available data showed that persons convicted by plea tended to receive shorter sentences than persons who were convicted by trial and that blacks were less likely to be convicted by plea than whites'.[88]

Nor did either group of evaluators consider such issues as the assignment of different drugs to different offence levels. I have to confess some ignorance of how drugs are made and sold. However, it does seem rather strange, on the face of it, that ten grams of 'crack' (a drug of choice, apparently, of poor blacks in inner cities) has the same penal value as a kilogram of pure cocaine (the drug of choice of the rich and famous). The fact that cocaine

---

[86] D. Weisburd, 'Sentencing Disparity and the Guidelines: Taking a Closer Look', (1992) 5 *Federal Sentencing Reporter* 149.

[87] For an additional critique of the United States Sentencing Commission's analysis, see W. Rhodes, 'Sentence Disparity, Use of Incarceration, and Plea Bargaining: The Post-Guideline View from the Commission', (1992) 5 *Federal Sentencing Reporter* 153.

[88] United States General Accounting Office, see above, n. 83, as excerpted in (1992) 5 *Federal Sentencing Reporter* 134, 135.

can easily be made into crack (thus increasing the penal value of the drugs in one's possession dramatically) is lost in the Guidelines.

Assignment of penal value to drugs can, in addition, create a form of systemic racial discrimination. Heaney, for example, suggests that for him 'the most disturbing systemic disparity [created by the Sentencing Commission Guidelines] is the apparent disparate treatment of young, black males, who on the average receive *Guidelines* sentences significantly longer than their white counterparts for similar offences'.[89] Clearly what is disparity for Judge Heaney is not necessarily disparity for the Commission. And, not surprisingly, when they exchanged arguments about 'disparity' in sentencing in an issue of the *Federal Sentencing Reporter*, they, for the most part, were not able to agree what the arguments were, let alone persuade each other.[90] In any case, different Guidelines for easily convertible amounts of drugs would not be considered to be a potential source of disparity. The drug equivalency table created by the United States Sentencing Commission defines equivalence once and for all.[91] The same is true of other differences created before the sentencing hearing: differences in definitions, charge practices, and plea discussions.[92] Because these differences in processing would not show up in case files, they would not be considered evidence of unwarranted disparity by the Sentencing Commission.

Identical twins with identical criminal records each of whom has just purchased an ounce of cocaine will get different sentences if one is caught before mixing his cocaine with an ounce of sugar and the other is caught after. It is clearly not disparity under the Guidelines that the twin who mixed fastest would be likely to get a sentence six months longer than his slower brother. I am sure that the Commissioners would be quite disturbed if someone were to suggest that this was not fair. Certainly the six-month difference would not be considered to be 'disparity' by the Commission or by the General Accounting Office in their analysis of the data.

Heaney notes that 'historically, the judiciary could restrain an abuse of discretion by the other branches through its ability to impose sentences which it considered were in the interests of justice. Now its authority is

[89] G. Heaney (Senior Circuit Judge, US Court of Appeals for the Eighth Circuit) 'The Reality of Guidelines Sentencing: No End to Disparity', (1991) 28 *Am. Crim. L. Rev.* 161, 165.
[90] See above, n. 59.
[91] The issue of race-correlated disparity created by the Guidelines is made salient by a trial court finding in Minnesota that 96.8% of those charged with possession of cocaine in its 'crack' form were black, whereas only 20.3% of those charged with possession of cocaine were black (L. Oberdorfer and D. Banks, 'The Four Year Reports of the Sentencing Commission and the General Accounting Office: Some Observations', (1992) 5 *Federal Sentencing Reporter* 158, 159. If one notes that the cocaine can very easily be turned into crack by any user with a metal spoon, some baking soda, and a match, the distinction made by the United States Sentencing Commission can, at best, be described as 'interesting'.
[92] See the discussion by Senior Judge Gerald W. Heaney, see above, n. 59, 237.

restrained.'[93] He goes on to show that in a variety of ways, similar cases are getting different sentences, but because of the nature of Guideline sentencing, these cases typically will not be seen, on the record, as 'disparity'.

8. SEVERITY AND PRISON POPULATIONS

Some of the explosion in the U.S. [imprisonment] figures may relate to a sort of inter-institutional misunderstanding. The institution of the law has come too close to politics, at the same time as utility-thinking borrowed from the institution for production seems to have been given what appears to be absolute dominance. . . .

It is impossible politically not to be against sin. This is a competition won by the highest bidder. To protect people from crime is a cause more just than any. . . . A crime-free society is such a sacred goal for so many, that even money does not count. Who asks about costs in the middle of a total war?[94]

There is little question that the Guidelines are having their desired impact on the sentences that are being handed down. In January 1984, about half (48.6 per cent) of the Federally sentenced defendants ended up in prison. This increased steadily (in pre-Guidelines days) until early 1987 when it levelled off at around 55–57 per cent. After the Guidelines were declared constitutional in January 1989, the proportion of convicted offenders sentenced to prison jumped to, and stayed near 60 per cent.[95]

The Federal prison population has been going up dramatically since 1980. In 1980 there were approximately 25,000 people in Federal prisons. By 1988 the figure was about 44,000[96] and in 1990, this figure was about 59,000. Commission estimates for 1998 are between 80,000 and 135,000.[97]

Knapp and Hauptly note that the Commission appeared to equate 'punishment' with 'imprisonment' and that 'compared with the state guideline efforts, the [USS] Commission was profligate with respect to correctional resources. . . . Unlike guideline states, the federal government's tradition has been to fund any and all correctional increases regardless of the source.'[98]

---

[93] See above, n. 89, 186.
[94] N. Christie, *Crime Control as Industry: Towards Gulags, Western Style?* (New York, 1993), 151–2, 167.
[95] United States Sentencing Commission, *Annual Report* (1990), Table C-6.
[96] M. Quinlan (Director, Federal Bureau of Prisons), (1988) 1 *Federal Sentencing Reporter* 105.
[97] United States Sentencing Commission, *Annual Report* (1990), Figure 11.
[98] K. Knapp and D. Hauptly, 'US Sentencing Guidelines in Perspective: A Theoretical Background and Overview', in D. J. Champion (ed.), *The US Sentencing Guidelines: Implications for Criminal Justice* (New York, 1989), 15.

Support for Knapp and Hauptly's view of the Commission's interpretation of the meaning of punishment comes from an explanation that former Commissioner Michael Block gave of the guideline for fraud:

Apparently mindful of the fact that deterrence, not incapacitation, is our primary concern in fraud sentencing, and that most recent deterrence research indicates that an increase in the certainty of punishment is a more powerful method of dissuading potential offenders than an increase in the magnitude of punishment, the Commission chose [in its initial fraud guideline that Professor Block participated in creating] to concentrate on increasing certainty. It intended no major change in the overall severity of sentences for fraud. The minimal (14%) increase in the expected (or average) time to be served under the Guidelines . . . resulted simply from the Commission's attempt to conform the sentences for fraud with those for larceny.

What the Commission did intend to be dramatically different under guideline sentencing was the likelihood of being sentenced to confinement. . . . [T]he Commission expected that the proportion of fraud sentences involving some confinement would rise under guideline sentencing from 41 percent to 76 percent. Because confinement was reasonably likely for offenders convicted of large frauds, even under pre-guideline practice, the Commission's restructuring of fraud sentencing was anticipated to have its most dramatic effect on the sentences for moderately sized fraud. . . . What the Commission intended in its restructuring of fraud sentencing was the frequent imposition of relatively short sentences.[99]

The Director of the Federal Bureau of Prisons hoped that by 1995, he would have 'reduced [his] overcrowding to a rate which would be about 20 per cent over [the prisons'] design capacity' by building 15,000 more cells. As head of the Bureau of Prisons, Quinlan argued that 'we have to look at other alternatives' to prisons.[100]

In many jurisdictions, massive increases in prison populations would be seen as a major source of concern. Aside from any social or personal costs of imprisonment, the economic costs, or at least opportunity costs, would enter into the debate. It is interesting to see how the General Accounting Office interpreted its mandate to look at 'the impact of the Guidelines on the operations of the federal criminal justice system'.[101] They focused on the courts and investigative agencies, apparently ignoring their impact on the prisons. Certainly, it was no surprise to Congress that by not rejecting the Sentencing Commission's Guidelines, it would be responsible for housing many more offenders in Federal prisons.[102]

More people are being sentenced to Federal prisons, and when they get there, they stay longer. Though most commentators of a liberal persuasion might be concerned about this increase in prison populations, those of a

[99] M. Block, see above, n. 38, 451.   [100] M. Quinlan, see above, n. 96, 105, 106.
[101] See above, n. 83, 10.
[102] See e.g. A. Alschuler, 'The Selling of the Sentencing Guidelines: Some Correspondence with the U.S. Sentencing Commission', in D. Champion (ed.), see above, n. 98.

more conservative bent are not. A former Commissioner (ex officio), former Attorney-General William Barr was, in January 1992, clearly an advocate for increased use of imprisonment:

If we want to reduce violent crime, we must press ahead unrelentingly with the policy of incapacitating violent criminals through incarceration. The choice is clear: more prison space or more crime. [During the 1970s and 1980s] many courts went far beyond what the Constitution requires in remedying purported Eighth Amendment violations. . . . Most burdensome of all, these decrees imposed limitations or caps on the population of state prisons. . . . The population caps, in particular, have in some cases wrought havoc with the state's efforts to get criminals off the streets . . . The federal system is not operating under burdensome court decrees, and in January 1991, operated at about 165 per cent of design capacity,[103] and did so in compliance with the Constitution. Many states, however, are required by judicial order . . . to operate *at*, or even *below* [emphasis in original] design capacity. Indeed, the overall state average in January 1991 was about 115% of capacity. If the states could operate at the level of the federal prison system, that would mean an additional 286,000 inmate beds . . . Now I am *not* (emphasis in original) saying that every state can operate at the same level of capacity as the federal system. . . . My point here is merely to point out the *enormous* potential in terms of additional bed space.[104]

If I understand the former Attorney-General correctly, he is not only advocating a 'crime control through incapacitation' model, but he is suggesting that part of the responsibility for crime levels in the USA lies with the wimpish states which appear willing to have levels of incarceration at only 115 per cent of their rated prison capacity. The Attorney-General, one might venture, would have been pleased, rather than appalled, to read recent articles reporting that 42 per cent of young black males (aged 18–35) in Washington, DC, and 56 per cent in Baltimore, Maryland, are under criminal-justice control on any given day. He might have been disappointed to discover, however, that only about 14 per cent and 12 per cent of the total population of young black males in Washington and Baltimore, respectively, were actually in custody.[105]

The Commission itself seems to be strangely ambivalent about the impact of its Guidelines on the Federal prison population. Indeed, they tend to give most of the credit for the increase in the prison population to Congress. In 1988, their (revised) Guidelines manual noted that:

---

[103] F. Zimring, ('Are State Prisons *Under*crowded?', (1992) 4 *Federal Sentencing Reporter* 347) points out that 'rated capacity' itself is a slippery concept, since prison systems do their own rating and such rated capacities can be affected by a variety of factors including political considerations.

[104] W. Barr, 'Department of Justice Excerpts of Attorney General's Remarks [to the California District Attorneys Association on 14 January 1992 in Palm Springs, California]', reprinted in (1992) 4 *Federal Sentencing Reporter* 345.

[105] J. Miller, '56% of Young Black D.C. Males 18–35 under Criminal Justice System Control', (1992) 3 *Overcrowded Times*; J. G. Miller, '56% of Young Black Males in Baltimore under Justice System Control', (1992) 3 *Overcrowded Times*.

The Commission has also examined its sentencing ranges in light of their likely impact upon prison population. Specific legislation, such as the new drug law and the career offender provisions of the sentencing law, require the Commission to promulgate rules that will lead to substantial prison population increases.... The Guidelines themselves, insofar as they reflect policy decisions made by the Commission ... will lead to an increase in prison population that computer models ... estimate at approximately 10%, over a period of ten years.[106]

Tonry[107] suggests that the Commission is being overly modest. He notes that the Commission, in effect, set its Guidelines for drugs from the base created by Congress' mandatory minimum sentences rather than setting drug sentences in line with an overall proportionality model and then, if the sentence was not as high as the mandatory minimum, instructing the sentencing judge to impose the mandatory minimum. Knapp and Hauptly are more blunt. They suggest that in order to give credit for the increased prison population to Congress, the Commission had to use mental gymnastics and 'an innovative methodology to understate the Guidelines' contribution to prison population projections'.[108]

9. PLEA BARGAINING

In this essay, I do not have space to go into the Guidelines and plea bargaining literature in detail. From the time of the discussion of the Sentencing Reform Act to this very day, many observers have expressed serious concerns about the impact of plea bargaining on the handing down of fair sentences.

Virtually every commentator has spent some time discussing the added power given to the prosecutor under the US Sentencing Commission's Guidelines' regime and has noted the added incentives on the part of offenders to go for a deal to avoid the full weight of what could be construed as the proper guideline. As the Commission itself points out: 'Within the guideline structure, charging and plea practices have a more visible impact ... on the severity of a defendant's punishment than under the previous indeterminate sentencing system.'[109]

[106] United States Sentencing Commission, *Federal Sentencing Guidelines Manual* (incorporating guideline amendments effective 15 June 1988), 1.11. A similar view is expressed by a (now former) United States Sentencing Commissioner and staff member (M. Block and W. Rhodes, 'Forecasting the Impact of the Federal Sentencing Guidelines', (1989) 7 *Behavioural Science and the Law* 51.

[107] M. Tonry, 'Salvaging the Sentencing Guidelines in Seven Easy Steps', (1992) 4 *Federal Sentencing Reporter* 355.

[108] K. Knapp and D. Hauptly, see above, n. 98, 15 and 17–18 (n. 7).

[109] United States Sentencing Commission, *The Federal Sentencing Guidelines: A Report on the Operation of the Guidelines System and Short-Term Impacts on Disparity in Sentencing, Use of Incarceration, and Prosecutorial Discretion and Plea Bargaining* (1991), Executive Summary, 24.

Without going into great detail the Commission in its own 1991 report presents evidence of varying levels of plea bargaining leading to an under-mining of the 'appropriate' sentence in various parts of the country. In one jurisdiction, for example, the Commission found evidence 'indicating some prosecutorial circumvention of guideline [charging and plea negotiation] policies . . . that went unchecked by judges who were generally opposed to the Guidelines or the resulting guideline range'.[110] About a quarter of the prosecutors interviewed by the Commission noted that 'they sometimes will not charge all known criminal behaviour' if the defendant is co-operating with them or if the penalty seemed too severe.[111]

Pleading guilty under the Guidelines can have a positive impact, of course: in 1990, 88 per cent of those who pleaded guilty received a two-level 'adjustment' for acceptance of responsibility compared to only 20 per cent of those who were convicted at trial.[112]

The Commission estimated that in 17 per cent of all cases the plea arrangement resulted in some other form of sentence reduction.[113] In drug cases, not surprisingly, the proportion of cases involving a plea 'advantage' was higher—about 27 per cent. Some estimates of the 'rate' of plea bargain-ing in particular locations for particular offences are even higher. All esti-mates based on examinations of files are, of course, almost certain to be under-estimates, since many of the issues that are the subject of plea bar-gains do not appear in the files that are created after the accused is indicted.

The added power of the prosecutors under the Guidelines, and the in-creased structural incentives to plea bargain, are so clear and almost univer-sally acknowledged that there is really no need to spend more space on the issue here. The nature of an effective bargain—'fact bargaining' or agree-ments to suppress facts about 'relevant conduct' or even about the offence of conviction or criminal record—is clearly encouraged by Guidelines such as those of the US Sentencing Commission.[114]

The other side of the coin, of course, is that sentences can be severe, and the system and the prosecutor so rigid, that defendants have nothing to lose by pleading not guilty and exercising their right to a full trial. The Sentenc-ing Commission presents data that appear to show that roughly 90 per cent of convictions are as a result of a guilty plea and this proportion has been relatively stable since 1987.[115] This is, however, a contentious finding, since it includes cases that were still being sentenced under the pre-Guidelines regime. A more detailed analysis of pleas comes from Massachusetts where, in line with the Commission findings, guilty pleas were in the range of 87–88 per cent in pre-Guidelines days, but by 1990/1991 had dropped to 81–82 per cent of cases sentenced under the Guidelines. This may not look like

---

[110] United States Sentencing Commission, 17.   [111] Ibid. 23.   [112] Ibid. ii. 410.
[113] Ibid. 412.   [114] S. Koh, see above, n. 5, 1120.   [115] See above, n. 109, 409.

much until one considers it in terms of trials. In pre-Guidelines days, one might expect about 12 per cent of cases to be decided on at a full trial. Under the Guidelines, the proportion increases to about 18 per cent. In other words there are, at present, *50 per cent more* full trials being held.[116]

10. THE ROLE OF THE PROBATION OFFICER

Heaney notes that one of the 'constants' of sentencing practice across districts is that:

The probation officer determines the essential sentencing facts to be included in the presentence investigation report from the files of the prosecutor and government investigators and from an interview with the offender. . . . Probation offices are compelled to rely primarily on the government files because they have neither the human nor material resources to make an independent investigation of the facts. . . . The version of the facts set forth in the presentence investigation report and the probation office's calculation of the sentencing range ordinarily are accepted by the sentencing court.[117]

In cases where there is a dispute on the conclusion of the pre-sentence enquiry, the probation officer apparently tries to resolve the dispute but if the parties cannot agree the probation officer apparently attaches an addendum to the report in which 'he finds the facts, states his conclusions, and recommends the applicable Guidelines range. In a majority of cases, the court accepts the presentence investigation report. Consequently, most often, it is the probation officer and not the court that determines the Guidelines range.'[118] Heaney points out that in the four districts he studied, the courts calculated a Guidelines range different from the pre-sentence investigation in only 10 per cent of the cases.[119]

Given the critical role that probation officers play in the implementation of the Guidelines, it is important to see whether they are able to follow the instructions that they receive from the Sentencing Commission in applying the Guidelines. In one study of probation officers,[120] a hypothetical drug case involving the sentencing of three people charged with conspiracy to distribute cocaine was written. The researchers chose 47 districts randomly (not haphazardly, but using actual random numbers), got lists of those probation officers in each district who prepared pre-sentence reports, and then chose, randomly, one of them. They managed to get 46 of the probation officers to participate. Each read the case and assigned a base

[116] F. Bowman, 'The GAO and Sentencing Commission Impact Reports: Where's the Impact?', (1992) 5 *Federal Sentencing Reporter* 164; M. Tonry (see above, n. 85) notes that in 1991 the trial rate increased even more.
[117] G. Heaney, see above, n. 89, 168–9.　　[118] Ibid. 174.　　[119] Ibid. 174, n. 42.
[120] P. Lawrence and P. Hofer, (1992) 4 *Federal Sentencing Reporter* 330.

offence level. Base offence levels varied considerably for each of the three people.

Defendant 1: Base offence levels ranged from 24 to 32 (A 'No record' sentence range from a median of 57 to a median of 136 months).
Defendant 2: Base offence levels ranged from 20 to 32 (A 'No record' sentence range from a median of 37 to a median of 136 months).
Defendant 3: Base offence levels ranged from 16 to 32 (A 'No record' sentence range from a median of 24 to a median of 136 months).

These are not trivial amounts of disparity. It would appear that the range could be explained, for the most part, by understandable differences in interpretation of the meaning of the 'relevant conduct'. It should also be noted that all of the sentences that would have resulted from these wildly varying applications of the Commission's Guidelines would have been deemed to have been conforming to the Guidelines. Indeed, given the way in which the Commission defines disparity, no disparity would have been evident from sentences for defendant three which might vary from 21 months (the bottom of base level 16) to 151 months (the top of base level 32). Had these been real defendants—and it is reasonable to assume that such wildly varying sentences are being given to 'similar' offenders—one wonders whether the defendants would agree with a Commission calculation that identical cases receiving sentences of 1.75 years and 12.5 years does not constitute evidence of unwarranted disparity.

One might even be tempted to agree with one commentator who asked, not rhetorically, I think, 'Was judge created disparity all that bad?'[121]

<h2 style="text-align:center">II. HOW HAVE THE SENTENCING GUIDELINES BEEN RECEIVED BY VARIOUS GROUPS?</h2>

Outside of Washington, DC, one can search in vain for writers who have been supporters of the United States Sentencing Commission and its Guidelines. The exceptions are those associated with the Commission itself and those involved in a few Federal agencies (like the Federal Department of Justice under the Republican administration). Perhaps the most positive support outside of the Commission and Department of Justice is provided by the Commission itself. The Commission, as part of its four-year review, surveyed 46 judges, of whom 30 (65 per cent) thought the Guideline sentences were mostly appropriate. Almost all (39 of 47 respondents or 83 per cent) Assistant US Attorneys (Federal prosecutors) thought the sentences were appropriate as did most (31 out of 45 or 69 per cent) probation officers

[121] J. Clarke (Federal Defenders of San Diego, Inc.), 'Ruminations on *Restrepo*', (1989) 2 *Federal Sentencing Reporter* 135, 136.

surveyed. Public defenders and private lawyers were generally of the view that sentences were inappropriate under the Guidelines.[122]

That survey was, however, the high point of survey support for the Commission's Guidelines. When asked about disparity, only 32 per cent of a sample of 415 judges thought that disparity had decreased under the guideline system, in comparison to the pre-Guidelines system. An almost equal number (28 per cent) thought disparity had increased, with 28 per cent thinking that it had stayed the same. Twelve per cent didn't know. A bare majority (51 per cent and 52 per cent) of prosecutors and probation officers, respectively, thought that disparity had decreased. Very few (11 per cent) Federal defenders or private attorneys (19 per cent) reported that in their view disparity had decreased.[123]

Almost everyone else who has ventured a full written opinion on the Guidelines has been unfavourable. Perhaps one extreme example of a publicly stated view of the Guidelines comes from a judge who served on the Federal Courts Study Committee that looked at the Guidelines. His view, supported by two other judges on the committee and expressed as an 'additional statement' in the report, was that 'The federal sentencing Guidelines are not working. According to the legislative history, the goal of the Guidelines was honesty, uniformity, and proportionality. The Guidelines are failing miserably in achieving any of these goals.'[124]

Another commentator noted that one judge testifying before the Federal Court Study Committee in early 1990 suggested that the Guidelines produce 'an illusion of justice' and that making most personal characteristics 'not ordinarily relevant' meant that:

[J]udges who feel constrained to remain faithful to the Guidelines must impose sentences of imprisonment on undeserving defendants simply because of the political view of the Sentencing Commission. The people who most frequently suffer such unfair sentencing consequences are the poor, disadvantaged, and minority defendants.[125]

One judge reportedly resigned rather than have his sentencing function reduced, as he put it, to the role of 'a clerk toting up numbers and imposing unjust sentences'.[126] By the end of 1989, over 200 judges had either written judgments or concurred in finding the Guidelines unconstitutional (a view which the Supreme Court eventually disagreed with). When the Federal

[122] United States Sentencing Commission, see above, n. 109, i. 103.   [123] Ibid. 114.

[124] Judge Keep, 'Additional Statement by Judge Keep, in which Mr. Aprile and Chief Justice Callow Join' (appended to the report of the Federal Courts Study Committee), reprinted in (1990) 2 *Federal Sentencing Reporter* 236.

[125] T. Hillier II (Federal Public Defender, Western District of Washington on behalf of Federal Public and Community Defenders) to the Subcommittee on Criminal Justice of the US House of Representatives Judiciary Committee, (1990) 2 *Federal Sentencing Reporter* 224, 225.

[126] D. Freed, see above, n. 8, 1686 n. 14.

Courts Study Committee heard witnesses on the Guidelines, 270 people came forward with their views. Two hundred and sixty-six spoke against the Guidelines; the four who spoke in favour of the Guidelines were three of the Commissioners and the Attorney-General of the United States.[127] Another judge suggests that 'the imposition of rigid Guidelines by an administrative agency on a sentencing system is destined to failure'.[128] Perhaps this is wishful thinking on the part of Judge Lay, since he reports that he and his colleagues do not perceive the Commission to be much interested in their views. Judge Lay notes that:

[M]any of the [United States Sentencing] Commissioners expressed their disdain for the views of certain members of the federal judiciary. One commissioner apparently told members of the second and eighth circuits that 'Congress took away the sentencing discretion of federal judges because they couldn't be trusted in the sentencing process' and that 'the [United States Sentencing] Commission is not interested in receiving input from the federal bench'.[129]

Former Commissioners have also not been kind to the Commission. A paper co-authored by Michael Block (a former Commissioner) pulls few punches when it reports that 'the festering problem of misconception within the Commission as to its proper role has now begun to be manifested in misguided policy decisions'.[130]

12. WHAT IS LIKELY TO HAPPEN, OR WHAT SHOULD HAPPEN TO SENTENCING IN THE US FEDERAL JURISDICTION?

As various people have pointed out,[131] the Commission did not appear to believe it had anything to learn from the experience of various states. Thus, for example, it did not, unlike the Minnesota Commission, see part of its role as one of gathering support (politically and within the justice system, and in particular, within the judiciary) for its position. Thus in contrast to the Minnesota experience, the US Sentencing Commission is described as having taken 'an ideological approach, even political approach to guideline development that disavowed constraints, suppressed discussion of purpose, closed decision making to interested and affected parties and departed substantially from past sentencing norms'.[132]

[127] D. Freed, see above, n. 8, 1686 n. 1719–20.
[128] D. Lay (US Senior Circuit Judge, 8th Circuit; previously Chief Judge, US Court of Appeal, 8th Circuit), 'Rethinking the Guidelines: A Call for Cooperation', (1992) 101 *Yale LJ* 1755.
[129] Ibid. 1768.   [130] J. Parker and M. Block, see above, n. 6, 318.
[131] See e.g. D. Parent, see above, n. 7. Parent was the first director of the Minnesota Sentencing Guidance Commission, the first legislatively created sentencing commission in the USA.
[132] Ibid. 1788.

Perhaps largely on the basis of the US Federal experience, Tonry[133] argues that the political climate of a jurisdiction must be considered in thinking about how to reform sentencing. In particular, of course, legislative intervention in sentencing is, by definition, going to be political and one must be careful to determine that the climate is right for reform. Thus, for example, in comparisons between the US Federal Guidelines and proposals for sentencing reform such as those of Canada,[134] one has to realize that the criminal-justice policy climate in the two countries is, apparently, quite different.

Daniel Freed[135] suggests that it would be possible to deal with many of his own and others' criticisms of the US Sentencing Commission Guidelines if the courts were to interpret the Guidelines in line with the legislation and if the Commission were to revise the Guidelines in line with a more liberal interpretation of the enabling legislation.

Similarly, the Federal Courts Study Committee recommended that 'the Guidelines ... should not be treated as compulsory rules, but rather as general standards that identify the presumptive sentence, and (2) the Guidelines, and if necessary the [Sentencing Reform Act], be amended to permit consideration of an offender's age and personal history'.[136]

Dale Parent has suggested, however, that opening up the Guidelines without principled guidance would, in effect, use 'departures to revise the Guidelines', a procedure which, he believes, 'is not a good way to draft fundamental policy changes'.[137]

One rather comprehensive set of suggestions comes from Michael Tonry. Tonry's solution to the problems of the Guidelines would, in effect, reduce the use of imprisonment and/or have the sentence reflect factors in addition to the severity of the offence category. Thus Tonry suggests that 'substantial assistance' given by the defendant to the prosecutor should be available to the court as a reason for departure (downwards) any time it is given, not just when the US Attorney makes a motion to that effect. The Guidelines should include the possibility that a first-time non-violent offender could receive a non-prison sentence; the Guidelines could be modified to increase the availability of probation, and other intermediate punishments as an alternative to prison; there should be a modification of the 'real offence sentencing' rules. In cases where Congress created mandatory minimum sentences, these mandatory minima should not be the starting-point for determining the sentence, but rather should override, if necessary, a pro-

[133] M. Tonry, 'The Politics and Processes of Sentencing Commissions', (1991) 37 *Crime and Delinquency* 307.
[134] For an interesting discussion of contrasting models, see A. von Hirsch, above, n. 34.
[135] D. Freed, see above, n. 8.
[136] Report of the Federal Courts Study Committee, 2 April 1990, as excerpted in (1990) 2 *Federal Sentencing Reporter* 232, 233.
[137] D. Parent, see above, n. 7, 1791, 1793.

portionate sentencing system.[138] Finally, he suggested that the size of the grid be reduced to something more manageable than 43 levels. Tonry concludes that:

The core objections are that the Guidelines are too rigid and too harsh, and too often force judges and lawyers to choose between imposing sentences that are wisely perceived as unjust or trying to achieve just results by means of hypocritical circumventions. Judges are forced by the Guidelines to choose between their obligation to do justice and their obligation to enforce the law. Many judges resent having so often to make that choice.[139]

The Commission itself admits that there are problems. But its assessment, not surprisingly, is that the problems are attributable largely to those who don't like the Guidelines. In its 'final note' in its 1991 report, the Commission suggests:

[S]o long as some number of judges resist this new guideline system, the reduction of unwarranted disparity, the increased certainty and uniformity, and the end to the pockets of undue leniency identified by Congress will be less than would otherwise be achieved. This must be kept in mind when measuring the early effects of the sentencing Guidelines.[140]

[T]o a lesser extent, a similar pattern is found among some federal prosecutors. The Commission's research suggests that in a minority of cases, federal prosecutors compromise the full potential of the Guidelines to accomplish the statutory goals by negotiating plea agreements that are not consistent with the Department of Justice policies and Commission policy statements. Because these bargains are given only

[138] S. Schulhofer (see above, n. 48), suggests that this would be a dangerous course of events, since it would place the Commission in direct opposition to the apparent will of Congress. He suggests that the Commission 'has a duty to accept policy judgements made by the legislature' (p. 172), and should not attempt to set an independent course from that set by Congress. His solution to this problem would, probably, end up being quite similar to that suggested by Tonry, but would be politically more acceptable. He would have wider drug quantity ranges which, in effect, would mean that there would be larger 'cliffs' (non-overlapping areas) between different drug-quantity guideline ranges. The result would be that there would be more clustering of drug sentences at the term required by the statutory mandatory minimum. Enhancements, if any, would be driven by factors other than quantity.

[139] M. Tonry, see above, n. 107, 359.

[140] See above, n. 109, ii. 419. One can only imagine what United States Sentencing Commissioners must have thought when they heard of a report of a US District Judge, who, in expressing his 'disdain of mandatory federal sentencing laws' told jurors at the conclusion of a seven-day trial that convicting the accused of possessing more than 50 grams of crack cocaine would lead to a mandatory sentence of life in prison without parole. The jury then acquitted the defendant after deliberating for three days. The judge gave his instruction in the context of asking the jury to make a special finding on whether the amount of the drug was under or over 50 grams. Defence counsel, described as 'elated by the judge's action' suggested that 'Now that judges no longer sentence, the jury, in effect, is the sentencing body by virtue of their verdict. The judge is saying the jury should be informed of what they are doing.' The case had originally been in a state court where the applicable maximum sentence would have been twelve years, as compared to life in the federal system where the case ended up ((1989) 2 *Federal Sentencing Reporter* 187–8).

to some defendants, the unwarranted disparity eliminated by the uniformity of sentencing Guidelines is compromised for this minority of cases.[141]

The overriding conclusion the Commission draws from this short-term evaluation . . . is that at this early juncture there is every reason for Congress to reaffirm the sentencing reforms it set in motion through passage of the Sentencing Reform Act of 1984 and no compelling justification for any significant alternation of those policies.[142]

There are scores of statements—from judges and others—criticizing the arbitrary, rigid nature of the Guidelines as they have developed over the past five years. Stephen Schulhofer, co-author of a paper with Commissioner Ilene Nagel on plea bargaining, and someone referred to by Michael Tonry as a 'Commission apologist',[143] suggests that:

The Sentencing Reform Act reflected a strong congressional commitment to preserving a place for offender circumstances and rehabilitative needs in the sentencing decision. Participants in the process find ways to allow for these considerations anyway, though their methods are too often haphazard, hidden and uncontrolled. To make the sentencing process more effective and more just, the Commission and the appellate courts must now take steps to permit a greater measure of structured flexibility. A sentencing system that eliminates unwarranted disparity will nonetheless choke on its rigidity, unless it finds a way to permit appropriate differentiation among differently situated offenders.[144]

With apologists like that, one might suggest that the Commission does not need enemies.

I would suggest, however, that most of these suggestions miss the fundamental issue. Though it is clear that some important changes (e.g. those suggested by Tonry) or a different interpretation and different set of judicial attitudes (e.g. those suggested by Daniel Freed) could have an important impact on the Guidelines, the issue is, ultimately, a highly political one. And the question one must ask is equally simple: what kind of sentencing structure does one want? As Tonry[145] points out, perhaps the most notable aspect of the evaluations carried out by the US Sentencing Commission and by the General Accounting Office is that neither of them asked themselves, or any of the principal participants in the system (judges, probation officers, lawyers, offenders, etc.), whether sentencing had improved under the Guidelines from what it had been before.

Perhaps, in all of this, the lesson is a simple one. Legislatures get what they ask for, and if they want something different, they had best ask for it rather explicitly.

It is hard to imagine that much can change without legislative intervention. A different set of Commissioners obviously could implement a new

---

[141] See above, n. 109, ii. 420. [142] Ibid. 420. [143] M. Tonry, see above, n. 85, 148.
[144] S. Schulhofer, see above, n. 48, 173. [145] M. Tonry, see above, n. 85, 183.

approach to sentencing without legislative change. However, leaving sentencing policy and approaches to the whim of government appointees does not appear to be an adequate solution.

Whatever happens in Federal sentencing in the USA, however, the rest of us should realize that the United States Sentencing Commission has performed an important function. It has demonstrated for better or worse that sentencing practice can be changed rather dramatically in a short period of time. We—and our governments—now know, however, that before we embark on a journey to reform sentencing, we should decide which direction we wish to go.

Michael M. Hihm, Chief Judge of the United States District Court, Central District of Illinois, summed up the problem quite well with a quotation from Yogi Berra, a legendary American baseball player: 'You have to be very careful if you don't know where you're going, because you might not get there.'[146]

---

[146] M. Mihm, 'The Roles and Responsibilities of the Judiciary in the Implementation of the Sentencing Reform Act of 1984', (1992) 5 *Federal Sentencing Reporter* 174, 176.

9

Reflections on the Role of the Sentencing Scholar

ANDREW ASHWORTH

The essays in this volume show, as do newspapers the world over, that sentencing is a matter of widespread concern. It is a central issue of social and legal policy. As a field for enquiry it is vast, and in this penultimate essay I draw upon merely a few of the themes mentioned by other contributors so as to raise some general topics for discussion. The essay is divided into three sections. First, some common confusions about sentencing reform are identified. Secondly, there is an exploration of what different groups of people expect of sentencing systems. Thirdly, the role of the sentencing scholar is held up for scrutiny; in a sphere strongly influenced by politics, public opinion, and practicalities, what should be the role of the academic?

I. SOME COMMON CONFUSIONS

Because discussion of sentencing takes place in so many different contexts—politics, the media, the courts, academic writings, etc.—it is not difficult for misconceptions to be repeated and take hold, particularly amongst those who wield influence. My goal here is to identify some possible confusions.

A frequent confusion at many levels of discourse is *the confusion of aims with methods*. The last two decades have seen renewed discussion of the possible rationales of sentencing, particularly 'desert', and also the development of numerical guideline systems of sentencing of one form or another. Far too frequently one comes across the assumption that the two are necessarily linked. This is a confusion. Accepting desert as the leading aim does not mean accepting guidelines as the method: the Swedish system, as Nils Jareborg shows,[1] is an example of desert without numerical guidelines, and the same could be said of Finland and perhaps of England and Wales. Nor does the acceptance of numerical guidelines as the method mean that desert must be accepted as the aim: the Federal Sentencing Guidelines in the United States, discussed by Anthony Doob,[2] demonstrate this.

[1] N. Jareborg, 'The Swedish Sentencing Reform', above, Ch. 4.
[2] A. Doob, above, Ch. 8.

Often connected with this is a further *confusion over the choice of rationales*. Some proponents of the 'cafeteria' approach to sentencing, whereby judges are free to select whatever rationale they wish to pursue in a particular case, have assumed that the only alternative would be a single rationale to cover all cases. They then criticize this as unworkable in practice, on account of the variations in types of cases to be sentenced. Correspondingly some proponents of the need for greater certainty and consistency have assumed that the only alternative to a single rationale would be the 'free for all' of the cafeteria approach, which they then criticize as allowing excessive judicial discretion. This is unnecessary polarization. It is perfectly possible in practice to structure a sentencing system so as to have a primary rationale which, in defined circumstances, gives way to certain other sentencing purposes. The Swedish law achieves this, as does the English law of 1991 in respect of the role of rehabilitation in the selection of community sentences and the place of incapacitative sentences for the 'dangerous'.[3]

Somewhat linked to this, but perhaps more prevalent in academic circles, is *the confusion over the completeness of rationales*. It is sometimes assumed that, once one has decided on a primary rationale, the answers to other sentencing problems follow by some process of deduction. This is true only to a limited extent. Even the most elaborate sentencing philosophies, such as Jeremy Bentham's, have found difficulty in covering all the ground in a coherent manner. In modern times critics have pointed to disagreements among desert theorists about the proper treatment of previous convictions, but there is more to the problem than that. There is a need to explore the principles and policies that should influence the approach to multiple offences, to aggravation and mitigation of sentence, to the impact of sentencing on offenders with different susceptibilities, and so forth. There are further questions about the proper approach to the sentencing of young offenders and of mentally disturbed offenders. The adoption of a primary or overall rationale for sentencing is necessary but not sufficient.

The same style of argument may be invoked to show *a confusion about the relevance of other principles and policies*. Perhaps the most obvious of these principles is non-discrimination or equality before the law. Sentencing policy, as a sphere of public policy, must ensure that this principle is honoured. Another principle much discussed in recent years is 'truth in sentencing', and there is now widespread support for the view that the sentence announced in court should not be emptied of significance by subsequent executive actions in granting parole or early release.[4] The claims of such principles do not depend on the primary rationale chosen for sentencing.

[3] Sections 6(2)(a) and 1(2)(b).
[4] See e.g. the discussion by A. Freiberg, Ch. 3, and by D. Thomas, Ch. 5.

Finally, there is *the confusion between judicial independence and unlimited judicial discretion.* This has manifested itself in the belief, sometimes strongly held, that any encroachment on the sentencing discretion of judges is an attack on the independence of the judiciary. In the constitutional theories of most countries, however, there is no doubt that the legislature has the right to pass statutes on sentencing which have the effect of restricting the discretion previously enjoyed by the courts. The confusion is between the principle of judicial independence, which protects the freedom of judges to administer the law without fear or favour, and the question of policy about the amount of discretion that courts should be able to exercise at the sentencing stage.[5] The principle of judicial independence carries a somewhat different implication in certain countries. For example, in some European countries judicial independence refers to the independence of each judge, who cannot be bound by any non-statutory rules, and in the Eastern European states it is often a banner of liberation from executive interference. But the principle has no particular bearing on the proper extent of judicial discretion in sentencing. That is likely to be determined by the goals and traditions of the particular system.

2. WHAT IS EXPECTED OF SENTENCING SYSTEMS

Widespread satisfaction has not always been one of the achievements of sentencing reform. Major changes have taken place in several jurisdictions, and yet, since sentencing is a high-profile form of public decision-making that has to deal with a wide range of cases and circumstances, dissatisfaction may remain in some quarters. What are the expectations of sentencing reform?

Some expectations may simply be unrealistic. A strong belief among some members of the public, politicians, and judges is that sentencing systems influence crime rates—the 'hydraulic' theory that if sentences go up, crimes go down, and vice versa. Many criminologists decry this as naïve. Only a small percentage of crimes ever result in the passing of a sentence,[6] and there is a low probability that anything other than very extreme penalties will have an impact on the recorded crime rate.[7] To this, some sentencers reply that if sentences are low, the word spreads quickly among offenders and potential offenders and they will take advantage. The trouble

[5] For elaboration, see A. Ashworth, *Sentencing and Criminal Justice* (London, 1992), ch. 2.

[6] For analysis, see, e.g. Canadian Sentencing Commission, *Sentencing Reform: A Canadian Approach* (Ottawa, 1987), 119; G. Barclay (ed.), *A Digest of Information on the Criminal Justice System* (Home Office, London, 1991), 31.

[7] e.g. D. Beyleveld, 'Deterrence Research as a Basis for Deterrence Policies', (1979) 18 *Howard Journal* 135, excerpted in A. von Hirsch and A. Ashworth (eds.), *Principled Sentencing* (Edinburgh, 1993), ch. 2.

with both sides of the debate is that we lack reliable evidence about types of offence, situational factors and many of the other matters that affect decision-making by various types of (potential) offender.[8] Similar problems beset most large-scale comparisons of trends: it has been argued suggestively that, whilst the doubling of the imprisonment rate in the United States in the last decade has been accompanied by a stable crime rate, reductions in the imprisonment rate in England and in other countries have been accompanied by rising crime rates,[9] but the lesson of criminological enquiry is that we should examine the causal steps with care. In this respect as in others, *perceptions* of changes in sentencing levels may be no less important than their actual effects. Lower sentences may be opposed on the basis that they devalue a certain interest or license certain conduct. The appearance rather than the reality may also be important in respect of fear and crime: higher sentences may succeed in allaying fear, even if they do nothing else. These possibilities demonstrate the complexity of the social issues surrounding sentencing.

A further difficulty with the assumption that raising sentence levels is the best way to deal with crime problems is that some opinion surveys suggest that members of the public, particularly victims, do not always subscribe to that belief. Take the findings of the first British Crime Survey—that 'if people are asked at a general level whether court sentences are adequate, a great majority answer that they are not. But if they are asked . . . about a specific incident involving themselves . . . victims' recommendations are broadly in line with present practice.'[10] Now this is a generalized finding expressed in a general way. What is interesting is that some judges disagree with it, saying that it does not represent the views of the victims and members of the public with whom they come into contact. If public opinions are to be relevant to policy-making, we need carefully constructed research designed to answer the key issues. Judges must be drawn into the

---

[8] For three studies of decision-making by offenders, see T. Bennett and R. Wright, *Burglars and Burglary* (Aldershot, 1984); N. Shover and T. Honaker, 'The Socially Bounded Decision-Making of Persistent Property Offenders', (1992) 31 *Howard Journal* 276; and R. Light, C. Nee, and H. Ingham, *Car Theft: The Offender's Perspective* (Home Office Research Study No. 130; 1992). On rational choice theory, see also R. Harding, 'Rational-Choice Gun Use in Armed Robbery', (1990) 1 *Criminal Law Forum* 427; and, more generally, D. Cornish and R. Clarke, *The Reasoning Criminal* (New York, 1986).

[9] See P. Farrington and P. Langan, 'Changes in Crime and Punishment in England and America in the 1980s', (1992) 9 *Justice Quarterly* 5.

[10] M. Hough and P. Mayhew, *The British Crime Survey* (Home Office Research Study No. 76; 1983), 28; for further British discussion, see M. Hough, D. Moxon, and H. Lewis, 'Attitudes to Punishment: Findings from the British Crime Survey', in D. Pennington and S. Lloyd-Bostock (eds.), *The Psychology of Sentencing* (Oxford, 1987), ch. 12. For international surveys, see N. Walker and M. Hough (eds.), *Public Attitudes to Sentencing* (Aldershot, 1988); and J. Roberts, 'Public Opinion, Crime and Criminal Justice', in M. Tonry (ed.), *Crime and Justice: A Review of Research*, xvi (Chicago, 1992).

planning of the research, since they tend to speak so confidently on these matters.[11]

The views and expectations of the public are therefore somewhat diverse. Politicians and the media can build upon and foster what Tony Bottoms, in his leading essay, refers to as 'populist punitiveness'.[12] Surveys by criminologists and others reveal a more complex picture. The aims and expectations of sentencing reformers also appear to be diverse. Some press for sentencing reform because of a belief that decisions of such importance should be taken on the basis of settled principles and in an accountable manner: the emphasis here is on consistency, on legality, and on 'rule of law' values in a sphere so often characterized by wide discretion. This may be termed the 'legality approach' to sentencing reform. Others press for sentencing reform primarily on the ground that a particular system has adopted aims and principles of sentencing that can no longer be sustained. Thus in some countries rehabilitative sentencing gave way to the desert principle because of doubts about the effectiveness of large-scale treatment schemes and because of claims that some offenders were being subjected to disproportionate deprivations. This may be termed the 'rationale approach' to sentencing reform. A third strand may be found among those who see sentencing reform as a means of altering the severity of punishment in a particular jurisdiction. In most instances the reformers promote parsimony in sentencing, and wish to reduce the use of imprisonment and replace it with more community-based measures.[13] Whilst there are occasional examples of sentencing reforms with no such concerns,[14] this will be termed the 'parsimony approach' to reflect the prevailing view, endorsed by the United Nations at its Eighth Congress on Crime Prevention (1990), that imprisonment should be regarded as a sanction of last resort. In practice it is not uncommon for sentencing reforms to be urged on at least two of these grounds, particularly rationale and parsimony, and one of the tasks that remains is to explore the implications and interactions of the three approaches.

3. WHAT SHOULD SENTENCING SCHOLARS DO?

Enough has been written to establish the diversity of expectations that the public and those who press for sentencing reform may have. The essays in this volume give plenty of examples of tensions between academic com-

[11] See A. Doob, above, Ch. 8.
[12] A. Bottoms, 'The Philosophy and Politics of Punishment and Sentencing', above, Ch. 2.
[13] Cf. the discussion of 'the community' by A. Bottoms, above, Ch. 2.
[14] See A. Doob, above, Ch. 8.

mentators and sentencing practitioners, as well as conflicts between politicians and either or both of the other groups. Granted the public importance
and sensitivity of sentencing, none of this is surprising. Indeed, these tensions underlie many of the compromises that shape sentencing laws the
world over. There is evidence that sentencing scholars can have an influence—sometimes direct, sometimes indirect—on the development of law
and practice. It is evident from the foregoing discussion that scholars may
have different concerns: many support sentencing reform because of a
desire to promote legality, rationales, and parsimony, but, as suggested
below, there may be occasions on which it is necessary to choose between
those approaches. The aim here is to venture a few suggestions about the
proper tasks of the sentencing scholar. At least six tasks merit further
discussion.

3.1. Sentencing Theory

The first task is to press forward with the development of sentencing theory.
This calls for the constant re-examination of the various rationales of sentencing, and it is good to see that debate in these quarters is in full vigour
again.[15] Through his reflections on just deserts, managerialism, and 'the
community' earlier in this volume, Tony Bottoms gives a fine example of
what the scholar can do in this respect.[16] Moreover, it is not just a question
of examining deep theories in terms of their social or philosophical creden-
tials and their empirical effects. It also involves the examination of other
principles that ought to have a bearing on the distribution of sentences by
courts. If there is evidence of racial discrimination in sentencing,[17] would it
be sufficient to declare such discrimination to be improper and to promote
training in racial awareness? Is it right that financial penalties should be
adjusted according to the means of the offender and, if so, how far should
the principle of equal impact be applied to other forms of punishment, such
as imprisonment and community sanctions? If it is accepted that criminal
courts should order offenders to pay compensation to their victims wherever possible, does it follow that the victim should be able to make a
statement to the court either on the effects of the crime or even as to
sentence?[18] There is also a need to devote further energy to the develop-

---

[15] Among books published in the recent past, see B. Hudson, *Justice through Punishment*
(Basingstoke, 1987); N. Lacey, *State Punishment* (London, 1988); D. Garland, *Punishment and
Modern Society* (Oxford, 1990); J. Braithwaite and P. Pettit, *Not Just Deserts* (Oxford, 1990);
A. von Hirsch, *Censure and Sanctions* (Oxford, 1993). For an anthology of readings, see A. von
Hirsch and A. Ashworth, *Principled Sentencing* (Edinburgh, 1993).

[16] Above, Ch. 2.

[17] For a recent English study, see R. Hood, *Race and Sentencing* (Oxford, 1992).

[18] For discussion, see e.g. D. Hall, 'Victims' Voices in Criminal Court: The Need for
Restraint', (1991) 28 *Amer. Crim. L. Rev.* 233; G. Hall, 'Victim Impact Settlements: Sentencing

ment of criteria of offence-seriousness and of the relative severity of sentences, two subjects often identified with desert theory but regarded as relevant in almost all approaches to sentencing. These are areas where it is far easier to be a critic than a constructive thinker, and yet their centrality to sentencing makes a strong case in favour of further attempts to develop criteria.[19] Both those who take the legality approach and those who adopt the rationale approach to sentencing reform should support these endeavours.

3.2 Rationales and Sentencing Systems

Secondly, there is the task of persuading sentencers and politicians that the rationales for sentencing do have consequences for people's liberty, and that it is important to be clear about priorities. The Council of Europe has recently made several recommendations along these lines, of which these are the first two:

1. The legislator or other competent authorities, where constitutional principles and legal traditions allow, should endeavour to declare the rationales for sentencing.

2. Where necessary, and in particular where different rationales may conflict, indications should be given of ways of establishing possible priorities in the application of such rationales for sentencing.[20]

The Council of Europe's recommendations then insist on proportionality as an upper limit, on parsimony in the use of imprisonment, and on non-discrimination, and they go on to propose the introduction of starting-points or 'orientations' to guide sentencers. This confirms that legality, rationales, and parsimony are not merely academic concerns. They affect such vital matters as the deprivation of liberty and the length of incarceration. As argued above, and as the Council of Europe has recognized, this does not mean that there must be a single all-embracing rationale without exceptions, but neither does it mean that courts should be left to choose among the various rationales at their will.

Unfortunately the 'cafeteria' approach to sentencing rationales remains influential in some quarters. It seems to have maintained its hold throughout the reform process in Victoria, largely on account of the power of the judicial lobby.[21] Equally, a law which referred to 'balancing' or 'taking

---

on Thin Ice?', (1992) 15 *New Zealand ULR* 143; A. Ashworth, 'Victim Impact Statements and Sentencing', [1993] *Crim. LR* 498.

[19] See A. von Hirsch and N. Jareborg, 'Gauging Criminal Harm: A Living-Standard Analysis', (1991) 11 *Oxford JLS* 1.

[20] Council for Europe, Appendix I to Recommendations No. R(92) 17 of the Committee of Ministers to Member States concerning Consistency in Sentencing.

[21] See A. Freiberg, above, Ch. 3.

account of' all the well-known rationales, without guidance on priorities, would be an abdication from the principle of legality. What the law should provide is a structure for sentencing that sets out the leading principle, and states clearly the ambit of any other relevant principles. In this way it would be perfectly possible to pursue different policies in respect of certain types of offence or offender whilst keeping faith with the principle of legality, as Paul Robinson has shown.[22] The Swedish sentencing law provides a practical example of this[23] and the English Criminal Justice Act of 1991 can be regarded as recognizing proportionality or desert as the primary rationale, with exceptions for incapacitation (in respect of certain sexual or violent offenders) and for rehabilitation (in choosing among community sentences of similar severity).[24] Once these issues have been decided at the level of principle, it then becomes a question of finding the machinery for ensuring that they are translated into practice. Whether the machinery be judicial development through appellate review, or guidelines created by a sentencing commission, or some other method, may well depend on local matters concerned with recent history and contemporary politics.[25] This second task is one for adherents of the rationale approach and the legality approach.

3.3. Structuring Sentencing

A related task, central to the concerns of reformers who adopt the legality approach, is to ensure that the sentencing system demonstrates a commitment to the rule of law and to the principles of natural justice. It should aim to have rules and principles that are clear and stated in advance; these should be applied to the facts that emerge from proper fact-finding procedures; and their application should be explained by reasons stated in open court, reasons that relate the actual sentence given to any relevant rules or principles of the system.[26] The great advantages of this are that law and legal values become part of the discourse of sentencing. As Nils Jareborg puts it,

[22] P. Robinson, 'Hybrid Principles for the Distribution of Criminal Sanctions', (1988) 82 *Northwestern ULR* 19, excerpted in A. von Hirsch and A. Ashworth (eds.), *Principled Sentencing* (Edinburgh, 1992), 241. For an adaptation of Robinson's approach that gives primacy to a restorative theory of justice, see D. van Ness, 'New Wine and Old Wineskins: Four Challenges of Restorative Justice', (1993) 4 *Criminal Law Forum* 251, with comments by A. Ashworth, 'Some Doubts about Restorative Justice', (1993) 4 *Criminal Law Forum* 277.
[23] See N. Jareborg, above, Ch. 4.
[24] For elaboration of this view, see A. Ashworth, above, n. 5, 69–72.
[25] Cf. M. Tonry, below, Ch. 10; and also A. von Hirsch, K. Knapp, and M. Tonry, *The Sentencing Commission and its Guidelines* (1987); and M. Tonry, 'Judges and Sentencing Policy: The American Experience', in C. Munro and M. Wasik (eds.), *Sentencing, Judicial Discretion and Judicial Training* (London, 1992).
[26] In the Council of Europe recommendations (above, n. 20), E2 states that 'what counts as a reason is a motivation which relates the particular sentence to the normal range of sentences for the type of crime and to the declared rationales for sentencing'.

the result is 'fairly detailed legal provisions and a legal structure where we earlier had a black box. Legal argumentation regarding matters of sentencing suddenly became acceptable.'[27] It is extraordinary that values which have long been regarded as important in the criminal law have tended to be neglected at the sentencing stage[28]—despite the fact that, in most common-law countries, a majority of defendants plead guilty and therefore have no 'trial'.

This approach is, of course, in constant tension with the need for discretion in sentencing. This, too, is a matter of some importance. Many sentencing decisions call for the exercise of judgment in assessing the strength of certain factors in a case (especially aggravating and mitigating factors) and in deciding what weight to assign to them where there are conflicting factors.[29] This is one element in the judicial argument for maximum discretion and minimum regulation or, as it is sometimes put, less 'interference'. A powerful expression of this view is the memorandum of the Victorian judges to the Starke Committee, which includes the following passage:

The fundamental concern of the judges . . . is with the justice of the sentence imposed. They regard it as vital that there be no disparity in the justice with which every offender is dealt and therefore believe that the widest discretion should remain with sentencing judges. It is only if judges retain a wide sentencing discretion that they can respond to current community views and problems, that they can reflect changing attitudes to particular crimes and that they can do justice in all the changing circumstance of life.[30]

It seems that the present Lord Chief Justice of England takes a similar view: in an extra-curial speech, Lord Taylor called for fewer restrictions on sentencers and expressed the view, widely held among judges and magistrates in this country, that Parliament's efforts in the 1991 Act provide clear evidence that the best policy is to leave sentencing to the judges.[31]

However, it is important to separate the various strands of the argument here. If it is contended that the 1991 Act is poorly drafted, that must be accepted. It fails to express the policies clearly, it is unnecessarily complex,

[27] Above, Ch. 4, 122.
[28] 'Decision-makers have extremely limited discretion when they assign liability, while they enjoy very broad discretion when they sentence' (P. Robinson, 'Discretion and Legality in the Distribution of Criminal Sanctions', (1988) 25 *Harvard Journal on Legislation* 393, 396).
[29] Note the suggestion by A. Freiberg (above, Ch. 3) that sentencers should openly state the basis for their calculations. In England and Wales only the discount for a guilty plea (which is an either/or question, not a matter of degree) seems capable of quantification: see further A. Ashworth, above, n. 5, ch. 5, esp. 129–33.
[30] *Victorian Sentencing Committee Report*, iii (1988), Appendix A; see also A. Freiberg, above, Ch. 3.
[31] Speech to the Law Society of Scotland, reported in *The Times* and other newspapers on 22 March 1993.

and it encourages a narrow, literal approach to interpretation. If it is contended that the growth of sentencing legislation in recent years has made the task too complicated—as David Thomas argues above[32]—the claim should be examined closely. Is it argued that we should jettison policies that are socially important, such as the compensation of victims or the deprivation of offenders' profits, simply because they make the task of sentencing more difficult? Surely not: the drafting should be far simpler, but it is right that there should be rules on these matters. Dreadful drafting should not be taken to indicate that the policies are wrong or that legislative rules are an inappropriate way of giving effect to them. At the very least it indicates a need for greater consultation and co-operation over the form of legislation. Some might go further and argue that it shows the folly of trying to express detailed sentencing guidance in primary legislation, where the vicissitudes of passage through the legislature can create inconsistencies that later haunt the courts. The legislature should lay down the broad lines of policy, but the experience of other systems shows that a more imaginative approach to the provision of detailed guidance—through delegated legislation, for example, under a power given to a Commission—is worthy of consideration.

It is not hard to obtain agreement for the proposition that the elimination of judicial discretion—as in the imposition of mandatory minimum sentences in certain jurisdictions[33]—is a policy that sacrifices the court's ability to do justice by way of individualizing the sentence in a particular case. As Schulhofer has remarked: 'a sentencing system that eliminates unwarranted disparity will nonetheless choke on its rigidity, unless it finds a way to permit appropriate differentiation among differently situated offenders.'[34] But it is equally objectionable to have wide judicial discretion which allows judges to decide on priorities among the rationales of sentencing, and which leaves issues of principle to piecemeal judicial development. This fails to accord with the principle of legality; it gives no weight to the need for maximum certainty; it reduces the amount of judicial accountability; and it does all these things in a sphere that concerns the deprivation of liberty, or at least restrictions on liberty. To conclude by stating that there must be a 'balance' between rule and discretion would be insufficient. Those who adopt the legality approach to sentencing reform should insist that we strive to articulate rules and principles so far as possible, and that the exercise of discretion should always be accompanied by the giving of concrete reasons that relate the sentence clearly to the legal structure.

The multiplicity of factors that may be relevant to sentencing is not, however, the only element in the judicial argument for maximum discretion and minimum 'interference'. Sometimes that argument is bolstered by ref-

---

[32] D. Thomas, above, Ch. 5.   [33] See M. Tonry, below, Ch. 10.
[34] Quoted by A. Doob, above, Ch. 8, 249.

erences to the principle of judicial independence, although it was argued earlier that this rests on a confusion. Sometimes the argument is supported on a slightly different ground—that it is wisest to leave the development of sentencing principles to the judiciary. The 'wisdom' is claimed to derive from the judiciary's ability to respond flexibly to different types of cases, their understanding of public opinion and yet their insulation from direct political pressure. However, the issues of social policy that arise in sentencing are surely too fundamental and too broad-ranging to be left to a small group of senior judges. Even if the workings of an appellate court were equal to the task of extensive and systematic guidance-giving, this would not be the proper approach. The framework of policies and principles should be established by law, although certainly after involving the judiciary to a greater extent than proved possible before the enactment of the Criminal Justice Act 1991 in England. Judicial experience in matters of sentencing is invaluable and ought not to be ignored, but it would be a mistake to regard it as the only relevant experience. I also believe, looking at the English system in the 1970s and 1980s, that 'leaving it to the judges' would result in inconsistency and incompleteness in sentencing guidance. David Thomas, on the other hand, takes the view that judicial self-regulation was just beginning to function effectively in 1982 when Parliament began its campaign of 'interference'.[35] We will never know, although it is fair to point out that the justly celebrated technique of the 'guideline judgment' was used very infrequently in the 1980s, and that the Court of Appeal has shied away from providing guidance in the everyday cases of burglary, deception, handling stolen goods, and many thefts, where guidance is sorely needed. Appellate review may be an excellent method of refining the details of existing guidance, but the evidence suggests that it is a much less successful way of generating the kind of wide-ranging and coherent guidance that is required. Whether a sentencing commission would be the best solution in a particular jurisdiction depends on a number of factors, including the legal culture.[36]

3.4. Workability

It is apparent from the previous discussion that the most suitable kind of sentencing reform may differ from jurisdiction to jurisdiction. That should not be taken to mean, however, that comparative study of the kind contained in this volume has no practical relevance. On the contrary, a number of worthwhile points can be taken. One is that study of other systems may bring to light different techniques of tackling familiar problems. Another is that comparative study shows the importance of attending to the practical

[35] See above, Ch. 5.   [36] For English proposals, see A. Ashworth, above, n. 5, Ch. 12.

details of any sentencing reform: on this point the dissatisfaction with many of the detailed provisions of the English Criminal Justice Act of 1991, strongly expressed by David Thomas,[37] may be contrasted with the efforts made in Victoria and described by Arie Freiberg.[38] At least four failures in the process of introducing the English legislation can be identified—the failure of consultation with sentencers about the details of the reform, the failure to explain and justify the changes publicly in a convincing manner, the monumental failures in drafting and the parliamentary process, and the failure to organize training for the new law in a way that not only attended to sentencers' concerns but also explained the policies and purposes of the legislation. The reaction of many English sentencers is 'surely we do not need more complicated legislation'; there is an answer to this,[39] but little has been heard of it.

A further, crucial aspect of 'what works' is to be aware of the ways in which any sentencing law can be diluted or even nullified in practice by the 'adaptive behaviour' of sentencers and other criminal-justice professionals. The Minnesota guidelines suffered a measure of erosion from practices of this kind,[40] and even mandatory minimum sentences tend to be circumvented to a certain extent in practice.[41] It seems that almost any sentencing law has what might be termed a 'drag co-efficient', the extent to which resistance can slow it down and blunt its effectiveness. But there have been notable successes: Arie Freiberg describes the effectiveness of the Victorian law requiring judges to shorten their custodial sentences.[42]

Whether judges and others who resist are regarded as heroes or villains may depend on one's approach to sentencing reform—whether the legality approach, the rationale approach, or the parsimony approach. Those who applaud the efforts of some Federal judges in the United States to escape from the clutches of the US Sentencing Guidelines are showing great concern for parsimony and little respect for legality. The three approaches may conflict, but this is not to suggest (as some have done) that they must conflict. For example, some critics of desert theory charge it with a tendency to produce greater severity of sentences; on this view, the rationale approach and the legality approach conflict with the parsimony approach. However, there is no inevitability about this: everything depends on the political context. Some desert-orientated systems have not been connected with a movement towards harsher penalties, as the experience of Finland and Sweden shows,[43] and one of the judicial criticisms

[37] See above, Ch. 5.　　[38] See above, Ch. 3.　　[39] See above, p. 260.
[40] See A. von Hirsch, above, Ch. 6, and R. Frase, above, Ch. 7; also K. Knapp in A. von Hirsch, K. Knapp, and M. Tonry, above, n. 25, ch. 8.
[41] See M. Tonry, 'Mandatory Penalties', in M. Tonry (ed.), *Crime and Justice: A Review of Research*, xvi (Chicago, 1992).
[42] See above, Ch. 3.
[43] For elaboration, see A. von Hirsch, *Censure and Sanctions* (Oxford, 1993), ch. 10.

of the 1991 English legislation is that it requires courts to impose some sentences that are too lenient. If the argument is confined to the legality approach, arguing that guideline systems tend towards increased severity, the experience of the first eight years of the Minnesota guidelines tells against this; what happened there in 1989 was a political change, born of 'populist punitiveness', that could have happened anywhere.[44] Indeed, such increases in severity did happen in other American states that had neither guidelines nor a desert rationale, New York State being a leading example. New York, like the US Federal jurisdiction and many others, has altered its sentencing laws largely by enacting mandatory minimum sentences for certain types of crime, notably those related to drugs and to guns, and for all second felony convictions. It is experiences like these that confirm some commentators in their view that sentencing should be left to the judges with minimal input from the legislature. It is evident, from what has been argued earlier in this essay, that such an approach builds upon a false notion of judicial independence,[45] and goes against the principle of legality and several other principles. But for those who assess sentencing by reference to overall parsimony in punishment rather than either legality or clarity of rationales, this is a possible judgment in the context of political trends in a particular country,[46] even though it is anti-democratic in its premisses.[47]

3.5. The Need for Research

A further task for sentencing scholars, particularly those who support the legality approach, is to engage in empirical research into the process of sentencing. Research into why judges and magistrates do what they do has long been advocated as a prerequisite of the successful development of sentencing policy,[48] but sentencers in many countries seem to resist research. Apart from the irony that judges sometimes berate academics for not understanding practice when it is the judges who bar the way to research by means of observation and interview, the social importance of sentencing is a powerful argument in favour of careful research. More ought to be known about the motivation of judges and magistrates. Such knowledge would assist in the formation of sentencing policy, and it might also help to extend a form of accountability into this sphere of public decision-making. No doubt research of this kind will be perceived as a threat and

---

[44] See A. von Hirsch, above, Ch. 6.   [45] See above, 253.

[46] See e.g. D. Downes, *Contrasts in Tolerance* (Oxford, 1988).

[47] Cf. J. Waldron, 'A Right-Based Critique of Constitutional Rights', (1993) 13 *Oxford JLS* 18, 38.

[48] See e.g. Council of Europe, *Sentencing*, Report by the Sub-Committee of the European Committee on Crime Problems (Strasburg, 1974); Council of Europe, *Report of the Select Committee on Sentencing* (1993).

may be resisted on this account. This has led some criminologists to advocate the 'Trojan Horse' approach of offering to assist the judiciary through
research rather than to propose an enquiry into their methods of working,[49]
but it seems to me that the public policy arguments for research must be
confronted. They are surely overwhelming.

3.6 Sentencing in its Context

A sixth task for sentencing scholars is to promote a sense of perspective
about the role of sentencing. It is well known that the passing of sentence is
merely one stage—albeit a public one—in a long series of decisions ranging
from the decision to charge, through prosecutorial review, mode of trial,
venue, plea negotiation, the presentation of facts to the court, and subsequently the enforcement of sentences and decisions on early release. Yet
this seems to be forgotten in many pronouncements. People expect courts
to control crime. Some judges and magistrates seem to think that crime
prevention is their main task, whereas it is a much wider issue of criminal-
justice policy in which the courts' part is less important than is commonly
believed. Moreover, the courts in many jurisdictions receive only a selection
of cases, and receive them only in the form in which they are constructed by
others in the criminal-justice system.[50] The tendency to overstate claims
about the effects of sentencing must be counteracted.[51]

4. CONCLUSIONS

The essays in this volume show that there is a range of questions to be
resolved in relation to sentencing reform. Each jurisdiction has to select the
most appropriate method of deciding on proposals for reform (e.g. committee of inquiry); it has to decide on the authority that should formulate
and promulgate the reforms (e.g. primary or delegated legislation, the
judiciary or a specially-constituted commission); and it has to decide on the
most appropriate style of guidance (e.g. numerical guidelines, narrative
guidelines, hierarchy of principles).[52] These questions of procedure are
accompanied by equally weighty questions of substance about purposes,
principles, and policies. As a participant in or commentator on such devel-

---

[49] See A. Lovegrove, 'Sentencing Guidance and Judicial Training in Australia', in C. Munro
and M. Wasik (eds.), see above, n. 25.

[50] A striking example of this is the influence on plea-bargaining of the US Federal Guidelines: see A. Doob, above, Ch. 8. The practices of prosecuting and defending lawyers are
influential in most systems.

[51] See above, n. 3 and accompanying text.

[52] For an international survey, see A. Ashworth, 'Sentencing Reform Structures', in M.
Tonry (ed.), *Crime and Justice*, see above, n. 10.

opments, the sentencing scholar must flit constantly between the realms of principle, practical implementation, and empirical research. Yet the agenda is often set by the politicians and the press. As Arie Freiberg observes: 'Sentencing structures are built upon unstable foundations. They are the result of, and vulnerable to, shifting social, political, and economic pressures. They will survive as long as they fulfil the needs of the dominant political elements of the society of which they are a product.'[53] In this context it is principle that is most likely to lose out, and this suggests that arguments of principle should be highest on the sentencing scholar's list of priorities.

[53] A. Freiberg, above, Ch. 3, 93; see also N. Jareborg, above, Ch. 4, and A. Doob, above, Ch. 8.

Sentencing Reform Across National Boundaries

MICHAEL TONRY

At first sight, sentencing looks much the same in most Western countries. In circumstances of some formality, after a process that signals the symbolic importance of the state's possible taking of a citizen's liberty or property, an impartial judicial official soberly announces the penalty the offender will suffer. It seems quite simple, almost universal. Without acceptable excuse or justification, an individual has done something that the law forbids, and the state has declared him blameworthy and deserving of punishment. The problems that can arise—that the fact-finding process is unfair or unreliable, that judges are capricious or biased or idiosyncratic, that penalties are ineffective or cruel or inconsistently applied—also are universal. Different legal systems should, it would appear, want and be able to learn from one another about such elemental problems. In recent decades, however, there has been relatively little transfer of sentencing technology and learning between legal systems. That is understandable, but a pity.

As the essays presented in this volume, and a small but accumulating empirical literature on sentencing research and policy, demonstrate, there are lessons to be learnt across national and sub-national boundaries that can help individual jurisdictions improve their systems while avoiding foreseeable mistakes. 'Improve' of course is a loaded term. Champions of reduced sentencing disparities, or greater control over officials' decisions, count as improvements legal and policy changes that many officials find abhorrent. No doubt the proponents of England's Criminal Justice Act 1991 saw its passage as a harbinger of improved sentencing while judicial opponents saw the repeal of key provisions in 1993 as an appropriate rejection of benighted legislation.

This essay distils from the empirical literature on sentencing policy a number of observations that seem relevant to any Western legal system. They relate to the simple, elemental nature of sentencing that can be seen behind the obscuring mechanical and procedural details of different legal systems. Three points stand out. First, just as estate agents cite 'location, location, location' as the key to property values, 'planning, planning, planning' is the key to effective implementation of new sentencing schemes. Secondly, well-planned and executed innovations can alter judges' behaviour and sentencing outcomes. Thirdly, while 'one size fits all' may work for bathrobes and synthetic socks, it will not work for sentencing policy. Different jurisdictions have different problems.

The preceding claims, at their most exciting, are prosaic. Anyone should know that solutions must be tailored to problems, that successful implementation of anything is facilitated by careful planning, and that well-conceived, well-executed changes should have some effect.

In practice, few sentencing policy changes are well planned or well implemented. Jurisdictions contemplating changes can learn from the occasional successes and frequent failures of others. This essay offers a preliminary overview of current literature on sentencing policy changes. Section 1 discusses discretion and disparity as common backdrops of sentencing policy in every country. Section 2 sets out a number of generalizations from past documented sentencing policy changes that can illuminate paths for other jurisdictions to follow. Section 3 circles back to discuss desert, the most commonly invoked modern rationale for sentencing policy, and its implications for policy changes.

1. DISCRETION AND DISPARITY

Proposals for sentencing change come from many quarters. Penal abolitionists, humanitarians, and political liberals typically want reduced severity. Law-enforcement officials, victims' groups, and political conservatives want penalties made tougher. Academics and civil libertarians want them made fairer. Utilitarians and crime-control spokesmen want them made more effective. Nearly all want sentencing made more consistent, whether in the name of justice, efficiency, effectiveness, or economy.

Whoever wants what, however, must confront the antipodean twins of discretion and disparity. Someone must in every case decide what to do. In most common-law jurisdictions, at least until recently, judges have been accorded great latitude to decide what will happen to individual offenders who come before them. The difficulty is that sentences sometimes reveal more about judges than about offenders, just as book reviews sometimes reveal more about reviewers than about books.

If sentencing is, at least substantially, about offenders' blameworthiness, systems in which judges have wide discretion are troublesome. Equally principled and thoughtful judges, call them Plato and Aristotle, Bentham and Kant, or Thomas and Ashworth, are sometimes going to impose different penalties on seemingly similar offenders. Unintelligent or unprincipled or unscrupulous or partial or egoistic or bigoted judges are often going to impose very different penalties on comparable wrongdoers. Research in many countries documents the existence of disparities in sentencing that cannot be accounted for by reference to the characteristics of offenders or the circumstances of offences. This is true even of the Netherlands, long the possessor of the developed world's lowest incarceration rates: a paper prepared for the Colston Symposium began: 'One of the striking peculiarities of the Dutch administration of criminal justice is the wide discretionary power of the judiciary concerning sentencing.'[1]

The association of unwarranted disparities with unstructured discretion seems inevitable to many observers and a self-evident problem. Curiously, however, that problem is not at all self-evident to many judges. In most English-speaking countries, at least, the prevailing judicial ethos rejects both the need to structure sentencing discretion and the appropriateness of doing so. By American standards, for example, the sentencing policy innovations represented by the Criminal Justice Act 1991 in England and Wales are quite modest. Much closer to Scandinavian declaration of general principles to guide discretion than to detailed American sentencing guidelines, the Act's most controversial provisions left substantial opportunity for judicial construction of undefined and elastic words like 'serious'.[2] Yet the Lord Chief Justice, in a widely reported speech, was subsequently moved to say that its provisions forced sentencers into a strait-jacket and that the new law, fashioned by 'penologists, criminologists, and bureaucrats', had created a system that was 'incomprehensible to right thinking people generally'. That key provisions of the 1991 Act, including the establishment of a unit fines system in the magistrates' courts, were repealed in 1993 is attributable at least in part to judicial hostility to the Act.[3]

Australian judges appear to be committed at least as strongly as their English brethren to the notion that judges in some sense own sentencing and that legislative encumbrances on that ownership are inherently inappropriate. Arie Freiberg's essay,[4] for example, traces the genesis of Victoria's Sentencing Act 1991, which abolished remission of sentence, to *Yates*,[5] a decision of the Supreme Court of Victoria. The central issue was whether sentencing judges should take the likely effect of remission into account when setting sentence. The answer was an emphatic 'no'. The court observed that the very existence of remission communicated to observers either that 'the court had no authority because little notice was taken of the sentence imposed' or that the court was engaged in a charade designed to mislead the public about the severity of sentences. The most telling bit of

---

[1] P. Tak, 'Sentencing in the Netherlands', a paper distributed at the Colston International Sentencing Symposium, Bristol, 1993.

[2] See D. Thomas, above, Ch. 5, and N. Jareborg, above, Ch. 4.

[3] M. Wasik, 'England Repeals Key Provisions of '91 Sentencing Reform Legislation', (1993) 4 *Overcrowded Times* 1, 16–17; D. Moxon, 'England Abandons Unit Fines', (1993) 4 *Overcrowded Times* 5, 10–11.

[4] See above, Ch. 3.

[5] [1985] VR 41.

rhetoric, 'the authority of the court is eroded whenever the executive is authorised to interfere with its orders', intimates that the central issue in sentencing is acknowledgement of the authority of the court rather than justice to the offender or achievement of the policy or practical aims of government.

If there were grounds for believing that legal doctrine, court rules, or tariff case-law assured that sentences were justly imposed, that they were reasonably consistent and proportionate, the focus on protecting the court's authority might seem less anomalous. At least in Victoria, however, there is little reason to believe this. Freiberg cites *Williscroft*, a decision of the Court of Criminal Appeal, on the sentencing process:

Now, ultimately every sentence imposed represents the sentencing judge's intuitive synthesis of all the various aspects involved in the punitive process. Moreover, in our view, it is profitless . . . to attempt to allot to the various considerations their proper part in the assessment of the particular punishments presently under examination. We are aware that such a conclusion [about appropriate punishments] rests upon what is essentially a subjective judgment largely intuitively reached.[6]

This belief in the 'intuitive synthesis', namely, that judges are uniquely qualified to set sentences and, presumably, despite the different experiences, values, and personalities of individual judges, that the sentences imposed are just ones, is not unique to Victoria. In New South Wales, in an important decision concerning the Sentencing Act 1989, the Court of Criminal Appeal in *R* v. *McClay* acknowledged a new approach but insisted that judges give 'appropriate weight to well-established principles of sentencing'.[7] To like effect, the High Court of Australia, in *Veen (No. 2)*, averred that 'sentencing is not a purely logical exercise. . . . The purposes overlap and none of them can be considered in isolation. . . . They are guideposts to the appropriate sentence.'[8]

Nor is belief in the judges' capacity for 'intuitive synthesis' unique to England and Wales and Australia. At the Colston Symposium, Manfred Burgstaller of the University of Vienna described the 'existential conversation' which is used in Austria as a metaphor to describe judges' mental processes when deciding sentences, and noted that observers of Austrian courts, like observers of courts everywhere, worry about the unwarranted disparities that appear to be common.

In many American jurisdictions, judges long denied the existence of sentencing disparities. Many still do. Disparity research is faulted as misleading because it fails to take all the relevant factors into account. At least a dozen times, while discussing seemingly anomalous sentences, judges

---

[6] [1975] VR 292, 300.
[7] (1990) 19 NSWLR 112.
[8] (1988) 164 CLR 465, 476.

have told me: 'if we were present at the sentencing, we would understand why the judge imposed that sentence'. I suspect that many judges in Western countries would similarly dispute disparity research, without acknowledging the assertion's inherent ambiguity.

Understood one way, the claim is about measurement. The model has not been adequately specified and more variables, especially qualitative variables, should be taken into account. This can always be true, but it is not a claim that disparity does not exist, merely that it has not convincingly been demonstrated. Understood another way, the claim is about judges. Had we been there, we would understand why that judge imposed that sentence. This will often be true, but it recasts the question from 'Has this defendant received a sentence that is reasonably consistent with those imposed on other like-situated offenders sentenced by other judges?' to 'Has this judge, in light of his environment, beliefs, and experience, imposed an unreasonable sentence?' Understood in this latter way, the refutation of the existence of disparity is instead a reassertion of judicial ownership of sentencing, an assertion that an 'understandable' or 'not unreasonable' sentence is a just one.

Belief in judicial ownership of sentencing has in England and Wales been remarkably influential. I have many times asked colleagues about their experiences as members of the English Parole Board and several times heard stories of prisoners coming before the board who were serving what appeared to all to be aberrantly long sentences. Each time, the stories go, someone observed that the judge must have had a good reason to impose such a long sentence, although nothing in the files revealed what that reason might have been, and as a result the board decided not to recommend release.

It is unclear how much of the opposition of American federal judges to the US Sentencing Commission's Guidelines that Anthony Doob describes[9] derives from objections to their severity and rigidity and how much from the Guidelines' explicit rejection of the notion that judges own sentencing. The more than 200 Federal district court opinions declaring the entire system unconstitutional, a conclusion with which none of the nine justices of the US Supreme Court in *United States* v. *Mistretta*[10] agreed, suggests that intrusion on judicial discretion was a major and emotional consideration.

There is, unfortunately, no way round the dilemma that sentencing is inherently discretionary and that discretion leads to disparities. In the United States, serious attempts have been made to objectify sentencing by establishing explicit standards to guide decisions in individual cases. At the extreme, as Anthony Doob's essay in this volume details,[11] the Guidelines

[9] Above, Ch. 8.
[10] 488 US 361 (1989).
[11] Above, Ch. 8.

adopted by the US Sentencing Commission for use in the Federal courts purport to be mandatory. They are all but universally criticized for their rigidity and their consequent inability to draw distinctions between cases that most observers believe should be distinguished.

Three major substantive lessons can be drawn from the sizeable American evaluation literature on the effects of major efforts to reduce disparities by changes in sentencing laws and practices.[12] First, newly established standards for sentencing can effect changes in the patterns of sentences that judges impose and can reduce sentencing disparities. Secondly, in so far as standards direct judges to impose sentences they consider inappropriate, they will often devise ways, sometimes in concert with counsel, to do something else. Thirdly, standards that aggressively try to eliminate disparities and achieve uniformity in sentencing, like the Federal Guidelines, often violate the second half of the equality injunction ('and treat different cases differently'), and are especially likely, therefore, to drive discretion underground as judges and lawyers try to achieve sentences that everyone agrees are reasonable.

Artifices in the Federal system to circumvent guidelines that the judge and counsel consider unjust are legion.[13] Judges sometimes simply refuse to find facts (for example, a larger quantity of drugs or use of a firearm) which, if found, would require a much harsher sentence. Judges sometimes consent to plea bargains which, because of the authorized maximum sentences they entail, make it impossible to impose the sentence required by the guidelines. Sometimes judges defer to proposed stipulated findings of fact that omit incontrovertible details that would require a harsher sentence; other times judges order probation officers to omit key facts from their pre-sentence investigation reports; both these practices are expressly forbidden by Sentencing Commission policies. Sometimes judges ignore the applicable guideline or an applicable statutory mandatory minimum sentence; unless one of the parties objects and appeals, that is the end of the matter.

There is some irony in this causal chain: in the interest of reducing disparities that the visible exercise of discretion makes evident, standards are set that operate to make the exercise of discretion invisible, which makes disparities all but invisible and nearly impossible to monitor. In a system like the Federal Guidelines, in which some judges feel ethically

---

[12] M. Tonry, 'Sentencing Commissions and their Guidelines', in M. Tonry (ed.), *Crime and Justice: A Review of Research*, xvii (Chicago, 1993).

[13] US Sentencing Commission, *The Federal Sentencing Guidelines: A Report on the Operation of the Guidelines System and Short-Term Impacts on Disparity in Sentencing, Use of Incarceration, and Prosecutorial Discretion and Plea Bargaining* (Washington, DC, 1991), A-1–A-90; I. Nagel and S. Schulhofer, 'A Tale of Three Cities: An Empirical Study of Charging and Bargaining Practices under the Federal Sentencing Guidelines', (1992) 66 *Southern California Law Review* 501.

bound to observe their oath to enforce the law and therefore apply guidelines they believe to be unjust, and other judges feel ethically bound to observe their oath to do justice and therefore circumvent the guidelines, it is likely that aggregate disparities exceed those in the system that the guidelines displaced.

The preceding paragraphs should not be construed as a counsel of despair. Some American states, for example Minnesota, Oregon, and Washington, have found a middle ground on which presumptive guidelines set standards that most practitioners find reasonable and on which the scheme is sufficiently flexible to allow meaningful differences between cases openly to be taken into account.[14] That balance has been hard to strike, however, and many more states have failed than have succeeded (though at the time of writing, promising new guidelines systems have recently taken effect or soon will in Kansas, North Carolina, and Arkansas).[15]

As a matter of policy, it is hard to imagine a persuasive argument why celebration of judicial ownership of sentencing is a more important policy goal than reduction of unwarranted sentencing disparities. The best I can devise would be a slippery slope argument that an independent judiciary is essential to the preservation of an ordered democracy and that any intrusion on the existing scope of judicial authority threatens the concept of judicial independence. This would be a silly argument, although some judges may believe it. Were it valid, it would apply as readily to codification of bodies of law like contracts, property, and torts that evolved under the common law as to establishment of rules for sentencing where formerly there were none.

Andrew Ashworth[16] has demonstrated why it is a confusion to conflate protection of the judge's power, within applicable law, to decide the facts of individual disputes and apply the law to them—a process at the core of judicial independence—with protection of the judge's preference to set sentences free from standards that might constrain his exercise of discretion. Discussions of this subject are difficult because the conflation is common and the suggestion that legislatures have the same legal and constitutional authority to set standards for sentencing as for the law of contracts is often met with an emotional defence of judicial independence.

American efforts at sentencing reform offer some insights into the discretion–disparity nexus. First, judges are educable. From a beginning in the 1970s, when indeterminate sentencing was ubiquitous and judges were

---

[14] See above, n. 12.

[15] D. Gottlieb, 'Kansas Adopts Sentencing Guidelines', (1992) 4 *Overcrowded Times* 1, 10–13; S. Proband, 'North Carolina Legislature Adopts Guidelines', (1993) 4 *Overcrowded Times* 4, 11–12; K. Knapp, 'Allocation of Discretion and Accountability within Sentencing Structures', (1993) 64 *University of Colorado Law Review* 679.

[16] 'Sentencing Reform Structures', in M. Tonry (ed.), *Crime and Justice: A Review of Research*, xvi (Chicago, 1992).

as opposed to constraints on their sentencing discretion as are English and Australian judges today, most American judges now are prepared to agree that sentencing should be guided by rules. That one of the earliest and most influential books calling for sentencing reform, *Criminal Sentences: Law Without Order*, was written by a Federal trial judge who decried 'lawlessness' in sentencing may have helped legitimize sentencing reform in judicial eyes.[17] As a result, and as Richard Frase's essay in this volume[18] documents, more and more states are moving to adopt sentencing guidelines. Secondly, intransigent opposition by judges to efforts to reduce disparities is a dangerous strategy.[19] Sometimes, as in England and Wales in regard to the Criminal Justice Act 1991, or as in Victoria and New South Wales generally, intransigence wins out. Other times, as in the American Federal system, intransigence excludes judges from the policy process, and the standards adopted in their absence are the worse for it.

In England and Wales, although the judges appear to have won the day in 1993, passage of the 1991 Act in the face of judicial dubiety suggests that judicial obstructionism may yet be swept away when a future reform wave rolls in. That is in effect what happened in the American Federal system. Bills calling for a sentencing commission and sentencing guidelines were first introduced in 1974, first passed in the Senate in 1979, and passed by both Houses of Congress in 1984, always over the opposition of most Federal judges.[20] America's Federal Sentencing Guidelines should be a lesson to judges everywhere that oppositionism can carry a high price.

2. LEARNING ACROSS JURISDICTIONAL BOUNDARIES

Sentencing policy changes in the English-speaking countries have seldom been the subjects of sophisticated impact evaluations. A dozen or two studies in the United States, a handful in England and Wales (mostly on the use of community-service orders),[21] and a few in Australia[22] make up the evaluation literature.

---

[17] M. Frankel, *Criminal Sentences: Law Without Order* (New York, 1973).

[18] See above, Ch. 7.

[19] M. Tonry, 'Judges and Sentencing Policy: The American Experience', in C. Munro and M. Wasik (eds.), *Sentencing, Judicial Discretion, and Training* (London, 1992).

[20] K. Stith and S. Koh, 'The Politics of Sentencing Reform: The Legislative History of the Federal Sentencing Guidelines', (1993) 28 *Wake Forest Law Review* 223.

[21] K. Pease, 'Community Service Orders', in M. Tonry and N. Morris (eds.), *Crime and Punishment: An Annual Review of Research*, vi (Chicago, 1985).

[22] e.g. A. Freiberg, 'Truth in Sentencing?: The Abolition of Remissions in Victoria', (1992) 16 *Crim. LJ* 165; A. Freiberg, 'Sentencing Reform in Victoria', (1993) 4 *Overcrowded Times* 7–9; A. Gorta, 'Impact of the Sentencing Act of 1989 on the NSW Prison Population', (1992) 3 *Current Issues in Criminal Justice* 308; A. Gorta, 'Truth-in-Sentencing in New South Wales', (1993) 4 *Overcrowded Times* 4, 11–12.

There are none the less things to be learnt by looking at sentencing policy changes across jurisdictional boundaries. Because I have several times surveyed the American literature,[23] the discussion here is not exhaustive. Instead, drawing on the American, Australian, and English literatures and experience, I offer a number of generalizations about efforts to change sentencing policies and practices. Much of what I say may seem and be self-evident. My defence is that, self-evident observations or not, many jurisdictions have failed to take account of them.

First, among ambitious innovations, more fail than succeed, and the explanations often can be found in the care and thoroughness of planning and implementation. Unit fines in England and Wales, a Continental import, were repealed in part because of opposition from magistrates and partly because of design failure such as their application only to magistrates' (but not Crown) courts, their application to traditional trifling tariff offences like motoring violations and littering, and the default provision that offenders for whom means information was unavailable received the highest possible unit fine.[24] By contrast, a day-fine pilot project in New York City was successful and was later implemented; day-fine systems are now being established in jurisdictions across the United States.[25]

There are other examples. Abolition of remission in Victoria was sufficiently well advertised and implemented that the prison population held steady because judges adjusted their sentences accordingly.[26] Abolition of remission in New South Wales produced a rising prison population when judges failed to make the necessary adjustments.[27]

In the United States, planners in Minnesota, Washington, and Oregon worked assiduously to win judicial support for sentencing guidelines.[28] The support won may often have been grudging, but it was won and most of the goals of sentencing reform were realized. In Pennsylvania, the judges were not successfully won over and many simply ignored the guidelines. In the Federal system, judges were excluded from the policy-development process, and treated as opponents rather than as collaborators. As a result, widespread judicial defiance and opposition continues seven years after the Guidelines took effect.

Secondly, sentencing policy changes can change sentencing practices. Examples include Victoria's successful abolition of remission, several

---

[23] M. Tonry, 'Structuring Sentencing', in M. Tonry and N. Morris (eds.), *Crime and Justice: A Review of Research*, x (Chicago, 1988); M. Tonry, 'Sentencing Commissions and their Guidelines', in M. Tonry (ed.), *Crime and Justice: A Review of Research*, xvii (Chicago, 1993).

[24] D. Moxon, above, n. 3.

[25] S. Turner, 'Day-Fine Projects Launched in Four Jurisdictions', (1992) 3 *Overcrowded Times* 5–6.

[26] A. Freiberg, above, n. 22.

[27] A. Gorta, above, n. 22.

[28] M. Tonry, above, n. 19.

American states' guidelines' effects on racial and other unwarranted disparities, and the American Federal Guidelines. Despite widespread dislike of the Federal Guidelines, no one disagrees that the Guidelines, vigorously policed by probation officers, the US Sentencing Commission, and the Federal appellate courts, have changed sentencing patterns and practices.[29] Whether disparities have been reduced is at best unclear. With sufficient vigour, however, even the most unpopular sentencing changes can achieve high levels of nominal compliance.

The lessons to be drawn from the American, Australian, and English experiences involve process and can be found in any introductory textbook on public management. Involve all affected agencies and constituencies in the planning and design work. Make the planning process open and accessible so that affected constituencies can voice their concerns early, and so that policy fights, and necessary resulting compromises, can be made before plans have become firm rather than afterwards. Anticipate and develop contingency plans for all foreseeable problems. Cultivate support from the mass media. Conduct extensive public relations and outreach programmes. Hold training sessions for officials and practitioners who must work with the new regime, so that its goals and rationales are at least understood and respected (even if they are not agreed with). Before implementation, establish monitoring programmes so that patterns and pockets of non-compliance will be apparent. Establish technical support facilities so that answers are available for questions about policies and procedures. None of this is glamorous, but it holds the key to whether policy initiatives succeed. No laws are self-executing. Sentencing laws and rules, because they impinge on judicial ownership of sentencing, may be even less likely than others to achieve widespread acceptance. The evaluation literatures have shown what can go wrong and suggest ways that the past's problems can be avoided in the future.

Anthony Bottoms in his essay in this volume[30] suggests that desert, managerialism, and community are the key ideas that underlie modern policy debates about the criminal-justice system. From them can be triangulated 'Proportionality with a Human Face' as a widely accepted goal of sentencing policy in most jurisdictions. Desert captures the widely shared intuition that just penalties should be proportioned to the offender's blameworthiness. Managerialism provides the means to achieve compliance with sentencing policy. Community expresses the recognition that questions of justice are generally best decided in local settings.

Desert does not have widespread appeal, I believe, because all reasonable people believe that retribution rather than general prevention is the

---

[29] M. Tonry, above, n. 12.
[30] Above, Ch. 2.

general justification of punishment, and because there is a widely shared intuition that justice is inexorably linked with fairness and that fairness consists in treating like cases alike. Even in an incapacitative or rehabilitative scheme of punishment, most people would find it appropriate that cases be dealt with consistently within applicable criteria and inappropriate that they be dealt with inconsistently. Fairness, not desert, is the key idea. Because desert implies a comprehensive approach to setting sentencing standards that can then be consistently or inconsistently applied, desert often serves as a proxy concept for fairness.

If fairness is a major goal of policy, managerialism with its interest in inputs, outputs, and throughputs, impact projections, accountability, and cost-effectiveness provides the tools to deploy in its pursuit. Managerialism is often used pejoratively as a codeword to express dissatisfaction with dehumanized technocracy, management as an end in itself, and evolution towards a Foucauldian future of discipline and surveillance. No doubt those are legitimate concerns but they overstate. Thought of another way, managerialism is a metaphor for bureaucratic rationality and the simple idea that policies worth setting are worth achieving, and that there are more and less effective ways to do that.

Bottoms's third idea, community, is the most important and the least acknowledged of the three. Notions of community abound in relation to sentencing—the movement for community-based sanctions, interest in devolving power to local levels, concern in an avowedly pluralist world that communities vary widely in their composition and in their predominant values and traditions. All these are important ideas and together they reveal a powerful constraint on national, provincial, or state sentencing policies—justice is local.

Tensions arise when sentencing policies direct judges to impose sentences that are discordant with local notions of justice. Many illustrations can be offered.[31] In American jurisdictions, for example, research nearly always shows that sentences for many crimes are harsher in rural areas than in cities. Sentencing policymakers invariably decide that the new standards should apply throughout the state. Not surprisingly, rural judges often resist and not uncommonly disregard the new too-lenient sentences. Mandatory minimum sentence laws often require judges to impose sentences that they, the prosecutor, and the defence lawyer believe are too harsh. Sometimes the sentences are imposed and all concerned believe that injustice has been done. More often the lawyers or the judge figure out a way to avoid imposing an 'unjust' sentence, thereby frustrating state policy goals.

[31] A. Blumstein, J. Cohen, S. Martin, and M. Tonry, *Research on Sentencing: The Search for Reform*, Report of the Panel on Sentencing Research, National Academy of Sciences (Washington, DC, 1983).

Bottoms might object that I am not describing community variations but differences in the views of individual judges and the court workgroups of which they are a part. That is at least partly true, though it is likely that the views and values of court functionaries are at least partly shaped by the predominant views and values of the communities from which they come. The key points, however, are that no one, including judges, is comfortable behaving in ways that they believe are unjust, and that dissonance between official policies and decision-makers' sense of injustice will often be resolved in favour of the latter.

Bottoms's analysis leads, I believe, to a notion of proportionality with a human face as the overall goal of sentencing policy. This means that there should be standards for sentences according to which cases can be seen to be dealt with consistently or inconsistently, and tools of public management should be used to develop, implement, promote, monitor, and enforce those standards, but they should be sufficiently flexible that local officials can adapt them to take account of local notions of justice and of meaningful differences between cases.

Like all calls for just the right amount of anything, not too much and not too little, a proposal for sentencing standards that are constraining enough to assure that like cases are treated alike and flexible enough to assure that different cases are treated differently is a counsel of unattainable perfection. None the less, that is probably what most people would want to see in a just system of sentencing, and we know some things about how a jurisdiction can move closer towards that goal.

3. DESERT AND DISPARITY

The maxim 'treat like cases alike' has as its complement 'treat different cases differently'. For jurisdictions in which unwarranted sentencing disparities are believed to be common, experience with sentencing and parole guidelines in the American Federal system and in some states shows that disparities can be reduced.[32] American experience and the Victorian experience with abolition of remission instruct that well-implemented sentencing policy changes can successfully change decision-making patterns.[33] The American Federal experience, however, as Anthony Doob's essay in this volume documents, also shows that sentencing standards can be so detailed and inflexible that they risk violating the equality complement's adjuration to treat different cases differently.

What David Thomas in his essay in this volume[34] calls 'the newly fashionable desert theory' provides the callipers by which most people measure the

---

[32] M. Tonry, 'Structuring Sentencing', above, n. 23.
[33] A. Freiberg, 'Sentencing Reform in Victoria', above, n. 22.   [34] Above, Ch. 5, 135.

extent of unwarranted disparity. 'Disparity' is an empty category that can be filled only by reference to some standard. In principle, the standard could be set by any criteria. In practice, both the empirical grounding and the normative consensus are lacking for sentencing standards based on deterrence, rehabilitation, or incapacitation. By default, most people appear to believe that fairness means 'treating like cases alike' which in turn means, at least, 'alike in respect to the crime they committed'.

Even the American Federal Guidelines, which are avowedly not based on a desert rationale, or any other explicit rationale, in practice look like a desert system. The Guidelines grid[35] sets out 43 levels of offence severity ranked from lowest to highest, much as desert-premissed guidelines might do, and six levels of prior record seriousness, also much as desert-premissed guidelines might do.

A considerable literature on proportionality in punishment argues that punishment is an exercise in blaming and that punishments must be commensurate to the offender's relative blameworthiness.[36] More serious crimes are more blameworthy and warrant harsher penalties than less serious crimes and crimes of comparable seriousness are equally blameworthy and warrant comparable penalties. Although spirited debates centre on the precise role proportionality should play in setting sentencing policy or imposing sentences in individual cases,[37] no one seems to argue that desert has no relevance to justice in sentencing.

For most people in most places, as a normative matter, 'unwarranted' disparities exist when sentences in general are disproportionate to the relative severities of the offences for which they are imposed. Systems in which judges are not subject to established and enforceable standards are presumably those in which the likelihood of unwarranted disparities is greatest.

This section considers when a jurisdiction should attempt to learn from the American experience and set policies that are intended to structure decision-making in order to reduce disparities. In effect, the question is: When is an American cure the right prescription for another country's sentencing ailments? The answer is: it depends on the distribution and severity of sentences that characterize a legal system. Where few offenders receive prison sentences, and those are typically short, the human costs of unwarranted disparities may be relatively slight and the iatrogenic risk that a structured sentencing system will fail to treat different cases differently may be unacceptably high. Where many people receive prison sentences, or sentences are often severe, the burdens borne by the victims of un-

[35] Above, p. 216.
[36] A. von Hirsch, 'Proportionality in the Philosophy of Punishment', in M. Tonry (ed.), *Crime and Justice: A Review of Research*, xvi (Chicago, 1992).
[37] See e.g. A. von Hirsch, above, Ch. 6, and R. Frase, above, Ch. 7.

TABLE 10.1. *Distribution of prison sentences, Sweden and Victoria*

Duration	Sweden	Victoria
10+ years	0	3.6%
4–10 years	1.7%	19.6%
2–4 years	3.3%	36.0%
1–2 years	5.0%	23.2%
1/2–1 year	12.0%	
1/6–1/2 year	28.0%	13.4%
under 1/6 year	50.0%	

Sources: For Victoria, percentages from Table 3.7, showing prison-term dispositions as a percentage of all dispositions in superior court, in Freiberg's essay in this volume were doubled because, as Freiberg reports, 48 per cent of all sentences were to imprisonment. For Sweden, data are taken from Nils Jareborg's oral presentation at the Colston Sentencing Symposium in Bristol.

warrantedly severe or otherwise disparate sentences may be unacceptably high and the risks of inflexibility worth taking.

Table 10.1 shows the distribution of prison sentences imposed in 1991 in Sweden,[38] and Victoria.[39] The data are from secondary sources and may not be fully comparable although, because each represents the distribution of dispositions within a single jurisdictional system, their non-comparability is not a problem for my purposes. In Sweden, Jareborg reports that 41 per cent of convicted offenders in 1991 received prison sentences and that 95 per cent of those were for two years or less. Where relatively few offenders are incarcerated, and the vast majority of those for very short periods, the human costs for individuals of unwarranted disparities are seldom likely to be great. If two like-situated offenders receive one and three-month sentences, or even one and two-year sentences, the absolute difference, while still a cause for concern, will not drastically alter the offender's life. In Victoria, Freiberg reports that 47.9 per cent of offenders in superior courts received prison sentences in 1991. Nearly a quarter of those received terms exceeding four years and nearly three-fifths received terms longer than two years. Where many offenders are incarcerated for long terms, the potential range of disparity is great and the case for standards is much stronger.

Table 10.1 is only a starting-point. Despite the dispersion of sentences in Victoria, for example, it is possible that a case-law tariff policed by appel-

[38] N. Jareborg, above, Ch. 4.
[39] A. Freiberg, above, Ch. 3.

late sentence review suffices to reduce the risk of unacceptable disparities. Or conceivably, local or national norms about punishment are so well established and so widespread that injustice from disparity is unlikely to be substantial.

For myself, I am sceptical that appellate sentence review anywhere is rigorous in the absence of reasonably precise standards whose appropriate application in individual cases can be assessed on appeal. The American Federal appellate courts have aggressively policed judicial compliance with the Federal Guidelines, but they are very mechanical and detailed, much more like income-tax regulations than a general sentencing tariff. The Minnesota appellate courts have been less aggressive in enforcing Minnesota's guidelines and have created some case-law doctrines of amenability and non-amenability to probation[40] that afford considerable opportunity to judges to avoid applying otherwise applicable guidelines. The few evaluations of appellate sentence review in American states that lack detailed sentencing standards have concluded that without standards appellate courts can do little more than make *ad hoc* decisions in individual cases and that typically only aberrantly severe sentences are overturned.[41] Even in England, where the publication and analysis of appellate sentencing decisions is more extensive than in any other English-speaking country, David Thomas, unquestionably the leading authority on the subject, acknowledges in his essay in this volume that statutory and policy changes in the late 1970s effectively brought to an end the hopes for a more ambitious review of judicial sentencing practice.[42]

Although few sentencing reforms that affect judges' discretion have leapt across national boundaries, there is an available body of evidence on the effects of sentencing policy changes that should be transferable. In the United States, the Washington Sentencing Guidelines Commission built on Minnesota's experience, as did Oregon's Commission on Washington's, and later commissions on their predecessors'. The Federal Commission for a variety of reasons made no effort to learn from its state predecessors; Federal courts and defendants will for many more years suffer the consequences. In Australia, Victoria has shown how to implement the abolition of remission while avoiding the unintended consequence of increased prison populations and crowding. New South Wales has shown how not to do it. The Germans in the early 1970s showed that a country can successfully adopt day-fines; the English recently showed how not to. Minnesota

[40] R. Frase, 'Defendant Amenability to Treatment or Probation as a Basis for Departure under the Minnesota and Federal Guidelines', (1991) 3 *Federal Sentencing Reporter* 328.
[41] H. Zeisel and S. Diamond, 'Search for Sentencing Equity: Sentence Review in Massachusetts and Connecticut', (1977) 4 *American Bar Foundation Research Journal* 881.
[42] Above, p. 130.

and Washington showed that judges can be persuaded to accept substantial diminutions in the scope of their discretion over sentencing; the recent English and American Federal experiences offer alternate scenarios of how things can go wrong when judges are not persuaded of the legitimacy of the new regime.

When I was asked to attend the Colston Symposium, I was sceptical whether we know much about sentencing policy that has cross-national relevance. I was mistaken. National and sub-national jurisdictions can learn a great deal by looking outside their boundaries to the documented experiences of earlier innovators. There are positive and negative lessons to be learnt. George Santayana observed that those who cannot remember the past are condemned to repeat it. Adapted to sentencing policy the aphorism might go: those jurisdictions that refuse to learn from the experiences of others are condemned to repeat their mistakes.

Index